America's Political Class Under Fire

America's Political Class Under Fire
The Twentieth Century's Great Culture War

By   David A. Horowitz

ROUTLEDGE
NEW YORK & LONDON

Published in 2003 by
Routledge
29 West 35th Street
New York, NY 10001
www.routledge-ny.com

Published in Great Britain by
Routledge
11 New Fetter Lane
London EC4P 4EE
www.routledge.co.uk

Routledge is an imprint of the Taylor & Francis Group.

Printed in the United States of America on acid-free paper.

10   9   8   7   6   5   4   3   2   1

Library of Congress Cataloging-in-Publication Data

Horowitz, David A.
    America's Political Class Under Fire: The twentieth century's great culture war / by
David A. Horowitz.
        p.   cm.
    Includes bibliographical references (p.   ) and index.
    ISBN 0-415-94690-5 (alk. paper)—ISBN 0-415-94691-3 (pbk. : alk. paper)
    1. Social classes—United States—History—20th century.   2. Elite (Social sciences)—
United States—Public opinion—History—20th century.   3. Classism—United States.
4. Intellectuals—United States—Public opinion.   5. Public opinion—United States—
History—20th century.   6. United States—Politics and government—20th century.
I. Title.
HN90.S6 H67   2003
305.5′0973′0904—dc21   2003003923

To the memory of Louis Filler (1911–1998), who introduced me to the passions of History as my first mentor at Antioch College

For strangers are risen up against me, and oppressors seek after my soul.

—Psalms, 54:3

CONTENTS

Acknowledgments

The initial draft of *America's Political Class Under Fire* was prepared during a full year's sabbatical leave in 1998–99, an opportunity to which I am indebted to Portland State University and the taxpayers of Oregon.

Historians depend to an incredible degree upon the goodwill of archivists and librarians. I would like to thank the assistants at the Western History Collections at the University of Oklahoma and the Special Collections Department at the University of Virginia Library for providing photocopies of key correspondence. The staff at the Portland State University Library, especially Cyril Oberlander and the interlibrary loan team, proved to be indispensable allies, as did the patient associates of the Multnomah County Public and Reed College libraries. Relevant congressional reports and hearings transcripts were accessed through the library facilities of Portland's Northwestern School of Law.

Crucial stages of this project were supervised by David McBride, an editor of broad vision and attentive detail who encouraged me throughout the entire process while steering me clear of potential pitfalls. The thoughtful suggestions and critiques of two anonymous reviewers and Robert D. Johnston were tremendously helpful in setting the agenda for early revisions. *America's Political Class Under Fire* assumed its final form under the watchful care and commitment of Routledge Publishing Director Karen Wolny, Editorial Assistant Jaclyn Bergeron, Production Editor Nicole Ellis, and Copy Editor Douglas Puchowski, to all of whom I am eternally grateful.

I have benefited immensely from the counsel and inspiration of friends and professional cohorts, including Peter N. Carroll, Justus Doenecke, Robert A. Goldberg, Michael G. Horowitz, Harry P. Jeffrey, Michael Kazin, Shawn Lay, Leonard J. Moore, David W. Noble, William G. Robbins, and Eckard Toy. Special thanks go out to my History colleagues at Portland State, particularly Bernard V. Burke, Gordon Dodds, Tim Garrison, David A. Johnson, William L. Lang, Thomas Luckett, Patricia Schechter, Friedrich Schuler, and chair Linda Walton. Gloria Myers Horowitz remains in a category of her own as special consultant and personal adviser.

None of the aforementioned individuals is responsible for any inaccuracies or mistakes of judgement contained within these pages, which are all my misfortune and none of their own.

Introduction: America's Controversy with the Guardian Class

Ku Klux Klan leader Hiram Wesley Evans referred to them as the morally suspect and culturally decadent "strangers" of the 1920s. Farm activist John A. Simpson pictured them as members of a powerful political trust whose policies threatened to leave the rural Depression economy in permanent ruin. Monetary inflationist, business advocate, and New Deal opponent William A. Wirt equated them with the despised "inner circle of Washington" and questioned their loyalty to American institutions and democratic rule. Texas representative Martin Dies, Jr. condemned them as "strangers to the American way" and sought to purge them from the federal government agencies of the World War II era. Senator Joseph R. McCarthy viewed them as a members of an over-educated, effete, and privileged elite whose treachery had betrayed the nation's ideals. A special committee of the House of Representatives associated their involvement with tax-exempt foundations of the 1950s as symptomatic of an emerging "interlock" –a shadowy intellectual cartel said to be exerting thought control over government, education, and politics. Alabama governor George C. Wallace saw them as the "bearded beatnik bureaucrats" alleged to be running 1960s Washington. And Ronald Reagan and his successors dismissed them as "margin scribblers" who defied the common sense of the people.[1]

The subjects of such colorful descriptions have been portrayed in scholarly literature and in polemical works as members of a New Class–an assortment of government planners, public administrators, social service providers, policymakers, academic specialists, and knowledge professionals comprising an influential segment of the civic intelligentsia. Because such practitioners often lent their expertise and concerns to the resolution of governmental problems and cultural issues, they have been branded as the policy intellectuals, the knowledge elites, and the guardian class of modern society. *America's Political Class Under Fire: The Twentieth Century's Great Culture War* chronicles the manner in which critics viewed and censured such public actors in the United States between the Progressive Era and the century's end. It uses the term "political class" to broadly describe publicly active professionals and their allies, particularly lawyers, officials of public institutions, government officers, social workers and therapists, academic consultants, university students, and selected activists and cultural ideologues.

Who, exactly, were the social guardians and members of the political class who aroused such contention and what issues were put into play by their convictions and public actions? Rexford Guy Tugwell offers a useful example. Raised in upstate New York during the 1890s, Tugwell received his academic training at the University of Pennslyvania and began teaching economics at Columbia University in 1920. A consumer-oriented theorist, he argued that lower prices were the key to prosperity and that government regulation and national planning could be harnassed to stimulate purchasing power. Tugwell believed that private sector profits induced instability because they created industrial overcapacity and encouraged excessive speculation in money markets and other securities. No socialist, he nevertheless insisted that professional economists and industrial leaders could coordinate production with demand and thereby regulate the distribution of goods in the private market.[2]

Tugwell's theories entered the public sphere when he became a member of Franklin D. Roosevelt's "brains trust," a small group of New York academicians who advised the Democratic candidate in the 1932 presidential election and served as consultants and managers in the new administration. As a top official in the Department of Agriculture between 1933 and 1936, Tugwell recruited a team of urbane lawyers who shared the conviction that farm producers should be seen as consumers whose purchasing power could help restore the economy. Yet the agency's emphasis on lower agricultural prices infuriated rural traditionalists, who discounted cosmopolitan New Dealers whose priorities seemed to penalize agrarian producers. Disturbed by a purge of planners from the Department of Agriculture, Tugwell further antagonized critics in 1935 when he publicly called for a class-conscious alliance among farmers, workers, and government reformers to overcome plutocracy and reconstruct American agriculture and industry.[3]

As an engaged political intellectual, Tugwell fused academic thinking with concrete policymaking. Yet the economist's controversial career illustrated the inherent difficulties facing the political class. Tugwell and his colleagues frequently were portrayed as unaccountable advisers and elite social planners whose collectivist ideas and arbitrary methods threatened ordinary producers and democratic rule. As the opposition of agrarian populists such as John Simpson and William Lemke demonstrated, hostility to policy intellectuals was not confined to the privileged classes. Suspected of hidden motives, urbane affinities, and a distaste for the commonplace, social guardians of this kind found their sincerity and goodwill challenged by a host of critics and adversaries.

Social scientists and political writers have been interested in the relationship of the experts and service professionals to society since James Burnham, a former American Communist, portrayed the administrators of private corporations as an ideologically neutral and autonomous elite in *The Managerial Revolution* (1941). The Austrian-born economist Joseph A. Schumpeter saw the professional elite as more political. In *Capitalism, Socialism, and Democracy* (1942), Schumpeter described intellectuals in the public sector as alienated from the market economy even though they depended upon business interests for financial and political support. He concluded that policy and social service professionals used their cultural influence and place in government bureaus to implement anticapitalist sentiments and socialist planning because they felt deprived of prestige and power.[4]

The connections between planning experts and state authority received further attention from Friedrich A. Hayek, the brilliant Austrian economist and bitter anticollectivist. In *The Road to Serfdom* (1944), Hayek insisted that coercive governments empowered technical specialists, who then used their expertise to further a statist political agenda. He argued that government bureaucracy and state regimentation resulted from the undemocratic agenda and self-interested aims of the intelligentsia's planning experts. The knowledge sector's participation in the centralized governments of Europe and the United States in the 1930s and 1940s prepared the way for Milovan Djilas's invocation of the term, New Class. A former official in Communist Yugoslavia who turned against the regime and suffered imprisonment, Djilas authored several works in the 1950s and 1960s that held that the political bureaucracy of the socialist state afforded unprecedented power and privilege to a select stratum of policy intellectuals. Offering "a Marxist critique of contemporary Communism," the exiled writer contended that the administration of collectivized property in socialized economies gave New Class managers and officials the chance to serve their own class interests.[5]

Djilas's introduction of New Class terminology led in two directions in the United States. First, it inspired 1950s and 1960s social scientists to apply the concept to the professional and technical intelligentsia or knowledge class of postindustrial society. Theorists such as economist John Kenneth Galbraith, social critic David Bazelon, and sociologist Daniel Bell tied the rise of the New Class to the gradual shift of the market economy from the production of goods to the provision of technical and social services. As participants in an expanding professional sector after 1900, members of the New Class supposedly benefited from a process in which education, communication skills, scientific training, and managerial ability replaced wealth and entrepreneurial talents as key prerequisites to political power, social status, and cultural influence. Bell suggested that knowledge professionals influenced the administration of corporate as well as educational and scientific institutions, and helped to shape public discourse over social issues such as the quality of life.In a similar manner, social critics Barbara Ehrenreich and John Ehrenreich pointed in 1977 to the growth of a "distinct class" of twentieth-century professional, technical, and managerial experts responsible for the maintenance of capitalist culture.[6]

The most complete academic analysis of professional culture appeared in sociologist Alvin W. Gouldner's *The Future of Intellectuals and the Rise of the New Class* (1979). Gouldner asserted that knowledge and social service practitioners used educational and conceptual skills to consolidate a hold on government power and monopolize the setting of cultural standards. Although New Class elites served as a "technical intelligentsia" to the monied sector, they often aligned themselves with organized labor by crafting policies involving state regulation of production and the provision of social welfare services. Such contradictory roles placed assertive professionals and managers in a virtual "civil war with the upper classes."[7]

Gouldner's emphasis on the reformist tendencies of the New Class pointed to a second direction for speculation on the subject after Djilas. While social scientists used New Class terminology to describe a politically neutral culture of professional experts, ideological opponents of centralized state power adopted the former Communist's model to depict a powerful cabal of pro-socialist government bureaucrats and planners in the United States. In *Capitalism and Freedom* (1962), free-market economist Milton Friedman asserted that deluded political intellectuals used the apparatus of the state to seek elusive and unrealistic social change. Neoconservatives of the 1970s, such as Daniel P. Moynihan, Michael Novak, and Norman Podhoretz, argued that the New Class deployed its favored position in American education, public health, and welfare bureaucracies to consolidate its power through the provision of social services to the poor. Neoconservative critics also portrayed knowledge elites in the media and academy as proponents of an adversarial culture promoting liberal social attitudes and values. The sharpest treatment of such influence emerged in Irving Kristol's *Two Cheers for Capitalism* (1978). By fashioning itself as the sole agent of the public interest, an educated establishment, asserted Kristol, used its power base in state bureaucracies to carry out a regulatory agenda and mold antibusiness sentiment.[8]

The harsh tones of Kristol's criticism were replicated in *The New Elite: The Death of Democracy* (1978), a polemic by University of Minnesota regent David Lebedoff. The author depicted the New Class as an inner circle of self-replicating white-collar professionals and managers whose status derived from the remoteness of its work from public scrutiny and ratification. Lebedoff maintained that membership in the elite coincided not only with the willingness to articulate secular and scientific social standards and judgments, but with the rejection of traditional cultural and political values. Negative assessments of the New Class became a mainstay of political journalism in the 1980s and 1990s. In *Arrogant Capital: Washington, Wall Street, and the Frustration of American Politics* (1994), popular author and commentator Kevin Phillips attributed pervasive policy stagnation to a "national governing class" of idea and concept "manipulators" who forged mutually beneficial relationships among government bureaus, the service professions, and public interest lobbies. Since the 1960s, wrote Phillips, a powerful Washington-based elite had come to regard itself "as the nation's proven guardian class."[9]

The ideological nature of such commentary has generated considerable controversy over the authenticity and usefulness of the New Class concept. Writing in 1979, Daniel Bell felt compelled to characterize the term as "a linguistic and sociological muddle." Bell insisted that neoconservatives too often confused the emergence of new social stratum with a set of adversarial cultural attitudes. He argued that by placing New Class policy intellectuals in widely diverse fields such as the arts, media, education, health, social service, research, engineering, and management, theorists had depicted the knowledge sector in overly broad terms. Bell maintained that it was impossible to put information and technical professionals in the same category as freelance intellectuals holding reformist and anticapitalist views. Without common objectives, sensibilities, and economic interests, the New Class, he concluded, was not a cohesive social class.[10]

Bell's frustration with the state of New Class theory received endorsement in 1983 from cultural historian Jean-Christophe Agnew. Writing in the leftist journal, *Democracy*, Agnew acknowledged the existence of a group of knowledge and service professionals whose generation of information and social symbols figured in the management of human relations. Yet Agnew suggested that theorists used the New Class concept "as a mirror in which to behold the reflection of their deepest misgivings and their highest ambitions as intellectuals." He recounted how scholars and polemicists had interpreted the disputed term to stand for the development of a vanguard of influential technicians between 1910 and 1930, of managers in the 1930s and 1940s, of administrators between 1950 and 1970, of professionals in the 1970s, and of intellectuals since 1980. The difficulty in defining the New Class caught the attention in the 1990s of leading cultural historian and social critic Christopher Lasch. In *The True and Only Heaven: Progress and Its Critics* (1991), Lasch insisted that neoconservatives condemned professional problem solvers and moral relativists because they sought to deflect resentment from their establishment allies in the corporate world. Opponents used the New Class idea as a polemical tool to discredit liberal political attitudes, he charged, not as a sociological concept of social class.[11]

Despite such misgivings, Lasch acknowledged the existence of a "professional-managerial class" of affluent salary earners whose common outlook included respect for educational credentials, commitment to free inquiry, skepticism toward authority, and a belief in cultural tolerance. Yet even by the terms of Lasch's minimalist definition, twentieth-century Americans have had difficulty accepting the legitimacy of an activist knowledge sector. "Although we defer to experts frequently and routinely," observed intellectual historian Thomas L. Haskell in 1984, "we do not do so happily." Surprisingly, little historical work has been done on the manner in which controversies over a politically and culturally active intelligentsia have played out in the past century's public life. The most significant contributions of this kind were produced by the legendary Richard Hofstadter. In *The Age of Reform: From Bryan to F.D.R.* (1955), Hofstadter framed a broad interpretation of early-twentieth-century Progressivism by pointing to the modernizing input of a "new" middle class of technical experts, scientific managers, and service intellectuals. The book's concluding segment demonstrated how professional practitioners, cosmopolitan reformers, and pragmatic political officials used the New Deal welfare and regulatory state to effect positive social change in the 1930s.[12]

Hofstadter's sympathies with the knowledge sector became even more explicit in his next work, the Pulitzer Prize-winning *Anti-intellectualism in American Life* (1962). Disturbed by accusations from Cold War anticommunists that the educated and governing classes lacked the moral fortitude to confront a relentless foe, the historian attempted to chronicle the cultural and political roots of animosity to the intelligentsia. *Anti-intellectualism* explored the "resentment and suspicion of the life of the mind and of those who are considered to represent it." Broadly defining the knowledge class as professionals who acquired marketable mental skills and lived off ideas, the book traced discomfort with American intellectuals to nineteenth-century creeds associated with evangelicalism, primitivism, Jacksonian politics, and the self-help ethic.[13]

Building on this historical legacy, Hofstadter tied twentieth-century hostility to professionals to the assertion of social expertise and ideological influence during the Progressive Era. This insight prompted the historian to express qualified concern for ordinary citizens buffeted by the modernizing and statist agendas of socially oriented and politically influential intellectuals. Sophisticated specialists and experts, he asserted, evoked "profound, and in a measure, legitimate fears and resentments," including powerlesssness, frustration, anxieties over manipulation, and concerns over the wrenching effects of the social change that the twentieth-century knowledge sector often promoted. "One cannot, even if one does not like their responses," explained Hofstadter, "altogether withhold one's sympathies from the plight of a people ... who have been dragged away from their 'normal' concerns, thrust into an alien and demanding world, and forced to learn so much in so short a time." Twentieth-century citizens had been compelled "to submit in matters of politics, taste, and conscience, to the leadership of a new kind of education and cosmopolitan America."[14]

Despite such empathy, Hofstadter equated the "underground revolt" against modern life with group hatreds and "the generally prejudiced mind" of an older culture. He pictured distrust of politically and culturally active intellectuals as greatest among the small-town lawyers and businessmen elected to Congress, describing their constituents as those tending to be "fundamentalists in religion, nativist in prejudice, isolationist in foreign policy, and conservative in economics." Because ideological intellectuals played a leading role in the legitimation of social and cultural innovation, argued Hofstadter, ordinary people irrationally attributed most of society's ills to their actions. The historian concluded that such logic led many Americans to suspect without evidence that the intelligentsia was at home with foreign ideologies like communism.[15]

By dramatizing the value and power conflicts separating certain knowledge professionals and social service practitioners from the rest of society, Hofstadter broke startling analytic ground. Nevertheless, sympathy for those following the life of intellect ultimately positioned him as a party to the profound disputes and confrontations addressed by his work. Hofstadter appeared to fall victim to a habit of mind described by political scientist Richard Hamilton, in which liberal academics identified themselves as "a tiny minority standing on the edge of an abyss." Seeing people like themselves as the sole inheritors of humane values and concepts of rational progress, intellectuals were said to fear the narrow-minded prejudices and archaic traditions of blue-collar and lower-middle-class people beneath them.[16]

Scholars such as Alan Brinkley and Catherine McNicol Stock have warned that social scientists and historians often fail to acknowledge how their status as knowledge professionals impacts their academic work. They have suggested that much of the scholarship on American society implicitly accepts the legitimacy of the progressive-liberal state and the rationalist and cosmopolitan ideologies associated with it. In an earlier work, *Beyond Left and Right: Insurgency and the Establishment* (1997), I attempted to distance myself from prevailing assumptions about twentieth-century political culture by focusing on those Americans who opposed all concentrations of power, whether based on economic control, cultural influence, or governmental ascendancy. My study concluded that populist fears about consolidated power explained more about American politics and culture than did conventional descriptions of liberal and conservative ideology.[17]

***

Segments of *Beyond Left and Right* examined how key actors opposed political intellectuals, social service experts, and secular ideologues as agents of consolidation and modernizing values. Yet these briefly treated episodes were a minor portion of a broad narrative and not the subjects of extensive scrutiny. After completing the manuscript, I became convinced that the pivotal relationship between socially oriented intellectuals and their adversaries called for fuller description, explanation, and contextualization. The present study, a historical monograph and synthesis using both primary and secondary sources, narrates and contextualizes numerous instances in which empowered members of the political class came under intense public fire. It focuses upon the social values, political concerns, economic interests, and specific grievances of those who tainted members of the knowledge sector as strangers–as shadowy cultural renegades or as privileged insiders and elites.

Although *America's Political Class Under Fire* occasionally references the New Class, use of the term should not suggest that knowledge practitioners and their cohorts existed as a cohesive or self-conscious social class, consistently shared common interests and ideologies, or were perceived by all opponents as a self-contained social entity. Nor do I wish to enter the sustained controversy over whether a vaguely defined New Class actually held power in the United States. Although much of the criticism of the political class social guardians came from conservatives, it is important to separate such discourse from predetermined categories. By describing the self-sustaining sets of values and interests shared by many of those who opposed policy intellectuals, information professionals, and social service providers, the present study seeks to analyze their protest in its own terms, to demonstrate the relative continuity of such denunciations over time, and to estimate their impact on the century's political culture. In tracing this American variant of class warfare, the book reexamines the relationship between intellectuals and their opponents once described by Richard Hofstadter. *America's Political Class Under Fire* seeks to shed new light on tensions between modernizing and traditional influences in the United States and to work toward a balanced and fair-minded assessment of the consequences of expertise for democratic life.

***

The opening chapter of the book focuses upon the cultural controversies associated with the rise of scientific expertise and a secular intellectual elite in the early twentieth century. It describes those moral traditionalists of the 1920s who questioned the presumed relationship between scientific authority and competence in the management of social affairs, as well as those who reacted against the guideposts of secular liberalism. By examining aspects of the Leopold-Loeb case, the Scopes trial, and the rhetoric of Ku Klux Klan Imperial Wizard Hiram Wesley Evans, the chapter sets forth the cultural foundations of the case against New Class guardians and the depiction of intellectual agents of modernization as "strangers."

Chapter 2 begins examination of the struggle against public service professionals, intellectuals, and administrators by tracing the campaign to controversies over the knowledge sector's involvement in government during the Progressive Era and the 1920s. As the narrative focuses on the 1930s Depression, it relates the producer values of the rural American middle class to accusations that President Franklin D. Roosevelt's New Deal brains trust lacked accountability. After exploring disagreements over Roosevelt's agricultural policies, the chapter moves on to a discussion of legislation regulating Wall Street financial practices, explaining how political disputes over vested economic interests spilled over into questions about the relationship of expertise to democratic procedure and the role of the executive branch of government during Roosevelt's first term.

The third chapter of *America's Political Class Under Fire* explores the way in which anxieties about the power of unelected presidential advisers heightened concerns about the fiscal and labor policies of Roosevelt's second administration. By investigating controversies over the executive reorganization bill, federal spending increases, the National Labor Relations Board, expanding bureaucracy, and social experimentation in the federal agencies, this chapter outlines how heightened concern over the role of New Deal political intellectuals was tied to legitimate differences in values and interests between elements of New Class guardians and their opponents.

The continuing debate over policy intellectuals, academic advisers, and social planners in government is the focus of chapter 4. This segment ties concerns over domestic bureaucracy during World War II to charges that intellectual "strangers" to the American Way were subverting national institutions and values with collectivist and experimental ideas and policies. By describing congressional investigations of wartime agencies such as the Office of Price Administration and the National Resources Planning Board, the chapter highlights the emotional power of disputes over expanded government power, increased federal spending, and the ideological affinities of New Deal personnel. Such expressions of anti-intellectual rhetoric are tied to wartime anxieties over the survival of democracy and traditional economic practices among independent producers and their representatives in Congress.

In chapter 5, fears of arbitrary rule by government administrators and concerns over the cultural loyalty of intellectuals are set within the context of the Cold War and the anticommunist crusade. By considering the confirmation fight of Atomic Energy Commission (AEC) head David E. Lilienthal, the furor over the Hollywood Ten, the rhetoric surrounding the Alger Hiss case, the criticism of Dean Acheson and General George C. Marshall, and the assaults on the Truman presidency by Senators Joseph R. McCarthy and Patrick McCarran, this segment chronicles the antielitist and antiestablishment implications of anticommunist social morality. The chapter attributes the effectiveness of attacks on selected policymakers, government officials, diplomats, and academics to the ability of opponents to depict them as members of a privileged elite of amoral and decadent ideologues serving their own class interests.

The controversial relationship between political intellectuals and the retention of traditional moral standards is highlighted in chapter 6 through examination of the flap over the security clearance of AEC adviser and atomic scientist J. Robert Oppenheimer. After a survey of populist imagery in McCarthy's pronouncements during the Eisenhower years, the chapter returns to the cultural foundations of the stance against New Class guardians through a detailed assessment of the 1954 congressional investigation into the role of tax-exempt foundations in sponsoring controversial social science research. It concludes its treatment of the tensions between expertise and democracy in the 1950s and 1960s with a description of the grass-roots campaign against fluoridated municipal water supplies and the manner in which activists demanded accountability on the part of public health experts.

Chapter 7 shifts the grounds of the narrative to those opponents of federal involvement in civil rights enforcement who replaced race-based arguments with populist denunciations of Washington bureaucracy, hostility to government-sponsored social experiment, and condemnation of the pluralist values and planning aspirations of the liberal intelligentsia. Such discourse receives further treatment in descriptions of the way in which 1960s politicians such as George C. Wallace, Barry Goldwater, Ronald Reagan, and Richard M. Nixon amassed powerful voting constituencies by playing upon public distrust of intellectual elites and their presumed responsibility for the period's social turmoil. This segment also highlights efforts among local officials and elected representatives to tie academics and other policy intellectuals to the disputed community-action component of Lyndon B. Johnson's War on Poverty.

The eighth chapter of *America's Political Class Under Fire* opens with a description of the Nixon administration's embrace of social interventionism through the pursuit of federal affirmative action in the construction industry. It places particular emphasis on the way in which workers' discomfort with civil rights administrators and planning experts framed organized labor's criticism of the controversial Philadelphia Plan. Chapter 8 then examines working-class opposition to New Left protest against the Vietnam War, and describes the manner by which Nixon and other 1970s leaders built powerful electoral coalitions on pervasive mistrust of the political intelligentsia. After delineating the president's attempts to marginalize the liberal establishment during Watergate, the chapter explores the rising popularity of populist conservatism and its influence in undermining the federal government's legitimacy under President Jimmy Carter.

Chapter 9 describes how Presidents Ronald Reagan and George H. W. Bush demonized New Class guardians as virtual scapegoats for the problems of the 1980s. It then uses the presidency of "baby-boomer" Bill Clinton to highlight continuing hostility to socially oriented professionals and cultural liberals. The chapter spans the views of political figures such as Ross Perot, Newt Gingrich, and Jesse Ventura, as well as those expressed in the popular literature of evangelical Christians and right-wing extremists. It concludes by examining the reaction to the Clinton administration's controversial federal health care reform package and by exploring the manner in which critics tied the president's personal conduct to his generation's mindset and culture.

The conclusion to *America's Political Class Under Fire* suggests how criticism of the knowledge sector and professional elite has contributed to the controversial legacy of the intellectual classes in the twentieth-century United States. It summarizes the argument that denigration of New Class guardians reflected conflicts over the social and economic consequences of expertise in American society and went beyond conservative attacks on the liberal state. After discussing the extent to which populist imagery defined the protests described in this work, the conclusion returns to the historical impasse over the role of knowledge elite and professionals in a democratic society with a series of suggestions for reconceptualizing the problem.

1

Secular Liberalism on Trial in the Turbulent 1920s

America had been taken over by "strangers," declared Ku Klux Klan Imperial Wizard Hiram Wesley Evans in 1926. The worst offenders, cried Evans, were morally suspect intellectuals who defended unlimited immigration and who validated the culturally decadent ideas and practices associated with the Jazz Age.[1] In making this charge, the Klan's leading official dramatized the discomfort with which traditionally oriented Americans viewed the presumed influence and power of scientific experts and secular intellectuals following World War I. As cosmopolitan elements of the middle class entertained the advanced theories of Charles Darwin, Sigmund Freud, and Albert Einstein, moral traditionalists tied the nation's intellectual guardians to the legitimation of disputed social and cultural change. By exploring key elements of the Leopold-Loeb case, the Scopes trial, and the rhetoric of 1920s KKK leaders, this chapter connects criticism concerning the social authority and influence of intellectuals and theorists to widespread anxieties over the fate of modern society.

***

Hiram Wesley Evans's diatribe against intellectual guardians occurred in an age of consumer prosperity and rapid cultural change. As new group identities emerged around race, ethnicity, gender, youth, and cultural affinity in the 1920s, success for the urbane middle class increasingly rested on self-commodification, manipulation of others, projection of personal imagery, and liberation from past standards. The postwar assault on organized religion and moral orthodoxy often came from biologists and social scientists. As suggested by the naturalist philosopher, Joseph Wood Krutch, it was difficult to maintain habits of reverence when scientific evidence undermined religious faith and humanity's central place in the universe. The postwar era "brought an acute consciousness of social and cultural change that challenged tradition, religion, rational order, and progress," cultural historian Lynn Dumenil has concluded. As familiar ways collided with a new ethic of commercialism and leisure, historian LeRoy Ashby has concurred, "traditional intellectual and cultural reference points wavered." Amid declining church attendance, fashionable intellectuals adopted a self-consciously secular perspective and an enhanced sense of their role as enlightened guides to social behavior.[2]

Daniel Bell has suggested that 1920s knowledge professionals embodied the spirit of modernity by replacing religious sanctions with endorsement of behavioral codes emphasizing individual self-expression, the quest for experience, and the importance of personality. The social authority that allowed academic specialists to claim such expertise stemmed from their association with institutions of higher learning, one of the key components of the rising information culture and professions. Elite colleges first sought to emancipate their curricula from traditional religious authority in 1868, when New York educator Andrew Dickson White, who helped found Cornell University, insisted that free scientific inquiry be separated from religious sectarianism and theology. Johns Hopkins University, the first institution to specialize in graduate and professional education, opened in 1876 with an emphasis on the natural sciences. Under the leadership of Charles W. Eliot, Harvard soon followed the trend away from the classics and moral philosophy by introducing the elective system and abandoning compulsory chapel. As undergraduate enrollment tripled between 1910 and 1930, many colleges and universities positioned themselves as progressive bastions of scientific empiricism and enlightened ideals by restructuring their curricula along the lines advanced by the elite institutions.[3]

University education was to generate students who were immune to folk myths and popular creeds. Learning must eliminate "passion, prejudice, partisanship, cowardice, and truculence alike," educator and philosopher John Dewey warned the newly formed American Association of University Professors (AAUP) in 1915. The organization's Committee on Academic Freedom reiterated the conviction that scientific progress was "essential to civilization." As long as loyalties were determined by nonsectarian and empirical standards, experts could counteract local prejudice and insulate democratic opinion from irrationality. Accordingly, university faculty had an obligation to protect freedom of inquiry, even when scientific conclusions were widely condemned.[4]

The shift toward scientific standards compelled American higher education to embrace secularization, a process which theorists like Daniel Bell subsequently associated with the knowledge sector's need to free itself from the constraints of traditional moral authority. As early as 1879, noted Harvard psychologist G. Stanley Hall had observed that "the most competent teachers of natural or physical science either tacitly accept or openly advocate the fundamental principles of evolution." Yet incorporation of Darwinian theories of natural selection into the curriculum represented a move toward moral relativism that prompted predictable rebuke from traditionalists. At Yale, college president Noah Porter, a former professor of moral philosophy, objected to the use of a textbook authored by pioneer sociologist Herbert Spencer because the Social Darwinist's work violated norms of doctrinal orthodoxy and used purely materialist criteria in advocating a free-market economy.[5]

For Protestant conservatives, the displacement of Biblical authority lay atop a slippery slope that led to the spread of relativist and materialist values, the breakdown of sexual morality, the loss of family cohesion, the deterioration of social decorum, and the eradication of personal behavior standards. Such anxieties were captured in "Blasting at the Rock of Ages," an opinion piece appearing in *Cosmopolitan* in 1909, which attacked colleges for teaching "that the decalogue is no more sacred than a syllabus; that the home as an institution is doomed; that there are no absolute evils; that immorality is simply an act in contravention of society's accepted standards; ... that the change from one religion to another is like getting a new hat; that moral precepts are passing shibboleths; that conceptions of right and wrong are as unstable as styles of dress."[6]

Concerns over the moral values of college youth intensified with James H. Leuba's *The Belief in God and Immortality: A Psychological, Anthropological and Statistical Study* (1916). A psychology professor at Bryn Mawr College and former Johns Hopkins student of G. Stanley Hall, Leuba used empirical data to buttress a polemic for modernist religion. His study concluded that traditional religious beliefs diminished as intelligence and education increased. The greater the eminence of scholars, asserted Leuba, the more the tendency to reject belief in a personal God and the existence of an afterlife. Similar trends held among students at the better colleges, nearly half of whom doubted or denied Christianity's "fundamental dogmas." A second survey of college youth, appearing in the *Yale Review* in 1923, found widespread indifference to religion and ignorance of the Bible. Five years later, another study concluded that no more than 25 percent of collegians attended church on Sunday.[7]

Academic specialists appeared to substantiate Leuba's connections between academic culture and agnosticism. At Syracuse University, a Methodist institution, the sociologist Edwin L. Earp declared that social science taught that moral beliefs were the evolutionary products of experience. Mocking the pretensions of organized religion, Earp proclaimed that it was "unscientific and absurd to imagine that God ever turned stone mason and chiseled commandments on a rock." At the University of North Carolina, where required church attendance had been dropped before World War I, and where graduates no longer received Bibles at commencement, sociology professor Howard W. Odum became the first editor of the *Journal of Social Forces* in 1922. The periodical featured works by social scientists such as Cornell's L. L. Bernard, who cooly dismissed the origin of divinities as "products of the folk imagination."[8]

Perhaps the most controversial contribution to the *Journal of Social Forces* was "Sociology and Ethics: A Genetic View of the Theory of Conduct," by Smith College professor Harry Elmer Barnes. Describing Christian views of sex as unhealthy and primitive, Barnes warned that inadequate birth control was fostering a population increase in "the least capable classes." Two thousand years of religion had failed to produce a "definitive body of rules for conduct," he complained. "Great periods of cultural efflorescence," concluded Barnes, had been characterized by freedom in sexual relations, while those "of the greatest degradation and decline" had been defined by sex repression and purity. Articles by Barnes, Bernard, and other scholars created a storm of controversy at the university, where Baptist, Methodist, and Presbyterian clergy vainly sought to stop the journal's state funding. Clearly, elite institutions like North Carolina were committed to the modernizing agenda, even if academicians offended the moral codes and authority of tradition-oriented elements of the middle class. Yet the ability to mount critical discourse depended upon the intelligentsia's skill in asserting universal competence. Accordingly, the role and status of experts became as central to public discussion in the 1920s as money and wealth had been in the 1890s.[9]

***

Academic intellectuals of the 1920s were intrigued by the idea that the methods and principles of the natural and social sciences could be applied to the study of human behavior and to the reconstruction of a rational and humane society. Knowledge professionals often assumed that adherence to scientific method would result in an informed consensus on all important matters of truth. Yet consideration of such issues was to be confined to those qualified to examine them. Noting that recent developments in science required mastery of complex techniques, the philosopher Morris Cohen saw an insurmountable barrier "between the uninitiated layman and the initiated expert." Elite press commentators like Walter Lippmann shared this view by maintaining the distinction between mere opinion and the empirical truth of objective experts invested with intellectual integrity.[10]

Immersed in empirical method, confident members of the 1920s knowledge sector demonstrated little awareness that a critical approach to established convention and authority facilitated their own rise to power as competitors to traditional elites. Nor did they seem to appreciate the extent of resistance to their efforts, particularly on the local level. Yet the controversy over the role and ideology of the intelligentsia played a major part in 1920s cultural disputes over the erosion of personal autonomy and community cohesion and over the perceived need to reinvigorate habits of individual discipline, duty, sacrifice, and social obligation. Was the price of scientific progress and material abundance to include the loss of customary folkways and spiritual values? Were metropolises such as New York and Chicago to taint the entire nation with vice, moral corruption, mindless artificiality, and decadent intellectual fashions?[11]

"There are certain individuals who hug to themselves the title 'intellectuals,' who contemptuously scorn all petty virtues," Republican senator Hiram W. Johnson, a self-styled progressive reformer and nationalist, told readers of the *New York Times Magazine* in 1923. Uneasy over the knowledge elite's tendency toward religious skepticism and moral experimentalism, many Americans wondered if public education was encouraging moral softness, social permissiveness, and intellectual irresponsibility. Were matters of faith and values to become the domain of professional experts who imposed their own agenda on local schools and colleges? Was adherence to scientific method to obscure the wisdom of elders and traditional authorities? Were institutes of learning to become instruments of social disintegration in which pupils were encouraged to reject the beliefs of their parents and defy community-based values? If the foundations of religious faith among youth were upset, could standards of moral behavior and decency be maintained?[12]

Concern over the troubled relationship between the advanced notions of cultural progressives and traditional precepts of individual responsibility exploded with stunning effect during Chicago's sensational Leopold-Loeb murder trial. In May 1924, Nathan Leopold, Jr., nineteen years of age, and Richard Loeb, eighteen, abducted Robert Franks, the fourteen-year old son of family friends, and killed him with a chisel blow to the head. Leopold had graduated from the University of Chicago at the age of eighteen, the youngest person ever to complete the institution's undergraduate program. An expert ornithologist, he was widely read in philosophy, metaphysics, and literature, as well as the sciences, and already had passed the entrance examination for admission to Harvard Law School. The athletically built and strong-willed Loeb, who also demonstrated intellectual brilliance, had been the youngest person to graduate from the University of Michigan at the age of seventeen. The offspring of Jewish families whose combined wealth exceeded $15 million, the two had begun a homosexual relationship five years before the murder.[13]

The perpetrators of the Franks murder were arrested when police found a pair of broken eyeglasses near the remote culvert where the body had been dumped and traced them to Loeb. Both men confessed to participation in the killing within sixty hours of their apprehension. Prosecutors then charged Leopold and Loeb with kidnapping Franks for $10,000 ransom and committing homocide to cover their identity. In the most controversial and publicized murder case of an illustrious career associated with the protection of labor radicals and the destitute, attorney Clarence Darrow agreed to represent the wealthy defendants to spare them the death penalty. Seven weeks after accepting the assignment, Darrow submitted a guilty plea, telling the judge that his clients "should be permanently isolated from society." The famed defense lawyer then stated that he hoped to offer evidence "as to the mental condition of these young men to show the degree of responsibility that they had."[14]

Seeking to have emotional illness accepted as a mitigating factor in sentencing, Darrow asserted that Leopold and Loeb were mentally diseased, a state halfway between sanity and insanity, and were not fully responsible for their actions. "One of the most obvious proofs of mental defect," Darrow recalled in his autobiography, "is that there is no adequate consciousness of the relation between the cause and effect in the conduct of the individual." Defense lawyers told journalists that "the killing was in response to an irresistible mandate of two criminally insane impulses." Darrow spent most of the $30,000 advanced by the families to hire prominent psychiatrists and neurologists to interview the defendants and submit thousands of pages of expert testimony. Prosecutors bitterly objected by charging that the defense ignored the moral sense of the defendants as the central issue of the hearing. State psychiatrists insisted that Leopold and Loeb were sane and mentally responsible. Anyone capable of the social courtesies demonstrated by the young men also "must sense the worth of actions, the worth of values," prosecution experts told the press. Testimony suggested that the Franks murder had been committed with conscious malice. The real defense in the case, declared Illinois state attorney Robert Crowe, was Clarence Darrow's philosophy of life.[15]

***

Darrow's advocacy of the mental illness defense and his characterization of capital punishment as state murder were intrinsic elements of a legal doctrine honed over forty-five years of practice. As a self-avowed agnostic and a student of modern science, the folksy lawyer placed major emphasis on the effect of heredity and the social environment on personal behavior. "The human machine moves in response to outside stimulation," he theorized in a 1922 treatise entitled *Crime, Its Cause and Treatment.* Instincts and emotions lay at the cause of every antisocial act. Each crime had "an all-sufficient cause for which the individual was in no way responsible."[16]

The views of crime advanced by Darrow were based upon Darwinian notions of evolution. The origin and development of all animal life was the same, he asserted. "The laws of growth and development which govern organic matter do not except man. Life begins with the cell and evolves according to pattern." Therefore, the emotions which controlled action were "hidden in the original cell, hidden in the germ or seed from which it sprang." Darrow contended that secretions from the ductless glands into the blood influenced behavior and emotions. This led him to suggest that human actions depended on the nature, strength, and inherent make-up of the individual, as well as the habits, customs, inhibitions, and experiences offered by the environment. Consequently, there was "no such thing as moral responsibility in the sense in which this expression is ordinarily used." Every process of nature and life, argued Darrow, was a continuous sequence of cause and effect.[17]

By placing human behavior in a state of nature, Darrow contested those who assumed that only humans were endowed with a soul and the power to tell good from evil. "As a matter of fact," he declared, "every scientific man knows that the origins of life is quite different from this and that no sane treatment of crime can follow this assumption of man's origin and nature." Darrow contended that criminal law evolved from "old customs and folkways based on primitive ideas of man's origin, capacity, and responsibility." His rejection of such notions led the famed attorney to insist that there was "really no such thing as crime." Management of behavior, not moralistic precepts of criminality, was the central challenge. If human actions were governed by natural law, reasoned Darrow, "the sooner it is recognized and understood, the sooner will sane treatment be adopted in dealing with crime." Once offenders were cured by psychiatric treatment, he believed, they should be returned to society if it was safe to do so.[18]

Darrow's ideas about criminality were summarized during a controversial address before the inmates of the Illinois State Penitentiary at Joliet. "I do not believe in the least in crime," he told the assembly. "I do not believe that there is any sort of distinction between the real moral condition in and out of jail. The people here can no more help being here than the people outside can avoid being outside. I do not believe people are in jail because they deserve to be. They are in jail simply because they cannot avoid it on account of circumstances which are entirely beyond their control and for which they are in no way responsible."[19]

Despite prosecution objection to evidence related to the emotional condition of the defendants, Darrow began the "functional mental disease" defense of Leopold and Loeb in late July. Emphasizing the role of heredity in psychological make-up, he theorized that the causes of emotional life were in the nerves, muscles, endocrine glands, and "vegetative system." The accused had been deprived of emotional feelings, argued Darrow. "I do not know what remote ancestors may have sent down the seed that corrupted" them, nor "through how many ancestors it may have passed," acknowledged the attorney. Yet he was convinced that diseased minds lay behind the crime. Was "Dickey Loeb to blame," asked Darrow, "because out of the infinite forces that conspired to form him . . . ages before he was born," he had come into the world without a sound emotional foundation?[20]

Moving beyond heredity, Darrow argued for the influence of the social environment in Leopold and Loeb's pathology. Correspondence between the two defendants suggested that the murder had been a thrill killing designed to execute the perfect crime and demonstrate German philosopher Friedrich Nietzsche's concept of the "superman." "In formulating a superman," Leopold had written to his cohort two years earlier, "he is, on account of certain superior qualities inherent in him, exempted from the ordinary laws which govern ordinary men. He is not liable for anything he might do." In a note to Darrow, Leopold confided that "the killing was an experiment. It is just as easy to justify such a death as it is to justify an entomologist in killing a beetle on a pin."[21]

The defense now speculated on the impact of Nietzsche's writings on the two young men. A student of the German philosopher, Darrow had for many years delivered a stock Nietzsche lecture on the Chatauqua literary circuit. "His idea was whatever a majority believed must necessarily be untrue," the attorney liked to say of his free-thinking predecessor. As he sought to build a case in Leopold-Loeb, Darrow now offered a darker twist to Nietzschean thinking. The great German philosopher believed that evolution was working toward the superman, he explained. Nietzsche taught that humans had no obligations, that a person "may do with all other men and all other boys, and all society, as he pleases." Darrow described the philosopher's *Beyond Good and Evil* as "a treatise holding that the intelligent man is beyond good and evil; that the laws for good and the laws for evil do not apply to those who approach the superman." Such notions were a species of insanity, Darrow acknowledged, the doctrines of a maniac. Yet the brilliance of Nietzsche's musing was so compelling, he noted, that the superman concept entered discussion at every major college and university.[22]

Having established that the collegiate environment exposed students to dangerous ideas, Darrow could ask if there was "any blame attached because somebody took Nietzsche's philosophy seriously and fashioned his life on it?" With "the impressionable, visionary, dreamy mind of a boy," Leopold made the mistake of taking Nietzsche too far, the defense argued. The Franks murder would not have been committed except for the intellectual dogma that Leopold had taken literally. It was hardly fair, contended Darrow, "to hang a nineteen-year-old boy for the philosophy that was taught him at the university," one that appeared in thousands of college library books. "The university would be more to blame than he is," the attorney asserted. "The scholars of the world would be more to blame than he is."[23]

Despite the originality of Darrow's plea, Cook County Criminal Court judge John R. Caverly found "no mitigating circumstances" or evidence of insanity in the Franks murder case. Yet Caverly spared Leopold and Loeb the death penalty by sentencing them to life imprisonment for the killing and to a concurrent ninety-nine years for the ransom kidnapping. As five thousand spectators waited for the decision outside the court house, the judge announced that "the dictates of an enlightened humanity" required that the defendants escape execution because of their status as legal minors.[24]

Although Judge Caverly sought to diffuse the issues of criminal responsibility raised by Darrow, the Leopold-Loeb case marked a turning point in American jurisprudence. As George W. Kirchwey, the former dean of Columbia University Law School and the warden of Sing Sing prison, pointed out in the *New York Times,* new knowledge of human psychology now was finding its way into the traditional system of criminal justice. Kirchwey contended that when the judge admitted Darrow's evidence, he opened the courts to a new concept of responsibility for crime and to an application of scientific principles from therapists and counselors. In concurrence, psychiatrist Leonard Blumgart told readers of *The Nation* that practically all the behavior of Leopold and Loeb could be viewed as compensation for a sense of inferiority, either physical or emotional. The time was coming, predicted Blumgart, "when all crime and all bad behavior will be approached as human illness is now, where moral questions do not enter in."[25]

Despite such viewpoints, the relationship between crime and punishment remained a sensitive matter. Two days before the start of closing arguments, someone left a human head, a pair of withered arms, and a single discolored leg in the shape of a skull-and-crossbones opposite the Loeb's Chicago home with the written message, "If the court don't hang them we will. K.K.K." Press comment on the sentencing brought mixed reviews. A New Jersey judge admonished that sympathy for minors should not disguise the fact that 80 percent of the nation's crime was committed by men under twenty-one years of age. Noting that poor adolescents in similar cases seldom received relief from the death penalty, the *Detroit Free Press* regretted that Leopold and Loeb had "enough money to hire a high-priced, emotional lawyer, who makes a speciality of cheating the gallows." As "jaded" murderers who killed a child "in order to get a thrill," the defendants were not entitled to mercy, editorialized the *Minneapolis Star*.[26]

The most provocative comments about Leopold and Loeb focused on the disturbing relationship between intelligence and evil. Even psychiatrist Blumgart acknowledged that Leopold's "superior intellect" did not mean that his behavior was "intelligent." Noting the defendants' lack of pity for their victim, the editors of *World's Work* observed that "intellectual genius may be housed in the same body with emotional imbecility." A similar view pervaded "Education and Murder," an editorial by British essayist G. K. Chesterton reprinted in the *Literary Digest*. Chesterton held that the Franks murder exposed the fallacy of college training as the foundation of a better world. Leopold and Loeb "reached the other end of nowhere, the last point of nihilism and anarchy," he wrote, "much quicker because of the speeding up of their mental development by education." The problem lay in "the philosophy of experience" taught at the university. As long as learning was "valued for the sake of experience, and not for the sake of right choice and for the truth," concluded Chesterton, "any miserable little diseased monkey is entitled to say that one experience is as interesting as another."[27]

***

The editors of the *New York Times* correctly concluded that Darrow's brief for modern penology largely had been ignored in the Franks murder sentencing.[28] Yet the highly publicized case dramatized a profound cultural controversy. The heart of the dispute lay in the perceived role of intellectuals and scientific experts in legitimizing societal standards that were premised on the belief that individuals were conditioned by circumstances beyond their personal control. By questioning whether criminals and others were morally responsible for the consequences of their actions, Darrow embraced a socially constructed explanation of behavior that challenged traditional precepts of accountability and appropriate conduct. Ironically, the famed attorney's widely disseminated endorsement of such a philosophy would return to haunt him less than one year later in a trial even more sensational than the Leopold-Loeb proceeding. As Darrow sought to defend the right of public school teachers to instruct students in the principles of scientific evolution in the celebrated Scopes trial of 1925, the expertise and authority of America's social guardians came under intense attack in one of the great courtroom confrontations of the twentieth century.

Controversy over Charles Darwin's theories of human evolution and metaphorical interpretations of Biblical text had simmered for decades among orthodox Baptists, Presbyterians, Methodists, and other Protestants. As a re-assertion of "the fundamentals" of evangelical Christianity spread through the Midwest, South, and Southwest in the early twentieth century, traditionalists insisted that the Book of Genesis and the Scripture offered believers an inerrant guide to divine plan and order. The association of the German military machine of World War I with a "might makes right" philosophy heightened concern over modern creeds, leading some theologians to wonder if evolutionary doctrines had caused the war. Even a moderate like Vernon Kellogg, a former Stanford biology professor, tied wartime Germany to the belief that evolution was "deter-mined by a vigorous and ruthless struggle for existence of the most combative type." By 1920, many evangelical worshippers linked evolutionary precepts to amoral education and the evils of modern atheism, secularism, immorality, materialism, and disintegration of the family.[29]

The evolution controversy quickly spread to the nation's colleges, the focal point of modern secularism and scientific expertise. By 1923, at least twelve professors, including several at the University of Tennessee, had been dismissed for advocating Darwinian views or defending the right of others to do so. At the University of North Carolina, Baptist minister A. C. Dixon assailed the secular influence of president Harry W. Chase, a Massachusetts native and former stu-dent of G. Stanley Hall. In 1924, North Carolina's governor personally intervened with the State Board of Education to ban two Darwinist biology textbooks from use at the institution. When a sociology professor at North Carolina College for Women at Greensboro conducted a class discussion in 1925 on Genesis as "a form of mythology," Ku Klux Klan chapters and religious groups invoked their power as taxpayers to demand that the "imported highbrow" from the University of Chicago be dismissed.[30]

Academics and educators responded to the threat of repression with sharply worded protests. The 1925 report of the AAUP Committee on Freedom of Teaching in Science condemned fundamentalists as "un-American" for seeking to control learning by popular vote rather than relying on the leadership of qualified experts. That same year the bulletin of the Association of American Colleges, a consortium of college presidents, admonished that religious educa-tion should not be based on "the desire to know what the people want, but ... to help the people want what they ought to have." Such expressions of academic privilege faced a tide of opposition in the 1920s, leading twenty state legislatures to consider banning the teaching of biological evolution in public schools. By the end of the decade, five states had enacted such restrictions.[31]

The first explicit prohibition of Darwinian teaching in the public schools came in Tennessee, where the Butler Act of 1925 forbade instruction in "any theory that denies the story of the divine creation of man as taught in the Bible, and teaches instead that man has descended from a lower order of animals."

Signed as a symbolic gesture by a governor who believed the statute was too vague to be enforced, the antievolution bill nevertheless aroused the attention of the American Civil Liberties Union (ACLU), which sought to test its constitutionality in a civil proceeding. Controversy over the Butler Act aroused the interest of the New York-born manager of a mining company in Dayton, a small town forty miles north of Chattanooga, who sought publicity for the community as a site for potential investment capital. Cooperating with the local school board president, whose pharmacy retailed required textbooks, the coal and iron executive arranged the arrest of a high school teacher for classroom use of a widely distributed Darwinian text, George Hunter's *A Civic Biology*.[32]

Dayton high school teacher John Thomas Scopes agreed to serve as the target of the complaint. The son of an agnostic railroad union leader and socialist, Scopes had studied chemistry at the University of Illinois and received a B.A. in physical sciences at the University of Kentucky. Following graduation in 1924, he had been hired as Dayton's science teacher and athletic coach. One month after passage of the Butler Act, Scopes agreed to a two-week stint as substitute for the school's ailing biology instructor. When his arrest compelled the state to press criminal charges, the first attorney to come to his aid was a University of Tennessee law school professor who had been dismissed for advocating the right of science instructors to teach Darwinist principles. Meanwhile, the World's Christian Fundamentals Association, organized in 1919 to fight modern theology in Protestant churches, retained William Jennings Bryan to assist the prosecution.[33]

Bryan has been heralded as the twentieth century's most important evangelical politician, certainly the central figure in American reform politics between the 1890s and the 1920s. The crusader's fusion of progressive politics and Protestant moralism led no less a source than John Scopes to depict him as "the greatest man produced in the United States since the days of Thomas Jefferson. . . . Anything that was for the good of the common man he favored." Remembered for his stirring 1896 presidential campaign in support of the free coinage of silver, Bryan used his influence in the Democratic Party to oppose the annexation of the Philippines in 1899 and to crusade against U.S. intervention in World War I. In 1910, the Boy Orator of the Platte added prohibitionism to a wide array of causes that included woman's suffrage, labor rights, regulation of monopolies, electoral primaries, and direct election of U.S. senators.[34]

The legendary status of the Great Commoner derived from an unwavering and persistent populism that permeated his views on culture and politics. In a 1916 interview with journalist John Reed, the nation's leading reformer confided that his favorite music remained traditional religious hymns or sentimental tunes; his preferred reading the Bible, Thomas Jefferson, or the democratic historian George Bancroft; and his art of choice the paintings found on the walls of the Young Men's Christian Association. Bryan considered sensual beauty without moral purpose to be a decadent play thing of the rich. As historian

LeRoy Ashby has suggested, the Midwest folk hero blamed social and economic elites for cultural corruption, holding them responsible for the excesses of the consumer economy and its accompanying hedonistic values.[35]

Bryan's political views were consistent with his suspicion of elites and his republican conviction that a rational, virtuous citizenry must remain at the center of human affairs. Espousing what he called "the democracy of the heart," he restated Jefferson's emphasis on human feelings as opposed to abstract reflection. An extravagant optimist who nevertheless acknowledged the existence of human frailty, Bryan insisted that the voice of the people reflected the will of God. "When reform comes in this country, it starts with the masses," he once observed. "According to our system of government, the people are interested in everything and can be trusted to decide everything." Crusader and politician, Bryan applied his expertise in democracy to science, which he saw as a revelation of God's purposes easily understood by the average person.[36]

Bryan took up the issue of evolution in 1920. A religious moderate who had sought to prevent a fundamentalist takeover of the Presbyterian church's general assembly, he previously had refrained from seeking the expulsion of Darwinian thought from the classroom. Yet World War I convinced Bryan of the connections between Nietzschean philosophy, belief in the survival of the fittest, and the social pathologies of war and violence. By the early 1920s, the reformer no longer was content to press schools to teach Darwin's principles as biological theory instead of fact. Instead, Bryan opened a broad assault on evolution in a series of addresses at state universities and seminaries, many of which found their way into print. Using his newspaper, *The Commoner,* he summarized his concerns in pieces such as "The Menace of Darwinism." In December 1921, Bryan began to teach an annual tourist Bible class in Miami. A weekly syndicated column, "What Commoner Bryan Is Saying," reproduced his Sunday school sermons. By 1923, Bryan was telling audiences that the antievolution crusade was the greatest reform movement with which he had ever been associated.[37]

The heart of Bryan's philosophy lay in the conviction that all morality and virtue depended upon religion and a belief in God. "Man is part of God's plan and is placed on earth for a purpose," he explained in a 1922 opinion piece in the *New York Times.* As an advocate of "applied Christianity," a version of the Social Gospel that integrated institutional religion into the world of politics and social reform, Bryan insisted that love, not force, was the key to human development. He bitterly objected to notions of the survival of the fittest, fearing that such thinking justified the employment of brutish behavior. Evolution, charged Bryan, was a doctrine "by which not the fittest but the fiercest and the most merciless survive." If young people learned that people came from beasts, that there was no divine plan in the universe, and that morality was simply man-made, materialism, hedonism, and selfishness would come to dominate the social arena. "All the ills from which America suffers can be traced back to the teaching of evolution," the religious populist told the Seventh Day Adventists in 1924.[38]

Bryan's deeply felt spiritual views placed him at odds with the dominant secular elements of the nation's intelligentsia. He mocked the "cultural crowd" that looked upon religion as fit only for the "superstitious and ignorant." Such intellectual superiority was unjust, he proclaimed in 1917, because reverence for God rested upon acknowledgment of human finiteness and sinfulness. Religious faith embodied a moral sense that took hold upon "those verities which man cannot grasp," and was therefore an avenue to truth. Through this perspective education became a means of nurturing the soul, not the brain. "The sin of this generation," Bryan told readers of *The Commoner* in 1921, "is mind worship–a worship as destructive as any other form of idolatry."[39]

Fashioning a folk wisdom that associated intellectual elites with moral decadence, Bryan warned that trained minds might wreck civilization if allowed to exercise authority without spiritual guidance. He castigated those highly paid teachers who embodied a "sham intelligence" that led students away from God. "We have allowed the moral influences to be crowded out" of education and undermined the faith of children, declared Bryan. To buttress his concern that state schools were destroying religious values, Bryan cited James Leuba's finding that nearly half the nation's college graduates denied or doubted the fundamental precepts of the Christian religion. Speaking before a commencement gathering at Kentucky's Asbury College in 1922, the Great Commoner attributed to Theodore Roosevelt a quotation suggesting there was "scarcely a conspiracy against the national welfare that does not have the brains of Harvard behind it."[40]

Bryan particularly objected to professional science's obsession with materialist values at the expense of religious sensibilities. "How long will they allow the search for strata of stone and fragments of fossil and decaying skeletons that are strewn around the house to absorb their thoughts," he asked in *In His Image*, "to the exclusion of the architect who planned it all?" Mocking academic scientists as "mind-worshippers," Bryan responded to an attack in the *New York Times* by characterizing professors as people who "misrepresent their opponents, look with contempt upon those who do not exhaust the alphabet in setting forth their degrees, and evade the issue which they pretend to discuss." In a magazine article published as the Scopes trial began, Bryan scored "the sublime self-confidence of the evolutionists" and mocked their presumptuousness for claiming an infallibility which they denied to the Bible. "While God does not despise the learned," the evangelical leader told a gathering at Dayton's Methodist Episcopalian Church the Sunday before the trial, "he does not give them a monopoly of His attention."[41]

Academic evolutionists had become another undemocratic elite for Bryan, a priesthood or "scientific soviet ... attempting to dictate what shall be taught in our schools." Insisting that control over education would contaminate religion, he dismissed the professoriat as "the smallest, the most impudent, and the most tyrannical oligarchy that has ever attempted to exercise arbitrary power." "Can a handful of scientists rob your children of religion and turn them out atheist?" asked the Great Commoner. Bryan had called upon Wisconsin taxpayers in 1922 to dismiss a university president whose toleration of evolution in the curriculum undermined the majority of the people's religious beliefs. Three years later, he used a sermon entitled "They Have Taken My Lord," to argue that no one could "rightly demand pay from the taxpayers for teaching their children what they do not want taught." Writing to co-prosecutor Sue K. Hicks in May 1925, the political evangelist insisted that Scopes was "the *easiest* case to explain I have ever found" because it involved the "*right of the people* speaking through the legislature, to control the schools which they *create* and *support.*"[42]

***

Bryan preferred not to address the teaching of Darwinism in a criminal context. Believing that instructors who violated the antievolution law should be given the opportunity to resign, he offered in advance to pay any fine assessed to Scopes. As the historian Garry Wills has suggested, Bryan was less interested in pillorying schoolteachers than in mounting a defense of the populace against secular experts and scientific elites. Such criticism, with its strong hint of anti-intellectualism and its impatience with academic freedom and reasoned discourse, infuriated the scholarly community and those who thrived on the exchange of ideas. The popular religion and politics of the average person represented by Bryan, asserted one contributor to *Scientific Monthly,* fashioned "an unsympatheic social milieu" for scholarship that made it difficult to raise the general level of intelligence. Edward Mims, an English professor at Tennessee's Vanderbilt University, lamented that the South's academies were threatened and confronted by "a negation of the very spirit of research and inquiry" required by such institutions. The region still had "a great mass of uneducated people–sensitive, passionate, prejudiced–and another mass of the half-educated," warned Mims, who had "very little intellectual curiosity or independence of judgment."[43]

Bryan's reputation among the intelligentsia may have been set in 1914 when Walter Lippmann pegged him as an opponent of the modern world of specialization and science, a man mired in a universe that had ceased to exist. Journalist and satirist Henry Louis Mencken sustained this view with portraits that ridiculed the reformer as a fraud, a "buffoon," a "zany," a "preacher of theological bilge," and "a teapot pope in the coca-cola belt." An admirer of the agnostic Clarence Darrow, whose work he had published in *The American Mercury,* and a trained engineer, Mencken urged his attorney friend to defend Scopes when news broke that Bryan was to assist the prosecution. Seeing the trial as an opportunity to make a fool out of an old adversary, the reporter volunteered to serve as a defense consultant. More technical advice came from the Institution for the Popularization of Science, a private foundation that recruited specialists in geology, zoology, anthropology, psychology, and sociology as courtroom witnesses.[44]

Darrow sought to quash the Scopes indictment on 13 July 1925 by arguing that the Tennessee antievolution law violated freedom of religion. Once Judge J. T. Raulston rejected the motion two days later, defense attorney Dudley Field Malone began his opening statement. Malone promised to present testimony from fifteen scientific specialists that there was no conflict between biology and religion over creation. "Science occupies a field of learning separate and apart from the learning and theology which the clergy expound," he declared. Yet the defense sought to demonstrate that there was no branch of science that could be taught without explaining the theory of evolution. A hymn, allegory, and work of religious interpretation, the Book of Genesis nevertheless could not be accepted as the basis for teaching science in public schools.[45]

Dr. Maynard M. Metcalf, a research professor in zoology at Johns Hopkins and a Congregationalist deacon, was the first to take the stand. Once Darrow asked the witness to define evolution, the prosecution objected that scientific views on the matter were irrelevant to the case. After the court dismissed the jury, all parties agreed that expert witnesses could testify about evolution before the judge, but only for purposes of permitting him to rule on the admissibility of such evidence. The next day, July 16th, Bryan delivered his only speech of the trial, a sixty-minute brief and sermon that ridiculed the applicability of expert testimony. "We do not need any expert to tell us what the law means," he declared. If Tennessee citizens had spoken through their legislature, it was not "proper to bring experts in here to try to defeat the purposes of the people of this state." The law simply concluded that "a minority" could not "compel a teacher to teach that the Bible is not true."[46]

Bryan took particular aim at academic theorists. "I suppose this distinguished scholar ... shamed them all by his number of degrees," he exclaimed as he pointed to Metcalf. The attorney then mocked evolutionists for not being able to state where life began and for failing to trace the transformation of one species to another. In their inability to fathom mystery and miracle, he persisted, materialists could not explain how humans "became endowed with the hope of immortality." Nor could they comprehend the need for redemption in a mechanistic universe in which "man has been rising all the time." Here Bryan taunted Darrow by citing Nietzsche, the center of controversy in the Leopold-Loeb trial, and the subject of Mencken's first book. Mencken had tied Nietzsche to evolution by describing the philosopher's superman as rising above the rejects of history. The journalist had described such a process as an unfolding of "the law of natural selection—that invariable natural law which ordains that the fit shall survive and the unfit shall perish."[47]

Bryan now used Darrow's Leopold-Loeb discourse on Nietzsche for his own purposes. His opponent had argued that because Leopold adopted Nietzsche's philosophy of the superman, he was "not responsible for the taking of human life." Darrow had sought to establish that the universities and professors who taught the German's creed were, in effect, more responsible for the Franks crime than the defendant. When Darrow objected that Bryan was misrepresenting him, the Scopes prosecutor cited the transcript passage in which the defense attorney had pleaded that institutions of higher learning, scholars, and publishers "would be more to blame." Tying the unconventional Nietzsche to Darwinism, Bryan concluded the brief colloquy by noting that Tennessee parents had taken the "necessary caution to write poison" on evolutionary theory through the state law at issue.[48]

Bryan returned his focus to the testimony of the academics by declaring "that all the experts that they could bring would mean nothing," even if specialists in Biblical texts. "The one beauty about the word of God is, it does not take an expert to understand it," he observed. Those who accepted Jesus and sought forgiveness knew more about the Scripture "than all of the skeptical outside Bible experts that could come in here to talk to the people of Tennessee about the construction that they place upon the Bible." The Holy Book was "not going to be driven out of this court by experts who come hundreds of miles to testify that they can reconcile evolution with its ancestor in the jungle, or man made by God in His image and put here for purposes as a part of the divine plan." Tennessee would not be humiliated because outsiders protested laws that did not conform with their own ideas, he concluded.[49]

On July 17th, the day following Bryan's performance, Judge Raulston ruled that scientific testimony on evolutionary theory was irrelevant if the prosecution could prove that the defendant had taught a theory contrary to Biblical notions of divine creation. Under Tennessee law, expert evidence was admissable "only when the issues involve facts of such complex nature that a man of ordinary understanding is not competent and qualified to form an opinion." Although Raulston permitted the statements of academic witnesses to be read into the record for purposes of appeal, his decision effectively ended the defense case. In the following days, both sides increasingly turned to the public arena to air their positions. In an outdoor meeting in nearby Pikesville on Sunday, July 19th, Bryan assailed the "gigantic conspiracy among atheists and agnostics against the Christian religion" and blasted journalists "who come from another state to call you yokels and bigots."[50]

As the trial moved to the courthouse lawn the following afternoon, Bryan ignored protests from the chief prosecutor and agreed to submit to questioning by Darrow. The defense ultimately induced Bryan to admit that he did not necessarily believe that the earth had been created in six twenty-four hour "days." Yet the evangelical received the crowd's most enthusiastic applause a moment later when he answered Darrow's taunt that "we have the purpose of preventing bigots and ignoramuses from controlling the education of the United States." "I am simply trying to protect the Word of God against the greatest atheist or agnostic in the United States," he responded. "I want the world to know that agnosticism is trying to force agnosticism on our colleges and on our schools, and the people of Tennessee will not permit it to be done."[51]

Bryan intended to put Darrow on the stand as a state witness but prosecutors forbade him from doing so. On July 21st, the last day of the trial, Judge Raulston further disappointed the reformer by expunging his testimony from the record on grounds of irrelevancy to a potential appeal. When the defense waived its right for summation, moreover, Bryan was deprived of the chance to present a concluding statement. Nevertheless, after eight minutes of deliberation, the jury returned with a guilty verdict and the judge assessed Scopes the minimum $100 fine required by the law. Days later, Bryan issued a public statement in which he protested that he had never been "called 'ignorant' or an 'ignoramus' . . . by any one except an evolutionist." Christians were "not enemies of education," he proclaimed.[52]

Four days after the end of the trial, Bryan traveled to nearby Winchester, where he addressed eight thousand followers at the county fairgrounds. The next day, July 26th, the Great Commoner died of complications from diabetes and other ailments. Mary Bryan released a printed version of her husband's undelivered closing argument laced with excerpts from his last speech. Bryan's testament described the Scopes trial as "the mountain peak" of a life's effort. At issue was the attempt of "a little irresponsible oligarchy of self-styled 'intellectuals'" who were leading children "into a starless night" by preaching irreligion under the guise of teaching science. Bryan's *Last Message* illustrated the perceived dangers of an ethically unaccountable intelligentsia by once again borrowing Darrow's quotations of Nietzsche in Leopold and Loeb. "To be obsessed by moral consideration," Nietzsche had written, "presupposes a very low grade of intellect. We should substitute for morality the will to our own end." Bryan recalled that the German writer had depicted supermen as "colder, harder, less cautious, and more free from the fear of public opinion," as men who were liberated from respectability and "the virtues of the herd."[53]

Stressing government's role in encouraging the young to reject destructive creeds, Bryan asked if the state would "be blameless if it permitted the universities to be turned into training schools for murderers," an obvious reference to Leopold-Loeb. He assailed psychologists who built upon the evolutionary hypothesis to teach that humans were "nothing but a bundle of characteristics inherited from brute ancestors," a further taunt to Darrow. Such emphasis on heredity would destroy all sense of responsibility and accountability, warned Bryan. College graduates needed religion for their own restraint and to assure society that their enlarged powers would be used for the benefit of society and not against the public welfare. Evolution's mechanical and materialistic view of progress, he concluded, paralyzed the hope for reform and discouraged those who labored for the improvement of the human condition.[54]

Although the metropolitan press sought to link Bryan's death to alleged humiliation at the Scopes trial, the significance of the proceeding was far more complicated. On appeal, the Tennessee Supreme Court reversed the Scopes conviction early in 1927 on technical grounds that the fine had been imposed by the judge instead of the jury. Yet in a 3 to 1 decision, the court sustained the Butler Act, which remained on the books until 1966. The 1920s also produced antievolution laws in Mississippi, Alabama, and Arkansas, while the populist governor of Texas, Miriam "Ma" Ferguson, banned all references to Darwinism in public school textbooks. Many educational publishers voluntarily followed suit. Meanwhile, John Scopes received a scholarship to study geology at the University of Chicago, the host institution of several defense experts. Hired by Gulf Oil, Scopes was sent to Venezuela in 1927, where he married the daughter of an American businessman and converted to Catholicism. After an additional year of study at Chicago, the geologist worked as a natural gas consultant in Texas and Louisiana until retirement in 1963.[55]

As Garry Wills has observed, the Scopes hearing constituted "a nontrial over a nonlaw, with a nondefendant backed by nonsupporters. Its most famous moment involved nontestimony by a nonexpert, which was followed by a nondefeat."[56] Wills also might have noted that the prosecution's most telling example, the Darrow plea for Leopold and Loeb, involved an argument largely irrelevant to the verdict in the earlier case. Nevertheless, Dayton provided an enormously revealing flashpoint of American cultural conflict.

For Darrow and most academics and intellectuals, the evolution controversy amounted to a battle over the right of teachers to counter backward superstition and intolerance with enlightened principles of modern science. For Bryan and the Tennessee prosecutors, however, classroom use of Darwinian theory constituted an "invasion" into the fabric of a tradition-based community by outside experts and social authorities, an external threat to the state's commonly shared moral order. In retrospect, the confrontation at Dayton addressed the enhanced role of newly emerging professional and academic elites in defining reality and in molding social institutions such as the public schools. At issue was whether the dissemination of modern ideas, practices, and policies addressed the intrinsic needs of a democratic constituency in an increasingly complex society, or whether the secularist agenda of the intelligentsia mainly served the aspirations and career goals of a rising professional elite that found itself dangerously removed from the general populace.

***

Less than two weeks after the conclusion of the Scopes trial, Ohio affiliates of the Knights of the Ku Klux Klan burned crosses to memorialize William Jennings Bryan. A week later forty thousand hooded and robed Klansmen paraded before 200,000 spectators through the streets of Washington, D.C. in a significant demonstration of the secret order's nationwide strength. As the weekend festivities in the capital concluded, a Klan delegation placed wreaths of red roses on Bryan's tomb in Arlington National Cemetery.[57]

More than any other popular movement of the 1920s, the Ku Klux Klan expressed Bryan's case against the secular and cosmopolitan orientation of America's intellectual social guardians. Reorganized in Atlanta in 1915, the "second" Klan confined membership to white, native-born Protestant men and committed initiates to a strict code of secrecy, obedience, fidelity, and organizational solidarity. As the segregationalist Invisible Empire spread from the Deep South and Southwest to the Northeast, Midwest, and Pacific Coast in the early 1920s, it embraced between two and six million adherents and fashioned itself as a vehicle of "100 percent Americanism." Under this rubric the Klan maintained its original commitment to racial supremacy while seeking to limit the political and economic influence of "hyphenated" immigrants and white ethnics, particularly Roman Catholics and Jews. Yet individual chapters often acted as local citizens' lobbies and focused on concerns such as law enforcement, civic improvement, social purity, support for public schools, and other reforms. The movement's espousal of traditional middle-class morality was particularly strong among Ladies of the Invisible Empire (LOTIES), its sister organization.[58]

As community reformers and purity crusaders, Klan leaders often cooperated with social work professionals, technical experts, and other civic elites. In Dallas, the Klan invested $85,000 in Hope Cottage, a professionally run home for abandoned children which the secret order subsequently turned over to the city. Denver's chapter head, Dr. John Galen Locke, used his professional expertise to warn city health officials in 1922 to take precautions against a threatened smallpox epidemic. In La Grande, Oregon, klavern officials asked the county health nurse to deal with a railroad worker who refused to make child support payments and backed the efforts of a Klan physician to obtain passage of a city bond issue for an artesian well system. In Washington, D. C., national leaders of both men's and women's Klans endorsed creation of a federal Department of Education to bolster the public schools, enhance teacher training, and provide better educational facilities and equipment.[59]

Klan activism also targeted elites accused of amorality, corruption, or mere arrogance. Knights in Buffalo, Youngstown, Indianapolis, and El Paso condemned politicians for failing to enforce anti-vice and prohibition measures. In Atlanta, Dallas, Denver, and Anaheim, Klansmen opposed city manager systems and establishment alliances deemed as unresponsive to the demands of ordinary citizens. Yet the most spirited Klan denunciations on both local and national levels were directed against the intellectuals and academic experts who appeared to legitimize social changes threatening to the secret order's predominately working-class and lower-middle-class constituency. Klan officials took particular aim at rationalist, secularist, and materialist social values attributed to the intelligentsia. A 1922 proclamation by interim Imperial Wizard Edward Y. Clarke denounced bolshevism "and other isms" receiving "much comfort and encouragement from a great number of silly, hair-brained Americans." "Some of the professors in some colleges and universities," a Texas Klan leader told a

1923 convocation, "are preaching doctrines that are detrimental to American ideals... [and] are not really and truly loyal to their state or to their nation."[60]

Although Klansmen seldom belonged to fundamentalist churches, biological evolution provided a fitting example of threatening social doctrine. When Knights in Oregon discovered that a political rival was a Darwinist, the klavern secretary described the culprit as someone who "firmly believes that man and monkey are true kindred spirits." Suspecting without evidence that their adversary's motives were ruled by local Catholic politicians, chapter officials concluded that he "needs a little fixing over," an apparent rhetorical threat. Yet ideologues like the editor of a Youngstown Klan newspaper professed assurance that "the so-called liberal element" were "campaign followers" of evil Catholics, atheists, and corrupt politicians. In Denver, Juvenile Court Judge Benjamin Lindsey, the broad-minded advocate of companionate marriage, became a prime target of KKK agitation in 1924 when he participated in the attempt to recall the city's Klan-backed mayor. Campaigning for the Georgia governorship six years later, a Klan officer predictably attacked "alien" beliefs and practices such as "atheism, communism, chain stores, and companionate marriage."[61]

Klan distrust of cosmopolitan social values was brilliantly captured in the rhetoric of Hiram Wesley Evans, the mastermind of the secret order's rise to mass movement status. The son of an Alabama judge, Evans completed high school in Hubbard, Texas, studied under a tutor for two years, and entered but never completed the dentistry program at Nashville's Vanderbilt University. Arriving in Dallas in 1900 at the age of nineteen, Evans set up a dental practice that mainly served African-Americans. Recruited from the Masonic Lodge as a charter member of the Dallas klavern and appointed as the chapter's first leader in 1920, he allegedly led a party of Klansmen in the kidnapping and branding of an African-American bellhop suspected of procuring prostitutes. After a temporary stint as great titan of the Texas Realm in 1922, however, Evans assumed the post of national Klan secretary, a position he used to denounce remaining vigilantism and terror among local chapters and to push the Klan toward purity activism, political lobbying, and national respectability. At the organization's Atlanta convention in November 1922, the Dallas dentist maneuvered himself into the top slot of imperial wizard.[62]

A life-long Democrat, member of the Disciples of Christ (Christian) Church, and devotee of fishing, Evans heralded himself as the most average man in America. Observers like the journalist Stanley Frost noted that the round-faced, undistinguished, and soft-spoken imperial wizard lacked high culture and educated sophistication. But they also described Evans as an excellent organizer, promoter, and administrator. Frost praised the Klan leader's practical common sense, intuitive understanding of ordinary citizens, and instinct for politics. Although Evans was said to possess a latent intellectual streak, Frost portrayed the imperial wizard's directly expressed thoughts and feelings as "those of the commonalty rather than the intellectuals." Such abilities enabled Hiram Wesley

Evans to rank as the undisputed advocate and defender of Klan views in the print media and public arenas of the 1920s.[63]

Evans first mounted the national stage when he addressed seventy-five thousand Klansmen and their families on Ku Klux Klan Day at the Texas State Fair in October 1923. Published the following year as a pamphlet entitled *The Public School Problem in America,* the address criticized the nation's inadequate commitment to quality public education. Evans underlined the urgency of school reform by delivering a jeremiad that confronted the spiritual impoverishment of the Jazz Age. America was "a wilderness in which predominates as much of stealth and more of vindictiveness than any jungle ever knew," protested the imperial wizard. Evans decried a spirit of lawlessness through legal evasion and subterfuge that disrespected and ignored national ideals and traditions. *"Truth, God's truth and man's truth,"* he declared, *"has become a vagrant–ragged, distorted, and discredited by selfishness."* [64]

***

Although Evans focused on the alleged threat of unassimilable Roman Catholics, Jews, and African-Americans, intellectuals held a special place in his demonology. Christian Knights, he told an interviewer in 1924, were "implacably opposed to atheistic intellectualism and to all the amatory and erotic tendences of modern degeneracy." Evans explained such terms in "The Klan of Tomorrow," an article authored in October 1924 for the *Imperial Night-Hawk,* the official KKK weekly. Although warning of foreigners who subverted national ideals with "moonshine patriotism," he placed the greatest blame on intellectual leaders who seemed "to accept the destruction of America as an accomplished fact." "Befuddled with the philosophy of a Communistic universalism" and the group mind of foreign creeds and ethnic identities, a cosomopolitan intelligentsia had paralyzed American nationalism. In a piece for the *Forum,* Evans insisted that liberals who permitted aliens to tear down the country prized toleration more than conviction.[65]

By the time of its Washington march in August 1925, the Ku Klux Klan appeared to have reached the apex of its power. Weeks after the demonstration Evans moved the organization's Atlanta headquarters to the nation's capital to enhance its role as a legislative pressure group. Yet the Invisible Empire was beginning to lose its mass appeal. Between the spring of 1924 and the end of the following year, an estimated 80 percent of the five million membership left the order. A second public demonstration of force in Washington in September 1926 would attract less than half the numbers of the previous year. Facing the potential dissolution of the movement, Evans published his most comprehensive defense of the order in the March 1926 edition of the mainstream *North American Review.*[66]

Transcending the obligatory concepts of white, Anglo-Protestant supremacy that defined Klan ideology, Evans conveyed a profound sense of loss and nostalgia in a perceptive and poignant critique of modern society. Nordic Americans, proclaimed the Klan's imperial wizard, were "increasingly uncomfortable, and finally deeply distressed," victimized by "confusion in thought and opinion, a groping hesitancy about national affairs and private life alike." "We began to find that we were dealing with strange ideas," wrote Evans, "policies that always sounded well but somehow always made us still more uncomfortable." Attributing a moral breakdown to the previous two decades, the Klan leader lamented that "one by one, all our traditional moral standards went by the boards, or were so disregarded that they ceased to be binding. The sacredness of our Sabbath, of our homes, of chastity, and finally even of our right to teach our own children in our schools fundamental facts and truths were torn away from us. Those who maintained the old standards did so only in the face of constant ridicule."[67]

Nothing was immune from the "invasion of aliens and alien ideas," complained Evans; "our great men, our historic struggles and sacrifices, our customs and personal traits, our 'Puritan consciences,'–all have been sacrificed without mercy." To add to such distress traditional Americans "found our great cities and the control of much of our industry and commerce taken over by strangers, who stacked the cards of success and prosperity against us" and came to dominate government. The Nordic American was "a stranger in large parts of the land his fathers gave him . . . , one much spit upon, and one to whom even the right to have his own opinions and to work for his own interests is now denied with jeers and revilings."[68]

Evans held out his sharpest criticism for liberal ideologues, the "enemy within" who served as the "intellectually mongrelized" apostles of "radicalism, cosmopolitanism, and alienism." Liberalism had "provided no defense against the alien invasion," proclaimed the imperial wizard, "but instead had excused it–even defended it against Americanism." But Evans went further to charge that as the province of "weaklings and parasites," liberalism had become "wholly academic, lost all touch with the plain people, disowned its instincts and common sense, and lived in a world of pure, high, groundless logic." Liberal ideology sustained a life "without moral standards," he asserted, one without any beliefs save "conviction in its own decadent religion of Liberalism toward everything." Guilty of undermining the Constitution and subverting the nation's customs and institutions, liberals had committed "nothing less than national, racial, and spiritual treason."[69]

Evans's contrast between traditional Americans and the intellectual liberals who legitimized modern practices and ideals clarified the evolving nature of the national culture and class war. Cleverly celebrating his constituents as "'hicks' and 'rubes' and 'drivers of second hand Fords,'" the imperial wizard offered a haunting collective portrait. "We are a movement of the plain people," he stated, "very weak in the matter of culture, intellectual support, and trained leadership. We are demanding, and we expect to win, a return of power into the hands of the everyday, not highly cultured, not overly intellectualized, but entirely unspoiled and not de-Americanized, average citizen of the old stock . . . the opposition of the intellectuals and liberals who held the leadership, betrayed Americanism, and from whom we expect to wrest control, is almost automatic." The Klan would succeed, declared Evans with bravado, because it was emotional and instinctive, rather than coldly intellectual, and because it could be trusted more than "the fine-haired reasoning of the denatured intellectuals."[70]

Evans's ethnocentrism led him to badly underestimate the adherence of immigrants and African-Americans to the traditional and patriotic values the Klan espoused. But his assault on intellectual liberals was far more grounded in the actual culture wars of the 1920s. As Robert A. Garson, a British scholar of American Studies, suggested in a landmark essay in 1977, postwar Knights and religious fundamentalists shared the fear "that the fashioning of society was being undertaken by a diverse but powerful economic group that was not bound by either historic tradition or an affinity for popular consent." Klan contempt for educational innovation, cultural pluralism, and hedonistic individualism reflected the conviction that the values of the new elite could not command public support and needed to be subjected to the scrutiny of the local community. At issue was the inability of ordinary citizens to influence the substance and spread of cultural beliefs and the desire of traditionalists to immunize families and communities from the forces of change that they had not themselves generated.[71]

Garson forged an evocative portrait of political fundamentalists who were profoundly disturbed by a generation of morally indifferent and purposeless leaders no longer committed to the cohesion and survival of society as they knew it. A favorite target of the orthodox were schools which prompted students to challenge their parents' way of life instead of inculcating venerated intellectual skills and moral values. Culture war in the 1920s, argued Garson, centered on a conflict between a growing professional elite and "a tradition-oriented society whose preoccupations had been ignored by the advocates of scientific rationality, objectivity, and modernism." Klan orthodoxy, he concluded, was not merely "a reactionary backlash" to the growing cosmopolitanism of American life. It was the political expression of a populace bewildered by a burgeoning culture it could not easily control or resist.[72]

Through Garson's interpretation of culture war, the rhetoric of Hiram Wesley Evans can be placed within the genre of modern alienation. Evans's evocation of the metaphor of the stranger anticipated Malcolm Cowley's observation that rootless 1920s intellectuals and literary exiles were "strangers in their own land." Lost Generation cohort John Dos Passos used similar imagery to condemn those who sanctioned the 1927 execution of the radical anarchists Nicola Sacco and Bartolomeo Vanzetti. "America our nation," protested Dos Passos, "has been beaten by strangers who have turned our language inside out, who have taken the clean words our fathers spoke and made them slimy and foul."[73]

Like the millions of Americans who cherished William Jennings Bryan's defense of religious faith, readers of the *North American Review* were familiar with the terms of Evans's critique of modern society and progress. Rather than serving as a mere conduit of exclusivist racial and ethnic codes, the Klan leader struck an early blow in the culture war between assertive professional elites and the forces of popular traditionalism. Fearful that uncontrolled societal change contributed to the character disintegration supposedly infecting the Jazz Age, grassroots defenders of moral orthodoxy insisted upon accountability from teachers, law makers, opinion makers, scientists, and other social guardians who legitimized ideological and cultural innovation. As historian Leonard J. Moore has argued, the roots of the twentieth-century confrontation between populist traditionalists and secular intellectuals lay in the turbulent and prophetic 1920s.[74] Leopold-Loeb, Dayton, and the angry rhetoric of the Ku Klux Klan all pointed to the controversial role of knowledge professionals and socially oriented intellectuals in the cultural debates unleashed by modernization and the rise of cosmopolitan values.

2

Shadow Government: The Brains Trust Under Fire, 1932–1936

Jazz Age prosperity offered a fitting context for wrenching debates over the cultural influence of academic professionals, scientific specialists, intellectual leaders, and other social guardians. Yet the terms of the debate changed dramatically following the Stock Market Crash of 1929, the onslaught of the Great Depression, and the advent of President Franklin D. Roosevelt's New Deal. Responding to rampant unemployment, falling demand for goods, deflation, and massive liquidation of investment, Roosevelt committed the federal government to unprecedented intervention in a peacetime economy and solicited the talents of leading academic and legal figures. Chapter 2 examines how the widespread use of unelected public service professionals, consultants, and aides during Roosevelt's first term intensified anxieties about the perceived political power of the knowledge sector. By exploring public discourse over the role played by policy experts and advisers in New Deal agricultural programs, in legislative regulation of Wall Street, and in the expanding influence of the executive branch, this chapter considers how interest group conflicts fed wider disputes over the relationship of social guardians to government power and the survival of democracy.

***

Although American suspicions about the political intelligentsia dated back to the presidency of Andrew Jackson, the issue attained new relevance during the Progressive Era. Between 1870 and 1920, educators, social scientists, physicians, attorneys, and social service providers organized over two hundred professional societies in the United States. Professionalization helped to protect the new middle class from the uncertainties of the market economy. It also enhanced the ability of the knowledge sector to participate in the creation and implementation of government policy. Prominent Progressive intellectuals like educator John Dewey, sociologists Lester Frank Ward and Edward A. Ross, and economists Richard T. Ely and John R. Commons argued that the state would have to rely upon the scientific and technical knowledge of professionals to further education, social ethics, and the general welfare. Ely and Commons established the American Bureau of Industrial Research in 1904. Three years later a group of ambitious social science professionals organized the New York Bureau of Municipal Research.[1]

Publicly oriented academics and scholars quickly won appointment to Progressive state and municipal commissions as nonpartisan experts and planners charged with regulating and administering market, labor, and social relations. In reform-minded Wisconsin, John Commons and other university advisers energetically applied their skills to the resolution of social problems through state regulatory agencies. Known as the Wisconsin Idea, the system encouraged the administering of "public interest" reform by service-oriented experts committed to political and economic efficiency. Commons worked on public utility and workers compensation legislation and helped to draft the civil service act that delegated the appointment of state officials to a nonpartisan commission. Social scientists and professionals also served as policy consultants and as members of investigatory commisions for Presidents Theodore Roosevelt, William Howard Taft, and Woodrow Wilson.[2]

As the Wilson administration recruited academic, professional, and business leaders to staff a variety of government agencies during World War I, planners like the philosopher and educator John Dewey promoted expert participation in the creation of centralized economic and social policy. Convinced that disciplined observation and reporting would improve public decision-making, Columbia University economist Wesley C. Mitchell established the National Bureau of Economic Research in 1920. By mid-decade, 150 business, professional, and reform lobbies were deploying academic specialists as expert witnesses before Congress to influence legislation. Despite frequent mistrust between officeholders and members of the academy, political leaders such as President Herbert Hoover viewed economic research and social analysis as an essential framework of policymaking. Organizing a scholarly survey of social patterns under the direction of Wesley Mitchell and University of Chicago political scientist Charles Merriam, the Hoover administration arranged for the publication of *Recent Trends in the United States* in 1933.[3]

The high profile of academic planning experts and technical specialists produced predictable controversy. Although he once had been a professional historian, political scientist, and college president, even Woodrow Wilson questioned rule by academic elites. "What I fear," Wilson once suggested, "is a government of experts. God forbid that in a democratic country we should resign the task and give the government over to experts. What are we for if we are to be scientifically taken care of by a small number of gentlemen who are the only men who understand the job?" Hostility to expertise even pervaded reform-minded Wisconsin, where the Democratic Party campaigned for the governorship in 1912 by attacking the new state income tax, wasteful regulatory commissions, and undemocratically appointed government officials. Voters were disdainful of paternalistic rule and "tired of being governed by the university clique; . . . tired of theorists, socialists, and sociologists," proclaimed one critic. Two years later, farmers and small businesspeople in the Home Rule and Taxpayers League denounced "tax-eating commissions" and remote bureaucrats, mounting the charge that "real democracy" had been destroyed because officials no longer trusted the people. Adopting the campaign query, "a state university or a University State?" a conservative Republican won the 1914 contest for governor.[4]

Concerns about planners and experts in government bureaucacies intensified in the years following World War I. Citing the "red tape, multitudinous officals, and inefficiency" of the wartime bureaucracy, critics tied postwar regulatory boards and social programs to the unwelcome prospect of concentrated political power. Sentiments against a permanent elite in the nation's capital were best summarized by Republican William E. Borah of Idaho, a fervent anti-monopolist and the Senate's leading authority on the Constitution. "The remorseless urge of centralization, the insatiable maw of bureaucracy," warned Borah, deprived "more and more the people of all voice, all rights touching home and hearthstone, of family and neighbor. There is not a practice, custom, or habit must soon be censored from Washington."[5]

Resentment of government bureaucrats could be particularly strong in the agrarian Middle West. In Iowa and Illinois, rural voters criticized the expense of state commissions and the demand for higher taxes to fund them. Midwesterners particularly objected to regulatory agencies that threatened to limit competition and access to traditional trades and occupations essential to local economies. Small-town voters in Iowa and Illinois resisted new training standards and licensing regulations for nurses, real estate brokers, architects, masons, construction contractors, plumbers, bakers, and cosmetologists. Ruralites also campaigned against public school spending that appeared to benefit big-city teachers and administrators. Taxation provided another arena for conflict. Farmers with land-based wealth and small businesses with tangible assets fought increased property levies, while calling for more taxes on the incomes and liquid holdings of urban professionals and salaried employees.[6]

***

Faced with a severe economic emergency in 1933, Franklin Roosevelt did not hesitate to draw upon the talents of academic policy experts and technical specialists. Roosevelt turned to policy intellectuals in an effort to broker the interests of investors, producers, organized labor, and consumers, while simultaneously restoring credit, individual economic security, and general prosperity to the capitalist market. Within the first one hundred days of the president's first term, Congress approved the creation of a host of new agencies such as the National Recovery Administration (NRA), the Agricultural Adjustment Administration (AAA), and the Federal Employment Relief Administration (FERA). The White House drew on planning and academic professionals to staff these bureaus and implement its programs. Indeed, much of the conceptualization behind New Deal reform originated with a network of 1920s management leaders, labor-minded social scientists, and unorthodox economists associated with consumer-oriented investment houses and business groups such as the Twentieth Century Fund, the Russell Sage Foundation, and the Taylor Society.[7]

The agenda of the industrial democracy innovators received widespread attention in 1932 when Columbia University law professor Adolf A. Berle and economist Gardiner C. Means published *The Modern Corporation and Private Property*. Arguing that corporate control rested in the hands of professional managers, the authors anticipated a "purely neutral technocracy" that would assume responsibility for distributing business income "on the basis of public policy rather than private cupidity." In the same year, *New Republic* editor George Soule published *A Planned Society*, a call for pragmatic reform and coordination that adopted both capitalist and socialist methods. *A New Deal*, a treatise by popular economist Stuart Chase proposing management of private enterprises in the public interest, also appeared in 1932. Meanwhile, John Dewey continued to insist that planners could bring cooperative control and social direction to industry and finance.[8]

In a period in which the professional labor market was in shambles, hordes of young lawyers, economists, political scientists, labor officials, journalists, and social workers flocked to Washington to offer their intellectual expertise to the executive agencies of the Roosevelt administration. Many of the new managers and bureaucrats were graduates of elite universities and law schools such as Columbia, Yale, and Harvard, where they had been taught that government had a positive role to play in regulating the economy in the public interest. Introduced to circles of power by cabinet officials such as Secretary of Interior Harold Ickes and Secretary of Agriculture Henry A. Wallace, the new arrivals formed an informal network of New Class insiders. New Dealer Thurman Arnold, a Yale law professor, anticipated that the capital's bright young professionals might adopt a "religion of government" and assume their place as "a competent, practical, opportunistic governing class."[9]

Roosevelt's turn toward the use of experts in national planning was heavily influenced by the academic advisers who joined his presidential campaign. Having used public administration specialists such as Columbia University's Raymond Moley to deal with statewide issues while governor of New York, Roosevelt convened a March 1932 gathering of policy-oriented scholars on national economic issues. One month later, the candidate used Moley's invocation of "the forgotten man" as the basis for a nationwide radio address that called for a government role in alleviating depression-imposed poverty. Subsequent remarks in St. Paul, shaped by Moley and Columbia economist Rexford G. Tugwell, described a "true concert of interests" requiring national economic coordination. Following a Moley memo setting forth the concept of a "new deal," Roosevelt delivered a speech at Georgia's Oglethorpe University that proposed federal action to stimulate purchasing power and regulate speculative production. The candidate's San Francisco Commonwealth Club address in September further pursued the advice of Moley, Tugwell, and Adolf Berle by advocating greater cooperation between government and business in economic planning.[10]

When candidate Roosevelt called a meeting of his three leading academic advisers and others at his Hyde Park estate in July 1932, a *New York Times* reporter in attendance came up with the the catchy term, "brains trust," to describe the gathering. True to their calling, the visiting scholars tended to dismiss politicians as opportunists and creatures of expediency. They shared Tugwell's conviction that public-minded intellects brought "fresh minds, clean motives, and unselfish aspirations" to questions of national policy. Through the application of scientific research and foresight, universities were to provide government with the inspiration, criticism, and expertise to usher in the new industrial state. By enlarging Washington's economic and social role, a civil service of professors and technicians would incorporate planning into a new constitutional order. Although differing on reform strategies, Roosevelt's brains trusters agreed that disinterested intervention by people like themselves would help to bring balance, stability, and order to the nation's ailing economy.[11] Like the biologists and social scientists of the 1920s, the self-confident professors had few qualms about asserting an historic role in the formation of public strategies and programs.

Once inaugurated, Roosevelt received his share of praise for the retention of academic advisers. After interviewing an anonymous member of the brains trust in May 1933, *New York Times* columnist Arthur Krock heralded the group's task as the creation of a benevolent form of state socialism to moderate labor-capital conflict, to regulate trade competition, and to provide security for workers. Two university presidents, Robert Hutchins of Chicago and Nicholas Murray Butler of Columbia, praised White House academics as pragmatic and trusted pursuers of truth. Criticism of the professors reflected the resentment of the "not very competent" in the face of expertise, scolded *Christian Century*. Similar approval came from the editors of *Collier's*, who argued that government was no more intelligent than the men who administered it and could not operate without the service of experts. Roosevelt received front-page coverage when he went to Yale in June 1934 to receive an honorary degree, where he told an audience of 2,500 that he would not abandon the practice "of calling on trained people for tasks that require trained people."[12]

Roosevelt's combative remarks at the Ivy League bastion suggested a defensiveness about the use of intellectual advisers that reflected underlying controversy. *New York Herald Tribune* correspondent and Roosevelt speech writer Ernest K. Lindley may have been correct when he noted in November 1933 that no aspect of the New Deal had been subjected to "hotter attack" than the brains trust. In the first month of the Roosevelt presidency *Business Week* had anguished about powerful Columbia University professors it described as "pure theorists . . . with a decided lean to the left." West Virginia's Henry D. Hatfield, chair of the Republican Senate Campaign Committee, expressed concern in

May 1933 that Tugwell and his associates had a controlling influence with the president. Critical press reports depicted a government of impractical economists and political scientists–a "professoriat" and "oligarchy of intellect" that overshadowed the cabinet and Congress and ran the country for its own good. Sensing potential political capital in the issue, Indiana Republicans gathered the following year to condemn "the sinister and hidden purpose of a so-called brain trust" that sought to change the nation's fundamental laws by indirection and implication.[13]

***

Discomfort with urban intellectuals and professionals had been particularly strong in rural areas during the 1920s, where economists often were suspected of ties to the dreaded Wall Street. Not surprisingly, many of the initial denunciations of academic political expertise in the New Deal focused on Roosevelt farm policy. Under Assistant Secretary Rexford Tugwell, economic counsel Mordecai Ezekiel, and finance adviser Gardiner Means, Roosevelt's Department of Agriculture pioneered centralized market planning under the assumption that individual farmers needed government help in adjusting production to sinking demand. Pressed by the president to limit agricultural output before surpluses completely leveled commodity prices, Tugwell embraced the domestic allotment plan of Milburn L. Wilson, a professor of agricultural economics at Montana State University. Wilson's scheme permitted farmers to vote on whether to reduce cultivated acreage for certain commodities if the government guaranteed higher market prices. A processing tax on millers would finance the program. Although the main task of domestic allotment was to increase farm values, Department of Agriculture economists viewed the plan as one that would introduce scientific and business techniques into agriculture while integrating academic experts into a permanent planning process.[14]

Rural producers responded in mixed fashion to a relief scheme that originated with economists, not farm leaders. Officials of the midwestern Farm Bureau Federation, mainly representing large growers, were among the leaders of major agricultural interest groups who endorsed the crop limitation concepts of the professional economists. Yet marginal competitors associated with organizations like John A. Simpson's National Farmers' Union, Milo Reno's Farmers Holiday Association, and William A. Hirth's Missouri Farmers Association, feared that the scheme had little to offer small producers and generally benefited absentee landowners. The dissidents insisted that any allotment plan incorporate a "cost-of-production" mechanism under which the federal government would license purchases of agricultural commodities and set legal minimum prices.[15]

Crop limitation opponents directed their anger at the New Deal brains trust. Days after Roosevelt's election, Missouri publisher Hirth castigated "professors and hairsplitters who are long on theories" but lacked familiarity with bank runs and unsalable surpluses. The allotment plan, complained a follower of John Simpson, was the creation of a college-bred economist who was ignorant about dirt farming. Testifying before the Senate Committee on Agriculture in January 1933, Simpson predicted that efforts to over-regulate agriculture would result in failure. Outright revolution among American farmers, he warned, only could be prevented by a price-fixing scheme based on cost of production in concert with an expanded currency to ease debt. At its March convention, the Farmers Holiday Association announced a nationwide strike in May unless Washington passed legislation setting minimum commodity prices and converted federal banks into public utilities. Government proposals for domestic allotment, charged FHA leader Milo Reno, were "a deliberate effort to palliate rather than remedy our agricultural ills."[16]

The rhetorical stakes of farm politics intensified when the Roosevelt administration incorporated domestic allotment in the proposed Agricultural Adjusment Act. Appearing before the Senate Agriculture Committee on the first day of public hearings in March 1933, Simpson protested that it was impossible to limit cultivated acreage and ridiculous to permit food to be sold below the producer's cost of production. As a struggling farmer and banker in the Oklahoma Territory of the 1890s, Simpson had supported the Populist Party. Forty years later, he blamed the Great Depression on poor distribution of wealth, diminished purchasing power, and the monopoly of credit he attributed to international bankers. "What we have overproduction of is empty stomachs and bare backs," Simpson told the Senate panel. The farm leader contended that the White House had produced a "consumer's bill" that would not allow half the nation's farmers to recap their costs. He insisted that the key to restoring rural prosperity was reemployment of the urban jobless and stimulation of demand for farm goods, not reduced acreage.[17]

The Senate responded to widespead criticism of domestic allotment by voting, 47 to 41, to insert a cost-of-production clause in the agricultural reform measure. Yet once the House eliminated the pricing provision, Congress approved Roosevelt's version of the bill one day before the proposed farm strike. The new legislation created the Agricultural Adjustment Administration, a powerful government agency endowed with the authority to provide crop price supports to farmers who signed acreage reduction contracts. Even AAA supporters such as Kansas Republican senator Arthur Capper admitted that the bureau extended "dictatorial" powers to thousands of federal agents. Moreover, the processing tax designed to finance the program was opposed by grain dealers, commission agents, millers, and agricultural attorneys. Direct government intervention in the market compelled Republican foes of the administration such as Massachusetts House member Joseph W. Martin, Jr. to charge that Roosevelt farm policies put Americans "on our way to Moscow."[18]

Martin's accusation particularly resonated with New Deal adversaries because of the influence of Assistant Agriculture Secretary Rexford Tugwell, the "impractical college professor" whom critics saw behind the AAA. A member of the Columbia faculty since 1920, Tugwell seemed to embody the characteristics that small producers most distrusted, partly because his economic philosophy focused on regulation of the market to assist consumers. In 1927, the professor visited the Soviet Union with a delegation of American trade unionists and intellectuals, but was critical of Joseph Stalin's agricultural programs and rejected socialism and communism. Nevertheless, Tugwell soon embraced experimental planning as a way of replacing nineteenth-century notions of unregulated markets. The fruition of such thinking appeared in a 1932 address before the American Economics Association, in which the theorist called for the replacement of the free market with a democratic system of planning and government controls. Tugwell proposed that profits be limited and enterprises run for consumers rather than for owners. By controlling prices and profit margins, government regulation was to adjust production to consumption.[19]

Tugwell endorsed domestic allotment because he believed that farm purchasing power was the key to recovery for the entire economy. Like Department of Agriculture financial adviser Gardiner Means, he preferred to treat growers as consumers and accept lower commodity prices as opposed to the higher rates sought by producer groups such as the National Farmers' Union. AAA officials like economic adviser Mordecai Ezekiel and general counsel Jerome Frank figured substantially in the agency's efforts to tie urban spending power to rural economic health. A legal philosopher and cosmopolitan liberal, Frank recruited department staff, including alleged radicals, from leading law schools. Like Frank, Ezekiel sought to stimulate consumption by working with the Department of Agriculture's Louis Bean and Commissioner of Labor Statistics Isador Lubin to promote high-volume production at lower prices.[20]

The consumer orientation of Department of Agriculture advisers infuriated economic traditionalists such as AAA administrator George N. Peek, who opposed acreage limitations, pushed for higher commodity prices, and preferred to dump the surplus overseas. Peek pictured Frank's Ivy League attorneys as "boys with their hair ablaze" who were involved in a socialist plot to collectivize agriculture. "These lawyers appeared distressingly inexperienced, radical, urban, and Jewish," the conservative administrator later recalled. In similar fashion, William Hirth's *Missouri Farmer* denounced "the visionary schemes of the so-called 'brain trust' who want to make the country over." Rather than practical men who could restore agriculture, complained Hirth, the New Deal produced "well-meaning theorists" who "babble about a 'planned society.'"[21]

Impatience with AAA restrictions and urban priorities led farm populists such as John Simpson to disparage the "brainless trust" held responsible for the controversial policies. In an open letter to the White House in September 1933, Simpson conveyed his fury. "Your 'Brain Trust' has justified my statement that they are bunch of impractical theorists," he began. "The best your economists propose is destruction of the things that could feed the hungry and clothe the naked." A month later, Simpson reiterated the complaint that Roosevelt's foolish advisers did not speak or understand the farmer's language when they sought to restore agricultural prosperity by lending growers more money instead of assuring them costs of production. "The best your 'Brain Trust' can produce as a remedy," he concluded, was "summed up in three words: drink, borrow, and destroy."[22]

Simpson's last attack on New Deal expertise came in "Modern Shylock," a January 1934 radio address inserted into the *Congressional Record* by Senator Burton K. Wheeler, a Montana Democrat with a long record of opposition to vested interests. People were "coming to feel that they have no control over the affairs of government," one segment began. "We know that something intervenes between the people and the control of their own affairs at Washington. It is not the people who have been ruling them." A second portion of the speech described a nation that "allowed itself to be governed by persons who were not invited to govern it ... They are the men who are never elected to anything. They operate behind closed doors in secret conferences." Simpson's chilling description had been taken verbatim from a 1912 campaign speech by Woodrow Wilson. Less than seven weeks after the farm leader's warning about shadow government, he died in the halls of the Senate office building after testifying against a proposed federal gas tax that threatened rural constituents.[23]

***

John Simpson's critique of the brains trust addressed major issues for those middle-class ruralites whose livelihood and social values stemmed from their status as independent producers or small enterprisers. Historian Catherine McNicol Stock has suggested that rural Americans often supported AAA because it promised immediate assistance. Yet many suspected that New Deal programs involved "interference by a centralized authority that knew little about the realities of their lives." Residents of the Great Plains feared that experts in Washington had little idea how recurrent dust storms, loss of crops, rising interest rates, increased costs, and deepening debt were making it difficult to retain modest land holdings and businesses even when marketing conditions were favorable. Farmers anguished that the government saw them as consumers and workers rather than as producers and businesspeople capable of running their own affairs. Welcoming state support to receive fair prices for their goods, they nevertheless worried that they could not maintain sufficient local and personal autonomy to sustain their communities and shared way of life.[24]

As historian Alan Brinkley has demonstrated, concerns over powerlessness and remote sources of authority helped to define the central social anxieties of the Great Depression. American farmers long had suspected outside experts who appeared unconcerned about their needs, interests, and sentiments. With the advent of the New Deal, the rural middle class confronted energized government professionals and managers whose reformist agenda looked to a "postproducerist" society of urban workers and consumers. On the basis of its credentialed knowledge, skill, and expertise, the new class of policy intellectuals, technical specialists, and social guardians legitimized centralized economic planning, presumed ideals of objectivity, and the spread of innovation. Accordingly, cultural authority coalesced on the 1930s Great Plains among a cosmopolitan elite of experts, including sociologists, economists, social workers, professors, attorneys, and government agents and advisers.[25]

The intervention of New Deal policymakers precipitated a predictable power struggle between rural communities and their benefactors. Stock has shown that during the Great Depression Dakotans desired government assistance in restoring prosperity, not help in redefining their business practices and goals. Convinced that the economic emergency placed material needs above notions of community and traditional morality, service professionals rarely showed interest in grass-roots concerns. Government agents "considered us a bunch of yokels living in a mess of geology poorly begun and never finished," a Dakota woman confided in her diary. As Stock has concluded, Dakotans worried that New Deal programs originated from outsiders who did not fully understand their circumstances but who had frightening power over their lives. Anxious to receive government financial aid, middle-class citizens of the Northern Plains were both thankful for and fearful of outside assistance.[26]

Dakota farmers were particularly nervous about the professors, economists, lawyers, and other trained experts who sought to apply their special skills to the social problems of the rural countryside. Newspaper editors and their readers often complained of contradictory policies, government paternalism, the urban biases and political radicalism of officials, the impractical nature of agricultural schemes, and excessive planning and control. Such views were perfectly embodied in the politics of North Dakota Republican William Lemke, elected to the U. S. House of Representatives in 1932. A short, chunky, freckled and nearly bald man with a heavy German accent, Lemke's "hick" image belied the fact that he was an accomplished graduate of Yale Law School and hence, a potential member of the New Class. Lemke launched his public career as an attorney and adviser to North Dakota's populist Nonpartisan League, became state attorney general in 1920, and promptly filed suits against the railroads and public utilities. Swept into Congress with an entire slate of League candidates, he disregarded party labels and identified with the early promise of New Deal reform.[27]

Lemke met with Roosevelt in the summer of 1932 and urged the presidential candidate to consider dumping agricultural surplus overseas and stimulating inflation at home. But once the Democrats assumed power, White House advisers painted the monetarist North Dakotan as a demagogue, a "prairie rebel, a madman from the sticks." Lemke had strong misgivings about the AAA package, which he publicly supported as a "toehold" but privately portrayed as an idiotic farm relief bill drawn by professors. The freshman legislator strongly preferred the Senate cost-of-production provision favored by the Farmers Holiday

Association. He also backed a Senate amendment by North Dakota's Lynn Frazier to establish a government program to refinance farm mortgages. "By the time the next session starts," Lemke wrote to a constituent following defeat of Frazier's proposal in the upper house, "even the President will see that he cannot follow Wall Street professors and expect them to write the farm program of the nation."[28]

As Dakota wheat prices remained unsatisfactorily low, Lemke became increasingly impatient with unelected agriculture administrators who lacked farm experience. He professed to be mystified by bureaucrats who argued about protocol and procedure during a dire emergency. Lemke castigated the fifty-five lawyers recruited by AAA general counsel Jerome Frank as social reformers with no interest in raising commodity values. When he learned that several Department of Agriculture attorneys had formed a Communist cell, the North Dakotan lost all faith. A speech in early 1934 borrowed John Simpson's image of the "brainless trust" and charged that "New York professors do not understand the agricultural problem of the nation." Pouring his heart out to populist monetary radical W. H. ("Coin") Harvey, Lemke complained that the House leadership had no remedies for the depression and had surrendered its powers to the president and the brains trust. "Here in Washington," he confided to a constituent in June 1934, "the farmers are being treated like a bunch of suckers and as if they don't know anything and need a guardian."[29]

Representing a state where foreclosures wiped out one-third of all farms between 1930 and 1944, Lemke saw Senator Frazier's mortgage refinance bill as an alternative to a failing agricultural policy. The measure allowed farmers whose debts exceeded the value of their depressed properties to meet mortgage obligations at 1 percent interest and to avoid foreclosure for five years if they continued to make reasonable payments. Overcoming the opposition of the Roosevelt administration, Lemke forced the proposal to the House floor in 1934 by gathering 145 signatures on a petition to discharge the bill from the Rules Committee. With the support of the National Farmers' Union, the legislation won passage in both houses and gained the president's signature. When the Supreme Court invalidated the act the next year, Lemke redrafted it to meet legal objections, gathered 218 signatures on a second discharge petition, and once again saw his bill become law. Although the North Dakotan failed to gain support for a more radical farm refinance scheme in 1935 and 1936, he had shown that it was possible for Congress to recapture the policy initiative from the brains trust.[30]

***

Suspicion of Washington expertise pervaded the political elites of Depression-era communities nationwide. In the predominately rural Dakotas and Carolinas, local merchants, bankers, real estate dealers, physicians, lawyers, and farmers bitterly resisted the recomendations of outside academics and reformers. As historian William R. Brock has demonstrated, politically sensitive officeholders in such big cities as Chicago, Philadelphia, and Pittsburgh shared an aversion to any change initiated from above. Locally elected officials especially resented the intrusion of social workers affiliated with the state and county relief agencies established by the Federal Employment Relief Administration. Frequently young and female, college-trained FERA directors were a new breed whose authority stemmed from professional competence in a barely respected field and from ties to a suspect federal bureaucracy. Social workers who made no distinction between the "worthy" and "unworthy" poor and ignored the wishes, condemned the methods, and questioned the integrity of popularly elected politicians, found middling success at the local level.[31]

The controversy over New Deal expertise took on particularly harsh tones during the campaign to enact federal law to regulate the stock market. In 1933 brains truster Raymond Moley suggested that Harvard Law School professor Felix Frankfurter aid in drafting securities legislation. A Viennese-born Jew of modest stature, Frankfurter had graduated from the City College of New York and received his law degree at Harvard. He first had served in government under Henry Louis Stimson, President William Howard Taft's Secretary of War. During World War I, Frankfurter chaired the War Labor Policies Board, a position that brought him into contact with Assistant Secretary of the Navy Franklin Roosevelt. A specialist in sociological jurisprudence at Harvard, Frankfurter advised New York governors Al Smith and Roosevelt. The ebullient professor taught that a legalistic democracy required disinterested public servants capable of organized and scientific thinking. Critical of business as narrowly selfish, Frankfurter hoped that a strong civil service might provide government with sufficient intelligence to resolve economic dilemmas and better serve the national interest.[32]

Described by historians as "the quintessential insider," Frankfurter delegated the task of drafting securities legislation to three former law school proteges, Harvard Professor James M. Landis, Thomas G. Corcoran, and Benjamin V. Cohen. Corcoran soon emerged as the conceptual leader of the team. Raised by a middle-class family of Rhode Island Irish Americans who looked down on unenlightened machine politicians, Corcoran graduated as the Brown University valedictorian and served as editor of Harvard's prestigious law review. Through Frankfurter, from whom he learned that the best public policy stemmed from intelligent and selfless administrators, Corcoran obtained a one-year clerkship in 1926 with Supreme Court Justice Oliver Wendell Holmes, Jr. After five years at a Wall Street law firm, he received a government position at Herbert Hoover's Reconstruction Finance Corporation, a post he retained with one interruption until 1940.[33]

Benjamin Cohen, portrayed by one journalist as "the most skillful legislative draftsman in America," had the responsibility of translating Corcoran's concepts into statutory prose. The son of a Jewish peddler from Poland who started a scrap-iron business in Indiana, Cohen studied economics at the University of Chicago before receiving his Harvard law degree under Frankfurter. After clerking for a federal judge in the 1920s and entering the private sector as a corporate attorney, he led the National Consumer's League's efforts in passing a New York State minimum wage law for women. Through Frankfurter's influence, Cohen served as associate general counsel to the New Deal's Public Works Administration between 1933 and 1934, and as attorney for the Department of Interior's National Public Power Committee from 1934 to 1941.[34]

Dispatching the Securities Bill to friendly Sam Rayburn's House Committee on Interstate and Foreign Commerce, Frankfurter's proteges easily ushered the proposal into passage in 1933. The legislation compelled full disclosure to investors of information concerning new stocks, required government registration of securities, and made corporate directors liable for improper trading practices. Enactment of the securities law was the first step in a process by which Corcoran and Cohen garnered a reputation as the most influential lawyer-intellectuals of the New Deal. Journalists described the two as "a pair of Washington backstairs wizards" who quietly composed legislation and coached acquiescent congressional Democrats. Despite their decision to remain in the background, noted one account, the support of the "legislative twins" meant that things were about to happen. The White House's top advisers were "roving centers, trouble-shooters, shock troops who go where the fighting is hottest," operators who knew "more about the inner workings of the New Deal than anyone except President Roosevelt."[35]

The next challenge for Corcoran and Cohen proved far more vexing than the Securities Bill. When Roosevelt sought more stringent regulation of Wall Street in 1934, the two attorneys drafted legislation creating the Securities and Exchange Commission (SEC). The new agency was to assume the Federal Trade Commission's power in licensing stock exchanges and be given the authority to prohibit price manipulation and other practices. Corcoran and Cohen also proposed that the Federal Reserve Board set margin requirements for down payments when securities were purchased. The new stock exchange measure reflected the skepticism about business morals and motives that characterized many New Dealers. Cohen had been influenced in the 1920s by economist John Maynard Keynes's notions of government spending and public regulation of investment. Corcoran believed that experts like himself were "technicians in democracy" who were compelled to confront entrenched interest and power groups like the Wall Street lobby.[36]

Battle lines between New Deal advisers and private sector figures quickly took shape when New York Stock Exchange President Richard Whitney denounced the Securities and Exchange Bill as a form of nationalization whose margin requirements would put the securities market out of business. Responding before the Senate Banking Committee, Corcoran denied that the measure enabled government to run the exchanges but insisted upon penalties for traders who made misleading statements. Although the legacy of the 1929 Crash assured broad support for the proposal, business leaders bristled at the influence of the inner White House cabal. In hearings before the House commerce panel in March 1934, manufacturer James H. Rand, Jr. charged that the stock exchange bill was pushing the nation toward communism. The measure had been drawn by "a group of radical young lawyers who hold no elective office," protested Rand. "Here in Washington," he declared, "a group of theoretically trained young men, sincere but totally inexperienced in government and business, wield great influence."[37]

Rand's statement prompted *Washington Star* columnist Paul Mallon to place responsibility for the stock exchange legislation on "Frankfurter's Hot Dog Boys." The cry was taken up the following month by House member Frederick A. Britten, an eleven-term Republican from Chicago's North Side. A graduate of a San Francisco business college, Britten had been a construction contractor before entering politics. Referring to the Washington residence shared by bachelors Landis, Corcoran, and Cohen, Britten now proclaimed that the government was run from a "little red house down in Georgetown," where between ten and eighteen of Felix Frankfurter's "little hot dogs" met nightly to formulate "the communistic legislation we all talk about in the cloakrooms."[38]

Two days before the vote on the stock exchange proposal in early May, the House engaged in a seven-hour debate, much of it focused on the bill's authorship. Britten insisted that the original draft had been written by junior members of the brains trust such as Telford Taylor, a recent Harvard graduate in the Interior Department. But "too much vodka and too little cream made it too hot for even the red-letter boys," charged the Illinois representative, and a milder version was prepared by Benjamin Cohen. Britten pilloried Cohen as one of "the scarlet fever boys down in the little red house in Georgetown" occupied by Felix Frankfurter and other officials. Frankfurter's "cheer leaders" sought control of all credit and corporate practices, he declared. "The real object of the bill," asserted Britten, was "to Russianize everything worthwhile" under government direction. After the representative noted Cohen's presence next to House Commerce Committee chair Rayburn, the young aide left the chamber. Britten then charged that Cohen had sat in on all executive sessions and practically directed the rewriting of the exchange legislation.[39]

***

Surprisingly, Republican members of the commerce panel took the initiative in disputing Britten's wild claims. When New Deal adversaries like Michigan Republican Carl Edgar Mapes and Indiana Democrat Samuel B. Pettengill assured colleagues that the securities bill would have a "minimum of interference with legitimate business" and would "kill the 'jackal' but save the 'hide,'" the House approved the measure by a one-sided margin of 280 to 84, although only twenty-eight Republicans sided with the majority. In the Senate, where all eastern Republicans opposed the legislation, the vote was 62 to 13.[40] Yet the easy victory could not disguise growing congressional discomfort with the executive branch's ties to unaccountable and radical intellectuals in the elite universities and law schools. Such concerns had taken an alarming turn during James Rand's March 1934 testimony on the Securities and Exchange Bill.

Weeks before Roosevelt's inauguration, the head of the Remington, Rand Company had appeared before the Senate Banking Committee to propose funding for a central industrial corporation to make low-interest loans to merchants. Days after the Democrats entered the White House, Rand joined leading business figures such as New York banker Frank A. Vanderlip, farm appliance manufacturer Vincent Bendix, Sears, Roebuck president Robert E. Wood, and publisher Frank E. Gannett, to form the Committee for the Nation, an organization committed to increased prices and purchasing power through planned monetary inflation. Traumatized by the collapse of retail values and the disaster in the rural economy, the committee demanded abandonment of the gold standard and devaluation of the dollar. Although Rand initially supported the National Recovery Administration because it gave businesses the authority to set prices, he criticized plans to restrict the work week as threatening to profits and economic recovery.[41]

In endorsing monetary reform, the three hundred industrialists and bankers of the Committee for the Nation shared the conviction of national farm leaders that a healthy agricultural market and inflated currency were essential to long-term purchasing power. The monetarist perspective of the reformers led Roosevelt adviser Raymond Moley to dismiss Rand's group as "Bryanism Reincarnated." Yet the committee also reflected the distrust expressed by New Deal critics like John Simpson, William Lemke, and Frederick Britten toward the hidden influence of presidential advisers in using government to restore an urban-based prosperity contrary to the perceived interests of ruralites and other producers. Such concerns surfaced when Rand read to the House commerce panel a statement attributed to Dr. William A. Wirt, a Gary, Indiana superintendent of public schools who served as an organizer for the Committee for the Nation.[42]

Published in complete form in the next day's *New York Times,* Wirt's manifesto declared that Roosevelt brains trusters were out to destroy the legacy of Washington, Jefferson, and Lincoln and to "reconstruct an America after their own pattern." In doing so, the culprits had overlooked the "great social progress" of a nation in which "the common man is getting his place in the sun." Wirt claimed that he once had asked some of the brains trust leaders "what their concrete plan was for bringing on the proposed overthrow of the established American social order." "I was told," he reported, "that they believed that by thwarting our then evident recovery they would be able to prolong the country's destitution until they had demonstrated to the American people that the government must operate industry and commerce." By destroying the ability of commercial banks to make long-term capital loans, the Roosevelt cabal would ensure that only the government could advance funds. Control and management supposedly would follow the flow of money.[43]

Wirt declared that New Deal officials felt "a superhuman flow of power from the flow" of the policies they set. "We are on the inside," one allegedly told the Indiana educator. "We can control the avenues of influence. We can make the President believe that he is making decisions for himself." Wirt reported that a well-placed administration aide had confided that "we believe that we have Mr. Roosevelt in the middle of a swift stream and that the current is so strong that he cannot turn back or escape from it. We believe that we can keep Mr. Roosevelt there until we are ready to supplant him with a Stalin. We all think that Mr. Roosevelt is only the Kerensky of this revolution." Wirt claimed that brains trusters were convinced that the country would need strong men in power once engulfed in flames. With Roosevelt's background, one adviser supposedly revealed, "we do not expect him to see this revolution through."[44]

Perhaps the most chilling portion of Wirt's statement pertained to the future practices of alleged New Deal subversives. The Indiana educator claimed that a brains truster had disclosed that the president's advisers would blame the administration's inability to engineer economic recovery on "the traitorous opposition." This would allow the government to use the full force of propaganda to crack down on political adversaries. For example, the print media could be threatened with truth-in-advertising legislation while potential exposure of crooked practices could be held over the heads of the financial community. Exploiting "the psychology of empty stomachs," Roosevelt officials supposedly planned to impose government control through manipulation of federal loans, contracts, subsidies, and aid to education.[45]

Interviewed in Indiana following Rand's presentation of his statement, Wirt told reporters that brains trusters had a blacklist of members of Congress who opposed administration efforts and who would be punished in time. He also claimed to have received a letter from a prominent citizen who asserted that a close friend had heard a similar story about the brains trust plan. Under the guise of relieving the economic distress, the correspondent had written, a social revolution was being promoted "by the inner circle at Washington." "Everyone knows that the radical group is working for a planned economy," declared Wirt. "But I don't want the new state to be created by the gradual substitution of the new ideas in government without the people being aware of what is going on." The educator said that he was concerned about the permanent nature of NRA industrial codes and other emergency measures. "The future Hitler of America is now in the background merely watching the formation of the mob," he warned.[46]

Wirt's broad attack on New Deal expertise received immediate support from Representative Harold C. McGugin, a Kansas Republican hostile to administration farm programs. "Those in control of the Agriculture Department are betraying the President and are merely using him," declared McGugin. Citing Tugwell as the dominating personality of the brains trust, the representative called for a congressional inquiry into the possibility that "someone closely associated with those behind the scenes" was following a designed plan to wreck the Republic. Three days later, fellow Republican Hamilton Fish, Jr., a New York House member from Roosevelt's Hyde Park district, described twelve New Deal officials as socialists, including Jerome Frank, James Landis, and Tugwell. In addition, Fish mentioned "about a score or more of young radicals, so-called economic experts and lawyers of the Felix Frankfurter school of thought, most of whom are disciples of Karl Marx," who were in government service.[47]

Despite such endorsements and Commerce Committee chair Rayburn's acknowledgment that presidential aides Thomas Corcoran and Benjamin Cohen had worked on the Securities and Exchange Bill, the sensational nature of Wirt's accusations left him open to ridicule. Raymond Moley protested that the brains trust included individuals from diverse backgrounds and differing philosophies, while Adolf Berle insisted that Roosevelt was "not the kind of man whose advisers run the show." Western Senate Republicans who supported the New Deal, such as Gerald P. Nye, Hiram W. Johnson, and William E. Borah, openly dismissed Wirt's charges as preposterous. Skeptical that any official had said what the Indiana educator alleged, Democrat Alfred L. Bulwinkle of North Carolina asked the House to investigate exactly who had discussed plans to "establish a communistic form of government."[48]

***

One day after Bulwinkle's announcement, Wirt assured journalists that when the welfare of the country demanded, he would read the names of brains trusters plotting to undermine the government. Alleging that one hundred intellectual conspirators already had demanded that Roosevelt adopt socialist policies or face their resignation, the educator claimed that naming two or three culprits would be a smoke-screen for the activities of the entire radical group. A week later the Committee for the Nation issued Wirt's ten-thousand word pamphlet entitled "America Must Lose–by a Planned Economy, a Stepping Stone to a Regimented State." Restating the charge that the Roosevelt administration was a Kerensky-like prelude to an American social revolution, the document set forth the monetarist views earlier popularized by Rand's committee. Meanwhile, after forty minutes of debate, the House appointed a special panel to investigate Wirt's allegations. With Democrat Bulwinkle as chair, the new committee rejected a Republican proposal to examine brains trust activities and voted along party lines to confine questioning to the potential plot to overthrow the government.[49]

Broadcast live over two radio networks, the Wirt hearings began on 10 April 1934, before a capacity crowd in the Caucus Room of the new House Office Building. Wirt told the committee that his charges were based on a dinner party conversation in Virginia the previous September. After asking several guests what the 'main idea' of the New Deal was, he allegedly had been informed that its purpose was to bring about a revolution against the established order. Wirt named Hildegarde Kneeland, the chief of the economics division of the Bureau of Home Economics in the Department of Agriculture, as his main source. The Indiana school official recalled that Kneeland had attributed to brains truster Rexford Tugwell the belief that the recent recovery was a speculative spree and that the stock and commodity exchanges eventually would be closed down. According to Wirt, Kneeland had paraphrased Tugwell by stating that if the "national plan" were carried out, it would be necessary to change the Constitution and "all our statutes . . . once and for all time." The indication that government action would lead to the disappearance of business, "was literally meant," insisted Wirt.[50]

The Indiana educator attributed to the "widely informed" Kneeland the belief that planners should take over the government, a sentiment supposedly shared by both Tugwell and Agriculture Secretary Wallace. With "so many of our people in the government, some in key positions," she allegedly had speculated, the question was "why don't we do something?" Wirt recalled that Kneeland then outlined a Tugwell plan to decentralize cities with the creation of new communities that would require the forced resettlement of existing populations. Such plans extended to the establishment of a factory town to manufacture government supplies near Fairmont, West Virginia. The homestead program, in which Eleanor Roosevelt was said to have a special interest, appeared to Wirt to be a communistic effort.[51]

Under cross examination, Wirt admitted that no one at the dinner party talked of overthrowing the government and that at best, the guests were "satelliltes" of the brains trust. Nevertheless, he insisted that the Roosevelt-Kerensky analogy had been made by Laurence Todd, a journalist with the Soviet news agency, Tass. The Indiana witness also claimed that he recently had been told by General William I. Westervelt, the former assistant to one-time AAA administrator, George Peek, that the farm agency had been asked by Consumers' Division head, Frederic C. Howe, if there was any way to reduce the diets of people on relief so that New Dealers could make better headway with a program "to inoculate them with the ideas we wanted to give them." In response, Assistant Agriculture Secretary Tugwell supposedly had assured Westervelt that he could get $1 million in public funds to start a school for unemployed college graduates to "inoculate" them with appropriate ideology. Wirt also reported that the general passed on a prediction by House Speaker Henry T. Rainey that the government would take over the nation's businesses after Congress adjourned in May 1934.[52]

Wirt's accusations received immediate backing from Edward A. Hayes, the national commander of the American Legion. Tugwell was one of many men in prominent places with communistic leanings, charged Hayes, who sought to destroy the nation from inside the universities and colleges. The Indiana educator also won support from Bulwinkle committee member McGugin, who denounced the panel's refusal to compel testimony from Tugwell and condemned its unwillingess to honor Wirt's rights to cross-examination. Nevertheless, the star witness' allegations were the subject of derision in the prestigious *New York Times,* whose front-page story included irreverent headings such as "Talk at a Dinner Party" and "Hostess Kept All Happy." News accounts noted that Wirt's rendering of Tugwell's ideas appeared to be based on the brains truster's previously published writings. Coverage in the *Times* also included NRA general counsel Donald Richberg's lighthearted doggerel: "A cuttlefish squirt, / Nobody hurt. / From beginning to end; / Dr Wirt."[53]

Wirt received his strongest rebuke from the participants of the notorious Virginia dinner party and the alleged sources of his other charges. Hildegarde Kneeland denied discussing the brains trust or Tugwell with the educator, and claimed never to have met the Assistant Agriculture Secretary. Tass's Laurence Todd and a second female employee of the Department of Agriculture insisted that Kerensky, Stalin, and revolution never were mentioned. David Cushman Coyle, a New York consulting engineer and member of the technical review board of the Public Works Administration, claimed that it was Wirt who dominated after-dinner discourse with talk of devaluating the dollar. Meanwhile, General Westervelt said he had never referred to a Tugwell plan for unemployed college graduates, although he did confirm the story concerning Frederick Howe and relief recipients. Yet both Howe and the AAA dismissed as "bunk" the possibility that government officials would seek to deprive the poor of aid. Finally, Speaker Rainey rejected Wirt's account of his alleged statements to Westervelt as "absolutely untrue," "silly," and "too absurd to warrant comment."[54]

***

Adhering to party lines once again, the Bulwinkle committee concluded by a 3 to 2 margin in late April 1934 that Wirt's charges were unfounded. McGugin and fellow Republicans protested that Democrats were minimizing the influence of "revolutionists" in formulating Roosevelt administration policy. But the panel's report, submitted two days before the House vote on the Securities and Exchange Bill, reiterated that Wirt's allegations were "untrue" in every sense.[55] By demonstrating that the sensational accusations of their opponents lacked veracity and were unrelated to the popular goal of stock exchange regulation, New Dealers won an important victory. Administration leaders hoped to show that the federal government sought to regulate selfish economic interests to serve the public welfare. Nevertheless, the Roosevelt team never completely overcame accusations that its authority and power rested upon a coercive apparatus of arbitrary officials, unelected strategists, and shadowy brains trusters, whose social values and political goals were alien to those of many Americans.

As the discomfort surrounding Rexford Tugwell and AAA demonstrated, the participation of academic experts and Ivy League lawyers in experimental farm programs provided a useful opening for opponents of New Deal policies. The political difficulties of regulating agriculture surfaced when reformer Jerome Frank helped to establish a Program Planning Division of AAA in 1933. Attempting to restore prosperity to impoverished regions like the rural South, the agency openly addressed the needs of marginal tenant farmers and sharecroppers, many of them African Americans. After commissioning a study on the question by Duke University professor Calvin B. Hoover, AAA sought to compel cotton planters to keep tenants on the land after owners agreed with the government to reduce cultivation. When local agents declined to enforce the proviso, Legal Division officer Alger Hiss issued an unpopular edict requiring landlords to retain their tenants for the duration of agreements. Growers also objected to government interference with their labor supply when the Department of Agriculture won a $25 million FERA grant in 1934 to resettle farm families on relief in new homestead communities. Relations with landlords further deteriorated the next year when Roosevelt appointed Tugwell to head the Resettlement Administration, an agency designed to use planning methods to relocate poor farmers off submarginal lands.[56]

Tugwell's association with New Deal experimentalism weakened AAA's political viability. Bitterly resented as an "un-American" snob with no respect for farm politicians, the Columbia University theorist encountered severe opposition when he was promoted to Under Secretary of Agriculture in 1934. Senator Harry Byrd, a conservative Virginia Democrat, labeled Tugwell a dangerous centralizer and collectivist. Ellison D. ("Cotton Ed") Smith of South Carolina, Demoratic chair of the Senate Agriculture Committee, complained that the post of Under Secretary should go to a farmer "instead of a professor." Such pressures took their toll on AAA, which critics accused of subservience to Jerome Frank's cabal of consumer-oriented attorneys. Concerned in 1935 with charges that the agency was fostering "social revolution" in the South, AAA administrator Chester Davis voided the Hiss edict, eliminated Frank's position as general counsel, fired Frederic Howe and several activist lawyers, and forced the resignation of Alger Hiss.[57]

Undoubtedly frustrated by the resistance of vested interests to economic and social planning, Tugwell responded with a tirade at an October 1935 meeting of Democrats in Los Angeles. The nation was witnessing the "death struggle of industrial autocracy and the birth of democratic discipline," he proclaimed. Yet there was no reason to expect that the unraveling of the "plutocracy" would be easy. "These historical changes never are pleasant," continued Tugwell, although Americans had "the duty of avoiding violence as the process goes on." The alternative to bloodshed, insisted the professor, was the establishment of "a farmer-worker alliance" that would allow the country to carry through "reconstructive" measures in agriculture and industry. "Our best strategy," he concluded, was "to surge forward with the workers and the farmers of this nation, . . . trusting the genius of our leader for the disposition of our forces and the timing of our attacks."[58]

Tugwell's portrait of a class-conscious presidency committed to the radical social planning of unelected advisers spoke to the undemocratic undercurrent that many opponents saw in the New Deal. Conservatives like former New York governor Al Smith responded that the under secretary should be shipped to Russia, where planning was appreciated. Critics long had accused White House assistants of collectivist leanings. West Virginian Republican Henry Hatfield had claimed during the Senate debate over the NRA that Roosevelt and the brains trust were forcing socialism upon the American people under the guise of industrial democracy. As early as 1934, a pro-New Deal banker had alerted colleagues to the "parlor pinks" of the president's inner circle. Appearing before five thousand upstate Republicans in August of the same year, the borough president of Queens, New York contrasted traditional survival techniques of self-reliance and individual independence with the allegedly unconstitutional methods of the college professors who served as the White House brains trust.[59]

Discomfort with the arbitrary rule and controversial methods of unaccountable strategists and policy intellectuals provided a major source of anti-New Deal fervor. Such concerns were compounded by the perception that unseen administrators were using their authority to marginalize ordinary producers and punish struggling enterprisers. Former AAA administrator George Peek shared such a perspective. Peek's forced resignation in December 1933 inaugurated the period in which the farm agency's experimental economists and urbane attorneys appeared less accountable to agricultural interests. His memoirs, published in 1936, bitterly recounted the capitulation of AAA and other agencies. Washington had been inundated with a "plague of young lawyers," recalled Peek, who "flooded airily into offices, took desks, asked for papers, and found no end of things to be busy about."[60]

Criticism of AAA theorists for alleged hostility to producers could be found in the continuing pronouncements of North Dakota representative William Lemke. The agency was a farce, Lemke wrote back home in 1935. As far as farmers were concerned, the New Deal was "a new shuffle with the cards stacked." By January 1936, the Gallup poll was reporting that 59 percent of nationwide respondents opposed the AAA. Lemke's Northern Plains constituents strained at government crop restrictions and resented Washington's inability to stop farm foreclosures. "We are fast approaching a feudal system, with farmers as the feudal serfs," the representative warned in a February 1936 speech. Lemke attacked "the little coteries of bureaucrats in Washington" who had declared war on agriculture. "We accept this challenge," he proclaimed, "and from now on the enemy will know where we are." The North Dakota politician had tried to bypass the agricultural bureaucracy the previous year by introducing legislation to refinance farm mortgages through low-interest government loans, but his

House discharge petition fell six names shy and the measure failed 235 to 142 when it came to the floor in 1936.[61]

* * *

Battered by small business and agricultural interests, the brains trust came under increasing scrutiny from Congress, many of whom saw the power of Roosevelt's advisers as a threat to the traditional prerogatives of the legislative branch. One of the most outspoken foes of executive rule was Representative Allen T. Treadway, a Republican from western Massachusetts who once had followed a career in the hotel business. In a May 1935 House speech that typified anti-New Deal sentiment, Treadway repeated the frequent assertion that Roosevelt policies were dictated by a professional brains trusts not responsible to the people. No one told voters in 1932, he complained, that the administration would "throw out everybody who had any experience in the departments and install second-grade college professors and establish a 'brain trust' such as is running the country today." Congress had surrendered virtually all of its powers to the executive, declared Treadway.[62]

Treadway's critique came less than two months after *New York Times* reporter Delbert Clark concluded that the brains trust had experienced a "fade-out" from the headlines as Roosevelt returned to reliance on practical politicians. In June 1935, Clark reiterated that the president's advisers were in the shadows and in a state of dispersal. The White House would not call for the re-emergence of theorists, he predicted. Yet within a week, brains trusters Thomas Corcoran and Benjamin Cohen returned to front stage as co-authors of the Public Utility Holding Company Bill. Abolition of the financial units of the electric power industry had been backed by the Federal Trade Commission, the National Power Policy Committee, the House commerce panel, and western Senate Republicans such as William Borah, George Norris, and Burton Wheeler. When Roosevelt signed on to a "death sentence" that mandated the dissolution of holding companies, Wheeler pushed senators to approve the clause by razor-thin margins. But as the sharply contested bill reached the House, conflict between presidential advisers and Congress once again erupted.[63]

The controversy took shape in late June when Alabama Democrat George Huddleston elicited House laughter and applause by referring to Corcoran and Cohen as "a couple of bright young men brought down from New York to teach Congress how to shoot." These were days, noted Huddleston, when experience and fidelity in public service were "exceedingly 'disqualifying.'" The question of White House meddling took on a sharper note four days later when Maine Republican Ralph O. Brewster told the House that Corcoran had threatened to stop construction on a $36 million dam in his district unless he voted for the "death sentence" clause. Brewster claimed that Corcoran had said that he was addressing the legislator with "brutal frankness." Although he described the co-author of the holding company bill as the personal representative of the president, Brewster discounted the possibility that Roosevelt was aware of such threats. Yet he called Corcoran's alleged actions "repugnant to every instinct of decency in legislation and proper regard for our constitutional oath of office."[64]

Corcoran refused to discuss the Brewster allegations, preferring to "let events take their course." Yet Representative Edward C. Moran, Jr., a Maine Democrat, claimed that the presidential adviser merely had suggested that if Brewster could not vote with the White House on the holding company matter, he was not the proper person to continue handling the legal work on the Maine power project to which the administration earlier had assigned him. Legislators in the lower chamber already had rejected the Senate version of the "death sentence" clause by a 216 to 146 margin. Further angered by alleged White House machinations, the House now voted, 258 to 147, to tie any dissolution of holding companies to the public interest. It then passed its own utilities regulation bill, 323 to 81. The House also adopted Indiana Democrat Samuel Pettengill's resolution to require the Rules Committee to investigate allegations concerning the exercise of undue influence by both the utilities and the president's team.[65]

As the showdown began one week later, Corcoran denied the charges as baseless. The presidential aide acknowledged that he had spoken with Brewster by telephone on 1 July 1935, the day the Senate version of the utility bill was considered by the House, and learned that the legislator would not support the "death sentence." "If . . . you are not a free man politically and must take power company support into your calculations," Corcoran reportedly said, "then you'll understand perfectly that from now on you can't expect me to trust you" to protect the dam project and win the necessary authorizations from the state legislature. Corcoran then claimed that he arranged to meet Brewster a few minutes later in the Capitol lobby. The Roosevelt adviser told House panelists that the Maine Republican said his political situation back home was "so delicate," that he could not support the administration's power bill. Yet, according to Corcoran, Brewster offered to mend fences by going back to his hotel and absenting himself from the vote. "You're a liar!" Brewster interrupted, as the hearing neared a break. "We'll see if I'm a liar," responded Corcoran.[66]

Brewster testified in the day's second session. The Maine Republican claimed that Corcoran called him on the telephone on July 1st, used profanity, and demanded that he support the "death sentence." He then met the presidential aide in the presence of Ernest Gruening, an anti-utility activist who was an official with the Department of Interior. According to Brewster, Gruening said it would be a "grave mistake" to oppose the amendment. The legislator then suggested that Corcoran interrupted and twice threatened that his negative vote would make "it necessary to stop work" on the Maine dam. At that point in the hearing, Representative Edward E. Cox, a Georgia Democat, asked Brewster how he could "let the gentleman talk to you in this way as though you were a hireling and you could do nothing about it." Brewster did not recall offering a response to Corcoran. "But when it comes to a fundamental issue of that kind and someone tries to use a club on me," he said, "there is only one answer–to tell them to go to hell and do the opposite."[67]

The following day, panelists cross-examined Corcoran. Although he acknowledged that he had become "very hot" when Brewster "lost his courage" and refused to support the "death sentence," the White House aide repeatedly denied that he threatened the Maine representative with reprisals. Gruening's testimony on July 11th completely supported Corcoran's version of events, leading Rules Committee chair John O'Connor to declare the incident closed. Five days later, House and Senate Commerce Committee chairs Sam Rayburn and Burton Wheeler assumed full responsibility for Corcoran's actions by acknowledging that they had encouraged the White House attorney to meet with members of Congress to lobby for the public utility holding company bill that he had co-authored.[68]

Despite the administration's vindication in the Brewster affair, Roosevelt aides faced the task of reconciling House and Senate versions of the "death sentence." As the matter went to a joint conference committee of both houses, Benjamin Cohen, the second author of the holding company bill, emerged as a primary symbol of congressional discomfort over executive-branch meddling by policy specialists. As recently as June 1935, Cohen had been mentioned as a possible nominee to the Securities and Exchange Commission. Yet the cerebral attorney had a reputation for being "too damned smart," as South Carolina senator James F. Byrnes bluntly put it. On July 24th, Alabama's George Huddleston broke up conference deliberations when he objected to the presence in the room of Dozier A. Devane, a Federal Power Commission lawyer, and White House attorney Cohen. Huddleston complained that the two advisers were outsiders, not employees of Congress, and therefore had no right to participate in executive sessions.[69]

Two days after the initial furor, the conference broke up again when Huddleston and two Republicans continued to protest the presence of White House aides. Roosevelt's lawyers were trying "to lobby" the deadlocked session, charged the Alabaman. On July 27th, the dispute erupted for a third time and conferees adjourned with little hope of settling differences over utility regulation. Five days later, the House reaffirmed its rejection of the Senate "death sentence" and voted, 183 to 172, to support Huddleston's resolution to exclude outsiders from conference sessions. On August 6th, conferees met without the presence of Devane and Cohen, but still were unable to agree on "death sentence" language. Finally, House Commerce Committee chair Sam Rayburn proposed a compromise by which the Securities and Exchange Commission would wait until 1938 to require holding companies to limit their operations and then would permit exceptions to dissolution. Rayburn's resolution passed the House, 219 to

142, the conference committee acceded, and the public utility holding bill won approval in both houses on August 24th.[70]

***

Allegations over interference with the legislative process by nonelected White House advisers pointed to the difficulty Roosevelt administrators experienced in legitimizing the involvement of brains trusters and legal experts in the formation of public policy. As the president positioned himself for the 1936 reelection campaign, Oval Office strategists could boast of a substantial role in New Deal reform and economic recovery efforts. In the same year in which Roosevelt signed the Public Utility Holding Bill, he assented to the Wagner National Labor Relations Act, approved landmark legislation for a comprehensive social security program of old-age pensions and unemployment insurance, and inaugurated the most extensive public works regime in history through the massive Works Progress Administration (WPA). Yet attempts to restore prosperity and initiate reforms appeared to place an unprecedented degree of influence among sinister officials in the executive branch who often were perceived as ideological opponents of free enterprise and open competition. As a result, Roosevelt critics often succeeded in tying the administration's alleged threats to their economic interests to challenges to democratic government, the accountability of elected leaders, and individual equality of opportunity.[71]

Impatient with attacks by conservative opponents, New Dealer Thurman Arnold blamed denunciations of reform on industrial and financial elites supposedly threatened by Washington's tampering with the profit system and their vested financial interests. Certainly, business titans who resisted government regulation were quick to demonize Roosevelt advisers as the source of their collective pain. As historians such as Ronald Radosh have pointed out, however, the most bitter New Deal adversaries tended to be independent producers, small business enterprisers, and self-employed professionals, whose mentality and interests mainly were rooted in economic individualism and the free market. In fact, Richard Hofstadter argued that it was the powerlessness experienced by such traditionalists that led to exaggerated notions of political intellectuals as irresponsible experimentalists whose conspiratorial methods dangerously impacted American society.[72]

Analyzing the hysterical qualities of mid-1930s agitation against the New Deal, historian Clyde P. Weed has placed such outbursts within the model of "creedal passion" first outlined by political scientist Samuel Huntington. Yet it is important to consider the bitter complaints of brains trust antagonists in full context. Despite public support for New Deal reform, historian Theodore Rosenof has suggested, Depression political culture continued to rest on enduring traditions of individualism, at once capitalist and democratic, in which central planning and dictatorship were inevitably linked as terrible dangers. Hostility to the rule of policy intellectuals stemmed in part from genuine discomfort over the troubling relationship between knowledge and power. Roosevelt theorists and experimenters often appeared as violators of fundamental ground rules who acknowledged no limits to their quest to build a new world mirroring their own values and interests. Former president Herbert Hoover summed up such concerns when he warned in 1934 that "some group somewhere gains benefits or privilege by the use of every power."[73]

Discomfort over perceived connections between radicalism and the ambitions of policy intellectuals and social guardians energized a group of midwestern Republicans who met in 1935 to denounce brains trust methods as demagogic. Similar concerns shaped the pronouncements of New York Representative and anti-New Dealer, Hamilton Fish. An American Legion founder who supported the 1936 presidential aspirations of anti-monopoly crusader and fellow Republican William Borah, Fish had chaired the first congressional investigation of domestic communism in 1930. Although careful to admit that Franklin Roosevelt was no Communist, the New Yorker accused the president of keeping "near Communists" like Rexford Tugwell in government service. Fish complained that Tugwell's "revolutionary speech" in Los Angeles implied that workers and farmers should rise and take over the government by direct action. He insisted that brains trusters like Tugwell had no loyalty to the nation's traditions or to established procedures of democracy. Instead, the president's advisers spread class hatred and, "like termites," undermined private property, capitalism, and the Constitution. Addressing a Republican meeting in 1936, Fish characterized New Dealers as architects of "a government of propaganda and ballyhoo . . . held together by the cohesive power of maintaining themselves in office at any cost."[74]

Roosevelt critics insisted that political intellectuals served their own interests and agenda by attacking commercial enterprise as illegitimate. Speaking before a conference of advertising executives in 1935, Harvard business school administrator Malcolm P. McNair deplored "the Tugwells, the Stuart Chases, all the brilliant young men, with their overweening pride of intellect, their pet panaceas, the blueprints of utopia, and their dense ignorance of the world of business." Corporate leaders like National Association of Manufacturers president C. M. Chester ridiculed public officials who could not "point to a single enterprise under their control competently and productively managed." Yet no critic attacked New Deal advisers and planners with as much glee as fellow intellectual H. L. Mencken, editor of the iconoclastic *American Mercury*. Looking to the 1936 election, the irreverent Mencken dismissed the shadowy brains trust as a "mob of mountebanks" promoting "unadulterated quackery." In the name of uplift and their own hegemony, he protested, Roosevelt's "medicine men" sought "a general overhauling and redesigning of human society and human nature." Questioning the moral integrity of New Deal policy specialists and social guardians, Mencken concluded that the president's advisers enjoyed "the solaces of the Marxian communion without actually submitting to baptism."[75]

3
The Welfare State
and Its Discontents, 1936–1941

Conflict between New Deal advisers and their critics reflected the knowledge sector's tendency to establish autonomous power bases in which its political and ideological influence contested the prerogatives of prevailing economic interests and independent enterprisers. As sociologist Alvin Gouldner noted in 1979, politically oriented intellectuals and policy specialists often used their government positions to generate social welfare policies that tied them to the working class in common alliances against narrowly focused business adversaries. Such efforts may have sustained corporate capitalism by mediating class conflict, but they simultaneously appeared to many defenders of private initiative as self-serving assaults on the integrity of the free enterprise system.[1] Chapter 3 examines how anxiety over politically intrusive social guardians during Franklin Roosevelt's second term figured in controversies over the expansion of the executive branch, experimental social programs in the federal agencies, Washington's consumer-oriented fiscal policies, and the administration's tilt toward organized labor. The chapter concludes with a consideration of the manner by which Depression-era anti-Semites depicted American Jews as the foremost initiators, beneficiaries, and symbols of radical sociopolitical change.

***

Contesting Franklin Roosevelt for the presidency in 1936, Republican nominee Alfred M. Landon condemned the New Deal's "tyranny of economic dictatorship" and its "bondage of bureaucracy." Landon's implicit assault on Washington political intellectuals emerged in more dramatic form from long-time Roosevelt adversary, William Lemke, candidate of the marginal Union Party. Lemke's run for the highest office represented the aspirations of a broad coalition that included the supporters of the late Louisiana populist Huey Long, followers of Roman Catholic radio priest Charles E. Coughlin, and adherents of Dr. Francis E. Townsend's plan to sustain the elderly through government pensions. Articulating the protests of small farmers, independent enterprisers in the old middle class, and industrial workers in traditional crafts, the Union Party celebrated local control and looked to solutions that were more cooperative than collectivist. The movement's rank and file recoiled at entrenched power and wealth in the banks and large corporations; it also suspected that hidden enemies in the intelligentsia were conspiring to socialize the American economy and enact statist controls over independent agriculture and small business.[2]

Relishing his role as Union Party kingpin, Father Coughlin proved masterful in exploiting the anxieties associated with brains trust rule. Since organizing his own network of syndicated radio commentaries in 1932, the Catholic priest had skillfully merged resentment of secular and privileged elites with suspicion of Communist subversion. By 1934, he was complaining privately about the "Pagan Deal" and referring to Roosevelt advisers as sycophants of the "Drain Trust." A public lecture in 1935 warned of the administration's "scientific social workers." Coughlin used the following year's presidential campaign as a forum for denouncing New Deal "'frankfurters' of destruction," "Stalinist relief" programs, and "Commies" such as Rexford Tugwell and Secretary of Agriculture Henry Wallace. Felix Frankfurter and the professors from the eastern universities, he told a gathering of twenty thousand at Brooklyn's Ebbett's Field, were "brain busted until they drew up blueprints and brought forth a beautiful pig," a reference to New Deal efforts to raise farm prices by restricting agricultural output and slaughtering stock.[3]

Union Party supporters like Dr. Townsend dismissed the legacy of the Roosevelt reformers as "a misdeal." Coughlin associate Gerald L. K. Smith, a Disciples of Christ minister, former Klansman, and one-time Long aide, delighted in branding the president's advisers as "a slimy group of men culled from the pink campuses of America with friendly gaze fixed on Russia." "Our president is being Kerenskyized in preparation for the chaos that is inevitable," Smith told thousands of Coughlinites in a recycling of the Wirt allegations of 1934. Similar themes became the mainstay of Lemke's presidential bid. The Agricultural Adjustment Administration was a national lunacy and farm secretary Wallace the greatest vandal in history, protested the candidate. As his first act as chief executive, the North Dakotan assured listeners, he would "fire the brainless trust and the bureaucrats that have been living on the taxpayers and tell them to go earn an honest living." Lemke promised to work with farm and labor leaders to restore "a government where all will have an opportunity to make a living, and let live."[4]

Although Lemke's message resonated with traditional populist themes and grievances, an impressive record of New Deal accomplishments and Roosevelt's ability to bond with ordinary voters dominated the campaign. The president prevailed in a landslide, taking 60.4 percent of the popular tally, losing only Maine and Vermont. Lemke captured less than 900,000 votes, 2 percent of the total. Meanwhile, Democrats assumed overwhelming majorities in both houses of Congress. Nevertheless, the forces of social change won no election mandate. Half the respondents in a January 1937 Gallup poll preferred that Roosevelt's second term be more conservative, while 35 percent thought it should remain the same, and only 15 percent hoped it would be more liberal.[5]

Skepticism toward additional government activity was based on a widely shared belief that Washington already had addressed the immediate needs of the Depression. "I regard the period of emergency at an end," Texas Democrat Martin Dies, Jr. told the House in April 1937, "and regardless of what crackpots and theorists think about it, I am going to vote from now on my own convictions." In an obvious blast at the reformers of Roosevelt's inner sanctum, Dies called for "an end to foolish, silly schemes." Days later, South Carolina senator James Byrnes endorsed relief cuts by noting that the administration had engineered recovery and "the emergency has passed." Impatient with prospects for continual White House experiment, House Republican leader Bertrand Snell observed that since 1933, the nation had "progressed from an emergency to a crisis." New Deal Senate supporters such as Republicans Hiram Johnson and Gerald Nye and Farmer-Laborite Henrik Shipstead also regretted that Congress had responded to the economic disaster by yielding excessive power to the executive.[6]

Controversy over the Roosevelt administration's assumption of contingent authority easily translated into distrust of White House advisers and brains trusters. "The emergency is over," a reader protested to the *New York Times* in February 1937; "the president has cast the money changers out of the temple; the theorists should now be cast out of the counting room." Indeed, when Agriculture Under Secretary Rexford Tugwell and Securities and Exchange Commission chair James Landis each announced their retirement early in the year, columnist Arthur Krock noted that Tugwell was often portrayed as "the personal devil of the New Deal" and Landis as one of its "most dangerous professorial products." By March 1937, White House correspondent Delbert Clark reported "the almost complete disappearance" of the brains trust and a new premium on administrators instead of planners and idea merchants.[7]

Although the influence of Roosevelt's theoretical advisers appeared to have diminished as the president began his second term, Benjamin Cohen and Thomas Corcoran remained key players on the executive team. Cohen continued to hold a nominal post as the general counsel of the National Power Public Committee, but remained a top adviser on electric power and legal issues. Corcoran maintained his position as counsel for the Reconstruction Finance Corporation, although he also served as the president's main speechwriter and as the conduit for hiring hundreds of federal government attorneys. Cohen's and Corcoran's most important function continued to be the drafting of reform legislation. Yet the "impressive anonymity" of the two presidential assistants returned to haunt the Roosevelt administration early in the second term.[8]

***

Concerned over the lack of cohesion in executive branch emergency programs, Roosevelt appointed a Committee on Administrative Management in the spring of 1936. Every chief executive since Theodore Roosevelt had called for reforms to facilitate the application of modern management to the federal government. The president hoped to reorganize the growing number of offices and agencies under his control to enable Washington to engage in more efficient, coordinated, and long-range planning. Reflecting the notion that public administration should be based on scientific principles, more than two-thirds of the twenty-six experts who served as reorganization committee staff were academics and over one-third Ph.D.s.[9]

The management panel's three members fused academic expertise with high-minded reform. Luther Gulick, the son of missionaries, graduated from Oberlin College, studied political science at Columbia, and had served as director of New York's Institute of Public Administration since 1921. Political scientist Charles Merriam also had trained at Columbia, taught at the University of Chicago in the 1910s, and been a Progressive Party activist. Seeking to apply academic scholarship to government policymaking, Merriam founded the Social Science Research Council (SSRC) in 1924. Five years later, he was appointed vice-chair of Herbert Hoover's Research Committee on Social Trends, a presidential panel supported by the SSRC and Rockefeller Foundation funding. Placed on the National Resources Committee by Roosevelt Interior Secretary Harold Ickes, Merriam urged executive branch coordination of New Deal emergency aid. Louis Brownlow, chair of the reorganization committee, was a Missouri-born journalist and municipal reformer who co-founded Chicago's Public Administration Clearing House in 1931 and advised Ickes and other New Deal cabinet officials.[10]

Submitted to Roosevelt in late 1936, the Brownlow report recommended an expanded Oval Office staff, placement of budget responsibilities within the White House, more presidential control over the civil service, conversion of independent commissions to twelve cabinet-ranked departments, and creation of executive planning agencies with authority over newly organized bureaus. Seeking to protect Roosevelt from criticism, the committee had met in strict secrecy and not consulted Congress, whose House panel on government reorganization was making little progress. The Brownlow report assumed that efficient administrative agencies would provide a policymaking alternative to the slow and cumbersome legislative process, the courts, and narrow partisan politics. Government planning would encourage the use of "social intelligence in determination of national policies," stated Merriam. The document asked that the president be given a free hand to execute the laws and administer the government. It proposed to fund six executive assistants whose qualifications Brownlow listed as "high competence, great physical vigor, and a passion for anonymity."[11]

Roosevelt submitted an administrative reorganization bill in January 1937 authorizing the president to issue executive orders to implement the Brownlow recommendations. Although Congress could reject such directives within sixty days, a two-thirds majority would be needed to override any subsequent presidential veto. After receiving the proposal in stunned silence, legislators created a joint committee to hold hearings with the Brownlow panel. Opposition assumed several forms. Senate leaders like Oregon Republican Charles L. McNary resented outside meddling by experts. "Is it up to me to pass my rights to you folks?" McNary asked Brownlow. Virginia senator Harry Byrd objected to the potential threat to fiscal responsbility raised by the advent of new welfare agencies. Other members of Congress feared that extension of the civil service would assure lifetime jobs to presidential appointees and jeopardize congressional patronage. Legislators also worried that the Brownlow reforms interfered with agency oversight, endangered control of programs affecting constituents, and disrupted their relationship with interest groups and lobbies.[12]

During the spring of 1937, the debate over executive reorganization assumed a more ideological tone. Responding to Supreme Court decisions in 1935 and 1936 invalidating the legal underpinning of the National Recovery Administration and the AAA, the White House proposed to restructure the federal courts just three weeks after requesting expansion of executive powers. By empowering the president to appoint additional federal judges for every unretired justice over the age of seventy, the Judicial Reorganization Bill would have allowed Roosevelt to add six of his own nominees to the Supreme Court. As the Senate Judiciary Committee began hearings on the controversial "Court-packing" measure, the White House faced increased accusations of "dictatorial ambitions." In March 1937, Democrat Burton Wheeler of Montana intensified the debate by naming Thomas Corcoran and Benjamin Cohen as the "young men" who allegedly had outlined the unpopular court reorganization plan to him a year earlier.[13]

Wheeler had hinted publicly on two previous occasions about the identity of the "bright young men" to whom he attributed the judiciary proposal. *New York Times* columnist Arthur Krock noted in April 1937 that Corcoran and Cohen had "been permitted to fade" into the background and hide from "the limelight they so deeply disdain" following the public utility holding company controversy. He also relayed Corcoran's and Cohen's insistence that the court bill had been prepared by Justice Department officials, not themselves. Yet Krock reported that rumors in Capitol Hill cloak rooms and corridors were suggesting that the names of the two presidential assistants would once again "fly in congressional debate."[14]

***

Predictions about Corcoran and Cohen proved to be accurate once the Senate sent the court bill back to committee in July and the House took up the Brownlow committee's proposal for six presidential assistants. One of the most outspoken opponents of the executive reorganization measure turned out to be Massachusetts Republican Charles L. Gifford, a former cranberry grower and school teacher. In a tirade aimed at the exclusive deliberations of the Brownlow panel, Gifford charcterized the bill as a bid for executive control that was so arrogant that it could not be openly discussed. Yet his fiercest fire was directed at Corcoran and Cohen, the confidential aides with "a passion for anonymity" who would scheme for the president under the cloak of secrecy. "It is now desired that they actually stay at the White House and not in the little red house on K Street," Gifford told colleagues. "They should live in the White House so it would not seem strange to be seen coming in the back door."[15]

Having ridiculed the secretive nature of Corcoran's and Cohen's activities, Gifford confirmed press suspicions by tying the pair to the discredited court reorganization bill. The judiciary reform package, he charged, was the product of "selfless, nonpublicized brain children lacking any practical experience in public affairs." Gifford pictured White House aides entering the corridors of Congress to "threaten a Brewster . . . if he did not vote for the program of the President." He marvelled at the gall of two existing secretaries urging the Brownlow committee to recommend the hiring of six additional executive assistants. "Unquestionably," he persisted, "the work of Corcoran and Cohen was the inspiration behind the Brownlow report. They are asking for more secretaries to write our legislation for us; brain children who will write our bills in such difficult language that even our own Sam Rayburn will need have them at his side."[16]

Gifford protested that presidential aides had "fastened themselves upon the very texture of our government in such a fashion that . . . a new house has been built on the original framework." Under the executive reoganization plan, he argued, anonymous secretaries would "bring and carry the president's messages, entertain him, and give him new ideas. . . . The cabinet and administrative officers will receive messages through them, salute, and send their replies by such liaison official." The proposal would enable the White House to "take over practically the whole executive function of government," leaving policymaking to appointees paid more than members of Congress. Such extravagant demands, warned Gifford, would "mean a sure dictatorship in this democracy of ours. . . . I have tried to suggest to you how extremely dangerous it might be to give the president any more Cohens and Corcorans."[17]

Congressional discomfort with brains trust rule had turned a housekeeping measure into a test of wills with the executive branch. "God only knows where the end will be," anguished Missouri Republican Dewey J. Short, a Methodist Episcopal pastor and a former college professor of ethics, psychology, and political philosophy. Short warned of "more political parasites placed on the public payroll to lobby, propagandize, and perpetuate the New Deal in power." "Are we to understand," he asked, "that the President can secure quicker and more accurate information from these satellites and sycophants, these theoretical, intellectual, professorial nincompoops who could not be elected dogcatcher," than from members of Congress, the cabinet, and leaders of his own party? If Roosevelt had consulted true Democrats and not "a few pseudo new dealers such as this putrid bill would create," he admonished, the chief executive never would have sought "to pack" the Court. Short won applause a month later by deploring the "half-baked panaceas and . . . wild economic and social theory . . . advanced by . . . experimentalists out of Columbia and dear old Harvard."[18]

Following what *Time* magazine described as "five hours of political rock-throwing," the House approved the addition of six personal assistants to the president's staff by a 260 to 88 margin. A second bill, which empowered the chief executive to regroup federal agencies and create a department of welfare, passed by 283 to 76. Yet the lawmakers balked at the entire executive reorganization measure, no doubt receptive to the plea of Oregon Republican James W. Mott that it was "time for Congress to resume its constitutional responsibilities as an independent legislative body." Not until 1938 did the Brownlow recommendations return to Capitol Hill for reconsideration. As the Senate provided the initial battleground, Montana Democrat Burton Wheeler assumed leadership of the anti-administration forces by introducing an amendment to require majority votes in both houses before reorganization orders could take effect.[19]

A long-time foe of corporate privilege, Wheeler had been Robert La Follette's vice-presidential running mate during the Progressive Party campaign of 1924. An early Roosevelt supporter, the Montana insurgent turned against the New Deal during the 1937 battle over judicial reorganization. Protesting against government regimentation by an unaccountable president, Wheeler bitterly objected to White House efforts to centralize the authority of the executive branch. "Some professor or some clerk," he told the Senate, was "going to sit down in some office in Washington, prepare reports and tell the members of the Senate and of the House what ought to be done." Wheeler reminded colleagues that voters had not elected "some of these professors from Harvard or some of these bureaucrats in Washington to do their thinking for them." With power concentrated in the capital's unelected officials, everyone was looking to government "for everything under the sun."[20]

Wheeler pictured the struggle over executive reorganization as a challenge to congressional virility. The task of restructuring federal agencies, he protested, would be taken on by "some little fellow" or by "some professor from Dartmouth, or Yale, or Harvard, or Columbia." The Montanan insisted that academics were not more competent than elected legislators and should not be granted constitutional rights assigned to Congress. He chided senators for going "with their little hats in their hands" to request favors from department heads with little or no experience about the problems under their jurisdiction. Wheeler recalled a visit concerning a reclamation project with a Public Works Administration attorney who came out of a New York banking firm and knew nothing about irrigation or Montana state law. He later complained about a Department of Interior specialist in western natural resources who had never been west of Chicago. Wheeler noted that almost every senator had anguished privately about the failure of agency heads and bureau chiefs to extend proper respect to members of Congress.[21]

Questions of congressional prerogative and administrative centralization turned nominally loyal Democrats against the Brownlow committee's reorganization proposals. Nebraska senator Edward Burke complained that no member of the panel had any faith in Congress or any use for the legislative branch. Noting that the presidential commission was composed of a former newspaper reporter, a college professor, and a professional reformer, Missouri Democrat Bennett C. Clark protested that the authors of the plan failed to understand that regulatory agencies were extensions of the legislative branch. Nevada's Key Pittman questioned how an urban lawyer like Interior Secretary Harold Ickes could possibly address the problems of the West if Congress permitted reorganization advisers to transfer the Forest Service from the Department of Agriculture to Ickes's jurisdiction. Yet Wheeler's amendment to require congressional approval over reorganization failed, 43 to 39.[22]

As the Senate debated whether to approve the executive reorganization bill in March 1938, public opinion polling indicated that only 38 percent of Roosevelt supporters backed the proposal. Meanwhile, 61 percent of farmers, 64 percent of small business operators, and 70 percent of white-collar employees opposed the Brownlow recommendations. Building on its success in resisting the previous year's court bill, publisher Frank Gannett's National Committee to Uphold Constitutional Government mobilized an outpouring of 300,000 telegrams to convince the Senate to defeat reorganization legislation. Father Charles Coughlin joined the fray with a radio address calling upon listeners to press their senators to oppose the measure. Nevertheless, once a motion to recommit executive reorganization to committee failed by 48 to 43, the Senate passed the bill, 49 to 42.[23]

Once the Brownlow recommendations moved on to the House, Roosevelt compromised by exempting several agencies from consolidation and by agreeing to Wheeler's proposal to permit congressional majorities to negate the bill's provisions. Yet the Republican decision to let Democrats dominate commentary succeeded this time when the House voted, 204 to 196, to recommit the measure to the Select Committee on Government Organization. All eighty-six Republicans, including the party's entire delegation of western progressives, supported the majority, but so did 118 Democrats. Humbled by this show of force, the White House agreed to further compromises in 1939 when Wisconsin Republican John Shafer denounced "the drunken orgy of spending by the New Deal crackpots, brain trusters, and nitwits." In the end, Roosevelt's two-year struggle for executive organization produced a 246 to 153 victory in the House, although the Senate insisted on an advisory amendment by Democrat Harry Byrd that tied approval of the plan to reduced federal spending.[24]

***

As the New Deal incorporated long-range planning, expansive public works, social welfare subsidies, and the stimulation of mass purchasing power between

1937 and 1939, the debate over government expenditures became the focal point of the conflict between Roosevelt officials and their critics. Seeking business growth through a healthy consumer market, a consortium of retail, banking, and labor leaders worked with administration economists toward an activist fiscal and monetary policy that ultimately embraced deficit spending. Public investment, progressive tax policies, and massive relief programs were to spur social mobility and private capitalization by redistributing income, providing government credit, and supplying undeveloped areas with essential infrastructure.[25]

The government's chief voice for consumer-based policy was the National Resources Commmittee (NRC). Initially created in 1933 as the National Planning Board, the agency first determined which projects would be financed by the Public Works Administration. Yet Charles Merriam, the board's most influential member, saw the office as a visionary force to promote rational decision-making. Refashioned the next year as the National Resources Board, an independent agency indirectly accountable to the president, the council became known as the National Resources Committee in 1935. The NRC's advisory group dominated the economic policy of Roosevelt's second term. It included Harvard economist and Federal Reserve Board assistant, Lauchlin B. Currie; Henry Wallace advisers Mordecai Ezekiel and Louis Bean; Department of Commerce aide Leon Henderson; Isador Lubin of the Department of Labor; Treasury economist Harry Dexter White; retailer and theorist Beardsley Ruml; and Gardiner Means, director of the NRC's Industrial Section. Other New Deal spending advocates included SEC chair Jerome Frank and economist Alvin H. Hansen.[26]

As the economy moved into a severe recession in 1937 and 1938, New Deal planners became convinced that unregulated capitalism threatened the functioning of the market. Under the supervision of Thurman Arnold, the Justice Department mounted a series of antitrust suits to police corporate price collusion. Yet Roosevelt's policy intellectuals rejected the notion that government policy should protect the interests of competing producers and increasingly accepted business concentration if it worked to the advantage of consumers and if corporations remained accountable to the state. On the same day in April 1938 that the president delivered an antimonopoly message to Congress, he called for "closer cooperation between business and government." Roosevelt also approved a new "spend-lend" program that included $3 billion for relief, public works, and housing. Using language provided by consultant David Cushman Coyle, the president now asked the country to accept federal budget deficits as a positive instrument of economic growth and full employment.[27]

As historian Alan Brinkley has suggested, New Deal theorists replaced punitive regulation of business and antitrust policing with a model of deficit spending long advocated by British economist John Maynard Keynes. Fiscal policy management offered a departure from confrontational approaches to the market as well as an abandonment of collectivist concepts once associated with Rexford

Tugwell. Yet in rejecting traditional budget balancing, countercyclical spenders introduced threats of inflation and high interest rates to private investors concerned about the normal flow of capital. Surveyed just before Roosevelt committed himself to budget deficits, 79 percent of business respondents preferred reduced taxes as a means of overcoming the recession to increased government spending for relief and public works.[28]

Keynesian economic policy also had important political and cultural implications. Macromanaging the market required that independent executive agencies and disinterested experts be freed from political and legislative pressures so that they might better serve the public interest. Yet Americans traditionally took pride in their refusal to extend deference to bureaucratic authorities. The use of state economic controls further violated another element of the national democratic heritage–the faith that virtuous citizens and producers competed with one another on an individual basis while a passive government simply enforced the rules of the game. By abandoning the creed that reward followed merit and by placing the decision to tip the scales of generosity in the hands of an unaccountable elite, Roosevelt officials found themselves in a highly vulnerable political position.[29]

Suspicion of New Deal advisers and managers understandably remained a constant theme of national press coverage. The major policies of the Roosevelt administration still were "shaped and perfected in the backrooms of the White House," Washington correspondents Joseph Alsop and Robert Kintner reported in June 1938. In periods of self-confidence, they asserted, the president withdrew into his circle of private advisers. Alsop and Kintner noted that a recent Roosevelt speech on taxation had been written by Herman Oliphant, an alleged radical serving as general counsel of the Treasury Department, and then been turned over to the president's "favorite left-wing advisers." They insisted that "the youngish liberal-radical lawyers and economists" of the administration had moved from responsibilities involving utilities supervision, securities regulation, and relief, to antitrust matters, and now were shaping fiscal and financial policy as spending advocates and supporters of greater taxation. The reporters noted that aides were preparing a new undistributed profits levy that would be used as a weapon against business instead of a mere source of revenue.[30]

Five months after publication of their story, Alsop and Kintner declared that some four hundred New Dealers had replaced the Roosevelt brains trust. Although high officials, government economists, business leaders, presidential advisers, and rank-and-file subordinates all were members of the team, the journalists contended that intellectuals chiefly expressed the president's will and were "the principal instrument" for carrying out his goals. Describing the White House group as "an offensive and defensive alliance of the left wing of the administration," Alsop and Kintner claimed that the New Dealers initially realized their strength during the 1935 Public Utilities Holding Company Bill fight and then coalesced when Thomas Corcoran and others gathered to draft the following year's Democratic platform and Roosevelt acceptance speech.[31]

***

Bitter divisions over relief demonstrated the controversial nature of the Keynesian elite's social welfare requirement. As far back as 1934, western Senate progressives such as Hiram Johnson and Minnesota Farmer-Laborite Henrik Shipstead had warned that relief should be viewed as an emergency measure to help the jobless and hungry. Sixty percent of Gallup poll respondents complained in October 1935 that government was spending too much money on welfare and recovery. By the end of 1938, 53 percent of people with an opinion believed that Harry Hopkins was doing a poor job as director of the Works Progress Administration, and nearly two-thirds of those with views registered their opposition to promoting Hopkins to be Secretary of Commerce. By 1939, only 28 percent of a national poll placed relief and the WPA among the best accomplishments of the New Deal, while 23 percent included them among its worst legacies.[32]

Instead of opposing relief to the poor, critics accused welfare agencies of inefficiency and corruption, particularly when political intellectuals seemed to reap underserved benefits. When the *Saturday Evening Post* estimated in 1937 that nearly two-fifths of poverty aid went to overhead, Indiana Democrat Glenn H. Griswold attacked "profiteers of relief" from the House floor and charged that foreign-born researchers, economists, and assistants held "swivel chair" jobs with the WPA. Indiana Republican Charles A. Halleck noted that the jobs agency once had hired twenty-seven publicity agents in his state. WPA's annual overhead surpassed $250 million, claimed New York Republican Robert Low Bacon. Painting Hopkins as the symbol of "a huge bureaucracy centered in Washington," Bacon pleaded that a larger percentage of funds go to relief recipients instead of administrators. The House barely defeated an effort to cut WPA appropriations by 20 percent in 1937, but two years later approved an investigation of agency expenditures by a vote of 352 to 27.[33]

Discomfort over the Keynesian elite's patronization of an economically dependent and politically subservient underclass fed the daring third-party crusade of Philip F. La Follette. Elected Wisconsin's governor as a Republican in 1930 and as a Progressive in 1934 and 1936, La Follette helped to enact a graduated income tax, state unemployment insurance, expanded relief and public works, and banking reform. Yet the independently minded politician maintained distance from radical groups such as the Farmer-Labor Progressive Federation, whose rallying cry of "production for use" appeared to symbolize socialism and big government. A New Deal loyalist until the 1937 recession, the young governor turned against Roosevelt's reliance on budget deficits and relief expenditures. La Follette hoped to restore prosperity through a nationalized credit and monetary system as well as a guaranteed annual income. Instead of redistributing wealth, he sought to expand production. In 1938, the heir to the La Follette political legacy formed the National Progressives of America (NPA), a movement aimed at fusing progressive and conservative principles.[34]

"How refreshing it is," declared columnist Dorothy Thompson, "to hear a speech from the non-Marxist left cut itself loose from the social work, settlement house, and benevolent feudal landlord mentality that has dominated the New Deal." Indeed, La Follette told *The Nation's* Max Lerner that he had contempt for intellectuals who bickered about specifics and "class" definitions in a period in which leadership qualities were more important than platforms. Although the governor correctly anticipated the opposition of liberal reformers, he underestimated the difficulty of gaining support from rank-and-file New Deal and Roosevelt loyalists. While the urban wing of Wisconsin's Progressive Party resented attacks on industrial unions and WPA relief, La Follette alienated the farmer-labor movement by neglecting to consult its leaders. On election day, 1938, the governor's fourth-term bid suffered a humiliating rebuke and the NPA soon expired. Nevertheless, a defiant La Follette refused to relinquish the conviction that the progressive faith was superior to "the high-falutin' dissertations of languid liberals and rocking-chair radicals."[35]

Ironically, the policy intellectuals denounced by La Follette figured substantially in the Roosevelt administration's disastrous performance in the 1938 congressional primaries and elections. According to unfriendly news accounts, radical attorneys and economists advised the White House to assist progressives facing anti-New Deal incumbents in that year's Democratic primaries. The *New York Times* reported that targets were selected by an "elimination committee" composed of Harold Ickes, Harry Hopkins, James Roosevelt, and Thomas Corcoran. Corcoran supposedly took the initiative in the primary fight against Iowa senator Guy M. Gillette. He also figured in the campaign to challenge Virginia representative Howard W. Smith, a former circuit court judge, banker, farmer, and newspaper publisher accused of obstructing public works bills. Smith's White House-backed challenger was William E. Dodd, Jr., an historian who was the son of the former ambassador to Germany and the preferred candidate of industrial labor union leaders. Roosevelt operatives also supported primary efforts to unseat senators Walter F. George of Georgia, Millard F. Tydings of Maryland, and Ellison ("Cotton Ed") D. Smith of South Carolina.[36]

Ignoring southern sensitivity to outside interference and resentment toward presidential advisers, the Roosevelt administration suffered a devastating defeat in the Democratic primaries. Representative Smith defeated Dodd by a 3 to 1 margin, while the four targeted senators survived the White House purge with ease. To compound the matter, the fall general election brought the Republicans eight new Senate seats and eighty-one in the House, many in the recession-battered Midwest and West. Accordingly, an anti-New Deal coalition of rural and southern Democrats and mainstream Republicans assumed control of Congress and provided Roosevelt critics with a powerful platform against federal spending, regimentation, government bureaucracy, and executive power. As New Deal programs tapped the expertise of economists and administrators in the interests of urban consumers, relief recipients, and organized labor, members of the new congressional power bloc exerted political muscle to protect their constituents and preserve their governing prerogatives.[37]

***

Not satisified with promoting the economic integration of southern farm tenants, sharecroppers, and relief recipients, the Roosevelt administration sought to modernize the South's tightly controlled labor market by freeing it from domination by old-style planters, merchants, and industrialists. The president's advisers therefore supported regional organizing efforts by textile unions affiliated with the Congress of Industrial Organizations (CIO) and endorsed the creation of nationalized labor standards through federal wages and hours legislation. Drafted by Thomas Corcocan, Benjamin Cohen, and Felix Frankfurter in consultation with CIO union leader Sidney Hillman, the Fair Labor Standards Bill of 1937 encountered initial resistance due to a wave of union-led sit-down strikes in the mass production industries, although the House approved an amended version late the next year. Yet even outside the South, the White House–supported labor movement continued to confront bitter adversaries in older industry and banking circles, among independent enterprisers, and within the more traditional elements of the skilled and semiskilled working class. The depth of anti-union sentiment was illustrated by the fact that 66 percent of Gallup poll respondents professed more sympathy with the Ford motor company early in 1938 than with its CIO opponents.[38]

New Deal labor policy was designed to stabilize worker-management conflict, promote economic recovery through higher wages and mass consumption, and maximize Democratic support at the polls. Such strategy underlay passage of the Wagner National Labor Relations Act of 1935, the landmark piece of legislation that transformed the American workplace by granting employees fundamental rights such as seniority privileges, grievances procedures, the freedom to organize without company harassment, and collective bargaining representation. Designed by Roosevelt advisers Leon Keyserling and Isador Lubin, the historic bill established the National Labor Relations Board (NLRB) to protect worker gains and serve as a last-resort mediator between unions and employers.[39] Yet as the 1938 elections strengthened anti-New Deal and anti-union sentiment, Congress turned away from the extensive reforms embodied in the Wagner Act and began to look at NLRB staff attorneys and administrators as culprits who endangered workplace due process and fair play.

The heart of the labor relations problem lay in the charge by some employers that the Roosevelt administration's political coalition with industrial union leaders prompted a stacked NLRB to side consistently with the president's allies in the CIO. The craft-oriented American Federation of Labor (AFL) also complained that its industrial union rival unduly benefited from the agency's jurisdictional rulings. Critics paid particular attention to the rapid expansion of the labor board's legal staff (from 14 to 226), and questioned the Communist ties of NLRB officials. Undoubtedly emboldened by the 1938 elections and infuriated at federal regulation of hosiery mills in his district, CIO adversary Edward E. Cox, a Georgia Democrat, demanded a House inquiry into the NLRB. When Virginia's Howard Smith, another powerful union foe, introduced a resolution to create a select committee to take on the task in July 1939, over one hundred Democrats, including Cox and seventy-one other southerners, prevailed in a 254 to 134 vote.[40]

Named as chair of the investigatory panel, Smith hired 22 attorneys and 109 examiners, seized NLRB files, and distributed 60,000 questionnaires to local unions, employers, and police. Public hearings were conducted between December 1939 and February 1940. NLRB chair J. Warren Madden, a former University of Pittsburgh law professor, testified that in its four years of operation, the board had sustained only 5 percent of the complaints against management, and that the annual number of working days lost through industrial disputes had declined by 31 percent. Yet the Smith committee exposed a series of embarrassing disputes among Madden's subordinates and charged the NLRB with incompetence. Investigators contended that unqualified attorneys reviewed and digested evidence that constituted the basis for board decisions. To illustrate their point, they disclosed that Bernard W. Freund, the twenty-seven year old nephew of New Dealer Benjamin Cohen, had been hired as an NLRB attorney despite little law experience and lackluster credentials. A staff lawyer had scribbled, "Ben Cohen's nephew," on the young man's application.[41]

According to newspaper accounts, Smith asked if Freund's uncle was "the junior member of Corcoran and Cohen?" In a note to Cohen the next day, the Virginian apologized for the remark but vowed to continue examining the qualifications of agency employees. The Smith committee contended that the NLRB had conspired to compel American industry and labor to subject themselves to the board's dictatorship. Investigators asserted that staff had attempted to blacklist employers by denying U.S. government contracts to companies accused but not yet convicted of Wagner Act violations. The panel claimed that the board solicited litigation to be brought before it for determination. It further cited extralegal activities by individual officials that amounted to aiding and abetting boycotts against firms involved in collective bargaining conflicts. Smith investigtors also accused NLRB employees of lobbying against legislation sponsored by the AFL in order to please allies in the industrial union movement.[42]

The committee reserved its strongest criticism for NLRB collusion with the CIO. It insisted that industrial union sympathizers, former labor activists, and radicals received hiring preferences as staff, field examiners, and review attorneys, sensitive positions that seriously undermined the board's neutrality.

Noting that the agency's Division of Economic Research produced the evidence upon which findings were made, investigators reported that research director and economist David J. Saposs had been a former member of the Socialist Party and an editorial board member of *Labor Age*. As recently as 1935, Saposs had described capitalism as characterized by "poverty, misery, and economic insecurity," conditions he saw as "ripe" for revolution if the middle class and workers had "the will to rise to the occasion."[43]

The twelve-volume Smith Committee Final Report was issued in December 1940, although it was not signed by the two other Democrats on the panel. Finding the NLRB "grossly partisan" to the CIO and "deplorably biased" in its operations, the document concluded that Congress should protect the right to collective bargaining without explicitly encouraging it. The report called for remedial legislation to amend the Wagner Act. It recommended that Senate consent be required for presidential nominations to the board, that the NLRB's judicial and prosecutorial functions be separated, and that the agency refrain from involvement in jurisdictional disputes among labor unions. The Smith committee also held that workers engaging in strike-related violence or unlawful acts should not be eligible for reinstatement. It called for a preponderance of testimony to establish management violations of labor law and suggested that employer failure to reach agreements should not be proof of bad faith.[44]

***

As anti–New Deal members of Congress ignored protests from labor supporters that the NLRB inquiry was designed to reverse the liberating achievements of the Wagner Act, Smith's amendments passed the House in June 1940, 258 to 129. Yet the proposals were shelved by the Senate Education and Labor Committee the following fall. By then, a bipartisan congressional coalition had agreed upon a more systematic method of limiting the influence of the professional regulators in the NLRB, the Wages and Hours Administration, the Securities and Exchange Commission, and other federal agencies. Between 1933 and 1940, the number of government employees in Washington had jumped from 75,000 to 166,000. The end of the Depression decade left the federal government with 500 bureaus in 135 departments and independent agencies, an investment estimated to surpass $5 billion. As a contemporary scholar suggested, the growth of regulatory commissions comprised the most important governmental development since World War I. Yet there appeared to be no limitations on the power of the "vast superstructure of corporate and semi-corporate entities" and little accountability to Congress or to ordinary citizens.[45]

Political commentator Walter Lippmann had addressed the issue of expanding government in *An Inquiry into the Principles of the Good Society*, a series of essays published in 1937. An elite of gradual collectivists exercised near-intellectual monopoly and absolute authority over the assumptions of modern politics, wrote Lippmann, but had not imbued the mass of people with their doctrines. In societies in which prosperity depended upon government assistance, he argued, the vital connection lay between wealth and state power. As the decade closed, such attacks on government spending, presidential power, and dictatorial agencies became a mainstay of anti-New Deal rhetoric. Concerns over concentrated power led western progressive Gerald Nye to complain to a national radio audience in 1939 that the Roosevelt administration was "a government of witch hunters and medicine men." First-term representative Karl Mundt, a South Dakotan Republican, described New Dealers as Tories preferring the centralized control of "a select coterie of Governors" to self-rule.[46]

Denizens of Capitol Hill were likely opponents of the usurpation of legislative powers by administrative agencies. Massachusetts representative John Taber vowed in 1939 that he personally would oppose the delegation of any further authority to the president. Pointing to federal departments of public works and welfare, Taber castigated bureaucrats who used propaganda to expand their operations and make citizens subject to their will. Freshman senator Robert A. Taft provided some of the sharpest criticism of the regulatory agencies. As a Republican, Taft had consistently argued that government should keep the peace, referee controversies, and adjust abuses instead of regulating personal and business activities. In a series of memoranda on administrative tribunals prepared by his staff in 1940, the Ohio senator found the evidence to buttress the case against rule by experts. Executive agencies had been delegated excessive power by Congress, exercised judicial powers not subject to review, were not bound by previous decisions, issued directives that violated due process, and made agreements among themselves without benefit of law.[47]

Congressional resistance to the regulatory powers of administrative bureaus became the subject of legislation in 1939 when Senator Marvel Mills Logan, a Kentucky Democrat, and Representative Francis Walter, a Democrat from Pennyslvania, co-sponsored a bill permitting individuals to appeal the rules, regulations, and orders of 130 bureaus and agencies in federal court. The proposal was favorably received by the Senate Judiciary Committee, which accused regulators of placing themselves above the statutes and of disregarding Congress and the bench. Yet only two weeks after Senate approval, Majority Leader Alben Barkley prevailed upon an ailing Logan to delay action on the measure until the next session. In February 1940, the House judiciary panel reported the bill out with the admonition that "the law must provide that the governors shall be governed and the regulators shall be regulated, if our present form of government is to endure.... The United States Government is not founded on autocracy." With the support of business groups, the American Bar Association, and the National Association of Women Lawyers, the proposal moved to the House floor.[48]

"It can never be admitted in this country," declared Francis Walter as the House dissolved into a committee of the whole, "that the administrative bureaucracies will control the legislative and judicial branches of this government."

The measure under question was "a warning to those who are more intent on . . . exercising greater autocratic powers . . . than the Congress conferred upon them." Georgia Democrat Edward Cox, a former superior court judge, reiterated that Walter-Logan sought to recapture powers that Congress never should have given away. Administrative edict involved the substitution of the discretion of bureaucrats for the rules of fixed, definite law, said Cox. Such mixture of legislative, judicial, and executive powers created a fourth department of government that undermined a system in which the supremacy of general rules of law had been established over personalized government. To applause from colleagues, Cox characterized the thinking of SEC and NLRB bureaucrats as rooted in a doctrine that emanated from Soviet Russia.[49]

Congressional fury toward administrative regulators surfaced in the remarks of Connecticut Republican Albert Elmer Austin, a physician and first-term representative. New Deal agencies had "wandered far afield in search of new laws to conquer or more vicitms to subdue," declared Austin. They were "overwhelmed with the idea that they are all sufficient in themselves, acknowledge no master, and proceed on the theory that they were in reality created to take over this government and promote it to a bureaucracy." Although Roosevelt Democrats contended that Walter-Logan would hamper the government's ability to function, Austin criticized opponents as advocates or creators of the bureaucratic system who could not admit "that their brain children had developed into agents of frustration or even destruction." House Judiciary Committee chair Hatton William Sumners reminded colleagues that federal regulators had the powers of a king, and that ordinary citizens had no ability to resist the mandate of an agent of the administrative bureaus.[50]

After approving an amendment by New Deal loyalist Jerry Voorhis that limited court appeals to regulations in effect three years or less, the House passed the Walter-Logan Bill in April 1940 by nearly a 3 to 1 margin, much of it provided by members with rural southern and midwestern constituencies. As the action shifted to the Senate, Majority Leader Barkley again requested a postponement. But Judiciary Committee chair Henry F. Ashurst of Arizona complained that "megalomaniacs" in the administrative agencies were seeking to prevent the proposal from coming to a vote, and the panel unanimously agreed to send the measure to the floor with minor amendments. Leadership delays, attention to the war in Europe, and the distractions of the 1940 presidential election campaign sidetracked the Walter-Logan Bill in October. Nevertheless, Virginia's Howard Smith soon opened a second assault on the administrative bureaucracy. Seeking to stop regulators "from amending the statutes by interpretation," Smith returned to a familiar theme by proposing that Congress overturn a Justice Department ruling that NLRB findings were "binding and conclusive" upon other agencies until reversed in court.[51]

Like Smith's amendments to the Wagner Act, the resolution failed to clear committee because of conflicts with the Walter-Logan Bill. Anticipating a presidential veto, Senate Democratic leaders allowed the long-delayed agency limit measure to come to a vote following Roosevelt's third-term reelection in November. As forty-three senators refrained from participation and ten members of the president's party lined up with the majority, the Senate passed Walter-Logan by a narrow 27 to 25 margin. Citing potential disruption of the national defense through the "chaos and paralysis" of government, and affirming that modern reform rested upon the administrative tribunal, Roosevelt vetoed the bill the following month. Within three hours, the action was sustained when the House voted 153 to 127 to override, far short of the required two-thirds margin.[52]

***

Despite such reverses as the Walter-Logan veto, the congressional war against professional regulators in the NLRB and other agencies continued to fester. In December 1938, newly appointed Secretary of Commerce Harry Hopkins had created a Division of Industrial Economics, and selected Richard V. Gilbert, a Keynesian economist recruited by Harvard colleague, Lauchlin Currie, as agency chief. Gilbert staffed the new bureau with academics who shared his views on the use of macroeconomic theory to sustain private investment. Yet several members of Congress took the Harvard professor to task for intellectual condescension and hostility to the free market. As a contributor to an anthology of essays by colleagues at Harvard and Tufts University, the economist had portrayed business aversion to government as irrational. The typical enterpriser was "caught in the foils of events he does not understand," wrote Gilbert, and was "merely seeking to lay the blame on something he thinks he does not understand, just as the savage in the face of the mysterious forces of nature seeks to make them more intelligible by inventing a host of gods and devils."[53]

As the House considered the Department of Commerce budget in February 1940, South Dakota Republican Francis H. Case protested that a $100,000 appropriation for the personal services of experts and specialists in Gilbert's division had no authority in law. Once the House eliminated the unit, Massachusetts Republican Henry Cabot Lodge, Jr. pleaded with the Senate to follow suit. Noting that the work of Commerce economists was duplicated by other agencies, Lodge mused that academic specialists were seeking to become permanent fixtures in Washington. "Shades of bureaucracy!" exclaimed West Virginia Democrat Rush D. Holt to sustained laughter. "Think of that–a secretary to the secretary to the Assistant Secretary of the Secretary of Commerce!" Once the Senate withdrew Gilbert's funding, division economists were transferred to other agencies. Yet Francis Case returned to the House floor in July to complain that Hopkins was so determined to maintain his "special 'brain trust,'" that he was forcing department retirements to free money for new advisers.[54]

Congress scored a second victory against Roosevelt administrators when it eliminated a controversial experiment in the Civilian Conservation Corps

(CCC). As the effects of the Great Depression began to abate, Corps officials announced in August 1940 that young men from moderate-income households could participate in the popular work program if state quotas were not filled by the offspring of poor families. At the same time, Department of Agriculture administrators sought the CCC's separation from the Department of War, which managed the youth camps. Hoping to shift the organization's mission from relief to the promotion of social service and citizenship, reformers planned to set up special facilities to train college students as Corps commanding officers. Congress had broadened the program's entry requirements in 1937 by permitting young men "in need" of work to participate alongside those whose families were on relief. Yet as legislators prepared to enact the first peacetime draft in U.S. history in September 1940, critics attacked the CCC for violating its legal requirement to focus on the unemployed.[55]

Expansion of the youth program's constituency coincided with the launching of an experimental project in rural Vermont. Seeking to establish "a new type of work service camp" to undertake rural conservation and reconstruction projects, six Dartmouth College students petitioned the CCC for financial assistance and for use of one of its former camps at Mt. Sharon. With support from columnist Dorothy Thompson and local farmers, Roosevelt asked Harvard Law School Dean and former White House adviser James Landis, two New Deal officials, and a Yale Law School administrator to study the proposal. In October, the president approved the creation of Camp William James under management by the Department of Agriculture, and sanctioned the appointment of Dr. Eugen Rosenstock-Huessy, a Dartmouth professor of social philosophy, as training consultant.[56]

Just before Camp William James opened in January 1941, the Youth Commission of the American Council on Education completed a four-year study engineered by General Electric board chair Owen D. Young. Calling for the merger of the CCC and the National Youth Administration, the panel concluded that the War Department should abandon its role in camp management. Despite the conviction of reformers that realignment would ensure broader application of the values of labor, congressional resistance to change remained high. Michigan Republican Albert J. Engel, a member of the House appropriations subcommittee overseeing the CCC, had protested for years that the youth agency spent more than half the funds awarded to enrollees on inflated salaries for political appointees. Following press reports on the Mt. Sharon experiment, Engel wrote to the Secretary of Agriculture to ask what the sons of the rich were doing in a CCC work camp. By February 1941, when the matter came to the House floor, the Vermont project had come under attack as "a starry-eyed and impracticable idea" and as "fancy experimentation."[57]

Engel's most pointed criticism centered on leadership training. Named after philosopher William James, the Mt. Sharon camp was dedicated to the idea that young men of "the educated classes" could join those of the lower orders in government service as a substitute for the spiritual energies normally aroused by war. The Michigan representative questioned whether such thinking addressed the welfare of participants or the attempt to instill a particular theory of government. He asked if the Roosevelt administration was going to make the CCC "a social guinea pig upon which these social students, including the professors, will experiment and dissect." Parents of enrollees had "a right to know that they are not going to be made the subject of social experiment," warned Engel. Pointing to Rosenstock-Huessy's role in organizing youth labor camps in Weimar Germany, the Michigan politician insisted that the Dartmouth professor had no business "telling us of American ideals." Ten days after Engel's speech, the War Department resumed management of the Mt. Sharon camp. Resigning in protest, twenty-four college enrollees began an independent labor colony nearby.[58]

***

As historian John Salmond has concluded, the first and only attempt by intellectuals to alter the CCC's structure and mission turned out to be a grave embarrassment.[59] Beyond a conflict between young idealists and military-minded bureaucrats, however, the Vermont controversy provided an important chapter in a bitterly sustained competition for national political and cultural legitimacy. In building a social order to reverse the failures of the Depression, Roosevelt planners and strategists hoped to universalize democratic and cooperative values among workers, farmers, and consumers. By assuming that planning and leadership responsibilities would be shouldered by an intellectual political class of social guardians, however, reformers failed to appreciate how their efforts mirrored their own interests and sensibilities. As participants in a power struggle with traditional political and business figures who buttressed their position by invoking principles of democratic procedure and free enterprise, New Deal enthusiasts failed to anticipate genuine resistance to their programs and to their enhanced role as government and societal leaders.

By the time Roosevelt began his third term in 1941, Thomas Corcoran had left the White House and the unity requirements of a prospective world war had prompted the president to replace brains trust theorists with business-oriented figures such as Edward R. Stettinius and Lowell Mellett.[60] Nevertheless, a skeptical Congress continued to assert vigilance over perceived excesses by executive branch agents in the administrative bureaus and other federal offices. Despite their near-universal dedication to market values and the promotion of a healthy consumerism, New Deal officials were suspect because their reliance on coordinated policies and economic management smacked of arbitrary manipulation and defiance of the customary rules of fair play. Associated with presumed foreign ideologies and practices such as class-conscious labor union activity, socialist national planning, deficit spending, and the welfare state, the Roosevelt political class easily could be cast as strangers who threatened the democratic way of life and compromised the interests of ordinary producers and middle-class enterprisers.

For some New Deal opponents, the Jewish background of powerful government officials provided a symbol of the alien nature of the New Class empowered by Roosevelt's New Deal. Although Jews constituted only 15 percent of the leading figures in the administration, key advisers such as White House counsel Samuel I. Rosenman, Harvard Law School Dean and Supreme Court Justice Felix Frankfurter, brains truster Benjamin Cohen, economist Isador Lubin, and AAA counsel and SEC chair Jerome Frank, were Jewish. Recruiting an unprecedented number of graduates of elite law schools, the Roosevelt administration also staffed agencies like the SEC, the NLRB, and the Agriculture, Labor, and Interior departments, with talented Jews and Roman Catholics.[61]

Apprehensive about the urban background of new recruits and sensitive to rural stereotypes of Jews and Catholics, agencies like AAA carefully screened new applicants. Even President Roosevelt had to circumvent ethnic prejudice. Secretary of the Treasury Henry Morgenthau, Jr. and other prominent Jews were so worried about the perception that Jews were responsible for New Deal radicalism that they implored the White House to refrain from appointing Felix Frankfurter to the Supreme Court. Fears of antisemitism were not illusory. Public opinion polling in 1938 showed that 31 percent of a national sample believed that Jews were less patriotic than other citizens, while 41 percent thought they had too much power. Nearly one-fourth the respondents were convinced that too many Jews held government jobs. Two years later, 17 percent of a national poll named Jews as a menace to America.[62]

Blamed for the killing of Jesus, Jews long had served as the targets of an antisemitic tradition that depicted them as strangers—as radical subversives, economic exploiters, social parasites, or morally unconventional iconoclasts. Such notions were reinforced in the United States, where Jews often were excluded from banking, insurance, corporate law, and other prestigious fields, and compelled to survive as professionals or middlemen in the consumer and service sector. Myth held that Jews avoided physical labor, valued profit more than life, and destroyed ethical standards in business, law, and medicine. Automaker Henry Ford summed up such thinking in 1921 when he dismissed the Jew as "a mere huckster, a trader who doesn't want to produce, but to make something out of what somebody else produces." Similar views underlay the revealing critique of Senator William Langer, a North Dakota populist, who privately fumed at Jews in 1941 for "wanting to be the American preferred stock of bankers, merchants, professionals, officials, and other wealth absorbers," while Gentiles were to serve as agriculturalists and laborers.[63]

The involvement of Jews in the service trades, professions, and knowledge sector made it easy to associate them with the wiles of the newly empowered political class. Jews represented the "new breed in Washington," historian Leonard Dinnerstein has noted. Accordingly, the government's Jewish attorneys and officals became a convenient symbol for those who perceived the Roosevelt revolution as a threat to their own interests and values. Such criticism sometimes came in the coded nuance of the upper-class. In December 1935, the Republican Committee of One Hundred gathered at New York's Savoy-Plaza Hotel to hear Elon Huntington Hooker describe White House advisers as "largely of foreign descent, radical associations, and questionable Americanism." More often, antisemitic attacks were phrased in the direct language of middle-class extremists like Father Coughlin, Gerald B. Winrod, or Gerald L. K. Smith, who pictured Felix Frankfurter as the leader of communistic Jews. The United Brotherhood of America (the Black Legion), one of a hundred antisemitic organizations nationwide, created a mild sensation in 1936 by attacking the "Jew Deal."[64]

Although the assault on Jewish members of the Roosevelt administration often originated in ethnic and religious prejudice, it embodied pervasive social anxieties over the inclusion of intellectuals and new professionals at the top levels of government. By 1938, 7,800 social scientists worked for the federal bureaucracy. Most experts in Washington served as administrators, not policymakers, and sought to use planning to initiate minor adjustments in a consumer-oriented political economy. Yet the struggle between the emerging knowledge sector and traditional power brokers in politics and business often assumed irrational and hysterical proportions, particularly when modern experts served to deflate criticism from elected leaders.[65] As the United States entered a world war to preserve its way of life and values against totalitarian foes in Europe and Asia, the conflict over domestic guardians would take on new intensity.

4

Planners versus Enterprisers: The Free World at Home during World War II

As the United States entered World War II, the debate over the ideological influence of socially oriented intellectuals and policy specialists reached new levels of acrimony. At stake was the nature of American war aims and the role of continuing political and cultural innovation at home. Were shadowy New Deal administrators and advisers plotting a "glorified worldwide WPA?" as Roosevelt critic Hamilton Fish, Jr. charged.[1] Were sinister strangers to the American Way about to use the wartime emergency to impose social experiments and collectivist policies on an unsuspecting populace and a powerless Congress? Chapter 4 grounds the assault on policy advisers and academic planners upon congressional efforts to control domestic bureaucracies such as the Office of Price Administration, the National Resources Planning Board, and the Rural Electrification Administration. Although questions of expanded government power and federal spending energized such activities, the political and cultural allegiances of New Deal personnel became an increasingly important focus of wartime controversy. Anti-intellectual rhetoric mirrored severe anxieties over the plight of traditional power brokers, the maintenance of economic and cultural orthodoxy, and the survival of democracy in a period of overwhelming change and uncertainty.

***

Repeatedly invoking the contents of the Atlantic Charter of 1941, Franklin D. Roosevelt and his top administrators depicted the global struggle against the Axis as a "free world" crusade for basic human freedoms and rights, including liberation from material want. Yet many anti–New Deal nationalists, former noninterventionists, and Republican politicians insisted that the fighting should be dedicated to a nonideological defense of U.S. interests. Roosevelt adversaries such as George N. Peek and Senator Robert A. Taft warned that the military campaign had to be directed toward restoring peace and protecting the United States, not changing the world. "This war does not belong to a little clique," protested William Lemke. "It belongs to all of us. It is not a social event for the international 400. It is a war in which our sons are dying."[2]

Reconciled to massive military expenditures, Roosevelt critics hoped to contain big government by limiting outlays for domestic or civilian purposes. On the same day in Feburary 1941 as the Senate raised the federal debt limit to $65 billion, Virginia senator Harry Byrd called for the appointment of a joint commission of Congress and the executive to explore ways of cutting nonessential government spending. Asserting that budget deficits irresponsibly shifted financial burdens to future generations, Byrd had played a key role in killing the administration's Works Financing Bill of 1939, a measure that would have allowed the Reconstruction Finance Corporation to loan $3 billion to government agencies for public works and other projects. The 1941 debt averaged out to $700 a person, claimed the senator, while local, state, and federal taxation threatened to absorb one-fifth of national income.[3]

Byrd received public support in July 1941 when a Citizens Emergency Committee on Nondefense Expenditures won the endorsement of several university presidents, economists, bankers, business figures, and farm leaders such as the National Grange's Louis T. Taber. As Congress sought to fund the defense program by increasing taxes by $3.5 billion the next month, the Senate Finance Committee approved the Byrd resolution. Congress organized the Joint Committee on Reduction of Nonessential Federal Expenditures in September 1941. Comprised of six senators, six House members, and two executive branch officials, the panel elected Byrd as chair the following month, a position he retained for twenty years. Early hearings included the testimony of Secretary of the Treasury Henry Morgenthau, Jr., who called for drastic cuts in soil reclamation projections, river and harbor improvements, agricultural aid, the National Youth Administration (NYA), and the Civilian Conservation Corps. Representatives of the Corps acknowledged that the agency's appropriation could be cut by half if it served only those on relief.[4]

Issuing an interim report less than three weeks after Pearl Harbor, the Byrd committee insisted that "every possible retrenchment" be made in the administrative costs of the civil departments and agencies. If the American people were to sacrifice and endure wartime hardships, it declared, the government should set the example. The panel contended that the restoration of prosperity made it possible to eliminate most relief spending. By deferring highway construction and public works, implementing substantial farm programs cuts, reducing WPA appropriations by 45 percent, and abolishing the NYA and CCC, the Byrd committee estimated that the federal government could save an annual $1.7 billion to help finance the war. It promised to review the budgets of all permanent agencies, government corporations, and emergency programs. Speaking before the Senate in Feburary 1942, Byrd observed that "the first battle we have to win is the battle of Washington." Jealousies between departments and officials could be ended, he said, by transfering "thousands of nonessential parasites" in government agencies to more useful activities.[5]

New Deal critics particularly objected to the use of public relations and propaganda experts in the government's nonmilitary bureaus. The Office of

Civilian Defense (OCD), an executive agency charged with bolstering public morale and preparing citizens for enemy attack, became a favorite target of the opposition. First Lady Eleanor Roosevelt, who headed the OCD's Volunteer Participation Division, held a reformer's view of the program's mission and hoped to incorporate physical fitness, cultural awareness, and social service into its activities. When Roosevelt appointed leftist actor Melvyn Douglas to head the OCD's Arts Council, New Deal activist Joseph P. Lash to organize the Youth Division, and radical literary figure Malcolm Cowley to enhance arts appreciation, skeptical members of Congress staged a revolt. In January 1942, an angry House voted, 187 to 169, to place the OCD under the authority of the War Department and to eliminate Director Fiorello La Guardia's position.[6]

One day after Congress acted, President Roosevelt blunted congressional criticism of the OCD by replacing La Guardia with former brains truster and Harvard Law School Dean James Landis. When the Senate restored the agency's funding, the House reversed its earlier elimination of the bureau by a narrow 172 to 167 margin. Yet the Volunteer Participation Division continued to come under sharp attack in a bitter floor debate in February 1942. Singling out Melvyn Douglas, Joseph Lash, and Malcolm Cowley as "leeches" upon the Treasury, New York Republican John Taber ridiculed the "frills and nonsense" of the OCD program. Civil defense did not not need the First Lady's "uplift program," protested Michigan Republican Paul W. Shafer. "Those who have heretofore been active in the effort to make over this country," concurred Georgia Democrat Edward E. Cox, "are taking advantage of the stress we now are in to promote and advance their scheme of collectivism."[7]

Opponents of New Deal experimentation such as Milwaukee Republican Thad F. Wasidweski took particular pleasure in targeting Eleanor Roosevelt's hiring of a modern dance instructor to assist the OCD physical fitness program. Noting the administration's penchant for "fan dancing," Missouri Republican Phillip A. Bennett mischievously passed on an exotic dancer's offer to serve the government without charge and to change the name of her act to the "Nude Deal." "These are wartimes," declared California Republican Leland M. Ford, "and I do not think that this country has to be sold by song and dance on the necessities of a need program." Sensing that the dance project was a vulnerable symbol of government frivolity, Ford attached an amendment to the OCD appropriation prohibiting expenditures for physical fitness instruction "by dancers, fan dancing, street shows, theatrical performances, or other public entertainment." Once the proviso was accepted without a recorded vote, the House approved a reduced OCD budget by a comfortable 258 to 112 margin.[8]

Eight days after the OCD appropriations passed the House, Eleanor Roosevelt resigned as assistant director for volunteer participation. When the Byrd committee questioned OCD Director Landis at the end of February 1942, panelists demanded that the agency abolish all frills. Noting that the OCD staff included sixty-one coordinators of sports and recreation programs who supervised ping-pong, horseshoes, marbles, and bowling, Byrd accused the agency of mounting a "gigantic plan of regimentation for physical fitness." The committee insisted that the OCD confine its mission to protecting civilians from air raids or risk termination of funding. In response, Landis reduced the importance of the Volunteer Participation Division and eliminated the agency's social service component.[9]

***

Although Congress managed to assert control over the role of policy professionals in the civilian defense effort, government public relations and propaganda activities continued to infuriate New Deal foes. In February 1942, Representative Phillip Bennett called for the dismissal of 90 percent of Washington's public relations experts. Senate Democrat Millard F. Tydings of Maryland joined the fray by characterizing the work of government press agents as high-priced "drivel." In May, Byrd accused the small Office of Government Reports of wasting nearly $28 million a year on publicity. When director Lowell Mellett, a close Roosevelt adviser, insisted that the agency had not spent one nickel on public relations and attacked Byrd's criticism as dishonest, the senator denounced Mellett as "an arrogant and proud bureaucrat." Whether the OGR put out information, publicity, or propaganda, charged the Virginian, it was wasting taxpayer money. Asserting that the agency's new headquarters had been built with funds transfered from another appropriation following a cut in its own operating expenses, Byrd castigated "the Mellett Madhouse" as needless and extravagant.[10]

The animosity between Byrd and Mellett offered a microcosm of the sharp differences between entrenched congressional leaders and the social interventionists and cultural innovators of the executive branch. The split took dramatic form in March 1942 when Tennessee Democrat Kenneth McKellar asked the Senate to abide by the Byrd committee's recommendation to abolish the Civilian Conservation Corps. McKellar's impatience with the once-popular agency was fed by his belief that CCC Director James J. McEntee was disdainful toward members of Congress. As wartime spending removed the remnants of Depression unemployment, moreover, an April 1942 Gallup poll found 54 percent of the national sample in favor of terminating the CCC. One month later, the House refused Roosevelt's request for nearly $50 million for the bureau's annual budget. After the House Appropriations Committee voted, 15 to 12, against funding in June, Michigan's Albert Engel, a persistent CCC foe, led a floor fight that resulted in a 158 to 152 decision to terminate the agency. Although the Senate initially deadlocked on the issue, conferees convinced it to agree to the defunding as of 1 July 1942.[11]

The Byrd committee's ongoing inquiries into government spending resulted in a November 1942 report that called for an end to draft deferments for federal employees, and for the dismissal of one-third of Washington's nonmilitary personnel. The panel cited a subordinate who characterized his supervisors as draft-dodgers who appeared "to do nothing but harass and needle the businessmen with . . . demands, suits, and everlasting forms of the most complicated order." Following the 1942 elections, Republicans gained nine seats in the Senate and forty-four in the House. Shortly thereafter, the 77th Congress completed its work by phasing out the WPA, a symbol of New Deal welfare statism and planning expertise whose projects often interfered with predominant agricultural pay scales in the rural South and West.[12]

As World War II raged, the growing power of domestic federal bureaucracy and rule by political intellectuals and social guardians loomed as major concerns for anti-New Dealers at home. Such opposition was validated by journalists who explained how standing among the government elite was measured by personal authority and the ability to use circumlocution to deflect criticism. Regulatory agencies had replaced the term, "order" with "directive," noted one Washington insider in 1943. The broad discretionary powers of government officials elicited response from mainstream groups such as the American Federation of Labor, but also from populists like William Lemke and North Dakota senator William Langer. Mocking bureaucrats who "hamper, harass, and hamstring with red tape," Lemke condemned administrative "bluff, bluster, blunder, and deception." Langer told union postal employees that most of the 750,000 men of draft age who held "swivel chair" positions and "cinch jobs" in Washington were products of "rather wealthy parentage and of families of rather great influence." Seeking the next Republican nomination for president, Ohio governor John W. Bricker complained that federal officials and government administrators were accountable to neither Congress nor the people.[13]

As the new House met in January 1943, Michigan's Roy O. Woodruff declared that Republican electoral gains showed that voters supported Congress "as their special instrument of control over their government." The representatives would "put an end to the defiance by bureaucrats of the expressed will and obvious intentions of the legislative body," he vowed. Fellow Michiganite Clare Hoffman used the election to celebrate the "clear-cut mandate to get rid of the bureaucrats, the crackpots, the Communists, and the New Dealers" who sought to remake America. After Senate Democrats Harry Byrd and Millard Tydings denounced agency transfers of funds without congressional approval, the House unanimously endorsed a prohibition on "hedge-hopping," a practice by which federal employees skirted budgetary restrictions by moving to other agencies. In March, both houses reversed a presidential order limiting after-tax salaries to $25,000, a reflection of the belief that Roosevelt officials were using the military emergency to engage in class warfare and antibusiness social experimentation.[14]

Two months after the confrontation with Roosevelt, a new Byrd committee report condemned overstaffing, inflated payrolls, and unwarranted promotions among the federal government's remaining three million civilian employees. Shortly thereafter, the president was forced to sign an urgent deficiency bill that included a ban on executive use of war emergency funds for projects for which Congress had refused to appropriate money. The Byrd committee took particular exception to the National Youth Administration, accusing it of duplication, extravagance, and ineffective results, and warning that the self-perpetuating agency threatened to instill bureaucratic control of education. In July, Congress terminated the controversial NYA, another vestige of the welfare state social planning and the ascendancy of policy intellectuals.[15]

Critics of New Deal experiment also questioned the activities of the Office of War Information (OWI). Established by Roosevelt in 1942 to coordinate wartime propaganda, the OWI used overseas radio, leaflets, magazines, and films to identify the U.S. cause with democratic goals. Yet the agency of 4,500 employees also contained a Domestic Branch to bolster morale at home. When OWI came up for House funding in June 1943, opponents jumped at the chance to question the high-minded reformism of government servants. The bureau was "attempting to propagandize the people of America in almost every walk of life," complained Republican Charles W. Vursell. "It is the best example of bureaucracy running rampant." Pointing to OWI Director Elmer Davis's former support of the Socialist Party, the Illinois representative accused the agency of "trying to influence the entire people of the United States on philosophies of government that have no connection with the propagandizing of or dissemination of war news."[16]

"America needs no [Joseph] Goebbels sitting in Washington to tell the American press what to publish," declared Alabama's Joe Starnes. Noting that the OWI insulted taxpayers by suggesting that they did not not know why they were fighting the war, Starnes called domestic propaganda "a stench to the nostrils of a democratic people." New Hampshire Republican Styles Bridges scored "the growing collection of misfits, political hirelings, and radical journalists" assembled in the OWI, which he compared to the propaganda machines of dictatorships. The agency was like "the cuttlefish which drowns itself in its own ink," he proclaimed. Pointing to OWI portrayals of Roosevelt as a benevolent opponent of toryism, congressional critics attacked the agency for New Deal and partisan propaganda. On June 18th, the House approved a Starnes amendment to cut off funds for the Domestic Branch by a vote of 156 to 80, and then abolished the unit by a vote of 218 to 114. Although members ultimately reversed the rash action, they slashed the bureau's budget by nearly two-thirds, stopped it from printing literature at home, and consigned it to a coordinating role between other agencies and the media.[17]

Despite the fact that the OWI survived until 1945, it faced constant threats from House and Senate critics suspicious of communications experts and New Deal reformers. Such animosity surfaced in a report of the House Civil Service Committee in 1943. Because college training was overemphasized as a qualification for government employment, asserted the committee, an excess of inexperienced youngsters dominated Washington personnel offices and agencies like the Office of Price Administration (OPA). Yet many college professors, economists, and young lawyers lacked the experience and tact required for public service. The report asserted that older, experienced participants in private industry often were rejected by federal employers, causing a bottleneck in recruitment. It also charged that subordinates of favored administrators were awarded dubious salary increases. The committee cited the case of a part-time clerk in a five-and-ten cent store who graduated from college, began work at an annual $1,320 as a junior classification analyst with the OPA, and quickly won promotion to the rank of associate personnel officer at $3,200 a year.[18]

***

Widespread dissatisfaction with the OPA contributed to public sanction of congressional monitoring of executive departments and agencies, a proposition endorsed by 72 percent of a Gallup poll in late 1943. Earlier in the year, Virginia representative Howard Smith won the support of the influential Edward Cox and House Republican Minority Leader Joseph W. Martin, Jr. by introducing a resolution to create an oversight committee to determine if administrative bureaus were adhering to congressional intent and observing due process. Smith's motion to create a "Select Committee to Investigate Acts of Executive Agencies Beyond the Scope of Their Authority" received a 294 to 50 endorsement by House colleagues and resulted in the seating of the persistent Virginian as panel chair. Significantly, no Republican voted against the Smith proposal, while 95 percent of southern Democrats and a majority of Democrats outside the South rallied to its support.[19]

Smith argued that the inquiry would give the House "an opportunity to take action on the things about which members have been complaining for months, but about which they have done nothing." He was interested particularly in objections by ordinary citizens and businesspeople to arbitrary agency actions, rules, procedures, regulations, orders, or directives. Smith suggested that the panel could ask bureaucrats "to point to the law by which they acted. If they can't point to the authority at law, we are going to ask them, 'well, where the hell then did you get the authority?'" When the bureaus knew that there was a committee "ready to look over their doings," he insisted, "they'll be more considerate of Congress, the law, and the intention of Congress."[20]

The Virginian's rage at the OPA stemmed from the agency's restrictions on price increases in southern cotton and land rentals. Yet hostility to the bureau's intrusive restrictions reached far into the producer culture of wartime America. Created by executive order months before Pearl Harbor, the OPA received its statutory powers from the Emergency Price Control Act, passed in January 1942 after six months of congressional deliberation. Under the law's provisions, the agency enacted retail price limits on nonfarm goods and instituted ten major consumer rationing programs to contain potential increases in living costs. Following passage of the Emergency Anti-Inflation Act later in the year, Roosevelt extended the freeze to most farm commodities, although he was forced to accommodate a resistant Senate by promising to forbid future wage and salary increases. By 1943, the powerful price-fixing commission had thirty thousand paid employees.[21]

OPA's problems were intensified by its first director, the controversial Leon Henderson. Born to a turn-of-the-century middle-class family in New Jersey, Henderson received his only academic degree as an undergraduate at Swarthmore College. Despite modest credentials, he taught at the Wharton School of Business and the Carnegie Institute before becoming the Director of Consumer Credit Research at the Russell Sage Foundation, one of the key sources of innovative business thinking in the 1920s. Henderson joined the New Deal as an adviser on consumer affairs to the National Recovery Administration's Hugh Johnson and later became the director of the agency's Research and Planning Division. His OPA appointment followed service as the executive secretary of Roosevelt's Temporary National Economic Committee, as a member of the Securities and Exchange Commission, and as economic adviser to Secretary of Commerce Harry Hopkins.[22]

Known as a brilliant and self-confident theoretician, Henderson had contempt for people of less intelligence, a category in which he placed the entire Congress. Like the Roosevelt brains trusters, he believed that politics should never interfere with disinterested public administration. Henderson was influenced by Columbia economist John Maurice Clark, who had advised him on planning matters at the NRA. Economists were "substantially unanimous" that price controls were necessary "in a defense emergency of the present magnitude," Clark informed Henderson in an August 1941 memo. Business leaders should not be the judges of price-fixing according to their own views, insisted Clark. Adhering to such advice, Henderson told Congress that the OPA needed to penalize "the chiseler" who raised prices. Running the OPA on nonpartisan lines, he encouraged no input from Congress on regional appointments and disregarded complaints from trade groups and individual producers as the products of self-interest.[23]

Seeking to protect consumer purchasing power, Henderson placed economists, not business leaders, at the forefront of price-fixing. He quietly abandoned the World War I model by which prices were structured to produce normal returns to high-cost producers. Instead, the OPA relied on commodity subsidies, a procedure which lowered consumer prices but reduced industry-wide profits. Selective price control was also the preferred method of Princeton economist John Kenneth Galbraith, who began his public career as the head of the Price Division of the Price Stabilization Program and later became OPA's chief operating officer. Galbraith believed that price control was necessary when supplies were limited because producer bottlenecks threatened inflation. Assembling a professional staff recruited from the major universities and New Deal agencies, the young economist devised OPA regulations to discourage consumer spending on durables normally produced by defense contractors.[24]

***

By the end of 1942, Henderson claimed that OPA's price-fixing economists had spared the federal government nearly $26 billion and consumers almost

$6 billion. Such savings had garnered the consummate New Dealer a positive public image, indicated by a 54 percent favorable rating in a mid-year Gallup poll. Yet the cerebral Henderson faced bitter denunciation from elected politicians such as Martin Dies, Jr., Robert A. Taft, and William Lemke, who condemned him as a technocrat and a stubborn theorist hostile to the interests of small producers and independent business enterprisers. The OPA, declared Lemke, was an "un-American child" of "an official clique in Washington" that thought more of "foreign institutions than our own." A short, muscular, cigar-smoking man whose clothes were baggy and rumpled, the tough, cocky, and impatient Henderson refused to compromise. "He never seemed to learn," noted one Washington journalist, that "a few good friends are worth more than a dozen good arguments."[25]

Henderson resigned as OPA director following Republican gains in the 1942 congressional elections. Yet the agency's political problems continued. The next April, administrators responded to a cost-of-living increase by freezing prices, wages, and salaries. Already disadvantaged by gas rationing, fuel restrictions, production limitations, and increased labor and supply costs, retailers and producers responded angrily. The president of the National Association of Retail Grocers told the House Committee on Small Business that his constituents were "not willing to submit to rules and regulations just to satisfy the whims and whams of some dreamer who uses the war effort as an excuse to change our economic system." OPA's "far-fetched rulings" had created "an American gestapo" of "power-drunk theorists," charged Representative Robert L. F. Sikes of Florida. When the OPA also subsidized consumer purchases of farm goods by selling agricultural commodities to distributors at less than cost, farm groups protested that officials were maintaining retail food prices at Depression levels in a program that Congress had never authorized.[26]

OPA critics concentrated their fire on the nonbusiness backgrounds of price administrators. In June 1943, Illinois Republican Everett McKinley Dirksen introduced amendments to reduce OPA funding by more than 20 percent and to prohibit payments of salaries to pricing officials who lacked at least five years business experience in the industries they regulated. Although fellow Illinois Republican Charles Vursell supported continued appropriations for the OPA, Vursell summarized the tenor of business hostility to New Deal political intellectuals. The administration needed to be cleared of "the theorists, crackpots, left wingers, college professors, and a thousand or more of its incompetent, inexperienced dreamers and planners," he stated, "who are attempting to control billions of dollars in business, most of whom have never had any business experience in the matters of which they set up as dictators." Vursell ridiculed the fact that price executives controlling nonferrous metals, iron and steel, industrial materials, paper products, and chemicals and drugs all were college professors. OPA needed men with practical common sense and proven business ability, he insisted.[27]

Dirksen's ban on OPA officials without business experience extended to deputy administrators and division heads like former Reed College president

Dexter Keezer, University of Texas economics professor George Stocking, and Yale Law School professor Robert Sessions. Yet Congress was most interested in academic economist John Galbraith, the thirty-four-year-old Canadian who served as OPA's deputy price administrator; and Harvard economics professor Richard Gilbert, the former Department of Commerce consultant who was the chief adviser to the price administrator. Using the two Keynesians as symbols of executive-branch rule by the Ivy League, Dirksen convinced the House to support his amendment by a 189 to 144 vote. Both houses of Congress also approved the Illinois Republican's proposal to end OPA consumer subsidies, but when the administration tied such payments to continued price supports for farmers, legislators agreed to extend the experiment for another six months. Another bill to require Senate confirmation of officials making at least $4,500 a year was abandoned as Congress prepared for the summer recess.[28]

Congressional challenges to executive-branch expertise came to a head with release of the Smith committee's interim report on the OPA in November 1943. The document concluded that the beleaguered agency had assumed unauthorized powers to legislate by regulation and had misinterpreted statutory law to set up a nationwide system of judicial tribunals through which the agency judged the actions of citizens relative to its own regulations and orders. Smith's committee accused the OPA of imposing "drastic and unconstitutional penalties" outside due process. It criticized the tremendous powers of price administrators who set confusing rules and regulations to carry out the provisions of the legislation that had established the bureau. The Smith panel contended that OPA had created its own penal code by criminalizing violations of rationing orders. Yet the only way to test the validity of price regulations was to proceed through an Emergency Court of Appeals in Washington. OPA was guilty of "a well devised and planned scheme" to control the gains of American industry by freezing profits at the 1936 to 1939 level, it concluded.[29]

Focusing on the explosive relationship between congressional prerogatives and executive power, the Smith committee accused top OPA officials of "entertaining the opinion that Congress lacks understanding of the legislation it has enacted." By granting itself executive and judicial powers at once, claimed the report, the agency threatened to bring about a complete breakdown of the price control law. The document recommended that Congress rewrite anti-inflation legislation and suggested that the OPA simplify its three thousand orders and regulations, many of which were "illegal, absurd, useless, and conflicting." Smith proposed that a joint congressional commission on appropriations be established to oversee executive branch expenditures and that a standing committee of both houses monitor administrative bureaus exceeding their authority.[30]

***

Representative Smith's recommendations for permanent congressional monitoring of federal agencies never took the form he anticipated. Nevertheless, political intellectuals in the OPA and other bureaus came under intense wartime scrutiny over their ideological views and loyalties, particularly alleged ties to communist philosophies and associations. As early as 1940, Texas Democrat Martin Dies, Jr. had called Roosevelt's attention to the affiliation of "high-bracket" OPA officials with Communist organizations and to their alleged opposition to free enterprise. In a House address the following year, Dies questioned whether price control, a symbol of intrusion into the producer market by policy intellectuals and academic professionals, should be administered by "strangers to the American way" who held decidely communist views.[31]

OPA administrators were not alone in attracting congressional attention as potential subversives. Michigan Republican Fred Bradley made similar charges in reference to training programs for block discussion group captains administered by the beleaguered Office of Civilian Defense. OCD was emulating the cell structure of the Communist Party and using social scientists to disseminate internationalist propaganda for a "super world state," charged Bradley. Anxieties concerning the involvement of intellectuals in radical change and in the assault on democratic institutions were deeply rooted in American society. Minnesota Farmer-Labor senator Henrik Shipstead liked to complain about the "long-haired men and short-haired women," the self-styled "brainy people," who thought themselves superior to voters and who presumed to do their thinking for them. The question of intellectual condescension was addressed in 1939 by the Wisconsin American Legion, which condemned radical educators who "suffered to teach and preach that we are all wrong in our democratic ideals." By 1941, teacher loyalty oaths were mandatory in over half the nation.[32]

No other issue symbolized the questionable loyalty of political intellectuals and social guardians to democratic values than the subject of communism. Republican Hamilton Fish, Jr. had led a House investigation into Communist activities in 1930. Four years later, a special panel on un-American activities focused on the alleged subversion of both the U.S. Communist and Nazi movements. Suspicious about the potential threat of New Deal officials to constitutional principles, Democrat Martin Dies proposed to create a new House committee in 1937 to expose "un-American propaganda." A Texas attorney, rancher, and law school professor, Dies was the son of a self-described reformer and progressive who had served in Congress from 1909 to 1919 as a noninterventionist, antimilitarist, and immigration restrictionist. Elected to the same seat in 1931, the younger Dies continued to express the sentiments of the district's small farmers by denouncing industrial and financial oligarchies and defending economic individualism. Opposing Wall Street concentration but fearful of bureaucracy, Dies battled chain stores, called for higher income taxes on the rich, denounced high tariffs, and supported workplace reforms. The Texas Democrat defended the New Deal until 1937, when he concluded that the economic emergency had ended and that sit-down strikes by industrial workers involved coercive methods.[33]

As Dies began to denounce Roosevelt administration bureaucrats, he employed the republican language shared by many of his rural constituents. Through the creation of innumerable boards, bureaus, and commissions, he stated, arrogant officials had amassed the power to run the government along radical principles while the influence of Congress waned. The Texas representative described "an array of paid parasites, swooping down on the country like the locusts in the east, eating away all the vitality and creative energy of the people." Dies forged support from rural Democrats, patriotic groups such as the American Legion, and urban liberals concerned about domestic fascism, to engineer a favorable 181 to 41 vote in 1938 on his proposal to create a Special Committee on Un-American Activities, of which he soon was named chair.[34]

Beginning its work in August 1938, the Dies committee reported that Communist cadres had infiltrated the CIO, the WPA's theater and writers' projects, New York's Brooklyn College, the farmer-labor movement, and the American Civil Liberties Union (ACLU). The panel demonstrated a special interest in "fellow-travelers," usually middle-class intellectuals like professors, writers, clergy, and government officials who were not party members but adhered to the Communist political line and cooperated with various "front" groups. It contended that 563 federal employees were tied to the American League for Peace and Democracy, formerly the American League Against War and Fascism, an alleged Communist front. Officers of the league's Washington, D.C. chapter included the assistant administrator of the Rural Electrification Administration, an economist with the Central Statistical Board, and the chief of the Forest Service. Among chapter members were the head of the Forest Service's public lands section, the Assistant Secretary of the Interior, the administrator for the REA, and the director of the Woman's Bureau of the Department of Labor.[35]

The Special Committee's first report in 1939 dramatized the issues at stake by alleging that some Roosevelt planning experts, social service providers, and public administrators were members of a Communist movement hostile to American principles. Instead of adhering to the notion of democratic government as limited by a divinely inspired set of individualistic rights and protections, contended the panel, suspect members of the New Deal bureaucracy subscribed to the class hatred, materialism, collectivism, and mindless regimentation associated with Communist dictatorship. The Dies committee viewed such individuals as members of a global revolutionary apparatus who knowingly subordinated truth, respect for law, and morality to the needs of violent class struggle and party supremacy. Those who sincerely held unorthodox economic views, a subsequent report explained, were to be distinguished from disloyal people who consciously aligned with dangerous foreign-controlled agencies and forces.[36]

Insisting in October 1941 that influential members of the Roosevelt administration were tied to the Communist movement, Dies sent a list of 1,121 alleged federal government subversives to the Department of Justice, including the names of Treasury official Harry Dexter White and the State Department's Alger Hiss. One of Dies's favorite targets was former *New Republic* editor Malcolm Cowley, chief information analyst for the government's Office of Facts and Figures. Cowley had seventy-two connections to the Communist Party and its front goups, charged the committee chair in a House speech in January 1942, making him "one of the most ardent Communist intellectuals in this country." Speaking to frequent applause from colleagues over a year later, Dies recast the link between New Deal reform and subversion by describing "supermen or social planners" who sought to establish a totalitarian scheme of bureaucracy and instill government by administrative edict. A united front of Communists, "crackpots," Socialists, and diverse totalitarians, he added, were engaged in a conspiracy to smear his investigations.[37]

In February 1943, Dies recommended that public funds be withheld from agencies employing forty suspect officials, each of whom he named. Congress had the right to guarantee that taxpayer monies were not spent "to achieve some social idea of a crackpot," he declared. "The contempt which these bureaucrats have for the Congress which appropriates their salaries is unbounded," proclaimed Dies. Despite the force of the presentation, the House decided, 153 to 146, to keep the salary restrictions out of the Treasury appropriations bill. Yet four days later, members voted, 302 to 94, for Edward Cox's resolution to extend Dies's Special Committee on Un-American Activities for another two years. The House also agreed to pursue the panel's charges against the forty named employees by ordering the Committee on Appropriations to establish an investigatory panel of five members, to be chaired by North Carolina Democrat John H. Kerr. Meanwhile, Dies announced that the special committee would refer to Kerr's inquiry any names from the larger list of subversives still on federal pay.[38]

***

The Dies committee paid particular attention to suspect government officials with academic backgrounds. The case of Goodwin B. Watson, chief analyst of the Federal Communication Commission's Foreign Broadcast Intelligence Service, illustrated the chasm between political intellectuals and mainstream politicians. A Methodist minister, psychologist, and professor at Columbia University Teachers College, the intelligence analyst had been a sponsor for rallies of the American League for Peace and Democracy, served on the advisory board of the American Student Union, and belonged to the League of American Writers, all alleged Communist fronts. In 1933, Watson joined New America, a group that promised to promote scientific planning in the full utililzation of productive capacity. The organization's founding pamphlet acknowledged the need to eliminate private property and the profit system when they interfered with the success of a planned and socialized economy. It envisioned a program of propaganda to win over the masses and to prepare them to use "coercive restraint" for the conquest of economic power that would build the new society envisioned by intellectual radicals.[39]

In response to questions about his past beliefs, Watson protested that in 1933 he thought it possible to combine political democracy with economic justice, but that he ultimately resigned from New America because of its coercive approach to social reconstruction. Although intellectuals who flirted with subversive ideas had a right to their views, answered Dies, they had no intrinsic claim to federal jobs and were not appropriate choices for government service. Such a perspective was conveyed in the Texas Democrat's November 1941 complaint to FCC chair James Lawrence Fly. Speaking of "a new influx of Communists and fellow travelers" into official Washington, Dies described Watson as "a propagandist" for communism and the Soviet Union. He expressed concern that "one of such outspoken Communists views and sympathies" should have important decisions entrusted to him. Watson's frequent eulogies on the Soviet system, wrote Dies, had "been coupled with emphatic disparagement of the American way of life" and an extraordinary amount of activity on behalf of Communist fronts. The committee chair vowed to expose the "sinister influence" allowing hundreds of Communists and their allies to occupy important positions in Washington.[40]

The Special Committee on Un-American Activities also targeted William E. Dodd, Jr., the assistant news wire editor for the Foreign Broadcast Intelligence Service. After receiving a Ph.D. at the University of Berlin in 1935, Dodd had taught history at several prestigious institutions. Between 1937 and 1938, he worked for the American League for Peace and Democracy, been a featured speaker at a rally of American Friends of the Soviet Union, and attended a conference of the League of American Writers. Dodd had been the favored candidate of the Roosevelt administration and the CIO in the 1938 Democratic primary campaign against Howard Smith. In addition to targeting Dodd, the Dies committee questioned the political associations of Robert Morss Lovett, U.S. Secretary of the Virgin Islands. A former professor of English literature at the University of Chicago and Harvard, and president of the socialist League for Industrial Democracy for twenty years, Lovett had aided groups such as the All America Anti-Imperialist League, the National Federation for Constitutional Liberties, the American Youth Congress, and the League of American Writers, alleged Communist fronts that Special Committee panelist J. Parnell Thomas described as "screwball and nitwit" causes.[41]

Lovett insisted that the Communist Party was nothing more than a political movement seeking to change existing conditions through constitutional means. Such a characterization was rejected vehemently by congressional leaders. When the Kerr subcommittee issued a report on the Dies allegations in April 1943, it first addressed the issue of subversion, which it defined as activity derived "from conduct intentionally destructive of or inimical to the government of the United States—that which seeks to undermine its institutions, or to distort its functions, or to impede its projects, or to lessen its efforts, the ultimate end being to overturn it all." Subversion involved any attempt, no matter how subtle or indirect, to replace the government with one that was hostile to and incompatible with the presumed ideals of American democracy. Those who fostered or associated with organizations working for the overthrow of the constitutional system were not to be entrusted with official responsibility.[42]

Although the Kerr panel cleared thirty-seven government officials, it reported that Goodwin Watson had admitted associations with at least twelve groups that the attorney general designated as Communist fronts or at least questionable. It also cited articles by Watson that criticized the capitalistic system and advocated its overthrow. Arguing that the responsibilities of the domestic war effort should not be extended to those who might destroy the nation from within, the subcommittee concluded that the activities of Watson, Dodd, and Lovett made all three unfit to continue in government employment. In May 1943, the full House Appropriations Committee approved an amendment to a spending bill that prohibited payment of salaries to the three professors. After Kerr described the three as out of sympathy with American principles and philosophies, only sixty-two House members opposed the rider on the floor. Following initial resistance, the Senate agreed by a 48 to 42 vote to set a November deadline for presidential reappointment of the three officials subject to its own approval. Pressed for wartime appropriations, Roosevelt signed on to the virtual firing.[43]

As supporters of Watson, Dodd, and Lovett protested that the professors had been unduly punished for their political and economic views with the financial penalties of a bill of attainder, the Civil Service Commission issued instructions forbidding loyalty investigators to question job applicants about their governmental philosophy or their belief in capitalism. The order specifically prohibited inquiries regarding sympathy with the Loyalists in the Spanish Civil War, the Socialist Party, the National Lawyers Guild, and the ACLU. Publication of the directive brought cries of protest from Republican anticommunists such as Illinois representative Fred E. Busbey and Michigan House member Clare Hoffman. If the new instructions were allowed to stand, warned Busbey, the nation's Communists would rejoice. Hundreds of party members and fellow travelers never would be removed if investigators could not examine their loyalties, he declared. Hoffman threatened to ask Congress to withhold appropriations from federal agencies that failed to clear prospective employees of Communist associations.[44]

As the Roosevelt administration sought to protect agency officials from political witch hunts, Watson, Dodd, and Lovett filed suit in the U.S. Court of Appeals to test the constitutionality of the congressional salary ban. The attorney general already had ruled that Congress had disqualified the three professors from office without due process. Although the plaintiffs maintained that the Kerr committee had acted as prosecutor and judge, denied them counsel, disregarded rules of evidence, and not offered them the right to summon witnesses, the court did not rule on the constitutionality of the measure that terminated their employment. Instead, it resolved the bitter dispute between the three political intellectuals and

Congress by ordering the government to provide the former officials with back pay and to purge all remnants of the case from their employment records.[45]

***

Congressional attacks on government academics like Watson, Dodd, and Lovett indicated the profound suspicion with which the majority of federal legislators viewed the executive branch's appointed policymakers and planners. Going beyond mere anti-intellectualism, elected officeholders often perceived the New Deal political class as a rival power whose authority rested on arbitrary rule, antidemocratic tactics, and hostility to the spirit of small enterprise. Such attitudes were previewed in a tirade delivered in 1939 by Dies committee panelist Joe Starnes following the testimony of a Roosevelt official who had once belonged to the suspect American League Against War and Fascism. "They are liberal in the use of refined invective," Starnes complained of the cerebral New Dealers. "They are liberal in the use of other people's money. They are very liberal in taking care of themselves at the expense of somebody else."[46]

Although pragmatic administration figures like David Cushman Coyle distanced the Roosevelt presidency from social engineering efforts, representatives of small business and rural interests such as Starnes recoiled at the tendency of government policy intellectuals to place themselves at the center of schemes for national economic planning. For wartime critics like Indiana Democrat and newspaper columnist Samuel B. Pettengill, members of the Washington intelligentsia like Rexford Tugwell and Adolf Berle stood for collectivist concepts and practices perceived as contemptuous of ordinary Americans.[47] Between 1939 and 1943, however, the leading focus of such anxiety was the National Resources Planning Board (NRPB), the Roosevelt administration's most ambitious agency in the use of planning experts and technical specialists to forge national economic policy.

Formed out of the National Resources Committee in 1939 as part of the reorganization of the executive bureaucracy, the NRPB first advised the president on land-use, water issues, transportation policy, public works, and wartime defense outlays. In 1940, however, a report on the use of resources placed the board firmly within the camp of Keynesian economists who saw deficit spending as a means of raising aggregate demand. Later in the year, Roosevelt directed the agency to explore how postwar planning could contribute to full peacetime employment. In a series of studies published in 1942 and 1943, NRPB economists like Alvin H. Hansen and Mordecai Ezekiel devoted themselves to the consideration of countercyclical fiscal and monetary policies to stimulate consumer spending, production, and investment once the war ended.[48]

As Alan Brinkley has shown, the activities of the NRPB demonstrated how the New Deal planning ideal had shifted from corporate regulation and production restrictions to the use of social security, welfare, and public works spending as a means to increase and redistribute purchasing power in the capitalist economy.

For Keynesian theorists, consumption had replaced production as the driving force of the modern market. Seeking to use the government as an instrument of economic growth, NRPB planners designed a postwar order that relied on social insurance, entitlements, expanded health and education programs, and ambitious work projects. A 1943 report entitled "Wartime Planning for War and Post-War" recommended that the federal government spend nearly $7.7 billion on a coordinated system of public works. "We have got to provide through planning," it concluded, "the means for sustaining the American concept of living, for full employment, security, and the pursuit of happiness."[49]

Through federal deficit spending and taxation, government economists hoped to manage the market without limiting the entrepreneurial freedom of corporations. Yet planners realized that jobs programs would involve expenditures that taxpayers were reluctant to pay. The NRPB also acknowledged that federal subsidies could place government "in certain fields traditionally regarded as the preserve of private enterprise." Testifying before the Temporary National Economic Committee in 1939, Adolf Berle had observed that efforts to promote purchasing power might entail the nationalization of investment through government capital credit banks and eventual public ownership of productive plants. An NRPB study of 1943 suggested that social security funds might be invested in industrial firms, many of whose assets were owned by wartime defense agencies. Planners also recommended that Washington could sell or rent out manufacturing plants that converted to peacetime use and maintained minimal levels of output and employment. Grants for conversion would depend upon the production priorities and regional industrial focus of the government.[50]

Although the NRPB was committed to a healthy capitalist order and to sustaining the economy's wartime recovery, public sanction of cooperation between centralized planners and urban consumers threatened traditional producers, local economic interests, and their customary allies in Congress. As Theda Skocpol has suggested, the planning board's academic consultants and social work administrators had little experience in formulating social policy and had no solid base within the Roosevelt executive branch or the war mobilization effort. In addition, the NRPB had the difficult task of winning support for expanded employment and public assistance programs during the wartime boom.[51] Seeing the bureau as a policy tool of the Washington bureaucracy and as a means by which rival political intellectuals and academics sought to impose a collectivist agenda that ignored small business concerns, Congress acted to reign in the most ambitious planning component of the Roosevelt New Deal.

The campaign against the NRPB began late in 1939 when a House subcommittee stripped all of the board's funding, although the Senate soon restored a $700,000 planning budget. Seeking to avoid future squabbling, Roosevelt asked Congress to make the NRPB a permanent federal planning agency in February 1942. Once again, the House rebelled, with Mississippi Democrat William M. Whittington leading the debate that resulted in a 252 to 104 defeat of the proposal. By assuring that the NRPB would remain dependent on annual congressional appropriations, chortled Pennyslvania Democrat Charles I. Faddis, Congress had denied "freedom of the seas to any board . . . of visionary, impractical, stargazing planners to work any or all of their rattle-brained ideas" for the postwar era.[52]

Following the Byrd committee's attack on expanding public debt in February 1943, the House Appropriations Committee eliminated the NRPB's $1.4 million funding for the coming fiscal year. Byrd celebrated the move and demanded that Congress take the initiative in postwar policy. Did Americans want to continue New Deal economic policies, bureaucracy, and centralized control, he asked? Legislators also rebuked the executive branch by cutting out programs they had not approved, including $3 million for state-administered childcare for employed mothers and $1.2 million for emergency grants for maternity and infant care for the families of military personnel. When Roosevelt sent two NRPB reports on postwar planning to Capitol Hill in March and April, a predictable furor ensued. "This is the most fantastic conglomeration of bureaucratic stupidity ever sent to Congress," declared Mississippi Democrat John Rankin, a bitter white supremacist, anti-Semite, and arch-conservative. Less ideological members nevertheless complained of the plan's projected $50 billion-plus price tag. A *Newsweek* columnist summarized congressional skepticism by dismissing the package as a blueprint for a postwar bureaucratic utopia reminiscent of economic fascism.[53]

Ohio senator Robert Taft, elected as an anti–New Dealer in 1938, emerged as the leading critic of the NRPB. If social welfare programs did not depend on prohibitive taxation, argued Taft, they would require deficit spending and unlimited public debt, leading to inflation and diminished private savings and investment. Singling out Harvard academics Alvin Hansen and Seymour E. Harris, the Ohio Republican condemned the NRPB as a propaganda agency for Keynesian economists. "I cannot understand," he told the Senate in May 1943, "why a Congress which believes . . . in one philosophy of government . . . should provide hundreds of thousands of dollars promiscuously for the making of plans by an agency which believes in an entirely different philosophy, which appears to be partly socialistic and partly the product of a dangerous financial imagination."[54]

In a well-publicized address before the Sons of the American Revolution in 1943, Taft insisted that the NRPB was attempting to establish a planned economy through compulsory bureaucratic orders directing every step of individual life. He particularly condemned designs for government ownership of transportation and for the operation of electric utilities and resource-based industries by public corporations partly funded by the Treasury. The program "which the Brains Trusters think desirable," he predicted, would lead to control of industry by administrative boards. "The danger is that most government bureaucrats of today will seek every opportunity to continue their own powers and their own jobs," declared Taft. Refusing to provide the standard of living with godlike status, the senator warned of the threat of arbitrary government and the centralization of power in unaccountable agencies in Washington. He argued that federal housing and health programs would undermine work incentives and erode traditional values of religious faith, morality, justice, and unselfishness.[55]

Following Taft's attack, the Senate defeated a reduced $534,000 budget for the NRPB by 43 to 31. Although $200,000 of the amount was restored on a limited basis, the House insisted that the planning board be abolished in August 1943 and that its functions not be transferred to another agency. When Senate conferees agreed to this provision of the $26.6 billion appropriation for federal agencies, Roosevelt was in no position to threaten a veto and the NRPB prepared to cease operations. As both houses created committees to plan peacetime reconversion based on the removal of wartime economic controls and the reduction of federal taxes, more than three-fourths of a 1943 Gallup poll indicated opposition to the social welfare reforms advanced by the NRPB.[56]

***

As the wartime emergency came to a close, a rebellious Congress took every opportunity to purge the federal agencies of professional reformers, policy intellectuals, and social guardians, a political class whose ideology and aspirations to power remained highly suspect. Animosity between elected officeholders and their rivals took on a particularly brutal form early in 1945 when the White House nominated Aubrey W. Williams to be the new head of the Rural Electrification Administration. With the support of key legislators like Texas representative Sam Rayburn, Roosevelt had created the REA by executive order in 1935 to finance electric power projects and economic development in remote areas, particularly in the Southwest and West. With domestic spending as a sensitive issue during wartime, however, even New Deal allies wondered about REA requests that would have doubled the agency's $500 million annual budget for postwar infrastructure. Spending critics in Congress also were alarmed at the administration's attempt to name Vice President and deficit budget advocate Henry A. Wallace as Secretary of Commerce.[57]

Concerns over the REA were compounded by the politically contentious track record of Aubrey Williams. An Alabama native who completed a social work degree at the University of Cincinnati, Williams worked with the Young Men's Christian Association and served as an Army artillery officer during World War I. The executive director of the Wisconsin Conference of Social Work in the 1920s, he went on to organize relief programs in Texas and Mississippi for the Reconstruction Finance Corporation in 1932. Joining the Roosevelt team, Williams became a regional field representative for the Federal Employment Relief Administration and deputy administrator for the WPA before assuming the directorship of the National Youth Administration in 1939.[58]

Williams's social work background raised the suspicion of rural producer groups such as the American Farm Bureau Federation, the National Grange, and the National Cooperative Milk Producers Federation, who jointly protested to the Senate Committee on Agriculture that the nominee was not qualified for the REA post by experience or training. The Grange also objected to Williams's work as organizing director of the National Farmers Union, a CIO ally that recruited agricultural workers. Yet it was the New Dealer's ideology that most disturbed opponents. Williams was one of the most radical men in the country, proclaimed Roosevelt adversary Hamilton Fish, Jr. Critics pointed to a speech before a 1938 conference of southern social workers in which the nominee had stated that some class warfare was necessary to achieve human dignity. The administration official also admitted that he once told a meeting of the socialist Workers Alliance to "stick together" and "keep our friends in power."[59]

Pressed on his views before the Senate Agriculture Committee, Williams denied that he favored forced distribution of wealth and insisted on his support for equal opportunity and democratic procedure. The nominee complained about the use of speech excerpts from a period in which the nation had experienced the shock of unemployment and depression. "It is pre-eminently unfair to argue that my contacts with suffering people at that time have permanently affected my mental status," Williams told the panel. Calling for a society predicated on Keynesian abundance, he argued that a large segment of people had been excluded from a just share in national wealth. Yet Williams's association with class-defined interests allowed critics to associate him with the communist cause. Appearing as an adverse witness, Tennessee senator Kenneth D. McKellar asserted that the nominee had consorted with, given assistance to, and praised the leadership of organizations pronounced subversive by the attorney general. Williams had wasted enough government money at the WPA and NYA, charged McKellar, and knew nothing about rural matters or electricity.[60]

The Senate agriculture panel also received a telegram from the former pastor of a Birmingham Presbyterian church alleging that Williams had denied the divinity of Jesus Christ after receiving a $700 college scholarship to study for the ministry. The nominee insisted that his failure to seek ordination was of no concern to the Senate and that the church had never requested repayment of the gift. Despite Williams's strong defense of his actions on this and other matters, the committee rejected his REA apppointment by a 12 to 8 vote in early March. The ensuing debate on the Senate floor further dramatized the issues at stake in Washington's war over the involvement of political intellectuals in government. Indiana Republican and former newspaper publisher Raymond E. Willis led the charge by describing the nominee as a member of a class-conscious group that sought to exploit economic resentment. The REA was "not an agency to be handed over to any Johnny-Come-Lately who has no qualifications other than the ability to speak beautiful words," snapped Willis.[61]

Questioning Williams's character, and implicitly attacking the secularism of the intellectual elite, the Indiana senator treated the church scholarship incident as a shabby chapter in the life of someone who did not recognize the sanctity of moral obligations. Willis dismissed the nominee's ten-year social work career in

Wisconsin as that of "a professional do-gooder" supported by state taxpayers. Williams had demonstrated incompetence and extravagance in government service, he complained. Farmers saw the REA as a servant instead of a master, declared the senator, and were "not hat-in-hand relief clients of the type for whom Mr. Williams is wont to shed his crocodile tears of professional sympathy." Willis blasted the New Deal official as "one of those social-minded star gazers" who were part of an entrenched group in government who believed that the free enterprise system had failed.[62]

Willis insisted that Williams was entitled to his own political philosophy as a private citizen. But he argued that anyone who did not believe in American democracy and the free market system should be disqualified for public office. The New Dealer's membership in the Communist Party was irrelevant, suggested the Indiana Republican. The key issue remained the political, economic, and social ideologies dominating his thought. Williams was threatening because his "social-worker solution" promised to make each citizen "a faceless unit in a static, anthill society." Under such policies, the federal government would become an enormous WPA whose clients would be guided, controlled, and dictated by "a self-perpetuating . . . elite corps of super social workers designed after the pattern of Aubrey Williams." The nominee's difference from the Communist utopia was merely one of degree, concluded Willis.[63]

In its first denial of an important federal post nomination in six years, the Senate voted, 56 to 36, against confirming Williams. The defeated candidate attributed the debacle to his open espousal of "the idea of getting power into the hands of the common people." His frank support of civil rights for African Americans in the South may have been more hurtful. Southern Democrats equated racial equality with radical socialism, collectivist social experiment, and coercive interference from reformers and planners who originated outside the region. It was easy to see Williams as the vanguard of a new political movement of blacks, industrial union organizers, and northern liberals and social democrats who hoped to revolutionize American life through an intrusive government bureaucracy. Not suprisingly, conservative Democrats such as Harry Byrd, Pat McCarran, Kenneth McKellar, and Millard F. Tydings joined Republican stalwarts like Raymond Willis and Robert Taft in opposing the Williams nomination. Self-styled populists such as Texas Democrat W. Lee O'Daniel and Republicans Arthur Capper, Hiram W. Johnson, Henrik Shipstead, and Kenneth S. Wherry also cast votes against the hapless New Dealer. Only when Congress provided the REA with independence from the suspect Department of Agriculture in May 1945, did the Senate feel free to approve the selection of a new director.[64]

***

As congressional attacks on Roosevelt planners intensified, Keynesian economists retreated to the Bureau of the Budget, where Alvin Hansen helped to advance a proposal for a national investment board with broad power to set taxing and spending policies. Produced in August 1944 with the title, "Postwar Employment Program," the study incorporated the reformist notions of the NRPB by linking the expansion of private sector job opportunities to a greater state role in the provision of social welfare protections. Yet Congress was unwilling to defer to the economists' desire to establish a universal safety net. Instead, it enacted the Servicemen's Readjustment Act (G.I. Bill) of 1944, which limited educational financial aid, low-interest loans, and additional unemployment and pension benefits to veterans perceived as an especially deserving class of citizens. When the administration introduced a full employment bill the following year, Robert Taft and critics in both parties protested that government job guarantees would raise labor costs and that executive-branch control of deficit spending would weaken congressional prerogatives.[65]

Opponents of the employment measure drew upon widespread anxiety over Washington officialdom. Anti-New Deal groups like the National Association of Manufacturers and the Committee for Constitutional Government contended that the proposal would allow bureaucrats to tell people where they could work and consumers what they could buy. Testifying before the House Committee on Expenditures in the Executive Department, George Terborgh, research director of the Machinery and Allied Products Institute and a former economist with the Federal Reserve Board, sounded the business community's alarm over the government's shadow elite. Economic analysis and policymaking in legislation, said Terborgh, "may be prepared and promoted by men unknown to the public, whose appointment has not been confirmed by Congress, and who have no formal public responsibility." Restating the argument against the Roosevelt brains trust, Terborgh warned of "behind-the-scenes manipulation by presidential advisers of the moment, possessed, it may be, both by a passion for anonymity and a passion for controlling economic policy."[66]

Concurring with such arguments, the House replaced the bill's references to government guarantees of full employment with language encouraging "maximum" job opportunities. Although the amended legislation required a White House Council of Economic Advisers to submit reports to a joint committee of Congress, the board was not to have the operational powers envisioned by Alvin Hansen and the Keynesians. Having met the objections of critics, the House passed the Employment Act by an overwhelming 320 to 84 in February 1946. Two days later, Taft and other former opponents permitted the watered-down measure to receive Senate approval without opposition and it soon was signed into law.[67]

Restrictions on the controversisal Office of Price Administration followed the vitiation of economic planning. After Howard Smith's Select Committee on Executive Agencies issued an interim report in August 1944, Smith introduced legislation to prevent government bureaus from taking punitive actions not specified in law. The powerful Virginian's gambit produced a commitment from the attorney general to reform the procedural rules of administrative bodies. Nevertheless, complaints continued to mount against arbitrary decisions by OPA officials. Only Congress stood between citizens "and a form of bureaucratic, dictated, coupon-rationed life which would combine the worst features of all known social systems," Nebraska Republican Kenneth Wherry told the Senate in June 1945. One of the most vocal critics of the OPA as an enemy of ordinary producers and small business interests, Wherry sought in vain to adjust price controls to costs of production. As rural resentment of the agency escalated, press reports described widespread violation of price regulations among farmers who saw Washington administrators as distant, alien, and antagonistic.[68]

Following the close of World War II, pressure for the unconditional surrender of the OPA intensified among producers fearing the permanent institutionalization of price control. Oklahoma Republican George B. Schwabe told the House that Americans suffered from "bureauitis." Ohio's Thomas A. Jenkins asserted that agency propaganda threatened to subject the nation to state socialism. Following an eight-hour anti-OPA filibuster in June 1946 by Texas Democrat W. Lee O'Daniel, the Senate voted, 47 to 23, for a compromise that prolonged limited price controls for a year. A decontrol board was to have the power to impose removal of price ceilings by calculating the relevance of production costs. When Chester Bowles, the director of the government's Economic Stabilization Board, resigned in protest, President Harry Truman vetoed the package and was sustained by the House in a 173 to 142 vote, since public opinion continued to support temporary controls during the postwar transition period. In July 1946, both houses approved a second compromise that continued some price and rent restrictions but allowed many producers to absorb production costs. The legislation also abolished ceilings on a variety of farm goods as well as on tobacco and petroleum products.[69]

Although widespread concern about consumer prices generated qualified support for the OPA, anti-New Deal members of Congress continued to use populist rhetoric to tie the agency to elite social and economic planners. Despite the relative popularity of price controls among working people, Washington's critics argued that when the values and interests of rural producers and independent enterprisers were attacked through the experimental schemes of academic professionals and intellectual policymakers, the basic freedoms and rights of all Americans were compromised. They insisted that Congress could begin the restoration of executive branch accountability and democratic procedure only by purging the government of the theoretical planners and radical ideologues whose allegiance to class warfare and consumer priorities endangered the spirit of enterprise and individual initiative that defined American life.

Criticism of intellectual policymakers in government had particular resonance during a war against totalitarian foes that underscored the potential relationship between concentrated state authority and human evil.[70] Significantly, the cold peace following World War II produced an international climate in which threats to the American Way of Life appeared as dangerous as they had during the fighting. As new anxieties over subversion and the dilution of core values overtook the nation after 1945, well-placed policy intellectuals and administrators came under renewed suspicion. Rather than focusing on allegations that shadowy elites endangered democracy through support of the social welfare state, the Cold War and global crusade against communism dramatized widespread insecurity concerning the intelligentsia's ideological loyalties and its covert methods of influence. The resulting confrontation nearly destroyed the fabric of national government and the cohesion of American society.

Pledging Allegiance: The Political Class and Cold War Loyalty, 1946–1952

Preparing to lead his party to triumph in the congressional elections of 1946, Republican House Leader Joseph W. Martin listed undue secrecy, arrogance, waste, and "crushing bureaucracy" as the leading sins of the reigning administration in Washington. Under Democratic presidents, asserted Martin, an unaccountable political establishment had perfected the use of deceit and trick phrases and resorted to "distortion and weird construction of law" to impose a collectivist agenda on the American people.[1]

Republican politicians and other critics of government centralization emerged from World War II with a renewed desire to portray New Deal administrators, regulators, and planners as illegitimate usurpers of democratic traditions. The Cold War against Soviet Communism offered an appropriate pretext for such efforts. Chapter 5 examines how allegations about the loyalty and judgment of federal bureaucrats reinforced suspicions concerning the moral and political accountability of policy consultants, communications specialists, and knowledge professionals inside and out government. By exploring the confirmation fight of Atomic Energy Commission head David E. Lilienthal, the controversy over the Hollywood Ten, the widely publicized Alger Hiss case, and attacks on State Department personnel by Joseph R. McCarthy and others, this chapter outlines how anticommunists sought to marginalize postwar members of the guardian class as a remote and untrustworthy elite.

***

Ohio Republican John W. Bricker based his 1946 race for the U.S. Senate on the notion that four years of wartime regulations and controls had left Americans fed up with "power-seeking, office-grabbing bureaucratic experimenters." Born on a small farm near Columbus, the lifetime Republican practiced law in the 1920s before serving as a consumer advocate on the Ohio Public Utilities Commission, as state attorney general, and as governor. Two years after winning the 1944 Republican nomination for vice-president, Bricker sought to go to Washington by advancing an anti–New Deal platform. Pointing to his longstanding support of workers' compensation, minimum wage laws, and state unemployment insurance, the former governor charged the Democrats with subservience to powerful and subversive union leaders allegedly leading the country toward collectivism and regimentation. Bricker insisted that high taxes, burdensome public debt, and increasing inflation victimized those whom the New Deal had "forgotten": those middle-class Americans whose ranks included white-collar clerks, bookkeepers, school teachers, stenographers, and pensioners on fixed incomes.[2]

American voters embraced Republican arguments in 1946 by ending fourteen consecutive years of Democratic dominance in the Senate and sixteen in the House. Republican leader Martin promised that the new Congress would ferret out all those who sought to destroy the American way of life. Although postwar inflation, widespread labor strikes, and delayed military demobilization contributed to the Republican victory, the election appeared to validate the party's repeated attacks on government economists, reform lawyers, and officials. Yet anti–New Dealers like Nebraska senator Hugh Butler liked to point out how the shift of congressional power had not affected the permanent breed of Washington insiders empowered by the Roosevelt and Truman administrations. Butler noted how former government attorneys were able to "feather their nests" by turning expertise in the regulatory process and access to powerful bureau chiefs to the advantage of lucrative postwar law practices, corporate lobbies, and influential consulting firms. The Plains Republican charged that the influence of erstwhile government servants like Thomas Corcoran outlasted their periods of public service when members of the political class guided clients through the very statutes and bureaucratic guidelines they had helped to draft, administer, and interpret.[3]

Simmering resentment toward the role of political intellectuals in the Washington establishment exploded in 1946 when President Harry S. Truman nominated David E. Lilienthal as the first chair of the Atomic Energy Commisison (AEC). Trained by Harvard's Felix Frankfurter, Lilienthal practiced utilities and labor law in the early 1920s with future New Dealer Donald Richberg. Establishing his own firm in 1926, the young attorney taught public utilities litigation at Northwestern University, represented the city of Chicago in a successful action to lower consumer telephone rates, and played a key role on Wisconsin's Public Service Commission. Barely thirty-three years old, Lilienthal received President Roosevelt's appointment as a director of the government-operated Tennessee Valley Authority (TVA) in 1933. An advocate of expanded electric power capacity and lower energy costs, he won promotion to the chairmanship of the TVA board in 1941. Five years later, Lilienthal worked with Undersecretary of State Dean Acheson and World War I industrial mobilization czar Bernard Baruch on plans for the international control of nuclear weapons.[4]

As senators on the newly created Joint Committee on Atomic Energy began hearings on the nomination in February 1947, Lilienthal won public support from corporate leaders at General Electric and some utilities, prominent university presidents, the Secretary of War, Dean Acheson, and Bernard Baruch.

Yet the appointment attracted resistance from utility and oil interests opposed
to publicly owned atomic energy, from congressional nationalists concerned
about internationalization of nuclear secrets, and from anti-New Dealers seeking to undermine the Roosevelt legacy and hamper President Truman's freedom
of action. Joining the hearings, Tennessee Democrat Kenneth McKellar grilled
the nominee on Communist activity in the TVA, his past political affiliations
and public power philosophy, and even his (Jewish) ancestry. When McKellar
pleaded that a single Senate vote should be enough to reject anyone for so important a post as AEC chair, the *New York Times* reported that the Lilienthal fight
might signal "all-out partisan warfare" between Republicans and Democrats.[5]

***

Seeking to demonstrate that the cerebral nominee did not understand that
democracy meant government by the people, McKellar convinced the Senate
committee to subpoena Arthur E. Morgan, Lilienthal's predecessor as TVA administrator. A conservation-minded water resources engineer and former president of Ohio's Antioch College, Morgan wanted TVA to revive small business
and handicrafts through cooperatives and other community ventures. Envi-
sioning a Jeffersonian society along classical republican lines, he hoped to free
the Tennessee Valley from domination by large corporations and the federal
government. This meant cooperation with smaller utilities in power-pooling
arrangements instead of reliance on huge public hydroelectric projects and
dependence on Washington expertise. Morgan's notions conflicted with New
Deal priorities on the generation of cheap electric power to foster consumer
prosperity and to sustain regional economic development. When the TVA director failed to respond to a series of White House questions during administrative hearings in 1938, Roosevelt fired him and named Lilienthal to head the
agency.[6]

Morgan insisted that the president's action had been taken to cover up charges
of mismanagement against Lilienthal and his allies. The former administrator
accused his rival of ruling TVA by intrigue, politics, and misrepresentation, of
faking electric power reports, and of colluding with the aluminum monopoly.
His sharpest critique, however, focused on the question of character, a theme
frequently broached by those objecting to the influence and power of cosmopolitan intellectuals. Morgan told Ohio senator Robert A. Taft that Lilienthal was
substantially lacking in ethical principles, an actor who instantly could play any
part to perfection. He accused the TVA administrator of using covert methods and false propaganda to mislead the public. Lilienthal was not a liberal by
personal conviction, Morgan complained to his hometown newspaper, Ohio's
Yellow Springs News, but one who used liberalism to further personal ambition.[7]

Senate members of the Atomic Energy Committee voted, 8 to 1, to support the
Lilienthal nomination, with only John Bricker in opposition. Nevertheless, Republican leaders Kenneth S. Wherry and Robert Taft opposed the appointment

as it reached the Senate floor. Taft issued a statement that criticized Lilienthal for failing to exclude Communist employees from TVA's nuclear installations and for being too soft on issues related to subversion and the Soviet Union. The Ohio senator also expanded upon Morgan's charges of intellectual dishonesty. Lilienthal was temperamentally unfit to head an important agency in a democratic government, charged Taft. He was a man who did "not care what means he uses to reach the end which he thinks happens to be desirable."[8]

Taft's statement described Lilienthal as a power-hungry bureaucrat and a secretive operator who stretched executive power beyond the limits of existing law. Calling attention to the nominee's public power philosophy, the senator tied the TVA administrator to New Dealers who sought government sanction to destroy private enterprise. To further his point, Taft quoted Lilienthal's definition of modern management as "the process of defining with skill and sense, what is to be done, and with it the fixing of responsibility for results, with wide freedom for judgment in the managers as to how it may best be done." Like Arthur Morgan, Taft saw Lilienthal as a coarse instrumentalist who placed ends over means in pursuit of his own agenda. Opponents such as Senator McKellar saw such behavior as totalitarian. Arguing that the New Deal administrator's every inclination was communistic, the Tennessee Democrat portrayed a bureaucrat "so slick, so double-dealing, so double-appearing, . . . he might well be a member of that party."[9]

Although Senator Homer Ferguson, a Republican reform judge from Detroit, acknowledged that Lilienthal was no Communist, he grouped the New Deal manager with government planners and crusaders who were not scrupulous about their tactics. The nominee was a "social aristocrat," asserted the senator–socialistic because he believed in government ownership and control, aristocratic because of his conviction that experts should be the new governing class. Such men "believe that this is the day of the experts of special managerial class to whom the people must grant broad powers," complained Ferguson. "They imply . . . that they know best what is good for the people, and that the people are to do what they are told to do." Seeking more power, regulatory officials would set up additional government bodies until they had erected an authoritarian state in which the people would become wards of the managers.[10]

Ferguson's remarks illustrated the hostility many elected politicians felt toward the administrative state's emerging political class. Seeking to reopen a confirmation process that once appeared resolved, Senator Bricker moved to recommit the nomination to committee in April 1947. The resolution lost by a close 52 to 38 margin and Lilienthal was confirmed six days later by 50 to 31. Nevertheless, opponents of government management and expertise had drawn blood in the bitter debate. Critics of the Roosevelt-Truman legacy also had touched a sensitive note in accusing agency heads like Lilienthal of callousness toward the threat of subversion. The former TVA head was not a Communist or a fellow traveler, insisted Robert Taft, but merely a New Dealer who saw communism as a benign and unthreatening form of democracy.[11]

***

Controversies over the loyalty and social philosophy of federal administrators intensified congressional interest in security against Communist subversion at home. Such concerns had crystallized in 1945 when an accidental discovery led government agents to recover more than a thousand classified State Department and military documents from the offices of *Amerasia*, a bimonthly sympathetic to the Chinese Communists. One of the six people arrested in the case was John Stewart Service, a foreign service officer who had turned over his own China policy reports to the magazine's editor, a well-known supporter of Communist causes. Yet FBI violations of due process and intervention by former brains truster Thomas Corcoran led to the abandonment of charges against Service and three others, while the editor and a minor official struck plea bargains to avoid prison. Anxieties over internal security nevertheless intensified when a trial in Canada exposed a Communist espionage ring of government officials and scientists. In March 1947, President Truman announced the creation of a stringent federal employee loyalty program in the United States.[12]

Set within the context of the Soviet Union's recent role as wartime ally against fascism, the *Amerasia* affair and the Canadian spy case reinforced the plausibility of collusion between foreign Communists and government officials. By offering an ideology and theoretical system that appeared to explain the breakdown of capitalism, the Communist Party had dominated political activity at major colleges and universities in the 1930s. Popular among antibusiness intellectuals and aspiring professionals, notions of Marxist class struggle and racial equality pervaded the guilds and unions of screenwriters, teachers, journalists, and social workers. Once the Communists turned to Popular Front unity with liberal Democrats to fashion a broad coalition against fascism in 1935, they attracted support from a political class seeking to mobilize state resources in the interests of social justice and economic equity. Although radical writers like Malcolm Cowley noted that most of the working class demonstrated a lack of revolutionary fervor, communist visions of a progressive folk-culture appealed to New Dealers and industrial labor activists who sought to lead the proletariat's fight against economic privilege and the status quo.[13]

As a dynamic vehicle for societal change and anti-fascist mobilization in the Depression decade, communist political culture fostered a variety of theoretical ideas, organizations, and social causes that gave the movement intellectual appeal but aroused the ire of critics. When New York University refused to fire two Marxist professors, newspaper publisher William Randolph Hearst attacked the school as a center of treasonable activity. In Wisconsin, the legislature condemned the state's major university as a haven of communistic teaching. The University of California became the first higher learning facility to make membership in the Communist Party grounds for dismissal in 1940. Meanwhile, the New York State Legislature commissioned the Rapp-Courdert Commission to investigate subversive activities in public undergraduate facilities and precipitated a purge of Communist Party members at the City College of New York.[14]

Anticommunists justified the repression of intellectual freedoms by pointing to the need to respond to the Communist Party, which they portrayed as a tightly organized, secretive, disciplined, and doctrinaire political entity whose primary loyalty was to the Soviet Union. Distrust of American Communists as agents of Moscow heightened after the party replaced its broad antifascist orientation with support for Joseph Stalin's nonaggression pact with Nazi Germany between 1939 and 1941. The subservience of Communist sympathizers to Stalin's influence was illustrated for members of the Dies committee in 1940 when a former commander with the Abraham Lincoln Batallion in Spain told the panel that he was not aware of the existence of any dictatorship in the elected government of the Soviet Union. Suspicion of Communist influence intensified in 1944 when the party temporarily disbanded, reconstituted itself as the Communist Political Association, and joined the CIO in supporting Roosevelt's reelection.[15]

Led by the Dies committee, wartime anticommunists insisted that Stalin's agents dominated New Deal agencies and were tilting U.S. foreign policy toward Soviet interests. As peace ended the wartime alliance with Moscow, anticommunist ideologues like FBI Director J. Edgar Hoover sharpened their assessment of the subversive threat. Hoover went public late in 1945 to declare that an ever broadening front of alien radicals sought to transform the United States into a land of class struggle. Standing only for "the license of their own," Communists supposedly were corrupting society through covert propaganda and the tricks of the intellectual confidence man. As postwar public opinion hardened against statist controls, domestic labor unrest, and Soviet foreign policy, a coalition of political activists, government prosecutors, congressional staffers, and conservative clergy joined Dies and Hoover in depicting communism as a menace to U.S. security, democratic freedoms, individual privacy, and religious values.[16]

Hoover often called attention to the alleged duplicity of Communist operatives. Appearing before a congressional committee in 1947, the FBI director pointed to the fact that the Young Communist League, a fixture on many college campuses, had changed its name to the innocuously sounding American Youth for Democracy. In "How You Can Fight Communism," an article written in 1948 for the *American Legion Magazine*, National Commander James F. O'Neill warned veterans that Cold War political and psychological campaigns had taken the place of military confrontations. Noting that party members disguised their agenda by posing as liberals, peace activists, trade unionists, and civil libertarians, O'Neill asked readers to beware of propaganda that was craftily conceived and carried out with "diabolic cunning and guile."[17]

Hoover depicted communism as intellectual secularism on the march, a materialistic religion that inflamed its adherents with destructive fanaticism. Former party member Elizabeth Bentley agreed that in its insistence on blind obedience, the movement was almost a religion. The cerebral attractions of communism were acknowledged in *My Son John* (1952), one of the few profitable anti-Communist films of the Cold War Era, which portrayed an intellectual protagonist seduced into the party by superior minds and daring thoughts. Yet anticommunist journalists like Eugene Lyons derided the intellectual and moral 'red terror' that spread through 1930s New York, Hollywood, and Washington, as well as many college campuses and the "more infected social sectors" of large cities. Describing Communist-leaning professors, scientists, entertainers, and diplomats as a new privileged class, Lyons warned that ideological swindlers and confidence men threatened American values with "Stalinoid" manipulations. Conservative radio commentator Paul Harvey charged that "two-faced" subversives relied on "sly innuendo, casual disrespect, printed mud, and verbal garbage."[18]

The association of Communist subversion with the hidden interests of untrustworthy political and intellectual elites was brilliantly portrayed in *Is This Tomorrow: America Under Communism,* a comic book published in 1947 by the Catechetical Guild of St. Paul, Minnesota. This clever piece of propaganda defined communism as an idea of government that planned to rule the world. The story line detailed the seizure of national power by a small Communist clique against the will of the American people. Significantly, the first step in the process involved the use of trained writers and educators to control the media and foment religious and class hatred. "Class conflict and the breakdown of bourgeois morals have been handled very well by our people in Hollywood," proclaimed one fictional activist. "People are giving up their silly ideas about the 'sacredness' of life." Once prominent politicians, popular front groups, and labor leaders were lined up, Communist organizers used the pretext of a drought to coordinate a series of national strikes, leading to the lynching of capitalists, race war in the cities, and a conspiracy to assassinate the president and vice president.[19]

With the nation's two leaders out of the way, the Communist Party used its prime agent of influence, the Speaker of the House, to declare a state of emergency. The fictional government immediately took over food distribution, burned produce storage facilities to further the crisis, and blamed anticommunists, who then were arrested. Real power rested with the party's top functionary, a goateed character who assumed the role of "Chief Advisor," received emergency authority, and created a one-party state. Officials now confined the issuance of food rationing cards to politically loyal and productive citizens. To consolidate their grip, Communist cadres shot the commander of the armed forces, dismissed Congress at gunpoint, dissolved all businesses, took over the press, nationalized banks and communications, placed unions under government direction, and assumed state ownership of church property. While religious artifacts were burned, dissidents were murdered by gangsters or sent to forced labor camps in North Dakota or Alaska. The final scene of the story revealed an inner circle of Communists in formal dinner attire raising a triumphant champagne toast.[20]

**

While Cold War rhetoricians, Truman loyalty administrators, and federal prosecutors sought to tie communism to actual subversion, a case seldom made in the 1940s with success, many Americans saw the issue in class terms. The totalitarian concept of communism sought "to keep the common man common," preached Republican House member, George A. Dondero, the former mayor of Royal Oak, Michigan, the working-class suburb of Detroit from which Father Charles Coughlin had preached. A similar perspective was endorsed by the Philadelphia Irish American whose letter pleaded with the Truman White House that communism was a reactionary movement reverting to the time when the individual was nothing and the state all-powerful, a stark contrast to the self-empowering and revolutionary force of American capitalism. North Dakota Republican Usher L. Burdick made the same point when he argued that only market societies permitted ordinary people to reap the fruits of their labor. "Congress must realize that this atheistic communism is not a working-class movement in this country and never has been," an angry correspondent informed Senator John Bricker. "It is a movement of frustrated intellectuals who are out to seize power."[21]

As Cold War tensions intensified between 1947 and 1949, the Republican-led 80th Congress launched twenty-two investigations of alleged Communist activity at home. The most important of these occurred in the old Dies panel, recreated with a new chair in 1945 as the House Committee on Un-American Activities (HUAC), the first permanent standing unit of Congress. Focusing initially on charges of subversive propaganda in government agencies, HUAC dissected the radio scripts of the Office of Price Administration. In 1946, the committee heard testimony from Louis Budenz, former managing editor of the Communist *Daily Worker*, who charged that the party used liberal intellectuals to defend its ideological line. Under Republican leadership in 1947, the panel interrogated Gerhart Eisler, a German refugee and accomplished intellectual it tied to the international Communist movement of the 1930s. Weeks later, J. Edgar Hoover testified that Stalin's agents had developed one of the greatest propaganda machines the world had ever known and targeted Hollywood as a potential springboard for Communist subversion of American democracy.[22]

Indeed, Communist Party organizers had established a film-industry branch during the Popular Front era in 1936. Its purpose was to garner financial support for Communist causes, enlist prestigious stars as allies, and keep anti-Soviet propaganda out of American films. As Eugene Lyons reported in 1941,

Communist affiliations sometimes proved a shortcut to success in the cohesive and socially conscious Hollywood community. HUAC had contemplated an investigation of the motion picture colony in 1945. Two years later, Republican chair J. Parnell Thomas directed a subcommittee to take closed-door testimony on Communist activities in Hollywood. The panel soon alleged that Communist screenwriters and directors had infiltrated the studios and projected subversive propaganda onto the screen. The film industry, it concluded, had become the principal vehicle for poisoning the American mind.[23]

To publicize its assertions concerning the corruption of a key communications industry by disloyal and subversive members of the intelligentsia, HUAC elicited open testimony from anticommunist allies in Hollywood, among them, Screen Actors Guild (SAG) President Ronald Reagan. A self-described New Dealer, Reagan had been dismayed in 1946 when the SAG was caught in a jurisdictional dispute between studio technicians affiliated with the American Federation of Labor and those aligned with the Conference of Studio Unions (CSU). Physically threatened when he opposed a strike called by the CSU, Reagan subsequently learned that the union was tied to the Hollywood Communist Party. He suffered further discouragement when the governing board of the liberal Hollywood Independent Citizens Committee of the Arts, Sciences, and Professions (HICCASP) refused to refer a resolution denouncing communism and supporting free enterprise to the general body. When screenwriter John Howard Lawson allegedly told Reagan that the membership was not politically sophisticated enough to make this decision, the actor joined eleven others in resigning from the organization, which changed its name in 1947 to avoid exposure as a Communist front.[24]

Reagan later claimed that the HICCASP episode taught him the connection between communism and the idea of government by an intellectual elite. "I knew from firsthand experience," he recalled, "how Communists used lies, deceit, violence, or other tactics." Offended at the takeover of liberal Hollywood groups by small but persistent numbers of party activists, Reagan ran for the SAG presidency. Once elected, he divulged information about alleged guild Communists to the FBI. When he appeared before HUAC, however, the affable Reagan simply stated that a small clique within the union was suspected of following tactics associated with the Communist Party. Rejecting government intervention, he testified that the SAG had exposed the lies and propaganda of Communist sympathizers and neutralized their impact. Reagan also insisted that Communists had not succeeded in using the movies as a sounding board for their ideology. Preferring the use of democratic methods in the good fight, he said that he hesitated to outlaw the Communist Party on the basis of ideology unless it turned out to be an agent of a foreign power.[25]

Following the voluntary testimony of Reagan and other Hollywood anticommunists, HUAC subpoenas led to the appearance of ten unfriendly witnesses, at least nine of whom had been or currently were party members. The group included the most talented and politically active writers and directors in the motion picture industry. Distinguishing between the expression of opinion and the confession of affiliation with a political organization, all ten collectively agreed to refuse to answer questions concerning former or present membership in the Communist Party. Instead of invoking Fifth Amendment protections against self-incrimination, however, the Hollywood witnesses based their noncooperation on First Amendment rights of free speech and told the committee that they would answer queries in their own way.[26]

The HUAC hearings of 1947 pitted political intellectuals who insisted on their legal rights to ideological nonconformity against career politicians and Republican partisans anxious to identify them as manipulators of the democratic process. John Howard Larson set the tone for the bitter confrontation. The founder and first president of the Screen Writers Guild and secret head of the Hollywood branch of the Communist Party, Larson was enraged by the committee's refusal to permit him to read an opening statement. Declining to discuss his political philosophy or activities, he adamantly invoked constitutional rights of free association. Dalton Trumbo, one of the highest paid screenwriters in the industry, and a party member since 1943, refused to acknowledge even his membership in the Screen Writers Guild. Equating committee efforts with fascist thought control, Trumbo protested that the hearings marked the beginning of an American concentration camp. Interrogators replied that the witness' evocative antiwar novel, *Johnny Got His Gun*, had been published in 1940 during the period of the Soviet-Nazi Non-Aggression Pact and had appeared serially in a Communist newspaper.[27]

Screenwriter Albert Maltz was the first to be given permission to read an opening statement. Drama critic for the Communist *New Masses*, Maltz had deplored the Marxist habit of judging literary works by ideological orthodoxy and then publicly recanted and confessed mistaken lines of thought when corrected by party superiors. He now told HUAC that it sought to destroy writers because of the strength of their ideas and their support for the New Deal. Choosing between the Bill of Rights and the committee's censorship of political thought, he insisted upon the right to think and speak freely regardless of consequences. Alvah Bessie, a Hollywood writer who had fought as a volunteer in Spain, told the panel that it was involved in a "patent attempt to foster the sort of intimidation and terror that is the inevitable precursor of a Fascist regime."[28]

Once witnesses failed to answer questions, an investigator read into the record detailed information about party-related activities, including the contents of Communist registration cards. In November 1947, the Hollywood Ten were cited for contempt of Congress. Following a meeting of fifty studio executives, the motion picture industry proclaimed that no Communists or subversives would be employed in film making. Reagan's Screen Actors Guild soon banned Communist Party activists and noncooperating congressional witnesses from membership and created a council to help people clear their names if they volunteered to appear before the FBI and HUAC. With the release of *Red Channels,* a pamphlet produced in 1950 by three former FBI agents, the blacklist expanded to 151 writers, directors, and performers accused merely of Communist front activity and affiliations.[29]

***

Despite the Hollywood Ten's desire to represent itself as the beleaguered vanguard of democracy, the HUAC hearings left a mixed legacy. Gallup pollsters reported nationwide support for the controversial contempt charges by a margin of 47 percent to 39 percent. The division in public sentiment was reflected by the fact that calls for punishment were greatest among manual workers and farmers, and less among professionals, businesspeople, and white-collar employees. Populist anger at the affluent radicals of the motion picture industry was captured by journalist Eugene Lyons, who derided "*deluxe* proletarians and three-car peasants . . . playing at cocktail communism." The ten unfriendly witnesses, Lyons reminded readers of the *American Legion Magazine,* included "no farmer or workman or so-called 'common man' . . . they were college graduates, Ph.D.'s, *summa cum laudes* and Phi Beta Kappas from Harvard, Yale, Princeton, and other great colleges." Cold War liberals within the film community also noted that many of those who sought protection for their constitutional rights had imposed collective discipline, thought control, regimentation, and strict secrecy in their role as functionaries of the Hollywood Communist Party.[30]

Critics who pointed to the perceived duplicity of Communist intellectuals and cultural figures tied such accusations to the charge that party members and allies were conscious agents or dupes of the Soviet Union. HUAC perceived its mission, according to a committee report of August 1948, as one providing citizens an opportunity to render a continuing verdict on public officials and those in private life who either openly associated with and assisted disloyal groups or covertly operated as members or fellow travelers. When the panel took testimony from Whittaker Chambers, a writer and editor for *Time* who had left the Communist Party in 1937, it received a first-hand account of the growth of Marxist study groups in New Deal agencies and the attempt of political intellectuals to shape government policy. Pressed for details, Chambers named eight Communists as former comrades, including Alger Hiss, a State Department official who had moved on to the presidency of the Carnegie Endowment for International Peace in 1946.[31]

Chambers told HUAC that disloyalty was a matter of principle with every member of the Communist Party. Yet his objections to the revolutionary creed were fundamentally philosophical, not security related. Communism brought not mere totalitarian slavery, he warned, but "spiritual night to the human mind and soul." Rejecting the premises of modern rationalism, Chambers equated communism with a vision of Man without God, one in which the human mind displaced God as the creative intelligence of the world. Traumatized by the signing of the Nazi-Soviet Pact in 1939, Chambers had relayed information about Hiss and former comrades to Assistant Secretary of State and former brains truster, Adolf Berle, and subsequently submitted to FBI interviews. Only when Hiss contested the charges in 1948, however, did the witness begin to achieve credibility.[32]

Two days after Chambers made his allegations, Hiss appeared before HUAC to deny ever being a Communist or knowing his accuser. Yet a subcommittee headed by first-term Republican representative Richard Nixon elicited graphic detail from Chambers about Hiss family life in the 1930s. When Chambers complied with Hiss's challenge to repeat the charges without congressional immunity, the ex-New Dealer sued for slander. To buttress his defense against the suit, the *Time* journalist produced copies of State Department documents that Hiss allegedly had provided in the 1930s for transmission to Soviet agents. In December, Chambers took Nixon and HUAC investigators to his Maryland farm where he produced five microfilmed rolls of State Department documents from a hollowed-out pumpkin in which they had been placed for safekeeping.[33]

The discovery of the sensational "pumpkin papers" led to federal perjury indictments against Hiss for lying about his Communist Party activities and his association with Chambers. Brought to trial in 1949, the former New Deal official produced two Supreme Court justices as character witnesses. Nevertheless, the prosecution showed that many of the microfilmed documents produced by Chambers had originated in Hiss's State Department office. Expert testimony also suggested that most of the material had been prepared on a typewriter once owned by the defendant. Despite such evidence, the jury deadlocked in an 8 to 4 vote for the prosecution. With looser rules governing admissible evidence, however, a second proceeding resulted in a conviction in January 1950 and Hiss received a five-year prison sentence.[34]

The Hiss case validated the widespread suspicion that lax procedures had enabled the Soviets to subvert government security and reaffirmed the assumption that Communists were tied to foreign conspiracies. It also reinforced the views of those who saw the New Deal as an elitist threat to democratic accountability. Hiss perfectly embodied pervasive fears concerning the trustworthiness of the permanent governing class. A graduate of Johns Hopkins and Harvard Law School who had served as a clerk to former Supreme Court Justice Oliver Wendell Holmes, Jr., he had begun his political career as a consumer-oriented activist in the Agricultural Adjustment Administration. Hiss then received an appointment as assistant to the assistant secretary of state for the Far East. A minor Roosevelt adviser at the Yalta Conference of 1945, the ambitious diplomat and reformer served as the secretary general of the meeting that led to the creation of the United Nations.[35]

Hiss's association with New Deal reform and internationalist foreign policy framed responses to the widely publicized case. Generally sympathetic to Roosevelt-Truman officialdom, the *New York Times* initially described the former diplomat as tall, slender, and youthful, as a witness who answered in strong tones and stood by his previous testimony. Chambers, in turn, was portrayed as heavyset and weary looking, as someone whose responses were dull and barely audible. The *Times* eventually distanced itself from Hiss. Yet the *Washington Post*, a newspaper that had forged a niche as the voice of the executive bureaucracy, maintained persistent support for the defendant, even following conviction. Meanwhile, the nationalist *Chicago Tribune* used the Hiss case to attack the moral iniquities of a bureaucratic class it accused of employing ridicule, smears, executive powers, the courts, and political pressure to hide the operations of Communists and fellow travelers within the government.[36]

Karl Mundt, the South Dakota Republican who chaired the HUAC subcommittee that investigated the pumpkin papers, summed up the discomfort over Hiss when he complained that the discredited New Dealer had placed a foreign creed above devotion to the American people. Days after the verdict, Mundt addressed the House on "What the Hiss Trial Actually Means." The former speech teacher marveled that there still were people in the country who believed "it inconceivable that a man who looks so smooth and so intelligent and speaks such an effective Harvard accent," could be guilty of betraying his country. Similar bitterness surfaced in an April 1950 editorial in the *Detroit Free Press*. "Yes, the 'intelligentsia' from the basements of Greenwich Village to the parlor pinks of the Park Avenue penthouse parlors glorified in how brilliant Hiss was and what a sucker he made of the authorities," exclaimed the editors. Noting that the defendant never missed an opportunity to express contempt for the ignorance and stupidity of the nation's people, the newspaper exulted that the "battered old typewriter" had no Groton-Harvard accent.[37]

***

The Hiss case pointed to the manner in which social class played into the profound animosities between reformist elements of the intellectual political class and their congressional adversaries. Representative Karl Mundt was particularly sensitive to this particular strain of culture war. Speaking before the national Kiwanis Clubs convention of 1949, Mundt recalled a debate on planned economies in which he had participated with a Harvard consultant to a federal agency. The South Dakotan's position was that government management could lead to police state tyranny because it rested on coercion. "This professor looked at me with the profundity which comes from a man with a Phi Beta key on his watch chain and no watch in his pocket," recalled Mundt; "this fellow looked at me as though I were something that should not have been down there in Washington at all." Angry at the way Ivy League academicians condescended those considered beneath their social status and intellectual level, the former high school speech teacher focused on how his rival had responded "with a delightful and convincing Harvard accent, which made me feel pretty small and unimportant."[38]

Social tensions over the role and accountability of the political class contributed to serious fallout from the Hiss controversy. Three days after the conclusion of the former official's second trial, Secretary of State Dean Acheson announced to reporters that whatever the outcome of an appeal, he did not intend to turn his back on his longtime friend and associate. Offered as a charitable gesture of personal support, Acheson's statement nevertheless attracted searing criticism for placing collegiality with an ex-colleague above loyalty to the nation. To add to the furor over the integrity and reliability of Washington officialdom, Hiss's conviction for lying about Communist activities came within seven weeks of the collapse of the Nationalist government of China and Mao Zedong's establishment of a Communist regime in Beijing. Blaming internal forces beyond U.S. control for the eminent disaster, Acheson had signed a State Department White Paper in August 1949 that announced U.S. refusal to risk full-scale intervention in behalf of a government that appeared to have lost the confidence of its own troops and people.[39]

As the Communists appeared on the brink of victory in China, State Department advisers on East Asia hoped to encourage the rebels to emulate anticapitalist Yugoslavia by remaining independent of Soviet control. But any accommodation with the Maoists infuriated American nationalists who believed that professional diplomats and advisers lacked the moral courage and judgment to recognize the inherent evils of communism. Led by lace importer Alfred Kohlberg, a "China Lobby" of business interests, journalists, and politicians such as Minnesota representative Walter Judd and California senator William F. Knowland sought support for the anticommunist cause in China and then held American foreign policy leaders responsible for its defeat. Republican nationalists blamed the Communist victory in China on appeasers in the State Department, whose duplicity and ideological sympathies were traced to the Yalta pact of 1945, an agreement by which the Allies consented to Soviet economic rights in Manchuria and secretly ceded postwar possession of two strategic Japanese islands to Moscow.[40]

The nationalist case against political intellectuals was presented in its sharpest form in *While You Slept* (1951), a bitter polemic by commentator John T. Flynn that accused New Dealers of using the liberal media to mount a propaganda campaign to cover up the conspiracy to sell out China. Anticollectivists like Flynn insisted that the State Department had lost in Asia what General Douglas MacArthur and the military had fought for and won during World War II. Like Alger Hiss, Dean Acheson was viewed by such adversaries as a symbol of the betrayal of the anticommunist crusade by career diplomats, professional reformers, and high-minded internationalists. Of Social Register background, Acheson had matriculated at Groton, Yale, and Harvard Law School before signing on as a senior partner in a Washington legal firm that specialized in international finance. Serving under the secretary of state between 1941 and 1947, the debonair diplomat won appointment to the department's top position in 1949. Yet six senators voted against the nomination because they viewed Acheson as an Europe-oriented globalist without sufficient moral backbone to pursue the Cold War in Asia.[41]

As a public service aristocrat, Acheson infuriated midwestern and western nationalists who distrusted the social elite of the East. His identification with Harvard strengthened not only an association with snobbery but reinforced an image of urbane sophistication and liberal paternalism that recalled the reaction to 1920s academics and to New Deal brains trusters. For its opponents, the State Department of Hiss, John Stewart Service, and Acheson embodied a dangerous mixture of cavalier security precautions, irresponsible internationalism, and corrupting cosmopolitanism. No critic expressed such disdain with the passion attributed to Nebraska senator Hugh Butler, a die-hard Republican non-interventionist and bitter foreign aid opponent. "I look at that fellow," Butler reputedly said of his arch adversary Dean Acheson, "I watch his smart-aleck manner and his British clothes and that New Dealism, everlasting New Dealism in everything he says and does, and I want to shout Get out, Get out, you stand for everything that has been wrong with the United States."[42]

The dangers of a callous foreign policy establishment of political intellectuals and a ruthless Communist conspiracy from abroad were most clearly drawn by Senator Joseph R. McCarthy. Raised by a hardworking Wisconsin farm family of Roman Catholics, McCarthy completed four years of high school in nine months and received a law degree from Marquette University before winning election at the age of thirty-one as a Democratic circuit court judge. Serving with the marines as a World War II intelligence officer, he changed political parties in 1944 and lost a Republican primary bid against an incumbent U.S. senator. Two years later, McCarthy won a narrow primary victory against the popular Senator Robert M. La Follette, Jr. by portraying himself as a robust and self-made product of the small-town working class. The candidate employed similar themes in the general election when he faced Democrat Howard McMurray, a University of Wisconsin political science professor with New Deal views.[43]

McCarthy cleverly exploited the perception that high-minded members of the Truman administration had accommodated to Soviet communism. "I'm just a farm boy, not a professor," he told debate listeners in Appleton, "but I'll be damned if I figure out this Henry Wallace view of Russia." Just as McCarthy raised doubts about the secretary of commerce, he attacked his Democratic opponent in the Senate race as "Communistically inclined." A McCarthy newspaper advertisement explained that "some of the Democratic candidates for high offices in the government have been repudiated by the party because they have proved to have Communist backgrounds and Communist ways of thinking." The Republican nominee insisted that he was "100 per cent American in thought and deed. No one can say that he believes in any of the foreign isms that have plagued the Democratic party throughout their reign."[44]

Elected to the Senate with the Republican class of 1946, McCarthy maintained a relatively low profile for three years. But in February 1950 he attracted national attention with a politically motivated speech to the Women's Republican Club in Wheeling, West Virginia, in which he claimed to have a list of 205 known Communists working and shaping policy in the State Department. Among the names cited by McCarthy were Gustavo Duran, a former foreign service officer working for the United Nations; Harlow Shapley, the director of the Harvard Observatory, a representative of the U.S. National Commission for UNESCO, and a left-wing advocate of international scientific cooperation; and John Stewart Service, the State Department China expert implicated in the *Amerasia* case. The senator soon amended the list to fifty-seven card-carrying Communists or party sympathizers. Appearing on the Senate floor eleven days after Wheeling, he altered the charges to eighty-one State Department "loyalty risks."[45]

McCarthy's aides were astonished at his ignorance about communism and his lack of preparation on the subject of domestic subversion. Although the senator insisted that "good loyal Americans" provided his staff with evidence, his speeches normally contained distorted, misleading, and inaccurate information. The numbers used at Wheeling had been calculated by manipulating and exaggerating selective data from a security files audit compiled in 1947 by the House Appropriations Committee. Yet the accuracy of the senator's irresponsible allegations and half-truths was not as significant as his skill in tapping deeply held resentments in midcentury political culture. With the help of speechwriter Ed Nellor,[46] McCarthy cleverly accomplished this task at Wheeling by expropriating the populist rhetoric and imagery of World War II's united front against fascism.

To orient troops to the dangers of the Axis enemy and to Allied aims in World War II, all members of the U.S. armed services had been required to attend screenings of *Why We Fight*, a series of film documentaries produced by Hollywood director Frank Capra at the request of Army Chief of Staff George C. Marshall. *Prelude to War*, the initial installment, had been placed into commercial production at the urging of President Roosevelt and won an Academy Award for best documentary of 1942. Capra brilliantly captured the urgency of the struggle against fascism and militarism. "The chips are down," proclaimed the film's narrator. "Two worlds stand against each other. One must die, one must live." In language borrowed from a speech by Vice President Henry Wallace, the sound track warned about a collision of freedom versus slavery, of civilization versus barbarism, of good versus evil. The war was "a common man's life and death struggle against those who would put him back in slavery."[47]

Applying Capra's folksy call for democratic unity in a battle against privilege and autocracy, McCarthy depicted the Cold War of 1950 as a confrontation between two diametrically opposed ideologies. "Today we are engaged in a final, all-out battle between communistic atheism and Christianity," he declared at

Wheeling. Repeating the warning that "the chips are down," McCarthy claimed that the United States was losing the anticommunist struggle and was "in a position of impotency" on every front. Unlike the war on fascism, the crusade against the Kremlin had been compromised at home by the professional foreign service and Washington's permanent political class. Cold War reverses resulted from the actions of an effete circle of liberal insiders who lacked the stamina, ruthlessness, or will to prevail in the deadly contest.[48]

Skillfully tying resentment toward the eastern social aristocracy with disdain for governing elites, McCarthy's blend of anticommunist politics decried the "traitorous actions of those who have been treated so well by this Nation." He focused on "those who have had all the benefits that the wealthiest nation on earth has had to offer–the finest homes, the finest college education, and the finest jobs in Government we can give.... The bright young men who are born with silver spoons in their mouths are the ones who have been worst." McCarthy used Alger Hiss, "a man who sold out the Christian world to the atheistic world," as the prototype of the domestic enemy. Dean Acheson, whom he castigated for maintaining loyalty to Hiss, was a "pompous diplomat in striped pants, with a phoney British accent." The Wisconsin Republican called for a moral uprising against "the whole sorry mess of twisted, warped thinkers" in government service. The Democratic Party, he contended, had lost control of the executive branch while a "group of twisted-thinking intellectuals" had taken over the State Department.[49]

***

Having reasserted dominance of both houses of Congress during President Truman's reelection in 1948, Democrats pressed McCarthy to substantiate his charges. Under the chairmanship of Maryland's Millard F. Tydings, a special subcommittee of the Senate Foreign Relations Committee took testimony from the Wisconsin Republican. McCarthy accused Ambassador at Large Philip C. Jessup, a character witness for Hiss and an editor of the China White Paper, of an unusual affinity for Communist causes. It turned out that Jessup had been one of many officials to sponsor a 1944 dinner held by the American Russian Institute, an organization subsequently placed on the attorney general's list of Communist fronts. McCarthy mirrored Alfred Kohlberg's charge that the former Columbia professor of international law had originated the myth of the democratic Chinese Communists. The senator also repeated allegations that John Stewart Service had tilted the State Department toward accommodation with the Maoist revolutionaries in China.[50]

The most dramatic confrontation of the Tydings committee hearings came when McCarthy took on Owen D. Lattimore, the director of the Walter Hines Page School of International Relations at Johns Hopkins University. Lattimore had been raised in China but been educated in Switzerland and England. After returning to the mainland as a journalist and entrepreneur, he received several fellowships to study the frontier dependencies of Inner Asia. Between 1934 and 1941, Lattimore edited *Pacific Affairs,* a magazine published by the Institute of Pacific Relations (IPR), a quasi-academic think tank that sponsored much of the research on East Asia in the 1930s and 1940s. He then served as a wartime adviser to the Chinese government of Jiang Jieshi and assumed directorship of the Pacific operations of the Office of War Information. Following the war, the China expert conducted State Department seminars on East Asia. In *Solution in Asia* (1945), he advocated recognition of the legitimate aims and strengths of the Chinese Communists so that the Soviets could be prevented from exploiting nationalist sentiments. Lattimore acknowledged the political appeal of the Maoist government in *The Situation in Asia* (1949), arguing that cooperation with the regime would promote regional stability.[51]

Characterizing Lattimore as "the chief architect of our Far Eastern policy," McCarthy read from a letter of 1943 in which the professor allegedly demonstrated pro-communist inclinations. Lattimore was a policy risk, insisted the senator. Testimony from ex-Communist Louis Budenz suggested that the party had considered the China expert helpful to its purposes. When the Lattimore inquiry provoked the wrath of congressional Democrats, McCarthy struck back. In an April 1950 speech before the American Society of Newspaper Editors, the senator denounced former Secretary of State George Marshall as "a pathetic thing . . . completely unfit" for supervising people such as John Stewart Service and Owen Lattimore. Complaining that "egg-sucking phony liberals" had branded him a "Revolving S.O.B.," McCarthy vowed not to be deterred by "the pitiful squealing of those who would hold sacrosanct those Communists and queers" who had sold China into atheistic slavery.[52]

Two weeks after the address to the editors, McCarthy told a gathering of midwestern Young Republicans that the Truman foreign policy had floundered on "Harvard-accented notes and powder puff diplomacy." When confronted with the "red-hot aggression of Soviet communism," chortled the senator, the State Department reacted with "a whimper of confusion and fear" and "a whining indecision that echoes around the world." Why must Americans "be forced to cringe in the face of communism?" asked McCarthy. Castigating "prancing mimics of the Moscow party line" who sold the nation short, he thundered that "the days of dilletante diplomacy are running out." As the plans of traitors were threatened, McCarthy told the Sons of the American Revolution in May, "the squealing will become louder and the fight will become tougher." Ten days later, the senator dismissed State Department criticism of his allegations as an attempt "to dishonestly protect reputations of the inner circle."[53]

McCarthy's attacks on the professional foreign service appeared to resonate with some segments of the public. Opinion polling in May 1950 revealed that 39 percent of the sample believed that the senator's accusations were good for the country, while 29 percent saw them as harmful or false. As the Tydings panel prepared a final report in July that labeled the McCarthy charges a fraud and a

hoax, 31 percent of Gallup poll respondents found the allegations to be literally true. Washington columnist John O'Donnell compared the subcommittee's
treatment of the Wisconsin Republican to the attempts to smear noninterventionist Senator Robert M. La Follette during World War I. O'Donnell also noted
that Tydings was the son-in-law of Joseph E. Davies, the former ambassador
to the Soviet Union whose *Mission to Moscow* had been made into a wartime
film romanticizing Allied cooperation with the Communists. Responding to
the Maryland Democrat's public characterization of McCarthy as a charlatan,
Indiana Republican William E. Jenner pointed to Tydings as a member of "a
select inner circle of a new political aristocracy."[54]

With the outbreak of the Korean War in June 1950, new tensions arose over
domestic security and the effectiveness of the global crusade against communism. In the fall elections, McCarthy campaigned in fifteen states, including
Millard Tydings's Maryland. At a gathering in Beaver Dam, Wisconsin, the senator declared that Dean Acheson was a "procurer of pinks and punks" and that
the Democrats were the "party of the puppets of the politburo." Vowing to expose "the dupes and stooges of the Kremlin," the unpredictable Wisconsinite
told a Maryland rally of Republicans that the American people were "entitled
to know the names of the traitors who plotted the Communist victory in Asia."
In Chicago, McCarthy used Ed Nellor's language to describe Democrats as the
"Commiecrat Party." For nationalists, Asia-firsters, and anticommunists, such
rhetoric had particular meaning when in April 1951 President Truman fired
General Douglas MacArthur as commander of U.S. troops in Korea.[55]

Once the Chinese Communists entered the Korean War in October 1950,
MacArthur had sought to expand the conflict to the mainland. "There is no substitute for victory," asserted the general in a letter to House Republican Leader
Joseph Martin. MacArthur believed that Asia, not a dying Europe, would determine the world's future. Yet the Truman administration saw the Korean conflict
primarily as a symbolic rallying point and opted for a negotiated settlement once
a stand against aggression had been made. Dismissed for publicly disagreeing
with military strategy and for failing to clear policy statements, MacArthur returned stateside to enthusiastic crowds of well-wishers and supporters. With
customary bluntness, Joe McCarthy embraced the celebrated general by attacking the political class in Washington as "a leadership which whines, whimpers,
cringes in fear, and urges that we dare not win a war which it started." The
Truman administration backed away from confrontation in Asia, said McCarthy,
because of concern over Communist nuclear weapons made possible by "secrets
stolen from us by spies which, according to the president, never existed."[56]

The philosophical implications of MacArthur's strategic differences with the
Truman administration became clear when the general published his memoirs in 1964. MacArthur castigated bureaucrats who used the proceeds of labor
to greater advantage than those who created it. He condemned American fiscal policy for moving toward a socialist and politically managed monopoly of

economic life. Yet the sharpest passages of the book used the context of foreign policy to offer a haunting replica of Hiram Wesley Evans's jeremiads of the
1920s. "Strange voices are heard across the land," wrote MacArthur, decrying
proven concepts of patriotism and suggesting a higher destiny of internationalism. The general lamented that military managers now disguised halfhearted
and indecisive wars with "some more euphemistic and gentler name."[57]

MacArthur's rhetoric suggested that the modern military had replaced the
leadership of traditional warriors with accommodating and duplicitous administrators. Nationalist supporters of the general believed that Secretary of Defense
George Marshall was a prime example of the new breed. After serving as army
chief of staff during World War II, Marshall became special presidential envoy
to China in 1946, where he vainly sought a negotiated settlement between the
Jiang Jieshi government and Communist rebels. Truman appointed his favorite
military adviser as Secretary of State in 1947. Two years later, the forces of Mao
Zedong took control of the Chinese mainland. When Marshall was nominated
as Secretary of Defense in 1950, eleven Republican senators voted against confirmation. An advocate of limited war, Marshall attracted further criticism for
joining Dean Acheson in the successful effort to extricate MacArthur from the
Korean command.[58]

McCarthy already had used the MacArthur firing to denounce Acheson as
"the great Red Dean of fashion," a key participant in the "lace hankerchief" and
"crimson crowd" that had betrayed the cause of freedom. Two months after
the general's dismissal, the Wisconsin Republican announced a major Senate
speech on George Marshall. Published in book form as *America's Retreat from
Victory: The Story of George Catlett Marshall* (1951), the 72,000-word polemic
may have been the work of Forrest Davis, a journalist who had served on the
staffs of Senator Robert Taft and Alfred Kohlberg. Read into the *Congressional
Record* in its entirety, the document sought to connect the activities of John
Carter Vincent, Acheson, and Marshall to Cold War reverses such as the "loss"
of China and the military stalemate in Korea. Describing the perceived amorality
of the nation's military and strategic leadership, McCarthy accused the highest
echelons of the Truman administration of moral debility, flabbiness, and lack
of resolve.[59]

McCarthy stressed that leftist-liberals in government had vitiated the national will to resist Soviet communism and instead sought accommodation
with a totalitarian foe. But the heart of his argument lay in the charge that such
irresolution was not accidental and involved more than ineptitude and folly.
"This must be the product of a great conspiracy," he declared, "a conspiracy
on a scale so immense as to dwarf any previous such venture in the history of
man." The Wisconsin Republican maintained that Washington's political class
had acquiesced in the effort to weaken the U.S. military role in world affairs,
to confuse the national spirit, and to impair the country's will to resist evil.
He attributed the "the high-pitched screaming and squealing of the Lattimores,

the Jessups, and the camp-following bleeding hearts" of the media to the fact that courageous investigators had uncovered the conspiracies of the government elite. McCarthy also reiterated the charge that the administration had used deceitful methods to protect Soviet agents in its ranks.[60]

America's Retreat from Victory stood as a perfect example of McCarthy's divisive style. Pressing ahead with his crusade against the diplomatic establishment of "the Commiecrat party," the senator appeared before a Senate Foreign Relations subcommittee in September 1951 to block President Truman's nomination of Philip Jessup as a delegate to the UN General Assembly. Recycling the allegations of Jessup's Communist front activity, McCarthy hinted that the former professor was effeminate and pointedly denounced the use of "kid gloves in perfumed drawing rooms." When the panel rejected the Jessup appointment in a 3 to 2 vote, Truman was compelled to make a recess appointment. McCarthy made similar charges the next year against Democratic presidential candidate Adlai Stevenson, whom he referred to in a televised address as "Alger–I mean Adlai," and ominously placed in the "Acheson-Hiss-Lattimore group." Seeking to separate the New Deal electoral constituency from Truman functionaries, the fiesty Republican pleaded that millions of loyal Democrats no longer had a party in Washington.[61]

***

McCarthy's pursuit of State Department experts and advisers helped to promote a skeptical view of Cold War Era intellectuals and knowledge professionals. As one scholar has suggested, "the widespread image of Communists as unscrupulous, duplicitous, and single-minded conspirators under the absolute control of an enemy power made it difficult to believe that Communist teachers and others were engaged in innocent activities." By 1950, twenty-five states required loyalty oaths of public school instructors. Hundreds of teachers, social workers, and journalists ultimately lost their jobs for failing to cooperate with state or congressional probes into Communist activity. Nearly one hundred college and university professors received similar treatment. Although some liberals criticized such action for violating free speech guarantees, academic institutions and professional societies often distinguished between heretics who advanced unpopular ideas and alleged conspirators serving foreign interests. The philosopher Sidney Hook argued that the former fairly competed in the marketplace of ideas while the latter subverted freedom through secrecy and deceit.[62]

McCarthy addressed the issue of communism and academic freedom in a compendium of views entitled *McCarthyism: The Fight for America* (1952), a book that featured a praiseworthy foreword by Northwestern University political scientist William M. McGovern. Citing an address by former HUAC research director J. B. Matthews, the Wisconsin Republican asserted that 28 percent of top collaborators with Communist-front groups in recent years had been college or university professors and that three thousand academics currently were affiliated with instruments of the Communist Party. Whatever the accuracy of such arbitrary allegations, McCarthy's solution was clear: the nation's educational system was to "be scrubbed and flushed and swept clean" of Communist influence. Restating William Jennings Bryan's disdain for those who imposed unwelcome views on local communities, McCarthy pictured Communist-minded teachers as insisting that academic freedom stood for "*their* right to force you to hire *them* to teach *your* children a philosophy in which you do not believe."[63]

Despite McCarthy's bravado, Senate Judiciary Committee chair Pat McCarran turned out to be the leading force behind congressional investigations of academic political activists. The son of poor Irish-Catholic immigrants to Nevada, McCarran dropped out of his senior year in college to support an ailing father. After a stint as a farmer, he won admission to the state bar, opened a law practice, and served five years on the state supreme court. Voters sent McCarran to the U.S. Senate during the Democratic sweep of 1932. After supporting early New Deal reforms, the independent-minded legislator opposed Franklin Roosevelt's "court-packing" bill, and campaigned after Pearl Harbor to terminate programs like the National Resources Planning Board and the National Youth Administration. By 1950, McCarran had taken his place as a major Senate force by parlaying the Judiciary Committee's veto over impending legislation into a powerful personal patronage and political machine.[64]

Suspicious of government social programs, McCarran was a fervent anticommunist. Following the outbreak of the Korean War, he authored the Internal Security Act. Passed over President Truman's veto in September 1950, the statute contained a requirement that Communist and Communist-front groups register with a Subversives Activities Control Board. Three months later, the powerful Nevada Democrat created the Senate Internal Security Subcommittee (SSIS) and stacked the panel with anticommunists like Mississippi Democrat James O. Eastland and Republicans Homer Ferguson and William Jenner. Committee staff included research director Benjamin Mandel, a Communist Party activist of the 1920s, and special counsel Robert Morris, both of whom had served with New York's Rapp-Courdert inquiry of 1940 to 1941.[65]

Following its predecessor, the McCarran committee addressed the institutional penetration of communism by investigating party-related activity in New York public colleges and the city school teachers union. Yet the panel's most persistent inquiry centered on the left-leaning Institute of Pacific Relations. Federal agents had taken possession of the Institute's files in a February 1951 raid on a barn owned by an IPR trustee in Lee, Massachussetts. The discovery led to a contentious series of hearings between July 1951 and June 1952 that generated twenty thousand documents, sixty-six witnesses, and a printed record of five thousand pages. The probe operated on the assumption that the IPR had played an important role in China's fall to communism through its questionable influence over academic experts in the United States and its covert ties to State Department officials.[66]

Seeking explanations for the unwillingness of the political class to defend Nationalist China, the McCarran subcommittee questioned John Carter Vincent, the former head of the State Department's Far Eastern Division, and John Paton Davies, Jr., another distinguished government Asia expert. Its most extensive examination, however, focused on Owen Lattimore, the former IPR journal editor and State Department consultant who had been the subject of extensive controversy between McCarthy and the Tydings committee. Described by columnist Joseph Alsop as someone with "an unfortunate habit of being silly" about Asian politics, Lattimore was treated as a classic fellow traveler. This view was sustained by the testimony of University of Washington professor Karl Wittfogel, a former Communist and IPR colleague. Wittfogel claimed that as editor of *Pacific Affairs,* Lattimore had published Soviet-oriented articles by a German Communist and retained a known Chinese Communist Party member as an IPR researcher. Testimony by Louis Budenz alleged that the Kremlin had asked Lattimore to convert the journal into a Communist Party–line organ.[67]

In a November 1951 letter to McCarran, Lattimore asked to appear before the SSIS to answer allegations he described as false and slanderous. Represented on a pro bono basis by influential Washington attorney, Abe Fortas, the Johns Hopkins professor navigated through three days of committee questioning in February 1952 while attempting to read a fifty-page opening statement. He insisted that previous clarifications concerning his ties to IPR had been "rather copiously provided" before the Tydings committee. Lattimore resented the impression that he was a Communist or dupe, that he ran the Institute, or that the editorial biases of *Pacific Affairs* were part of an IPR campaign to influence State Department policy. "My views proceeded from the facts," he protested, "and not the facts from my views." Maintaining that complete openness of discussion of data and ideas prevailed at the Institute, the witness portrayed *Pacific Affairs* as a journal that offered information and "well-informed opinion" to State Department personnel as well as anyone else.[68]

Lattimore sharply objected to allegations by former IPR colleagues that he knew certain Institute associates to have been Communists. Characterizing their testimony as a "nightmare of outrageous lies, shaky hearsay, and undisguised personal spite," he criticized the SSIS for failing to cross-examine witnesses against him. Although he refused to state categorically that the McCarran panel was acting in bad faith, Lattimore saw no hope that the committee would fairly appraise the facts of his case. The professor characterized assertions that he promoted Soviet interests or sympathized with Communist propaganda lines as nonsense. Suggesting a difference between alleged Communists working at IPR and outright control of the Institute, Lattimore persistently mocked the notion that the organization was an instrument of the Soviet conspiracy.[69]

Despite such responses, Lattimore conceded several points. Among documents presented by the committee were the minutes of a 1936 meeting of IPR officials in Moscow in which Lattimore had argued that "if the Soviet group would show in their articles a general line, a struggle for peace, the other articles would naturally gravitate in that line." The former editor of *Pacific Affairs* also admitted that during that same year he had pushed into publication a German Communist's piece about China, although he previously had told the SSIS that he had not done so. "The distinction between forcing it through and overriding an objection" was "not very significant," explained Lattimore. Another contradiction involved a 1937 letter in which Lattimore had described a *Pacific Affairs* author as a Marxist although his sworn testimony indicated that no Communist had ever written for the journal without identification. The panel saw a further conflict between Lattimore's claim that he had advocated noncommunist leadership of the Chinese reform movement in 1938 and a private letter in which he had supported a pro-Soviet international policy without Kremlin slogans or an impression of subservience.[70]

Lattimore scored the McCarran committee for "going into questions of what people knew or thought about Soviet Russia in the 1930s from the point of view of what we know and think about Russia in the 1950s." Reminding the panel that most people were not yet aware of the danger of Communist conspiracy in the period in which he served as editor of *Pacific Affairs,* the East Asia expert acknowledged that he once had held an optimistic view of the possibility of cooperating with Moscow. Nevertheless, Lattimore's romanticization of the Chinese Communists, underestimations of Soviet influence in Asia, and defensive rationalizations of Joseph Stalin's Purge Trials of the late 1930s suggested an ideological partisanship that countered the professor's assertions of academic objectivity and scholarly detachment. To buttress its contentions, the McCarran committee produced a letter of 1940 in which Lattimore told an IPR colleague that the recent Soviet invasion of Finland could be defended as an example of "self-protective aggression."[71]

As the cross-examination of Lattimore concluded in March 1952, Chairman McCarran observed that "the committee has been confronted here with an individual so flagrantly defiant of the United States Senate, so outspoken in his discourtesy, and so persistent in his efforts to confuse and obscure the facts," that the panel felt constrained to take notice of his "contumacious and contemptuous conduct." Lattimore had delivered a deliberate affront to the nation's people, said McCarran. Instead of an objective analysis of U.S. failings in Asian policy, the professor had offered a fifty-page "fusillade of invective, and a consistently evasive, contentious, and belligerent attitude." Describing Lattimore's language as insolent, overbearing, arrogant, disdainful, intemperate, provocative, and abusive, the chair accused the witness of intending to offend and outrage the committee and staff. Moreover, McCarran contended that the professor's willful unresponsiveness demonstrated that he was an expert at splitting hairs with "glib facility." The Nevada Democrat asserted that Lattimore's flagrant untruths involved a deliberate attempt to deny or cover up pertinent facts.[72]

The McCarran committee concluded that IPR used financial support from benevolent corporations and foundations to establish close relations with legitimate Asia scholars and researchers. Utilizing eminent academics and public figures as an impressive screen, a small core of Communist and pro-Communist officials and staff supposedly had taken control of the Institute. The final report on IPR, issued under the imprint of the Senate Judiciary Committee, held that a considerable portion of Institute activities were channeled toward a partisan effort to influence public opinion. As an instrument of Communist policy and military intelligence, the organization allegedly had used Soviet and Communist sources as the basis for the false information conveyed in its propaganda, public relations, and lobbying. Portrayed as a veiled influence on popular attitudes and State Department strategies, Institute leaders were accused of exploiting IPR's prestige and using agents such as John Carter Vincent to promote the international interests of the Soviet Union.[73]

Beyond its criticism of the IPR, the McCarran subcommittee sharply questioned the details of Lattimore's testimony. The panel chair noted that the former editor had stated that he had lunched with the Soviet ambassador after the nonaggression pact with Nazi Germany had ended but that documents showed that the meeting had occurred during the life of the agreement. McCarran also questioned Lattimore's inability to remember a meeting with President Roosevelt preceding a White House directive in 1945 that replaced several anticommunist State Department officials in China. Labeling Owen Lattimore "a conscious articulate instrument of the Soviet conspiracy," the Judiciary Committee's final report concluded that the star witness had testified falsely on five separate matters of relevance and substance.[74]

FBI and Department of Justice investigators had considered perjury charges against Lattimore for denying ties to Communist associates during his Tydings committee appearances. Ironically, the former IPR official set new allegations in motion when he argued that Louis Budenz should be prosecuted for lying about him before the McCarran committee. Preferring to believe Budenz, and anticipating a repeat of the Alger Hiss scenario, the committee chair pressed federal authorities to charge Lattimore with misstatements under oath. Subsequent indictments accused the witness of falsely denying 1930s Communist sympathies and of failing to acknowledge awareness of the Communist backgrounds of one-time IPR associates.[75]

A federal judge ultimately dismissed each of the charges against Lattimore as obscure and insufficiently focused.[76] Yet the controversial McCarran probe involved more than questions of perjury. At issue was the continuing struggle between elected career politicians and Washington's permanent governing class of public administrators, academic consultants, and policy architects. Certainly, SSIS investigators failed to prove that pro-Soviet elements in IPR had brought on the downfall of the Chinese Nationalists, influenced State Department strategy, or subverted U.S. foreign policy. Nevertheless, by suggesting that high-minded advisers were subject to poor judgment, cavalier disregard for national interests, ideological partisanship, disingenuous posturing, and pretentious arrogance, the inquiry helped to question the legitimacy of Washington's political intellectuals and social guardians.

For all their mean-spirited bullying and partisan bravado, intemperate investigators like Joe McCarthy and Pat McCarran conveyed pervasive bewilderment at the perceived inability of well-placed government managers, professional diplomats, and advisers to pledge unreserved allegiance to the moral implications of the Cold War anticommunist crusade. As the stakes of loyalty appeared to intensify in a period of national insecurity and crisis, politically active knowledge professionals found themselves vulnerable to widespread criticism and resentment of their privileged status as a governing class. Significantly, the assault stemmed not merely from questionable domestic policies and global strategies, but from widespread mistrust of an elite whose moral and cultural beliefs seemed at odds with the majority of the nation.

6

Hidden Persuasions: The Disputed Agenda of 1950s Policy Elites

By the time anxieties over Cold War loyalty peaked in the 1950s, a mature service economy had catapulted knowledge professionals and technical experts into a central role in American society.[1] Increasingly secular in outlook and independent of traditional mores, these social guardians became a fitting target for Cold War anxieties over the remote sources of political and cultural authority. Opportunistic anticommunist crusaders of the period pointed to Ivy League universities, Hollywood film studios, New York intellectual centers, and Washington governing circles as suspect influences on the national psyche. Chapter 6 relates how political intellectuals of the tension-filled 1950s found themselves the targets of intrusive congressional and governmental inquiries into their ideological loyalties and moral credentials. After delineating the controversy surrounding the security clearance of nuclear weapons consultant, J. Robert Oppenheimer, the chapter reexamines Joseph McCarthy's broad assault on the governing elite after 1952. Its last segments highlight the disputed status of Cold War knowledge professionals and social experts by examining the House investigation of links between tax-exempt foundations and the academic social sciences, as well as by exploring the nationwide campaign against public health management of fluoridated municipal water supplies.

***

Sensing public desire for accountability from members of the knowledge elite and sensitive government agencies during the height of the Cold War, congressional leaders stepped up the use of anticommunist investigations to great political advantage in the 1950s. The House Un-American Activities Committee renewed its inquiry into the activities of political intellectuals in the motion picture industry in 1951. Testifying after completion of a six-month prison sentence, former Hollywood Ten director Edward Dmytryk reversed an earlier refusal to respond to questioning by naming twenty-six former associates as Communists. Dmytryk said that the Hiss conviction and the Korean War had convinced him that party members might be recruited to commit treason. He also condemned the vanguard's methods of infiltration and thought control. "The battle for freedom of thought" in Hollywood's Communist community, Dmytryk told readers of the *Saturday Evening Post,* "had been twisted into a conspiracy of silence."[2]

Budd Schulberg, a successful screenwriter and novelist, appeared before HUAC in May 1951 to acknowledge Communist activities in the late-1930s and to name fifteen associates as former party members. Like Dmytryk, Schulberg attributed totalitarian tendencies to a movement he described as overly disciplined, manipulative, and regimented. In April 1952, film director Elia Kazan spoke of his Depression-era Communist Party membership and named eight members of a movement theater group to which he had belonged. Apologizing for earlier testimony that withheld names, Kazan warned that secrecy only served the Communists. Subsequent appearances by screenwriters Isobel Lennart and Roy Huggins included admissions that the two ex-Communists had lent themselves to a cause that appeared mainly to serve the interests of the Soviet Union. As Victor Navasky has suggested in an authoritative treatment of the subject, HUAC's ritual of naming names served to enforce a state-sanctioned exorcism of political deviance. Yet confessions by former Communists also helped to soothe anxieties about the questionable agenda and allegiances of influential knowledge elites and political intellectuals.[3]

Discomfort with the intelligentsia became an important ingredient of national politics as the popular General Dwight D. Eisenhower restored Republican stewardship of the White House in the 1952 presidential election. Eisenhower won an easy victory over the cerebral Adlai E. Stevenson, the Democratic governor of Illinois who had once served as a minor New Deal official. As Republicans once again took control of both houses of Congress, HUAC directly confronted the issue of high-minded subversion with a widely publicized investigation in 1953 into the alleged Communist ties of Harvard University's prestigious faculty. Stunned by public fears concerning ideological penetration of the classroom, most academic institutions disregarded the First Amendment rights of faculty by accepting the findings of congressional probes, submitting to hiring blacklists, and dismissing professors unwilling to renounce former or present Communist associations.[4]

Amid Cold War reverses, fears of subversion, and accusations of espionage among the intelligentsia, the stakes concerning loyalty were highest in the scientific community. Physicists had produced the atomic bomb that ended World War II in a top-secret project at Los Alamos, New Mexico. In September 1949, however, President Truman revealed that the Soviet Union had exploded its own nuclear device. Just after Truman announced plans to build a hydrogen bomb in early 1950, British authorities brought espionage charges against Klaus Fuchs, a German refugee physicist who acknowledged that he had given the Soviets atom bomb plans while working at wartime Los Alamos. A chain of further disclosures culminated in the arrest of two American Communist Party members, Julius and Ethel Rosenberg, who were tried for atomic espionage, convicted, and executed in June 1953.[5]

Historian Ellen W. Schrecker has described the Los Alamos laboratory as the scene of a cultural conflict between independent, radical-minded scientists, and military intelligence officers seeking to prevent leaks of wartime information. The bitter animosity between physicists and security officials resurfaced in November 1953, when William L. Borden, former executive director of the Joint Congressional Committee on Atomic Energy, sent the FBI a letter charging that J. Robert Oppenheimer, wartime head at Los Alamos, had "more probably than not" served as a Soviet spy. Raised as a secular Jew in an affluent New York family, Oppenheimer had studied quantum mechanics in Europe and at Harvard in the 1920s. A popular physics professor at the University of California at Berkeley during the Depression, he supported progressive causes embracing farmworkers, faculty unionization, and the Communist-backed struggle in the Spanish Civil War. Following his Los Alamos service, Oppenheimer was appointed to the General Advisory Committee of the Atomic Energy Commission (AEC), which elected him chair in 1947.[6]

Borden charged that Oppenheimer had been a monthly contributor to and organizer for the Communist Party before 1942; that his wife, brother, mistress, and close friends had been Communists; that the physicist knowingly had employed party members at Los Alamos; that he had frequent contact with Soviet espionage agents; and that he had given false information about his past to superiors. Borden also asserted that Oppenheimer had tried to block work on the hydrogen bomb following World War II. When President Eisenhower responded to the allegations by ordering the suspension of Oppenheimer's security clearance, the scientist asked for a loyalty-security hearing. After four weeks of closed door sessions ending in June 1954, the Personnel Security Board of the Atomic Energy Commission found Oppenheimer to be loyal but voted, 2 to 1, to label him a security risk. On appeal, the full AEC confirmed the administrator's loyalty, 4 to 1, but upheld the removal of his security clearance by the same margin.[7]

The Oppenheimer case raised important questions about the privileges of the policy elite and the standards by which its members were to be judged. Air Force leaders told the review board that the physicist had opposed the buildup of postwar strategic air power, discouraged the use of nuclear-powered aircraft, argued against the development of thermonuclear weapons, and sought the internationalization of atomic energy. According to colleague Edward Teller, Oppenheimer hoped to curb the nuclear arms race by limiting the size of weaponry and by stressing the use of tactical atomic devices. Fearful that toleration of such views invited political reprisals against the nuclear program, AEC chair Lewis L. Strauss had worked for Oppenheimer's removal by arranging for FBI wiretaps on the scientist, by placing unfriendly witnesses before the review panel, and by stacking the composition of the board itself. Meanwhile, the Eisenhower administration recognized the need to respond to the inquiry in a resolute manner to prevent any exploitation of the case by Joe McCarthy or others.[8]

Although officials like Strauss had political motivations for opposing Oppenheimer, the denial of clearance also rested on reasonable grounds. The physicist's conduct and associations since 1942, concluded the Personnel Security Board, reflected a serious disregard for the security system. Arguing that Oppenheimer had shown "a suceptibility to influence" with intelligence implications, the panel cited FBI files indicating that the Los Alamos administrator had associated with known Communists during the war and promoted the hiring of former students with Communist backgrounds. More damaging, Oppenheimer falsely had denied his own party activity and withheld from investigators information concerning a wartime associate's attempt to recruit him for Soviet espionage. The high-powered consultant gave the FBI further details about his past associations in 1946 and went before a closed session of HUAC three years later to name a former student as a Communist. Yet public statements about his political background and personal ties appeared inconsistent with sworn testimony on these matters.[9]

The most disturbing aspect of the Oppenheimer case was the Personnel Security Board's conclusion that the physicist had been less than candid when appearing before it. The review committee particularly objected to Oppenheimer's contention that he had opposed a crash program to develop the hydgrogen bomb in 1949 on tactical grounds when documentation suggested that he had objected to the project's concept, not merely its timing. Such inconsistencies led the board to express concerns about Oppenheimer's motives and character. The AEC reinforced these judgments on appeal when it ruled that the scientist was a security risk because of "fundamental defects in his character" and continued associations with Communists. By repeatedly exhibiting "a willful disregard of the normal and proper obligations of security," concluded the commission, Oppenheimer had "consistently placed himself outside the rules that govern others."[10]

As historian Barton J. Bernstein has suggested, the Oppenheimer controversy centered on the exceptional treatment the physicist had been afforded by government authorities. Having lied to and occasionally failed to cooperate with investigators and then misrepresented his advice on strategic policy, Oppenheimer nevertheless sought to exempt himself from the loyalty-security standards that applied to lesser government employees. Were academic advisers, expert consultants, and policy elites to be judged by special criteria because their intellectual talents were essential to the state? Although removal of Oppenheimer's security clearance did not mean that all scientists were under attack, it suggested that talented public servants were not entitled to distinctive privileges.[11] Under intense political pressure, the Eisenhower administration felt compelled to demonstrate that members of the political class would not be exempt from the discipline and loyalty standards required by Cold War solidarity and by popular distaste for communism.

***

As historian James Gilbert and sociologist Edward A. Shils have explained, Cold War scientific experts and administrators were special targets of public anxiety.

Like the evolutionists of the 1920s; physicists and other theoreticians were respected for their technical competence but widely distrusted on moral grounds. The scientific priesthood aroused concern because its iconoclastic secularism and moral neutrality conveyed an aloofness toward prevalent social mores. Nuclear physicists were particularly suspect because their professional culture emphasized international cooperation and knowledge sharing, a position that led Oppenheimer and others to support political projects like world federalism. The tension between moral-political unconventionality and the loyalty required to maintain nuclear security contributed to the widespread unease. Perceived as doctrinaire individuals whose impatience with normal politics facilitated allegiance to internationalism, communism, or other forms of 'highbrow technocracy,' scientists and other intellectuals easily could be portrayed as potential spies or traitors.[12]

The profound chasm between the political class of the governing bureaucracies and congressionally based politicians was dramatically illustrated by the continuing activities of Joe McCarthy. Once the Republican Party regained control of the Senate after 1952, McCarthy garnered the chairmanship of the minor Committee on Government Operations, a position he used to appoint himself head of a Permanent Subcommittee on Investigations. Using the power of committee subpoenas, the Wisconsin senator cleverly mounted a wholesale attack on the continued tenure of alleged subversives and Communist sympathizers in federal employment. Like the Oppenheimer hearings, the McCarthy inquiries placed knowledge class assertions of cultural and ideological autonomy against populist demands that sociopolitical elites conform to society's core values and beliefs.[13]

Committed anticommunists like McCarthy believed that the world view and sympathies of the liberal secular elite rendered it unfit to lead a free society. In *The Lattimore Story*, a biting polemic published in 1953, journalist John Flynn claimed that U.S. foreign policy had fallen under the control of "an alien web of intrigue, artifice, and deceit." Rejecting patriotism as a "social vice" and placing faith in the emancipatory potential of Soviet brotherhood, high-ranking government officials and agents supposedly had joined with eminent educators to promote Stalinist policies and cooperate with subversive elements. Long jealous of executive-branch intellectuals and advisers, many members of Congress welcomed the opportunity to demonstrate the contamination of communism on such individuals. Acknowledging that subversion and conspiracy were states of mind, ideologues like McCarthy and Pat McCarran nevertheless claimed that America's inability to stop Soviet and Chinese advances was a result of collusion between Communists and the politicized knowledge sector at home.[14]

McCarthy insisted that the Subcommittee on Permanent Investigations sought to overcome continuing government corruption and inefficiency by publicizing confidential information about subversives and "fifth-amendment Communists" still working in federal agencies. During the first year of his chairmanship, the panel conducted 157 investigations, 445 preliminary inquiries, and

1,745 interviews, 215 of the latter in public session. Initial efforts concerned government publicity and propaganda, a vital matter in a cold war embracing nonmilitary modes of struggle in which the loyalty of the knowledge elite was particularly important. McCarthy first targeted the Voice of America (VOA), an overseas radio news network run by the State Department's International Information Agency (IIA). Yet the inquiry fizzled when committee staffers found no evidence of subversion and were compelled to limit testimony to tidbits of political philosophy from the distant past of VOA officials.[15]

The panel's attention soon turned to the presence of books by Communists and fellow travelers in the IIA's Overseas Library Program. After committee counsel Roy Cohn and aide G. David Schine compiled a list of questionable authors during a highly publicized tour of the agency's European libraries, Louis Budenz and other witnesses testified about the Communist backgrounds of the targeted writers. McCarthy claimed that State Department libraries contained over thirty thousand books by known Communists, party sympathizers, or pro-Soviet propagandists. He asserted that three hundred had been written by people with Communist front records, and that twenty-one of the authors had invoked Fifth Amendment protections in congressional testimony. Protesting that the presence of such works indicated government approval of the authors, McCarthy subpoenaed a list of writers including mystery novelist Dashiell Hammett and Marxist historians Herbert Aptheker and Philip Foner. A fourth target, newspaper editor James Wechsler, had produced two of the books in overseas libraries while a short-lived member of the Young Communist League in the 1930s.[16]

With few results from his forays into State Department information programs, McCarthy opened an investigation into the Fort Monmouth Army Signal Corps Engineering Laboratories, the base where Julius Rosenberg worked during World War II. Once again, the best the senator could muster was an expose of the past associations and personal beliefs of civilian personnel. Yet McCarthy used the pretext of the loyalty-security inquiry to harangue his favorite adversaries. When Nathan Pusey, a Wisconsin college president, moderate Republican, and McCarthy critic, assumed the helm of Harvard University in the summer of 1953, the senator denounced Pusey as a snobbish phony and anti-anti-Communist. In the fall, the McCarthy subcommittee subpoenaed Harvard physicist Wendell Furry as part of the Fort Monmouth investigation, although the scientist never had worked at the laboratory. Following an executive session with Furry, the Wisconsin senator went out of his way to characterize the Ivy League bastion as "a smelly mess," a disreputable institution in which students were subject to indoctrination by Communist professors.[17]

Using the testimony of Louis Budenz, McCarthy criticized Army intelligence studies such as "Psychological and Cultural Traits of Soviet Siberia" for relying on the work of Communist and pro-Soviet writers like Harvard graduate Corliss Lamont. The senator also threatened to expose alleged Communist sympathies among Ivy Leaguers in the Central Intelligence Agency. Yet McCarthy attracted

the greatest attention when he took on the bureaucratic ridigity and faceless
depersonalization of the modern military. The immediate pretext for this confrontation was the subcomittee's investigation of Army loyalty procedures. Late
in 1953, McCarthy discovered that an Army dentist named Irving Peress had
been promoted to major and then honorably discharged despite the fact that
intelligence officials previously had recommended his dismissal for subversive
and disloyal tendencies. Hauling the dentist's commanding officer before his
panel in Feburary 1954, McCarthy complained that any general who protected
those who shielded Communists was not fit to wear his uniform.[18]

The stand-off between the Wisconsin senator and the U.S. Army led to an
explosive series of televised hearings in 1954 in which each side noisily accused
the other of bad faith and abuse of power. McCarthy relentlessly attacked military
leaders as soulless paper pushers who refused to take personal responsibility for
their actions. At one point the senator objected to a brief described as "Filed
by Department of Army," protesting that the document merely was the work
of Pentagon politicians who hid behind the Army title. McCarthy also refused
to reveal the names of civil servants who supposedly had provided him with
confidential files. He complimented those who passed on information despite
the fact that "some little bureaucrat" had stamped it 'secret' to defend himself.
There was no loyalty to a superior officer, stated McCarthy, that could prevent
federal employees from exposing the government's record of graft, corruption,
communism, and treason.[19]

McCarthy's denigration of agency heads and bureau chiefs reflected the lin-
gering suspicion that untrustworthy bureaucrats had subverted Washington's
administrative apparatus. Suspected since the early New Deal of reliance on
expertise at the expense of common sense, the governing class was highly vulnerable due to its perceived habits of secrecy and its aversion to legislative
scrutiny. Although McCarthy was a demagogue who often pursued crude and
unwarranted confrontations for their own sake, his radical and class-conscious
version of anticommunism cleverly targeted the weaknesses of the political-
ized knowledge sector. Congressional critics like the Republican senator sensed
that government social management had undemocratic, even totalitarian, implications. Similarities between liberal and communist social engineering, for
example, gave further credence to the far-fetched suggestion that the United
States was turning toward the Soviet model. Yet as Richard Hofstadter suggested, communism was not McCarthy's target but his weapon. Beneath the
senator's bluster lay a call for revenge against the perceived political and cultural
dominance of the nation's post-1932 elite.[20]

***

Although Joe McCarthy did not lead a mass movement, the Wisconsin senator could make claim to a broad following. As late as January 1954, Gallup
polls assigned the bombastic anticommunist a 50 percent favorable rating

(29 percent unfavorable, 21 percent no opinion). A national figure in Cold War politics, McCarthy offered a mesage that reached beyond the traditional Republican constituents of his home state. Portraying communism and New Dealism as products of the socially and politically privileged instead of the working class, McCarthy identified himself with a culturally infused brand of anti-establishment populism. Although anticommunists rejected the statist agenda associated with industrial workers and their reformist allies, popular figures like McCarthy fashioned their own version of class warfare by questioning the moral legitimacy of Washington's key policy intellectuals and public administrators. Admittedly, the unpredictable solon overreached himself during the Army-McCarthy hearings when he antagonized both the revered military and a popular president of his own political party. In December 1954, Senate colleagues voted, 67 to 22, to censure the Wisconsin Republican for conduct deemed contrary to the body's rules, traditions, and standards of decorum, effectively ending his political career.[21] Nevertheless, the ideological war on knowledge professionals resonated throughout the 1950s.

The tension between elected politicians and Washington policy intellectuals surfaced in dramatic form during the highly publicized controversies over John Stewart Service, Alger Hiss, and Owen Lattimore. In each case, congressional probes led to apparent connections between the Truman State Department, prestigious universities, favored think tanks, and tax-exempt foundations. Spurred by Hiss's former presidency of the Carnegie Endowment for International Peace, McCarran committee investigators revealed that the contentious Lattimore had been one of the beneficiaries of the foundation's financial generosity. They also disclosed that the Rockefeller Foundation had contributed to the support of the suspect Institute of Pacific Relations over a twenty-five year period. When Georgia Democrat and anti-New Dealer Edward E. Cox chaired a select House committee investigation of tax-exempt foundations in 1952, the panel concluded that subversives had penetrated the administrative hierarchies of the charities and often directed funding to like-minded associates.[22]

Following Cox's death and the assumption of Republican control of Congress in 1953, Tennessee's Brazilla Carroll Reece, a former economics professor, proposed to expand the investigation. American communism and socialism were financed by "a diabolical conspiracy" that used industrial fortunes to finance capitalism's destruction, charged Reece. When the House voted, 209 to 162, to organize a new select committee to explore the relationship between multimillion dollar foundation funding and the formation of public policy and social attitudes, Republican leaders named their Tennessee colleague as chair.[23]

Hearings began in May 1954 with a series of foundation critics. The most controversial testimony emerged from the two-day appearance of committee research director, Norman Dodd. A career investment adviser interested in the influence of education and finance on social concepts, Dodd had been recruited by Reece panel counsel, René A. Wormser. Releasing a staff report based on six months of study, Dodd argued that tax-exempt foundations were financing ideas and practices incompatible with the fundamental concepts of the Constitution. By building up the social sciences, he contended, charities such as the Rockefeller Foundation and the Carnegie Endowment were creating a form of mass education that threatened to alter American thought. Dodd cited internationalism, centralized government, the adoption of antitraditional curricula, and the politicalization of classroom learning as essential aspects of the new agenda. The ultimate purpose, he insisted, was the wholesale abdication of education to social purposes.[24]

Reece committee investigators believed that institutional sponsorship of the social sciences concentrated educational authority under the control of organizations and persons little known to the American public. Foundations, educational bodies, and government agencies formed a triangle of influences, asserted the staff report. The alleged aim of professors, politicians, and attorneys was to adjust citizens to the idea of planning and an evolving collectivism. To bolster his analysis, Dodd cited a 1934 report of the American Historical Association's Commission on Social Studies which had envisioned an "age of transition" in which people would abandon the "popular faith in economic individualism" and accept the "consciously integrated society" and "new social order" of the future.[25]

The week following Dodd's appearance brought the testimony of Albert H. Hobbs, an assistant professor of sociology at the University of Pennyslvania, and the author of *Social Problems and Scientism* (1953), a critical look at social science methodology. Hobbs observed that foundation-sponsored scholarship concentrated on empiricism, which he described as an experiment-centered form of research whose conclusions often were derived from manipulated or computed statistics. Arguing that the adoption of materialist methods involved a suspension of moral standards and principles, the sociologist discussed the controversial works of Alfred C. Kinsey and Stuart Chase.[26]

Kinsey's initial study on male sexual behavior, published in book form in 1948, had been financed by a Rockefeller Foundation grant administered through the National Research Council of the National Academy of Sciences. But Hobbs contended that the biologist's conclusions concerning the widespread incidence of male extramarital sex did not follow the data collected by his research team. Criticizing Kinsey for adopting pseudoscientific techniques by projecting the results of a poorly selected sample of 5,300 interviews to the entire population of men, Hobbs insisted that the study merely had shown that certain forms of sexual activity sometimes occurred among some individuals. More to the point, the sociologist questioned the assumption that traditional sexual codes were mere rationalizations, while homosexuality and extramarital relations were normal and legitimate. Hobbs also scored the results of a second Kinsey study that concluded that premarital sexual experience taught women to adjust emotionally to various types of men and to improve the overall effectiveness of their social relationships.[27]

Hobbs sharply disputed the tendency of journalists and academics to invoke Kinsey's interpretations when implying that controversial changes in social and moral values were rooted in scientific fact. Citing a *Harper's* article that claimed that the report's startling revelations "would be unbelievable but for the impressive weight of the scientific agencies backing the survey," the sociologist questioned whether Kinsey's research should become the basis of fundamental changes in social behavior and mores. To illustrate the problem, Hobbs pointed to a psychologist's review in *Scientific Monthly* of Kinsey's first study which blandly concluded that "current laws do not comply with the biologic facts of normal sexual behavior."[28]

The Reece committee witness used the popular economist, Stuart Chase, to illustrate the manner by which social scientists supposedly masked the advancement of a sociopolitical agenda with academic scholarship. Supported by research grants from the Social Science Research Council and the Carnegie Corporation, Chase had published *The Proper Study of Mankind* in 1948. According to Hobbs, the book was based on the principle of scientism—the point of view that science could solve all problems and take the place of tradition, belief, and religion. Hobbs held that the economist subscribed to the cultural lag theory—the notion that beliefs, ideas, and sentiments about the family, church, and government should be brought up to date with technology. The sociologist attributed to Chase a model in which individual beliefs and actions were determined by the social environment, one in which humans were puppets of culture. By manipulating society, argued Hobbs, social scientists like Chase believed that they could change human nature to lay the groundwork for collectivization and social planning.[29]

***

The controversial nature of the Dodd report and the Hobbs testimony produced a firestorm of protest inside and outside of the Reece committee. Panelist Wayne L. Hays, an Ohio Democrat, criticized the staff for issuing a document based on preexisting conclusions. The Dodd report, charged the research director of the American Jewish Committee's commission on community relations, was irresponsible and prejudiced and attempted to politicize scientific inquiries into human behavior. Hays and other critics noted that the Reece committee had issued a report on foundation behavior before holding public hearings and had limited testimony to a small group of hand-picked witnesses. After the Ohio representative forced a two-week suspension of hearings in mid-June, the committee voted, 3 to 2, to confine the remainder of the inquiry to written statements from foundation representatives.[30]

Partisan bickering guaranteed repudiation of the Reece committee's final report by the panel's two Democrats, who dismissed the account as a "crack-pot view" by those who suffered from "fear sickness." Nevertheless, the document illustrated the depths of the national cultural and class war that pitted social agencies and their academic allies against old-line politicians and advocates of traditional values. The main concern of the Reece committee was not communism, stated the report, but the undermining effect of collectivist movements. It argued that major charitable groups directly supported subversion by undermining productive concepts and principles. Foundations allegedly weakened the social and political system by financing the promotion of socialism and collectivist ideas. As one example, the report cited a history textbook funded by the Rockefeller Foundation that advocated public ownership of banks, key industries, and basic natural resources. The *Final Report* also accused foundation projects of denigrating American nationalism in favor of internationalist creeds.[31]

The Reece committee pictured the Ford, Carnegie, and Rockefeller foundations as part of an intellectual cartel that threatened thought control in government, education, and politics. Foundations formed an interlock through mutual operations, interchanging personnel, and shared directorates. By supplying executives and advisers to federal agencies, foundation leaders allegedly were in a position to formulate government research policies and steer contracts to favored social scientists. Along with the leaders of intermediary research organizations, the executives of major foundations were said to constitute an "effective *elite*" with virtual control of the nation's intellectual direction. As a professional class of administrators, foundation officials supposedly used the disbursement of funds to further their own position and influence. By utilizing selective patronage, preference, and privilege, concluded the panel, managers could impel finance-starved social science researchers to legitimize policies and projects they favored.[32]

The Reece report noted that the Ford Foundation devoted nearly all its $500 million capital to social science research. The enormous power and immense influence of grant money, argued investigators, promoted uniformity in a field highly vulnerable to bias and error, tending to induce educators to become agents for social change and propagandists for collectivism. The report suggested that the tentative results of social science scholarship were often promoted for the purpose of altering the opinion of the intellectual professions and the public. Reece staffers accepted the argument that empiricists and quantitative researchers monopolized the study of society. They criticized the prevalence of models of causality based on materialistic and deterministic concepts of human behavior as a type of intellectual nepotism. Associating such notions with Marxism, the *Final Report* expressed little surprise that social scientists veered toward collectivism and doubt concerning the validity of moral precepts.[33]

For Reece committee investigators, the most notorious characteristic of empiricism was ethical relativism. They noted that, by basing conclusions solely on sensory observation, social scientists relied on an empirical method which ignored moral precepts, principles, and accepted norms of behavior. Quantitative research paid no attention to cultural traditions or actual experience with people, Albert Hobbs had testified. The report's authors suggested that, by validating a social engineering approach to human life, social scientists conveyed the impression that they alone were capable of guiding the nation's people into better ways of living and improved principles of action.[34]

The promulgation of relativist theories, concluded the Reece report, dissolved "the religious basis of ethics and the Fundamental principles of democratic government." Recycling the brief against cultural elites and academics that dated back to the early years of the century, investigators warned "that there is a strong tendency on the part of many of the social scientists whose research is favored by the major foundations toward the concept that there are no absolutes, that everything is indeterminate, that no standards of conduct, morals, ethics, and government are to be deemed inviolate, that everything, including basic moral law, is subject to change, and that it is the part of the social scientists to take no principle for granted as a premise in social or juridicial reasoning."[35]

Did Americans wish "to permit the *'best minds'* . . . virtual control of intellectual direction in our country?" the Reece panel asked in its final document. Committee counsel René Wormser condemned the foundations as supporters of change for its own sake. By attempting to destroy national institutions and values before society had agreed on substitutes, charged Wormser, the powerful agencies were guilty of a pathological rejection of the judgment of most Americans. Wormser blamed "fog-bound intellectuals" for leading the foundations astray. Remote from economic realities, impractical, and alienated from business enterprise, social scientists and academic allies were subject to collectivist and revolutionary fashions of thought. In turn, privileged members of the intelligentsia received financial backing for their sociopolitical agenda through well-placed research grants and subsidized educational experiments.[36]

Concerned that foundations disguised political undertakings as tax-exempt educational activity, the Reece committee recommended that Congress deny tax exclusions to any charity organization holding more than 5 to 10 percent of its capital in the securities of a single enterprise. The *Final Report* also proposed that the federal government place a trustee on every foundation board. Amid protests of unfairness in the investigation and cries that politicians were attempting to exert thought control on private institutions and researchers, the House Ways and Means Committee failed to act on foundation reform.[37] Like William Jennings Bryan's assault on scientific elites in the 1920s and congressional probes into political dissent during World War II and after, the Reece inquiry proved insensitive to the requirements of intellectual freedom and leaned toward conspiratorial models. Nevertheless, the investigation clearly demonstrated how the sensibilities and interests of social service professionals and knowledge elites continued to collide with career politicians and others who identified with the legacies of traditional morality and economic individualism.

***

One of the most remarkable instances of conflict between 1950s social guardians and their critics came in the controversial field of public health. Since the first years of the twentieth century, groups such as the American Medical Liberty League had attacked the arbitrary power of organized physicians and demanded the participation of lay persons on state health boards and bureaus. In 1916, Oregon activist Lora C. Little campaigned for a ballot measure banning compulsory vaccination against smallpox, a procedure she pictured as unnecessary and involving poisonous toxins. Little warned against arrogant health professionals and "the learning that vaunts itself and proposes to tyrannize over the common sense of the common people." Although state health officials and opinion makers viewed the referendum as a test of scientific expertise, the measure passed in the county incorporating Portland, Oregon's largest city, and lost statewide by a mere 374 votes. Antivaccination campaigns soon took place in Toledo, Ohio; Rochester, New York; Kansas City, Missouri; Milwaukee, Wisconsin; and Providence, Rhode Island, culminating in an effort to block compulsory innoculation of U.S. soldiers during World War I.[38]

By the 1950s, fluoridation of municipal water supplies had become the issue of choice for critics of the medical establishment. Researchers with the Aluminum Company of America had discovered during the 1930s that the chemical fluorine discolored yet somehow strengthened teeth. Beginning in 1944, the U.S. Public Health Service (USPHS) sought to determine if fluorine reduced tooth decay by adding one part per million of the substance to the water systems of Grand Rapids, Michigan; Newburgh, New York; and Madison, Wisconsin. When the USPHS declared the experiment a success in 1950, the American Dental Association (ADA) endorsed fluoridation. The following year, the American Medical Association (AMA) approved the practice, as did the Children's Bureau and several federal social service agencies. As local health professionals took the lead in the crusade to fluoridate public drinking water, seventy-two cities with populations over ten thousand adopted the procedure in 1952. By the end of the decade, nearly one-third the nation's municipalities had fluoridated water systems.[39]

Although fluoridation won the support of local physicians, dentists, public health officials, newspaper publishers, educators, scientists, businesspeople, and civic leaders, the program quickly ran into bitter criticism from an assortment of grass-roots activists. The first rebellion occurred in September 1950 when voters in Stevens Point, Wisconsin rejected a fluoridation referendum by nearly 2 to 1. As the antifluoridation campaign took on national parameters two years later, the city of Seattle turned down a fluoride proposal by even greater proportions.

In La Crosse, Wisconsin, a measure to fluoridate public water supplies received less than 20 percent approval in 1954. Two years later, voters in Portland, Oregon defeated a fluoridation referendum by a 3 to 1 margin after public opinion polls showed the measure attracting twice as many supporters as opponents. By the time New York City shelved its fluoridation plans in 1957, seventy-five cities, including San Diego, Akron, and Baton Rouge, had abandoned the experiment after brief trials. Between 1950 and 1961, voters rejected fluoridated water in 60 percent of six hundred municipal referenda.[40]

Fluoridation opponents included dissenting physicians and dentists, Christian Scientists, health food advocates, naturopathic practitioners, and chiropractors. These critics depicted fluoride as a dangerous poison when found in concentrated quantities and warned that treated water might produce additional perils yet undiscovered. One of the early activists in the movement was Dr. Frederick B. Exner, a Seattle radiologist who had lectured on medical ethics and economics at the University of Washington Medical School and served six terms as secretary of the Association of American Physicians and Surgeons. Despite support for fluoridation by the Seattle branch of the American Dental Association, the city health director, and the municipal council, Exner helped to defeat the city's 1952 fluoridation referendum by describing the procedure as a hoax that brought increased probabilities of heart disease, cancer, and diabetes.[41]

Days before the Seattle referendum, the U.S. House of Representatives conducted hearings on the fluoridation controversy. Organized in 1950 under the chairmanship of New York Democrat James J. Delaney, the "Select Committee to Investigate the Use of Chemicals in Food and Cosmetics" now received testimony from proponents and adversaries of the flouride treatment. After hearing positive reports from representatives of the large dental and public health organizations, the panel listened to mildly critical statements from scientists and medical researchers who warned about the hasty use of the chemical as an antidecay agent. Witnesses cautioned that there were sufficient numbers of unanswered safety questions to warrant a conservative approach toward a process involving involuntary medication of entire populations.[42]

The central figure of the Delaney hearings turned out to be committee member Arthur Lewis Miller, a former physician and Nebraska state health officer. In two separate House addresses in March 1952, Miller informed colleagues that scientific experts had testified that fluoridation experiments were not far enough along to evaluate adequately. He was sorely disappointed that the USPHS now advocated that "every single soul in the community" should submit themselves to universal medication by flourine before all experimentation had been completed. The hearings had "sort of opened my eyes to some things I did not know," confessed Miller, who declared that he was "wiser today than yesterday." Two years later, the House Commerce Committee held three days of hearings on a bill to prohibit any government agency from introducing a fluoride compound into the water supply, but panel members decided that fluoridation should remain a local matter and the measure died with adjournment.[43]

The medical community reacted harshly to the Delaney committee's reluctance to embrace the fluoridation crusade. It was archaic and illogical to deny the dental benefits of fluoride to the nation's children, declared the journal of the American Dental Association. The scientific facts about fluoridation spoke for themselves, insisted the editors, and were recognized and accepted by every important national organization concerned with public health. Three years later, the prestigious City Club of Portland, Oregon backed up a fluoridation endorsement by declaring that no valid evidence had indicated that fluorides were harmful. *Chemical Week* dismissed antifluoridation activists in the same year as "a relatively small handful of Americans who have caused a stir out of all proportion to the merits of their arguments." Meanwhile, *Scientific American* recorded the health profession's perception that a "national epidemic of irrationality" and anti-intellectualism was feeding the dispute.[44]

What began as a technically conceived and rationally considered public health measure, wrote social anthropologist Arnold L. Green in 1961, had been transformed into the subject of bitter local disputes across the nation. The emotional controversy over fluoridation, concurred sociologist Robert L. Crain, was the single issue of greatest dissension in American cities of the 1950s and 1960s. Although opponents entered campaigns on an unorganized basis, with few political qualifications or supporters among civic groups or governmental officials, they nevertheless succeeded in sustaining long and noisy crusades that often brought victory. The results infuriated some, leading *Consumer Reports* to describe the controversy in 1978 as "one of the major triumphs of quackery over science in our generation." Studied in more detail than perhaps any community health measure of the twentieth century, the struggle to fluoridate public water supplies intrigued analysts as an issue that refused to obey traditional political rules.[45]

***

Public opinion specialists have suggested that the outcome of fluoridation referenda frequently depended on the political organization of municipalities, and included such factors as the degree of centralized authority and the disposition of community leaders toward change. The more people involved, the less chance of adoption, noted political scientist James Q. Wilson. Voters also hesitated to support fluoridation proposals when civic and elected officials refused to take a stand on the issue or when communities lacked a special constituency with a deep commitment to the cause beyond the abstract appeal of progress. With no means of assessing the power of the opposition, moreover, local governments tended to remain neutral on issues like fluoridation when criticism arose.

Although the matter posed little risk to individual careers, elected politicians seldom invested energy in a concern that generated modest political reward and considerable controversy.[46]

Such explanations may help to explain the electoral success of antifluoridation measures. Yet they do not offer an understanding of the commitment of the movement's leaders nor of the emotional effectiveness of the imagery they employed. As Arnold Green noted in 1961, fluoride opponents defied the experts by insisting that infusion of the chemical in public water supplies posed a substantive threat of poisoning. Rather than the embodiment of individual fantasies, the poison argument was shared by many of those who rallied to the antifluoridation cause. Yet Green maintained that the obsession over toxicity was best understood symbolically. Poisoning involved an attempt by an external force with malicious intent to deceive a human target and render it weak, helpless, and totally under control. Significantly, the victim was unable to identify the specific danger or locate its source. Those most sensitive and responsive to the poison symbolism, suggested Green, felt victimized and manipulated in crucial areas of life and feared that their autonomy and integrity as individuals were under severe attack.[47]

Green reported that fluoridation opponents who did not focus on literal health dangers remained intrigued by the metaphor of poisoning. Fluoride critics were convinced that there were disguised motives for initiating a program that was neither urgently necessary nor entirely safe. Antifluoridation activists feared the loss of individual rights concerning free choice and the right to decide what might be ingested into their bodies. "It's just the beginning of something much bigger to come," a Massachusetts movement leader told an interviewer. "Pretty soon they'll have people eating the same sort of thing."[48] Rather than expressing general anxieties about personal autonomy in modern society, however, fluoridation opponents specifically targeted the scientific community, the public health profession, and government bureaucrats as the hidden forces behind society's evils.

As Robert Crain indicated, overzealous proponents may have contributed to the dissension over fluoridation in the early 1950s by seeking to obtain adoption by local communities before scientific research clearly supported the program. By the time the medical community embraced fluoridated water, however, opponents had organized a nationwide campaign that treated endorsements by health experts with severe mistrust. Public opinion scholars of the 1950s suggested that ordinary people saw scientists as strange and distant persons whose lack of common sense and whose abstract reasoning made them difficult to comprehend and trust. Consequently, lay persons found it easy to believe that scientists might lend themselves to nefarious conspiracies. Since fluoridation adversaries tended to see the world as menacing, it was not surpising that they were significantly more likely to express unfavorable evaluations of scientific elites than were supporters.[49]

Antifluoridation rhetoric pictured water treatment programs as the product of a public health bureaucracy bent on regimentation. "Face to face with an overbearing man like him," a movement leader said of a USPHS official, "it gives the feeling of what it's like to be in Russia or Hitler . . . it gets to be a matter of compulsion. . . . The individual can be swallowed up, could be lost, ridiculed, misunderstood." Fluoridation was chemical rape, a Springfield, Massachusetts dentist told a House committee in 1954, an experiment conducted by "Godless medical tehnocrats" and imposed on communities through the thought control methods of modern public relations. Resentment toward scientific elites surfaced in descriptions of ordinary people as guinea pigs entrapped by government programs of mass medication, experimentation, and random treatment of whole populations. The idea of the greatest good to the greatest number, protested Seattle dentist Frederick Exner, was "decided by 'experts' who compel others to behave accordingly" and who used fluoridation as a legal precedent for compulsory medication.[50]

The controversy over fluoridated water afforded ordinary Americans the opportunity to express deep misgivings about the inordinate power of scientific experts, distant bureaucrats, and remote government officials. As a social psychologist noted in 1961, fluoridation symbolized "the buffeting one takes in a society where not even the water one drinks is sacrosanct" and where large and powerful organizations pursued their own aggrandizement and ability to control people. Polled a week before a 1953 referendum in Northampton, Massachusetts, 82 percent of fluoride opponents stated that water commissioners had not adequately consulted residents and had rigged public hearings. Ninety-three percent of the sample said that individuals should not be forced to drink something without their consent. Public authorities should not "arrogate to themselves the right to decide for all people what is good for them," an activist protested to the *New York Times* in 1957.[51]

The fluoridation issue reached deep into 1950s politics. Researchers found that fluoride opponents in Fairfield, California were less favorable than supporters toward racial integration of public schools and internationalist foreign policies. Connections with anticommunism were more blatant. Fluoride advocates in Northampton, Massachusetts more often criticized Joe McCarthy than opponents. Golda Franzen, a San Francisco homemaker and antifluoridation activist, claimed that the Communist-inspired process would result in "moronic, atheistic slaves" and weaken people's minds. In Michigan, an antifluoride lobby insisted that the Public Health Service's "vicious attempts to keep the people from voting on socialized medicine and against a Federal health dictatorship" were another manifestation of communism. "If we are to have freedom here in America," declared the group, "people should be permitted to eat, drink, wear, and live where they wish." Republican House member Clare Hoffman placed the organization's statements in the *Congressional Record* in 1954.[52]

Fluoridation had amazing staying power as a public controversy. In New York City, where a national committee led by pediatrician Dr. Benjamin Spock promoted the plan, the water commissioner reversed a positive recommendation by the municipal board of health in 1956. Following boisterous hearings the next year, the Board of Estimate once again put off the decision to fluoridate. Finally, after a second round of testimony and support from the City Council, the Board approved fluoridation in December 1963. In Portland, Oregon, supporters failed to get sufficient signatures to qualify for a municipal ballot measure in 1964 but succeeded in amending the city charter to permit fluoridation in 1978. Yet a 1980 county initiative repealed the city amendment and led to a law suit by fluoride opponents charging that county commissioners illegally had used federal funds to run election campaign advertisements providing information on fluoridated water.[53]

By the 1970s, antifluoridation activists had abandoned earlier arguments and insisted that the compound was linked to cancer. The new allegations were rejected by the scientific community with the same vehemence induced by earlier charges. In 1975, the World Health Organization reported that "the only sign of physiological or pathological change in life-long users of optimally fluoridated water supplies" was less tooth decay. The excesses of antifluoride rhetoric led scientists and their allies to question whether society could permit lay persons to influence complex and technical issues requiring trained expertise. Yet the campaign for pure water conveyed an unresolved distrust of academic experts and policymakers that accurately reflected key tensions in American society. As early as 1953, political scientist Alan Keith-Lucas pointed to the problems associated with the concentration of social expertise in a special class of consultants and practitioners. The danger lay in the fact that once positivist science became the rule of law, or once a group took on the right to treat others by scientific findings, no adequate checks remained to control the experts. Keith-Lucas saw an unsettling connection between the increased knowledge of "the self-appointed 'social physician'" and the assertion of "a benevolent or paternal dictatorship" by doctors over patients.[54]

The contradictions exacerbating class conflict between professional elites and those they served were examined in a 1961 analysis of the fluoridation controversy by Harvard School of Public Health researcher Arnold Green. Green reminded readers that power in the United States was dangerously concentrated in distant centers and enriched itself through "the exercise of coercive authority, hidden behind a baffling screen of vast government bureaucracies and giant corporations." Deception had become a practiced art in public affairs, he noted, an arena in which actual motives rarely were revealed by professed reasons. With individuals increasingly manipulated, the scope of personal initiative steadily contracted. Society was moving to an end that would find most people totally dependent on impersonal agencies, he concluded. As a result, a mood of despair and estrangement pervaded common citizens and led them to recover by striking out at perceived agents of discontent.[55]

Beyond framing the battle over fluoridation, Green's sensitivity to power-lessness and alienation helped to explain the larger struggle between modern society's knowledge elites and traditionally minded constituencies. Although opponents of expert rule and scientific prerogative often resorted to unreason-able arguments, hyperbole, and partisan posturing, the core of their concerns related to the state of the democratic process. Unsubstantiated allegations of Communist influence and unwarranted concerns about U.S. security against foreign subversion thereby functioned as metaphorical references to the intru-sion of remote elites in the lives of ordinary people and their congressional representatives. As Americans moved into the 1960s, new divisions over race relations and social policy would preoccupy the nation's attention. Neverthe-less, social interventionists and political intellectuals would continue to play a dominant role in public controversies. In fact, additional conflicts served to harden existing tensions between experts and guardians who wielded new forms of power and influence and those seeking to retain the legitimacy of older forms.

7
Zero Sum Governance: Social Interventionists and Race Politics, 1954–1968

Complaining to Senate Majority Leader Lyndon B. Johnson in 1957 of intolerable government impositions upon the nation's citizenry, a woman from Tyler, Texas named fluoride poisoning and the forced mixing of the races as the two leading threats to American liberty.[1] The juxtaposition of these seemingly diverse concerns hinted at the sense of powerlessness and alienation some Americans brought to the social and political arena. With far more implications than the fluoridation issue, the nationwide controversy over federal involvement in race relations and antipoverty policy between 1954 and 1968 called attention to the strategic role of the political intelligentsia in public life. As white reformers within the sociopolitical sector embraced demands by African Americans and other activists for racial and economic justice, opponents retorted with populist attacks on Washington bureaucracy, outcries against government social experiment, and protests about the assumed hegemony of liberal planners and social interventionists. Chapter 7 examines the context and significance of such rhetoric, with particular emphasis on the manner in which 1960s politicians such as George C. Wallace, Barry Goldwater, Ronald Reagan, and Richard Nixon translated a debate over race into one focusing on the trustworthiness, reliability, and intentions of social guardians and New Class insiders.

***

A broad spectrum of white political reformers, social service providers, government administrators, and radical activists long had served as crucial allies in the African-American struggle for racial justice and civil rights. Significantly, the Communist Party was the first predominantly white organization to endorse full racial equality, even calling for the creation of a separate black homeland in the Deep South in the 1920s. Communist lawyers, many of them Jewish, solidified the party's leadership on the race issue by defending the "Scottsboro Boys," nine black Alabama teenagers convicted on contradictory testimony for raping two white prostitutes on a freight train in 1931. Striking at the core of white supremacy, movement attorneys won a dramatic reversal of the verdict by convincing the U.S. Supreme Court that the defendants had been denied a fair trial because Alabama systematically excluded people of color from juries. Communist organizers also defied the southern caste system by enrolling twelve thousand people in the biracial and militant Alabama Share Croppers Union, and by forging the Southern Negro Youth Congress as a civil rights action group. Meanwhile, the Socialist Party mobilized twenty-five thousand followers of both races in the Southern Tenants Farmers Union, and led demonstrations in Arkansas and elsewhere against inferior education, the poll tax, and civil liberties infringements.[2]

New Deal political intellectuals played a major role in reshaping southern race relations in the 1930s. Although Roosevelt administrators and agency heads often deferred to regional notions of white supremacy by segregating government relief and job programs, Washington's huge influence on the economy threatened the stability of the South's social structure. By imposing restrictions on cotton acreage and by offering higher pay scales in government work projects, federal agencies encouraged African Americans to move off the land, away from the control of local elites. Federally sanctioned collective bargaining, which provided an entry into the region for CIO industrial unions, further antagonized white politicians by contributing to pressure for increased wages and by augmenting the potential influence of labor leaders and liberals of both races in the Democratic Party.[3]

Southern fears of outside interference by reformers and political intellectuals increased during World War II, when white liberals in the North committed themselves to the eradication of race prejudice and bigotry as part of the global crusade against Axis creeds of racial supremacy. As northern New Dealers and some industrial labor leaders supported African-American demands for an end to job discrimination in defense work in 1941, President Roosevelt created the Fair Employment Practices Committee (FEPC). During the war, members of the biracial Fellowship for Reconciliation formed the Committee of Racial Equality (CORE), an action group that organized sit-ins to desegregate restaurants and other public facilities in northern and border-state cities. White progressives in the South also joined black activists in mounting a national campaign against the poll tax, a levy that discouraged voting in most southern states by African Americans and other poor people. The evolving alliance between black protesters and white sympathizers became evident in 1944 when Swedish sociologist Gunnar Myrdal published *An American Dilemma*, a 1,500-page study of white racism and discrimination funded by the Carnegie Foundation.[4]

Historians Alan Brinkley and Steven F. Lawson have described how consensus-oriented reformers of the 1940s replaced their commitment to the economic populism and labor solidarity of the Depression era with a rights-based focus on individual entitlements and equal opportunity for racial minorities. Responding to increased African-American voting power in northern cities, President Truman appointed legal experts and human rights specialists to a federal Civil Rights Commission in 1946 and requested permanent status for the wartime Fair Employment Practices Committee. After Minneapolis mayor

Hubert H. Humphrey electrified the Democratic National Convention of 1948 by pleading for an end to political dependence on the white South and by demanding federal civil rights protections in the workplace and military, Truman desegregated the armed forces. As the struggle for racial justice threatened to eclipse the anticommunist crusade by the mid-1950s, white intellectual liberals and social activists took their place as indispensable allies of the movement.[5]

⌐Alan Brinkley and political scientist Jerome L. Himmelstein have noted that white civil rights supporters of the 1950s often derived from a professional or "post-industrial" sector embracing government, education, communications, and information services. Open to sociocultural change, quality of life concerns, enhanced personal freedom, and an idealistic toleration of diversity, progressive elements of the postwar upper-middle class sought an enlightened society that reflected the cosmopolitan values they embraced. By breaking down provincial customs, traditions, and prejudices that impeded rational assessment of individual talents and merit, moreover, Jewish and Roman Catholic professionals joined their Protestant cohorts in replicating a social order that enlarged upon and legitimized their own expertise and rise to cultural prominence.[6]

The cosmopolitan human relations agenda of liberal social interventionists was immensely controversial, however, particularly in the South, where the history of radical, communist, and Jewish involvement in civil rights gave elites the opportunity to ostracize white activists as outside agitators. Social equality for the races was a "socialistic threat," Virginia senator Carter Glass proclaimed in 1937. Support for black voter registration drives by southern CIO affiliates in the 1930s gave credence to the notion that Communist subversives fueled the drive for racial justice and industrial unionism. Southern Democrats alleged Communist Party infiltration in such agencies as the Federal Theater Project and the Office of War Information by pointing to their nondiscriminatory policies or their invocations of racial equality. During World War II, Texan Martin Dies, Jr. insisted that radicals and "crackpots" in government agencies were using the race issue to bring African Americans "within the sphere of their influence." In turn, southern objections to President Truman's nomination of Aubrey Williams as administrator of the Rural Electrification Administration partly reflected the social worker's support for racial equality and fair employment practices.[7]

⌐Outside the South, white liberal support for civil rights was interpreted as radical agitation by conservatives such as journalist and writer John Flynn, the former antimonopolist and noninterventionist who bitterly opposed state planning and regulation as collectivist. Flynn saw the struggle against racial discrimination as part of a carefully conceived campaign by revolutionary elements to induce social disorder by arousing the passions of Jews, African Americans, and others. "We are now in an extraordinary period of social revolution," the writer-activist wrote to New Hampshire senator Styles Bridges in 1949. Dimissing calls for a second fair employment practices committee as a bid for black votes,

Flynn proposeed to use the fililbuster as a last weapon in defeating the "social war machine" of socialist revolutionaries. Having made the northern Democratic Party their prisoner, he informed Senator Walter George of Georgia, "socialist-labor" elements sought to complete the capture of southern African-American minds and votes begun years earlier by Communists and other radicals.[8]

Flynn and other critics were quick to note the threads of radicalism that connected civil rights supporters in the academic social sciences, tax-exempt foundations, and alleged Communist fronts. They noted, for example, that Gunnar Myrdal's landmark study had been commissioned by the suspect Carnegie Foundation. Tennessee's Brazilla Carroll Reece told the House of Representatives in 1953 that Paul Hoffman, former president of the Ford Foundation, was chair of the Civil Rights Congress, a group on the attorney general's list of subversive organizations, and that Ford's Fund for the Republic had underwritten projects to popularize concepts of racial integration. Opponents of federal involvement in race relations questioned whether tax-exempt foundations should be engaged in molding public opinion. "We are told to pattern our behavior and to change our society" on the basis of social engineering arguments promoted by foundation-sponsored social science researchers, Professor Albert Hobbs warned the Reece committee in 1954.[9]

***

Two days before Hobbs's appearance before the foundation inquiry, civil rights activists and social scientists won a stunning victory when the Supreme Court ruled in *Brown v. Board of Education of Topeka* that states could not require students of different races to attend separate tax-supported schools. Attorneys for the National Association for the Advancement of Colored People (NAACP) built their case by using expert psychological testimony to assert that segregation eroded the self-esteem and learning ability of African-American children. The following year, the Court decreed that public schools were to be integrated with "all deliberate speed." Federal intervention through the legal system sent shock waves across the white South. In a 1956 Declaration of Constitutional Principles, 101 southern members of Congress criticized the Court's "clear abuse of judicial power" as a substitution of social ideology for established law. Legislators protested that school segregation confirmed the habits, customs, and traditions of the region's people and gave parents power over their children's lives and education. Tensions over the issue escalated in 1957 when President Dwight Eisenhower enforced a federal court's integration orders by sending U.S. paratroopers to Central High School in Little Rock, Arkansas.[10]

Although racial antagonism and white supremacy beliefs played an undeniable role in the defense of segregation, opponents of federal activism often linked their stance to a critical assessment of the liberal and academic social values defining the ideology of northern interventionists. The essence of such criticism was captured by an East Texas lumber dealer, who complained to readers of his hometown newspaper in 1957 that the Supreme Court had committed judicial usurpation by subverting the Constitution with a "sociological hodge podge." With similar logic, a Waco physician castigated Chief Justice Earl Warren as a "socio-communist." White community leaders in the South contended that the Court had replaced traditional and organic standards of human relations with overly rationalistic legal decrees. Race mixing, they argued, was a first step toward compulsory equality of association, a violation of the principle that social status should be earned and that interaction among democratic people should be voluntary.[11]

Reacting to the social science tenor of the *Brown* case, integration adversaries protested that the Supreme Court had facilitated the coercive intervention of an oppressive government bureaucracy into private areas of personal and social relations. By creating the conditions for extended federal authority, they contended, the Warren tribunal was preparing Americans for the tyrannical invasions of Communist dictatorship. Anticommunism had served as a pretext for southern opposition to social change and the empowerment of labor since the 1930s. Yet by raising alarms over the prospective issuance of orders and edicts by federal attorneys and human rights professionals, civil rights opponents touched upon widespread anxieties over modern powerlessness and depersonalization. Critics were able to tie racial equality to communism because they pictured the rights movement as relying on state coercion to erase the ethnic, national, and racial differences that supposedly preserved the distinctive features of human personality and culture. "Isn't the basic drive in civil rights to make the individual the mass, to make everyone the same, . . . to make everyone dependent on big government?" a California correspondent asked Indiana senator Homer E. Capehart in 1957. An Alabama realtor worried about "trying to put everybody in the same mold" by forcing the mixture of the races.[12]

Given the widely held association of communism with collectivist uniformity, it was not surpising that civil rights foes portrayed integration as an excessively reasoned attempt to alter social relations. "The final determinant in all human action," a Houston physician warned President Eisenhower following Little Rock, was "*emotion* and *not reason*." Similar sentiments pervaded a newspaper editorial produced in the same year by Nacogdoches, Texas lumber dealer, T. G. Tilford. Although Tilford claimed a half-century of "unbroken, close, harmonious association" with members of the local African-American community, he insisted that he had "no desire to integrate with them, and I can think of no reason on earth why they should desire to integrate with me." Limiting associations to those of one's own race did not deprive anyone of civil rights, he insisted, because no one had the right "to intrude on the rights of others." Contending that segregation carried no inherent stigma, a tenuous proposition at best, Tilford nevertheless dismissed integration as an artificial attempt to fuse two or more entities so that the component parts no longer were distinguishable.[13]

Despite attempts like Tilford's to portray race relations as an organic product of historical custom rather than a tool for social planners, southern leaders of the 1950s faced an agonizing choice. They could opt to maintain the region's hallowed racial traditions at all costs. Or they could seek to build an open, democratic, and biracial society that attracted outside investment. Seeking to stabilize the South's racial problem while placating northern African-Americans and liberals, the Eisenhower administration struck the first blow for regional modernization by introducing a federal civil rights bill in 1956, the first such attempt in eighty-one years. The measure proposed to create a new Civil Rights Commission and allow the Justice Department to initiate suits to desegregate state schools, integrate public accommodations, and end exclusionary voting. After bitter protests from southern members of Congress, Eisenhower signed a milder bill the next year that eliminated the provisions regarding public schools and accommodations. Nevertheless, many white southerners viewed the Civil Rights Act of 1957 as an attack on the region's way of life and a blow to the credibility of their elected representatives. A Texas theater owner reflected this sense of betrayal when she chastised Senate Majority Leader Lyndon Johnson for supporting the rights bill with press statements reminiscent of "a diplomat in an alien country."[14]

White southerners complained that the Washington political establishment considered civil rights opponents "so many morons who do not know what is good for the country." Yet television coverage of heavy-handed and often-violent responses to the racial equality crusade turned national public opinion against segregationalist die hards. Between 1955 and 1956, followers of Reverend Martin Luther King, Jr. faced arrest and harassment as they conducted a nonviolent and religiously inspired boycott of the segregated bus lines of Montgomery, Alabama. In Little Rock, Arkansas, NAACP activists won sympathy for the civil rights cause as they daily escorted nine well-dressed and dignified African-American students through cursing and violent mobs resisting the integration of the city's central high school. Black college students in North Carolina and Tennessee bore personal witness against the exclusionary practices of downtown lunch counters in 1960 by mounting a highly publicized campaign of nonviolent sit-ins at establishments refusing to serve African-Americans. The next year, white violence flared with ugly results when an integrated group of protesters staged a series of "freedom rides" across the Deep South to compel the federal government to protect the right of blacks and whites to travel together on interstate buses.[15]

By emphasizing spiritual redemption, personal sacrifice, and moral witness, the civil rights crusade induced considerable sympathy from many white Americans. The campaign elicited further support in 1962 when President John F. Kennedy federalized the Mississippi National Guard to ensure the integration of the public university at Oxford over the objections of the state's governor.

The following year, Reverend King led thousands of African-American children to face arrest, police dogs, and fire hoses in nonviolent street demonstrations aimed at municipal segregation ordinances in Birmingham, Alabama. On the same day that Kennedy nationalized the state's National Guard to counter Governor George C. Wallace's well-publicized intention to block black enrollment at the University of Alabama, the president went on television and dramatically announced his endorsement of federal civil rights legislation to address discrimination in public accommodations, schools, employment, and voting. In August 1963, an integrated gathering of 250,000 marchers rallied at Washington, D.C.'s Lincoln Memorial to hear the ringing oratory of King and other speakers demand congressional action to honor the nation's democratic heritage and pass the rights bill.[16]

Although opponents denounced the civil rights measure as a government edict for "compulsory love," a broad coalition of movement activists, labor leaders, and liberal reformers invoked traditional precepts of personal dignity and inclusion in sustained lobbying for the proposal. New Frontier operatives never succeeded in getting the legislation passed. Yet in the year following Kennedy's assassination, President Lyndon Johnson marshalled enough Republican votes to overcome a fifty-seven day Senate filibuster and win approval for the Civil Rights Act of 1964. The landmark statute, one of the fundamental triumphs of the rights campaign, empowered Justice Department attorneys to sue to desegregate public facilities and schools. Through creation of an Equal Employment Opportunity Commission (EEOC), moreover, officials in Washington could order unions and businesses to end workplace discrimination based on race or gender. The historic law also provided for the withdrawal of funds from federally assisted programs that practiced discrimination.[17]

By the summer of 1964, Lyndon Johnson had committed his administration to the vision of Great Society reform. Embracing civil rights leaders, human rights activists, and liberal policy intellectuals, Johnson sought to bring the amenities of life within the reach of all Americans, extend the New Deal to neglected minorities, and expand the Democratic Party's (and his personal) electoral support. Following passage of the Civil Rights Act and the outbreak of rioting in several urban African-American communities, the president pressed for a massive antipoverty program to maximize equal opportunity for all. The idea of a national war on poverty had originated with Kennedy's White House Council of Economic Advisers and been framed by a legislative task force of middle-level bureaucrats led by Adam Yarmolinsky, a former official of the the Ford Foundation's Fund for the Republic. Having pushed an assertive racial integration policy while a Pentagon official, Yarmolinsky approached antipoverty planning as a self-confident social interventionist. In March 1964 Johnson acted on Yarmolinsky's ideas by asking Congress for nearly a billion dollars to create a Job Corps training program, a domestic Peace Corps entitled VISTA (Volunteers in Service to America), and a network of community action programs to provide employment, occupational training, education, health, and legal services for the needy.[18]

Despite the pragmatic components of the war on poverty in a period of social unrest, Johnson's economic opportunity bill faced serious obstacles. The proposal initially was stalled by House Rules Committee chair Howard Smith, a veteran opponent of government social programs, who viewed it as excessively wasteful. In June 1964, the measure faced additional problems when Representative Peter Frelinghuysen, a moderate New Jersey Republican, demanded that the states be given more control over the Office of Economic Opportunity (OEO), the massive bureaucracy designed to administer the program. In the Senate, however, the Select Committee on Poverty overrode such objections and prepared the way for approval by the full chamber, 62 to 33. Following this victory, Smith's Rules Committee reported the measure out to the House by the closest possible vote, 8 to 7. On the floor, nevertheless, a group of North Carolina Democrats tied their support for the bill to Yarmolinsky's departure from OEO. Only after poverty administrator Sargent Shriver consented to their request did the Economic Opportunity Act of 1964 pass the House by a tight 228 to 190 margin.[19]

***

Johnson's Great Society symbolized the extent to which 1960s liberalism rested on the cooperation of African-American leaders and white activists, policy intellectuals, and government officials. Yet the involvement of white social reformers enraged opponents of government-mandated racial equality and raised the stakes of their opposition to imposed integration. Up to the 1960s, most incidents of segregationalist violence and terror targeted either African Americans or white Communists, often Jews. During the 1950s, White Citizens Councils in Mississippi and Alabama organized economic boycotts and intimidation campaigns against local black activists. More ominously, a revitalized Ku Klux Klan turned to shootings, beatings, bombings, and arson after 1954 to protest school integration and punish those who defied regional social traditions. Shortly after President Kennedy's endorsement of the civil rights bill in 1963, a white supremacist murdered Medgar Evers, the chapter head of the NAACP in Jackson, Mississippi. That September, Klan terrorists bombed an African-American Baptist church in Birmingham that served as a youth movement center, killing four young girls attending Sunday school.[20]

During the summer of 1964 militant resistance to the Civil Rights Movement and its white allies intensified in Mississippi. In response to the terror directed against African-American voter registration drives in rural sections of the state, activists in the Student Nonviolent Coordinating Committee (SNCC) and other civil rights groups invited one thousand white students from northern colleges to join a Freedom Summer project. Organizers reasoned that any attack on white, upper-middle-class youngsters would attract media attention and create the pretext for federal protection for rights workers. Predictably, rural whites in the state viewed the northern collegians as an outside elite seeking to impose social revolution on the South. Mississippians often complained that the students were slovenly dressed, discourteous to white elders, sexually promiscuous, and drawn to communism. Certain white southerners believed they had "the same right to exterminate civil rights workers that a farmer has to kill rabid dogs," presidential aide George E. Reedy advised Lyndon Johnson. The situation in Mississippi took on tragic proportions in the summer of 1964 when the FBI belatedly arrested a county sheriff and several Klansmen for the killing of a local African-American and two Jewish volunteers from the North. When the state refused to prosecute, the federal government tried the defendants under the Civil Rights Act.[21]

Reedy warned President Johnson that federal endorsement of racial equality amounted to a symbol of powerlessness for southern whites who sensed a loss of control over their lives and communities. Indeed, passage of the Civil Rights Act of 1964 prompted regional critics to charge that radical experts and government bureaucrats now extended special privileges to racial minorities at the expense of less favored whites. No single figure of the 1960s and 1970s embodied such attitudes as much as Alabama Governor George Wallace. Raised in a middle-class farming family in the impoverished southeast corner of his state, Wallace worked his way through law school with an assortment of jobs. After serving as a Pacific flight engineer in World War II, he joined the Alabama state legislature in 1946. A supporter of the breakaway States Rights Party that walked out of the Democratic Convention in 1948, Wallace won election as an Alabama circuit court judge four years later. He gained statewide acclaim in 1958 by refusing a federal court order to turn over voting records to the new federal Civil Rights Commission. Acquitted on contempt charges, the judge marched into the governor's chair four years later in the culmination of a campaign in which he pledged to "stand up for Alabama."[22]

Wallace's reputation spread across the nation following a stunning inaugural address early in 1963. Invoking the image of the Confederacy, the governor defiantly proclaimed "segregation now, segregation tomorrow, segregation forever." Five months later, he announced that he would defy a federal court injunction against interfering with the enrollment of African-American students at the University of Alabama. Although Wallace ultimately deferred to President Kennedy's command to "step aside," the fiesty politician promised that the future would bring victory over Washington's interference in state affairs. Meanwhile, he opposed the civil rights bill as an unwarranted extension of federal power over businesses and unions. As Wallace mounted a highly publicized tour of the North and West in early 1964, morever, he seemed to sense that the best way to legitimize his message was to distance himself from vigilante terrorism in the South, deemphasize white supremacy and race, and focus on the universal dangers of government intrusion into civil rights. Impressed by the resonance of this approach with working-class and middle-class audiences across the country, the Alabama governor entered several Democratic presidential primaries in 1964 against stand-ins for Lyndon Johnson.[23]

Placing himself in the national political arena, Wallace minimized the defense of racial segregation and transformed opposition to government-imposed civil rights into a campaign against political intellectuals and the liberationist strategies of the professional elite. Journalists covering the 1964 primaries reported that Wallace enthusiasts appeared more motivated by reactions to perceived double standards of racial injustice and by threats of African-American urban violence than by residual expressions of white supremacy. In racially tense Maryland, the Alabaman ran well in the same districts that easily returned supporters of civil rights legislation to Congress. Wallace continually assured northerners that he was not a racist and that it was ungodly to hate people because of their skin color. The problems of race would be resolved by "common sense and massive education," he told a Chicago television interviewer. Neither did the candidate seek an endorsement of segregation. Although he believed that both races benefited from separate spheres, Wallace explained, the issue was for each state to decide. "A vote for this little governor," he told northern audiences, was "a vote for the right to run your schools, your business, your lives, as you and you alone see fit" without help from the social engineers in Washington.[24]

Wallace cleverly played on rampant hostility to the perceived elitism of middle-class professionals and liberal social interventionists. As an astute biography of the Alabama politician has suggested, the combative governor had inherited "a touchy sensitivity to slights and condescension" from his father. Keenly aware of his rural background and lack of polish and sophistication while a college student, Wallace quickly had learned to resent patronizing by social betters. The candidate used class resentment and his identity as a beleaguered southerner to bond with white ethnic Americans and young industrial workers similarly sensitive to their own lack of cultural sophistication. Assailing "limousine liberals" in the populist tradition of Joe McCarthy, the governor insisted that people who had known poverty first-hand could "better understand the poor than the self-flagellating liberals who were born with silver spoons in their mouths."[25]

Like McCarthy, Wallace tied untrustworthy liberals and race relations interventionists to the evils of Communist dictatorship. Federal intervention into social interactions, he warned campaign audiences, reflected "a socialist ideology under which a few men in the executive and judicial branches of our government make decisions and laws without regard to our elected representatives who reflect the decisions of the people." Communists applauded government by executive or judicial edict, proclaimed Wallace, because powerful individuals could be brainwashed or corrupted, in contrast to Congress, which remained unwieldy and impossible to control. The Great Society threatened to subject individuals "to the caprice and whim of an autocratic, all-powerful government structure," he told an enthusiastic gathering in Cincinnati. The result would "amalgamate us into a unit of the one," with a powerful central authority "designed to equalize us into the common denominator necessary for a slave people."[26]

***

By discussing federal intervention in race relations in terms of modern depersonalization, class conflict, and arbitrary government, George Wallace managed to win one-third of the votes cast for Democrats and 25 percent of the total in Wisconsin's open primary in 1964. A few weeks later, the Alabama governor gathered 30 percent of the Democratic vote in Indiana and 43 percent in Maryland. Once Lyndon Johnson signed the Civil Rights Act and received the Democratic nomination for a new term, however, the Wallace candidacy ended and Republican presidential aspirant Barry Goldwater assumed the stage as the nation's leading Great Society critic. Since the late 1950s, American conservatives had targeted the bipartisan political elite as excessively secular and tainted by the New Deal legacy. As a native Arizonan, Goldwater skillfully mobilized western and southern Republicans by painting the eastern establishment as insufficiently concerned about communism, statism, and social issues such as crime and welfare dependency. Using direct and unpretentious language, the Republican insurgent rallied Sun Belt enterprisers and old-style professionals who resented the enhanced role of Washington's social guardians and Republican complicity in big government.[27]

Goldwater had emerged on the national political scene in 1952 by defeating Democrat Ernest McFarland of Arizona, the Senate Majority Leader. "Now is the time to throw out the intellectual radicals and the parlor pinks and the confused and the bumbling," he declared. In 1957, the first-term senator distanced himself from Eisenhower Republicanism by attacking deficit spending as "the siren song of socialism." Winning reelection the next year, Goldwater denounced Democratic political activists and labor leaders as collectivists. Such views found their way into *The Conscience of a Conservative*, a 123-page best-selling primer compiled in 1960 by *National Review* editor and Goldwater speechwriter, L. Brent Bozell. Denying that conservatism served privileged reaction, the senator defended his political philosophy as an expression of expanding freedom. Since federal managers had been corrupted by the pursuit of power, he argued, they needed to be restrained from interference in citizens' private lives. Washington had no constitutional authority to compel racial integration of schools or public accommodations, declared Goldwater. Nor should it impose socialism through social welfare programs.[28]

Days before John Kennedy's 1961 inaugural, Goldwater introduced "A Statement of Proposed Republican Principles, Programs, and Objectives." Written by Senate Labor Committee Minority Counsel Michael Bernstein, the declaration denounced the collective power of special interest groups. It asserted that the modern American political system submerged individual concerns and jeopardized voluntary social and economic relationships. The heart of the manifesto called for the Republican Party to address the needs of those "forgotten" and "silent" Americans "who quietly go about the business of paying and praying, working and saving. They mind their own business and meet their responsibilities on a day-to-day basis. They are the group who, for too long, have had their voices drowned out by the clamor of pressure groups which increases in volume as their number decline."[29]

By offering to rally ordinary people behind an antielitist banner that borrowed from Franklin Roosevelt as well as the lesser-known John Bricker, Goldwater restored populist conservatism to a central role in the Republican Party. Thirty-two business leaders, lawyers, small-town newspaper publishers, independent oil entrepeneurs, and regional bankers from the Midwest, South, and West soon called upon the Arizona senator to run for president. As the candidate prepared to enter the fray in 1964, Phyllis Schlafly's approving biography, *A Choice Not An Echo*, urged "grass-roots Americans" and fellow anticommunists to oust the liberal eastern establishment. Once in motion, the Goldwater campaign bypassed screening by leading political commentators through the innovative use of direct mail and advertising, techniques that also offset large contributions by Lyndon Johnson's political allies. In response to fifteen million solicitations, Goldwater staffers retired one-third of their $17 million campaign debt. The insurgent nature of the Arizonan's 1964 crusade was illustrated by the fact that 69 percent of Democratic contributions derived from donations of $500 or more during that year while only 28 percent of Republican gifts came in such large sums.[30]

Democratic activists insisted that Goldwater appealed to a "new class of affluent 'noncommunity-minded people'" who cared only for personal material comforts. Such analyses underestimated the depth of the social issues and political outrage tapped by the Republican nominee. Like George Wallace, Goldwater lashed out at disruptive civil rights demonstrations and black rioting in northern cities during the summer of 1964. The Arizona senator also emulated Wallace's focus on government bureaucracy as the prime symptom of social malaise. Goldwater accomplished this by tying federal administrators to a perceived breakdown of personal responsibility, long a theme of welfare state opponents. The government doctrine of "the fast buck and the fast answer," he asserted, perfectly reflected a national mood of "easy morals and uneasy ethics." Speaking in Salt Lake City, the candidate charged that the moral fiber of American life had been beset by "rot and decay" and that immorality started at the top. In a *New York Times* piece in November, he described a bartering White House as infected with "corruption, immorality, and cynicism."[31]

Like George Wallace, Goldwater shifted the focus from race relations to the federal political establishment and its liberal allies. He insisted that government civil rights administrators had deceived the country by incorrectly addressing the moral controversy over individual rights of association as a constitutional issue. Asserting that racial justice activists had transferred emphasis from equal opportunity to equal outcomes, the senator told the Republican National Convention that the nation had been misled by the "false prophets" of collectivism. The result, he concluded, was an arbitrary government of "centralized planning, red tape, rules without responsiblity, and regimentation without recourse." The presidential campaign of Barry Goldwater rested on the promise that Americans might retrieve control of their lives from the permanent political class in Washington.[32]

***

Although Goldwater's evocation of social issues contributed to Republican voting strength in the South, West, and white ethnic districts of the Northeast and Midwest, Lyndon Johnson successfully marginalized his opponent as an extremist on domestic issues and foreign policy. On Election Day 1964, the president amassed an impressive 61 percent of the popular vote, sweeping the Electoral College except for Arizona and the five states of the Deep South.[33] Despite the apparent vindication of Johnson's Great Society, however, the administration's identification with professional social activists and African-American rights organizers placed enormous political burdens on the White House. As social tensions escalated in the next four years, the government in Washington once again would be subjected to sustained condemnation by those who charged that the federal bureaucracy had fallen into the hands of an irresponsible and unaccountable elite.

The racial dimensions of the crisis over government legitimacy dated back to the Freedom Summer of 1964, when civil rights organizers created the Mississippi Freedom Democratic Party (MFDP) and attempted to replace the magnolia state's all-white delegation at the Democratic National Convention. Offered a token pair of at-large seats by liberal associates of President Johnson, the contingent walked out. The experience soured grass-roots civil rights strategists on the reliability of white allies and intensified efforts by black activists to stage voter registration campaigns among southern African-Americans. In Selma, Alabama, SNCC field workers requested help from Martin Luther King and the Southern Christian Leadership Conference (SCLC) when organizing efforts met adamant opposition by local officials. Seeking support for national voting rights legislation, King presided over daily demonstrations at Selma's county court house. As police harassment intensified, the local movement gained its first fatality in February 1965 when Alabama state troopers attacked a nighttime march in an adjoining jurisdiction and shot a nonresisting young black man to death.[34]

Seeking to condemn the brutality of state police and to protest Governor George Wallace's refusal to protect rights of peaceful assembly, six hundred demonstrators set out on a nonviolent march from Selma to Montgomery in March 1965. In an event immortalized as "Bloody Sunday," club-wielding

Alabama troopers teargassed and savagely beat the participants. The nationally televised episode became a flashpoint of the struggle over racial equality. Following King's request, over 450 white clergy and hundreds of northern social activists flocked to Selma to bear witness to Wallace's policies. Tensions escalated two days later when a group of white Selma locals clubbed to death a white Unitarian minister from Boston. When Wallace still refused security for the proposed march to Montgomery, a federal judge nationalized the Alabama National Guard, permitting the controversial parade to begin on March 21st. Four days later, a white homemaker from Detroit was shot and killed by a carload of Klansmen as she and a black male volunteer drove to the capital to ferry marchers.[35]

The Selma confrontations brought additional sympathy from those favorably disposed to the civil rights movement and widespread anger at Governor Wallace's apparent unwillingness to discourage violence in his state. Yet they embittered those Americans who saw mandated racial equality as a social experiment imposed by professional reformers, radical agitators, and outside adventurers. Criticism of the protests surfaced in a Colorado woman's admonition to President Johnson that the martyred volunteer from Detroit should have kept her place "at home, not in another state helping to cause trouble." "I hope you will remember all the people who stay at home and care for their families," she wrote to the White House, "who spend their money to keep the home together, and to support their church. Just because we don't march, it doesn't mean we have no cause, and are not thinking." A California homemaker complained that the government had deserted people like herself and given support to "rabble rousers and communists." In Alabama, the managing editor of the *Montgomery Advertiser* blamed the Selma troubles on "the forcible disruption" of local traditions "by an all-powerful government."[36]

Although critics were by no means free of racial slurs, the sharpest condemnations of the civil rights movement focused on the white intellectuals and social activists who rallied to the cause. One week after the Selma to Montgomery March, Reverend Bob Marsh of the First Baptist Church of Andalusia, a mid-sized town in south central Alabama, delivered a colorful and frank radio sermon condemning recent visitors to the state. Marsh began by disassociating his neighbors from white vigilantism. "I am afraid that we have too often allowed the ugly, God-defying, bottle-swinging, gun-shooting, bush-wacker and hate-monger to represent the image of Alabama and the South," he confessed. Yet the minister barely contained his fury at the supposed hypocrisy of "pungent beatniks and social revolutionaries" who participated in Selma street prayers when they presumably had no belief in God. "We are at the mercy of skillful and well-financed social planners," he warned, "who set forth to plan, promote, and push a social order based on naturalistic premises."[37]

Viewing the Western world as mired in mental stagnation, apathy, and immorality, Reverend. Marsh claimed that the elimination of laws against homosexuality, degeneracy, promiscuity, obscenity, and pornography served communist interests. He contended that subversive elements had created the impression that violence and insurrection were legitimate aspects of the American tradition when they served progressive causes. The Alabama cleric warned that the liberal media had fallen into a dangerous double standard. "You can be an unbathed beatnik, immoral kook, sign-carrying degenerate, a radical revolutionary," he complained, "one who treats the sacred with disdain, have no regard for decency and honesty, an out-and-out Marxist, an anarchist advocating the overthrow of everything in sight . . . and that is O.K.!" Yet those who stood for presumed principles of righteousness and individual initiative found the "guns of public opinion" turned on them as reactionaries and members of the fanatical right.[38]

Marsh insisted that white radicals sought to force racial integration and amalgamation on the South and that disruptive violence, not voting rights, was their underlying goal. His harshest critique centered on outside clergy who made the pilgrimage to Selma. "Long after you have returned to your Northern paradises, received your certificate of acclaim by the 'scape-goat seeking society,' and made your oratorical barbs against our 'corn-pone civilization,'" he claimed, "we Alabama ministers are going to have to pick up the shambles of your sanctified rudeness, try to explain to our people why those of you who deny the deity of Christ call yourselves Christian, attempt to understand why you left your strife-torn cities and pulpits to defy law and order, goad our people into strife, and disgrace the name of Christianity. We will have deep feelings of racial tension to heal after you have smugly faded into the sunset on your way to other social revolutions."[39]

***

Critics like Marsh were caught between the indefensible violence of civil rights opponents and local officials on one hand, and the social disruption attributed to the movement's supporters on the other. Yet Alabama's brutality in sustaining white supremacy pushed public opinion toward constitutional balloting guarantees for racial minorities, a proposal supported in March 1965 by more than three-fourths of a national poll and nearly half of the southern sample. Lawyers with the Civil Rights Division of the Justice Department and the Solicitor General's office earlier had drafted a voting rights bill, for which the administration had received promises of Republican support. Eight days after "Bloody Sunday" and two days after a consultation with a delegation from the National Council of Churches, President Johnson addressed a televised session of both houses of Congress and eloquently pleaded for passage of voter registration reform. Signed in August, the Voting Rights Act of 1965 suspended literacy tests and enabled the Justice Department to appoint federal registrars to replace local polling officials in counties with statistical patterns of low participation by minority voters.[40]

Once the Johnson administration broke down the barriers to African-American balloting in the South, it renewed efforts to address the problems of poverty and dependence that characterized many of the North's urban black communities. Just as New Deal political intellectuals had turned to government programs to promote the inclusion of working people into the economic mainstream, so did their Great Society counterparts seek similar treatment for the poor of the 1960s. In a period in which the Ford, Rockefeller, and Carnegie foundations subsidized experimental projects in New York, Cleveland, and other northern cities to replace welfare assistance with minority jobs programs, the White House acknowledged the importance of employment opportunities in the crusade against racial discrimination. In a precedent-setting June 1965 commencement address at predominantly black Howard University, Johnson embraced the new agenda by proclaiming that economic justice was "the next and more profound stage of the battle for civil rights." Noting that individual choice was not sufficient for people historically "hobbled by chains," the president called for affirmative action to redress past wrongs. "We seek not just freedom, but opportunity," Johnson stated in the landmark address, "not just equality as a right and a theory, but equality as a fact and as a result."[41]

The rhetoric of the Howard University speech reflected a growing sentiment among civil rights activists and policy advisers that pervasive discrimination could not be addressed completely by legislation because racism was too systemic. Johnson had been the author of President Kennedy's executive directive of 1961 mandating equal employment opportunities in federal government contracts. In September 1965, the Texan cited the Civil Rights Act in issuing Executive Order 11246, an historic directive that stipulated that all federal contractors cease hiring discrimination against racial minorities. By laying the foundation for affirmative action in employment, the Johnson administration initiated a profound policy revolution in which government managers would shape workplace rules in the name of racial equality. An interlocking configuration of federal agencies, congressional committees, academic theorists, and civil rights organizations now began to buttress congressional mandates on equal opportunity with new concepts of compensatory justice and group rights.[42]

Great Society officials first sought to apply the emerging synthesis by using the war on poverty to bring minorities into the economic mainstream. Although the White House was careful to state that poor whites, Hispanics, and Native Americans also experienced economic deprivation, the Office of Economic Opportunity became the central agency of Johnson's drive to break the historical correlation between race and impoverishment. In resorting to an experimental crusade against poverty, however, the administration was compelled to strike alliances with social activists and policy experts whose standing with elected politicians and voter constituencies was problematic. The resulting stalemate helped to discredit the president's personal reputation and left the Great Society with a controversial and mixed legacy despite enormous accomplishments like Medicare, Medicaid, urban development, aid to education, and civil rights legislation.

The complex class alignment surrounding antipoverty efforts was illustrated by Mobilization for Youth (MFY), an antideliquency program that served as the inspiration for the war on poverty's community action component. Developed in a New York City settlement house in 1957 with assistance from Columbia University sociologists, the Ford Foundation, and the National Institutes of Health, MFY received Kennedy adminstration funding to deploy neighborhood people in the crusade against youth crime. Significantly, the agency's board of directors consisted mainly of upper-middle-class professionals, while its staff was recruited from New York social activists and leftists who sought to mobilize the poor against the elected political establishment. These efforts backfired in the summer of 1964 when newspaper reports charged MFY with financial irregularities and ties to rent strikes and black rioting in Harlem.[43]

Despite negative publicity about the New York project that served as the model program for the Economic Opportunity Act, Congress appropriated $250 million for community action antipoverty organizations and "maximum feasible participation" by the poor in 1964. Pushed by Kennedy administration juvenile delinquency aide, Richard Boone; and OEO Inspector-General William Haddad, a New York reform Democrat, political machine opponent, and former Peace Corps executive; the war on poverty rejected the social service model in which planning originated with skilled experts and administrators in Washington. Instead, OEO encouraged the creation of more than a thousand neighborhood action boards between 1964 and 1968, most of which distributed government funds and services. As Great Society historian Irwin Unger has noted, "never before had the federal government sought to make informal grassroots organizations the primary agents for planning programs."[44]

Despite attempts by Johnson officials to inspire local organizing, however, poor people were slow to set up citywide antipoverty boards. In their place, Washington devised 'demonstration' projects and assigned them to local governments and agencies. Great Society administrators subsequently funded community groups that adopted 'national emphasis programs' as prepackaged entities. Philadelphia's war on poverty plan was devised by city officials and initially implemented by an existing antidelinquency panel created by the Ford Foundation. The mayor then appointed an antipoverty action committee consisting of local businesspeople, civic leaders, clergy, social workers, and political supporters. Mayors in Cleveland, New York, Los Angeles, and San Francisco soon followed suit. Yet as lucrative staffing and patronage machines emerged among the minority professionals and entrepreneurs who dominated neighborhood community action boards, elected officials in the major cities found their authority and legitimacy undermined in a confrontation of political and social interests that OEO never succeeded in resolving.[45]

Class tension over the war on poverty first surfaced in Syracuse, New York. In a demonstration project, Syracuse University received a $314,000 OEO grant in February 1965 to fund a community development association to teach techniques for mobilizing the poor. The group recruited nineteen African-American organizers, many of whom identified with the style of participatory democracy practiced by SNCC field workers in Selma and the Deep South. Another influence came from empowerment activist Saul Alinsky, a spiritual father to the emerging New Left of radicalized white college youth. Hired to conduct organizing workshops by a Syracuse University social work professor, Alinsky urged antipoverty staffers to bring the poor into the mainstream of community life through demonstrations and confrontations with the local power structure. Targeting middle-class politicians and landlords, organizers mounted voter registration drives and sit-ins, pickets, and rallies designed to protest unfair rental practices and the quality of municipal social services.[46]

The colonization of favored clients by professional antipoverty administrators clearly emerged in New York City, where the crusade against poverty involved the merger of two Kennedy-era antidelinquency programs in HARYOU-ACT (Harlem Youth Opportunities Unlimited-Associated Community Teams). The resulting agency quickly became a bonanza for administrators. By the spring of 1965, forty full-time staffers enjoyed $10,000 annual retainers, with salaries accounting for 80 percent of the program's federal funding. When Director Livingston Wingate contended that Harlem faced an incipient uprising that summer, he devised Project Uplift and added four thousand black youngsters and a staff of five hundred to the payroll. Similar policies characterized San Francisco's war on poverty after the mayor's racially mixed community action board lost control of funding to area development advisory panels dominated by civil rights militants. Press reports described the local agencies as dominated by a new class of subprofessionals and aides who specialized in attending meetings, providing contacts, interpreting needs, and making resources available.[47]

The enhanced role of middle-class social activists emerged dramatically in the government's antipoverty effort in Newark, New Jersey. In the summer of 1964, Students for a Democratic Society (SDS), the vanguard organ of the emerging white New Left, began one of twelve community mobilization projects in the city's African-American district. Attracting a core following of fifty residents, organizers led rent strikes, neighborhood cleanup campaigns, demands for improved city welfare services, and demonstrations at municipal police headquarters. The next year, OEO officials overrode objections from Newark's mayor and agreed to let SDS sponsor the local VISTA outlet. This relationship led to the government's retention of student activists such as Newark project leader Tom Hayden as per diem consultants on community organizing. After the city's community action agency had been taken over by civil rights leaders and a major riot erupted in the African-American ghetto in July 1967, Washington antipoverty administrators shut down the Newark program.[48]

***

Although OEO expenditures never exceeded an annual $1.78 billion, the war on poverty received more press coverage than any other domestic program of the 1960s except those involving civil rights. Providing sinecures for politically favored representatives of the poor and spending most of its funds on salaries, the campaign was subject to stringent criticism. The vulnerability of the crusade was captured by the Oklahoma critic who complained to President Johnson in 1965 that "your poverty program is another farce and a complete socialistic deal. A bunch of parasites paid from $22,500 to $30,000 per year and nothing but a waste of taxpayers' money." Rather than a controversy over assistance to the poor, the war on poverty pitted locally elected politicians in a power struggle with social activists and professionals for the right to legitimately represent the interests of the nation's economically disadvantaged.[49]

Advocates for the poor insisted that they were far more qualified to manage the antipoverty crusade than municipal officeholders. In Cleveland, a black minister joined the secretary for a group of fifty welfare mothers in charging that the directors of the city's antipoverty program had a vested interest in preventing poor people from becoming a political force in the community. Levying a similar accusation, a Chicago clergyman maintained that impoverished people in his city were being pushed out of antipoverty organizations "by men who drive Cadillacs, eat three-inch steaks, and sip champagne at their luncheon meetings." Yet the class dynamics to the antipoverty dispute were far more complex than suggested by such statements. In Chicago, where activists roundly criticized Mayor Richard Daley's personal control over the welfare bureaucracy, the citywide community action board dispensed more than twice as much federal money to each poor family as similar agencies in New York or Philadelphia. Despite Daley's dictatorial methods, Chicago antipoverty officials opened service centers more quickly and had better records in handling funds than units in other cities.[50]

By mid-1965, big-city politicians began to take the offensive against the perceived capture of the poverty program by social activists. Los Angeles mayor Sam Yorty inaugurated the campaign by objecting to efforts to replace his Youth Opportunity Board with a twenty-two person committee chosen by officials from the city's private antipoverty agencies. Pointing out that only two seats on the proposed panel would represent Los Angeles city government, Yorty argued that public policy would be established without accountability to voters or elected representatives. The poverty program should not be used as a "stepping stone for those with political ambitions," warned the mayor. In Syracuse, where officials charged that the war on poverty had fallen into the hands of Marxist ideologues, the mayor asked OEO to cut off funding to political training workshops. Angered by the intrusion of professional intermediaries, the city housing director agreed to meet with tenants complaining about services in public housing projects but not with the university-trained organizers of the protest.[51]

Concerned that social activists were mobilizing the poor against urban officeholders, elected officials objected to OEO policies requiring representation of economically disadvantaged people on community antipoverty planning boards. In May 1965, Yorty and San Francisco mayor John F. Shelley brought a resolution before the U.S. Conference of Mayors charging that Washington had failed "to recognize the legal and moral responsibilities of local officials who are accountable to the taxpayers for expenditures of local funds." Syracuse Republican mayor William F. Walsh added that the antipoverty program was "the most diabolical social work I have ever heard of." The rebellion against nonelected antipoverty organizers partially was pacified when delegates agreed to table the motion in exchange for an opportunity to convey their sentiments to the White House through a personal meeting with Vice President Hubert Humphrey. OEO administrator Shriver also addressed the controversy by issuing informal guidelines that stipulated that only one-third of community action board members had to be neighborhood residents and with a verbal acknowledgement that they did not have to be poor.[52]

As the Johnson administration fielded local complaints over the perceived influence of service professionals and social activists, congressional Republicans demanded greater control of the antipoverty program by state and city officials. During House consideration of OEO appropriations in the summer of 1965, Ohio Republican William H. Ayres distributed a list of 250 antipoverty consultants and experts, many of them top Washington lobbyists and journalists, whom the government had retained at between $35 and $100 a day. A voice vote defeated an amendment by Minnesota Republican Albert H. Quie to give governors a veto power over OEO projects. Yet after the House limited the ability of states to oppose antipoverty undertakings, the Senate allowed governors to hold informal hearings when objecting to community action projects. The impasse was resolved in September when Congress renewed the poverty agency's funding with an $1.78 billion appropriation that removed language concerning "maximum feasible participation" by the poor. The compromise also permitted governors to veto the location of projects (subject to Shriver's discretion) and required more input by state or local officials.[53]

Despite verbal support for the empowerment concepts underlying the crusade against poverty, Great Society officials began to reduce the emphasis on community action in the fall of 1965. Budget Director Charles Schultze privately warned President Johnson that OEO attempts to organize the poor were needlessly politicizing the program. In December, the government announced that the controversial Syracuse University community action project would receive only a token renewal of funding and would have to request further support from the mayor's antipoverty agency. Although community action projects accounted for 45 percent of OEO appropriations for the agency's second year, the bureau de-emphasized social experimentation in 1966 and concentrated on providing client services. As the administration requested a $1.75 billion appropriation for the next fiscal year, local officials in fifteen major cities and counties received long-awaited veto power over poverty projects.[54]

Not content with minor victories, Republican congressional leaders pursued their campaign against the antipoverty crusade in the spring of 1966. When

House Labor and Education Committee chair Adam Clayton Powell, a Harlem Democrat, allowed only supportive witnesses during OEO's appropriation hearings in March, Republicans Albert Quie and Charles E. Goodell denounced the proceedings as "a travesty on the legislative process." Two months later, all but one of the panel's nine Republicans signed a one-hundred page manifesto charging the poverty program with political influence, poor administration, and corruption. Calling for a fresh start to the entire effort, the Republicans recommended that most OEO programs be transferred to cabinet departments and that private industry be brought in to train, educate, and motivate the poor. In September, the House defeated a Republican proposal to narrow OEO's jurisdiction before it passed the agency's appropriation by 210 to 156. Yet after shifting a portion of the community action budget to modest job creation efforts, the Senate reduced its version of the bill to the lower House figure of $1.75 billion.[55]

***

Distracted by the growing demands of the Vietnam War, nervous about the backlash against black rioting in major cities, and concerned about criticism of community action programs by elected officials, the Johnson administration retreated from the war on poverty's once-ambitious goals. When a group of social work students organized a Manhattan teach-in on OEO's demise in December 1965, the *New York Times* reported that "educators blamed government functionaries, spokesmen for the government blamed educators, persons involved in neighborhood radicalism blamed social workers, and social workers blamed most of the others." In contrast, voters appeared to hold the Democrats responsible for the Great Society's failures. With escalating welfare costs, rising inflation, increasing crime rates, rioting in the cities, and the racial militancy of groups like the Black Panther Party in the headlines, Republicans gained forty-seven seats in the House, three additional positions in the Senate, and eight new governorships in the off-year elections of 1966.[56]

The most stunning upset of the 1966 campaign occurred in California, where Republican Ronald Reagan won election as governor. Reagan's success in the nation's most politically polarized state had been facilitated by Max Rafferty, a conservative social critic who emerged into the public arena six years earlier as superintendent of schools in a Los Angeles suburb. Rafferty maintained that public education was producing "spineless, luxury-loving, spiritless creeps," because teachers trained in progressive methodology stressed relativist values instead of eternal verities. The life adjustment philosophy and peer group cooperation stressed by modern schooling, he argued, left young people with no positive standards or competitive ethic. With the support of leading state figures in oil, banking, and real estate, Rafferty won election as California superintendent of education in 1962 and continued to influence the political and cultural debate.[57]

One year after Barry Goldwater's race for the presidency, a state speaking tour convinced Ronald Reagan how deeply voters resented California's high taxes, bloated crime rate, and inefficient social services. "People were tired of wasteful government programs and welfare chiselers," Reagan later claimed, "and they were angry about the constant spiral of taxes and government regulations; arrogant bureaucrats, and public officials who thought all of mankind's problems could be solved by throwing the taxpayers' dollars at them." As the former actor swung into the 1966 campaign, he drew a distinction between the "intellectual clique in Sacramento" and the "common sense answers" to social problems that baffled political class guardians. Reagan pictured working-class voters and business entrepreneurs as equally virtuous and law abiding. In contrast, he criticized privileged academics and remote bureaucrats as parasitic nonproducers who sustained the dependency of welfare recipients and excused criminals and moral offenders.[58]

By focusing on the Great Society's social welfare bureaucracies, Reagan liberated conservatives from unproductive attacks on New Deal programs like social security or from disruptive race baiting. Instead, the self-proclaimed "citizen politician" followed the example of George Wallace and Barry Goldwater by blaming a cultural elite of liberal politicians, intellectuals, and bureaucrats for sacrificing standards of individual responsibility and accountability in the desire to serve ungrateful and undeserving beneficiaries of the welfare state. Reagan's empowerment rhetoric, cheery demeanor, and folksy approach blunted the shrill edge of the Goldwater message without sacrificing its driving force. Winning 40 percent of the California labor vote in 1966 while simultaneously uniting the moderate and right-wing elements of the state Republican Party, the former entertainer went on to easy victory and revitalized the legacy of populist conservatism.[59]

Like George Wallace, Reagan sensed that voters were assured by an approach that mocked the condescension and self-serving attributes of the political class. "With terms like 'guidelines' and 'consensus'," he told a Los Angeles gathering of the National Sand and Gravel Association one month after taking office, "we face a controlled and planned economy, and sometimes, when you look at the efforts of the planners at every echelon of government, you wonder if they aren't a little like that fellow in the dark of the theater who sits there winking at the chorus girls. He knows what he is doing, but nobody else does." Reagan quoted Franklin Roosevelt's observation that legislation by trusted "masterminds" was too apparent in Washington. Bureaucrats never made decisions against their own interests, Roosevelt had warned. The California leader subsequently demonstrated his approach to government when he vetoed an OEO project that would have assisted seventeen chronically unemployed workers in one California county but earmarked half the grant for the salaries of seven administrators.[60]

Reagan cut across party lines by conveying the view that Great Society social experiments were the product of a culturally permissive elite of special interests who dominated a liberal political establishment. The same message characterized George Wallace's crusade against federal intervention in race relations. Rather than opposing the upward mobility of African-Americans, Wallace's white supporters appeared to object to the enhanced political influence of black elites in national affairs. As the Johnson administration cooperated with civil rights activists by drafting far-reaching laws and policies that altered the rules of competition, members of the white working class and middle class experienced the frustration of outsiders whose interests no longer appeared compelling to politicians. Reagan and the Alabama governor both succeeded in directing the attention of a national constituency from racial minorities to Washington's political class, a category that embraced lawyers, federal judges, academicians, elite opinion makers, and government planners and bureaucrats in the regulatory agencies.[61]

Wallace's rhetoric provided a safety valve for the resentments unleashed by federal involvement in civil rights and by examples of black violence such as the Watts Riot of 1965 in Los Angeles. "Bearded beatnik bureaucrats" had laid the ground for urban rioting by contributing leadership and public funds to finance discord, he told a national gathering of police officers in 1966. In an oral report to his state legislature the next year, Wallace tied Washington's perceived excesses to an alleged assault on democratic procedure and to disrespect for the abilities of ordinary people. "The people of this country are simply fed up with the antics of strutting bureaucrats lording it over them–telling them when to go to bed at night and when to get up in the morning," he stated. "They are fed up with bureaucrats telling them that they haven't got sense enough to run their own schools and hospitals and local governments." Laws of Congress, complained Wallace, were "now amended, supplemented, or repealed at will by mimeographed regulations and guidelines–by oral directives and penciled memorandums issued by faceless petty executives."[62]

As the Alabama governor's message resonated with national audiences, he went on television's *Meet the Press* in April 1967 to announce a possible run for the presidency on a third-party ticket. Declaring himself the leader of a people's crusade to alter the nation's domestic affairs, Wallace quipped that it did not "make any difference whether top, leading politicians endorse this movement or not." In fact, he asserted, public figures who resisted the backlash against big government would "get run over by this average man in the street–this man in the textile mill, this man in the steel mill, this barber, the beautician, the policeman on the beat . . . the little businessman." Once in gear, candidate Wallace insisted that the real issue of the 1968 campaign was the tendency of elites in "pseudo-intellectual government" to look down their noses at "the little people" who were the country's source of greatness.[63]

Like Goldwater and Reagan, Wallace tied high taxes, inflation, and government spending to a political class that seemingly tolerated crime, civil disorder, disrespect for authority, and the decline of the work ethic and traditional family.

As a populist, the Alabama governor denounced the tendency of Washington's elites to intellectualize societal problems and simultaneously ask ordinary taxpayers to fund their visionary social programs. Polling suggested that two-thirds of the support for Wallace's American Independent Party came from an unlikely coalition of Goldwater Republicans and Democratic union members. Once the ballots were cast, the Alabaman carried the entire Deep South and took nearly ten million votes, 13.5 percent of the nationwide tally. Despite the late return of traditional Democrats to Vice President Hubert Humphrey's fold, Wallace ran particularly strongly in blue-collar and white ethnic districts of northern industrial cities and suburbs.[64]

***

The real beneficiaries of the issues raised by Goldwater, Reagan, and Wallace were 1968 Republican presidential candidate Richard M. Nixon and his running mate, Spiro T. Agnew, Maryland's Greek-American governor. Addressing voter concerns about moral disorder and social instability, the Nixon-Agnew team tapped white fears of black street crime, widespread anger at inner-city rioting, resentment of student demonstrations against the Vietnam War, and opposition to perceived racial preferences in government programs. An astute politician, Nixon exposed the connections between high-minded liberals and the underclass. "In a time when the national focus is concentrated upon the unemployed, the impoverished and the dispossessed," the candidate told Republican followers, "the working Americans have become the forgotten Americans. In a time when the national rostrums and forums are given over to shouters and protesters and demonstrators, they have become the Silent Americans."[65]

Looking beyond its historic strength in the eastern business and financial establishment, Nixon's Republican Party exploited the political and cultural antagonisms between so-called Middle America and the liberal cosmopolitanites of the professional classes. The party's populist approach highlighted the traditional social values of white southerners and rural westerners. But it also addressed the antielitist sensibilities of white ethnic Catholics, blue-collar workers, union affiliates, and lower-middle-class Jews in the urban Northeast and Midwest. Nixon and Agnew reached out to these constituencies by expropriating Wallace's attack on liberalism as the self-indulgent lifestyle of the affluent and overly educated. In one of the closest presidential elections in U.S. history, the Republican team outpolled Democratic candidates Hubert Humphrey and Edmund S. Muskie by 43.4 percent to 42.7 percent.[66] The party of John Kennedy and Lyndon Johnson would return to the White House for only four of the next twenty-four years. Richard Nixon had orchestrated an electoral revolution that threatened to eclipse the social interventionism and cultural liberalism of government managers, policy intellectuals, and New Class professionals.

8

Class War: The Liberal Establishment Besieged, 1968–1980

Richard M. Nixon's 1968 electoral victory successfully exploited resentment over the federal government's role in addressing racial and economic inequities through broad social policies and programs. Yet the Nixon administration turned to the interventionist model of the political class when it undertook a controversial affirmative action program in the construction industry. Chapter 8 outlines the manner in which the president's turn to government policy planners and social managers on the minority job front offered an ironic contrast to White House efforts to marginalize New Left students and opponents of the Vietnam War as cultural elitists. By describing the pro-war rhetoric of organized labor leaders and politicians such as Nixon, Vice President Spiro T. Agnew, and George C. Wallace, this chapter explores the class dimensions to public disagreements over the war and the role of political intellectuals. It then examines how the White House sought to shift public debate to the issue of the "Liberal Establishment" and how Nixon's obsessions with the guardian class influenced his participation in the Watergate scandal. Chapter 8 concludes by outlining how liberal policymakers, social activists, and cultural liberals became prime targets of populist conservatives in the late-1970s and how disaffection with government undermined the presidency of Jimmy Carter.

***

Despite Richard Nixon's rhetoric, the new president had surprising difficulty in dismantling the government presence his speeches condemned. Nixon was unable to reverse a trend in which federal funding of state and local governments tripled while Washington's budget doubled between 1960 and 1970. After one year of Republican rule, 47 percent of high-level federal officeholders remained Democrats and only 17 percent Republicans. An explosion of government regulations, standards, and guidelines contributed to a sixfold increase in the size of the *Federal Register* during Nixon's tenure. Despite White House criticism of welfare, more households received family assistance under the Republican administration than during the Johnson years. Furthermore, government spending on applied social research more than quadrupled to nearly $1 billion between 1965 and 1975. Significantly, one third of the career civil servants and top federal appointees of the 1970s had social science degrees.[1]

The growing influence of the political class appeared to be strongest in race relations, the area of domestic affairs in which Richard Nixon compiled one of his most contradictory records. Supporting the principle of racial equality, Nixon legitimized the Kennedy–Johnson legacy of rights reform by accommodating to it. The president signed a second Voting Rights Act in 1970. He also accelerated public school desegregation in the southern states by allowing officials to replace administrative funding cutoffs under Title VI of the Civil Rights Act with Justice Department lawsuits promoting busing. During Nixon's first term, the percentage of African-American children in southern segregated public schools dropped from 68 percent to 8 percent. Yet the president managed to shift the onus of racial busing from the White House to the courts. Nixon's judicial appointments and public discourse also discouraged compulsory busing from spreading to northern suburbs predominated by white Republicans and George Wallace Democrats. By 1974, more than half the black pupils in northern and western states attended schools that were 95 percent or more African-American.[2]

The paradox of the Nixon administration's civil rights policy was most apparent in its controversial pursuit of affirmative action in employment. By promoting minority hiring programs in heavily unionized fields such as construction, the executive branch sought to repair its image as a lukewarm supporter of racial justice. Yet White House focus on economic rights and market freedoms pleased traditionalists who distrusted government sponsorship of intrusive changes in social patterns or policies that threatened to distribute income. Nixon operatives also reaped political advantages by pitting trade union Democrats against their historic allies in the civil rights and liberal community. Since affirmative action came out of the Department of Labor, moreover, the reforms consolidated executive authority and freed the administration from reliance on a Congress controlled by the opposition party.[3]

Although affirmative action in construction came to symbolize civil rights activity in the 1970s, its origins lay in the Kennedy and Johnson era. Three years after an NAACP report outlined racial discrimination in the railroad and building trades, a 1961 inquiry by the U.S. Commission on Civil Rights concluded that exclusion of African-Americans from construction apprenticeships was a major cause of black poverty. An executive order by President Kennedy required unions engaged in government work to eliminate discrimination. Although nearly all leaders of the American Federation of Labor-Congress of Industrial Organizations (AFL-CIO) signed a voluntary pledge to comply, the building trades unions refused. In 1962, Kennedy issued a second order requiring federal contractors to eliminate racial bias under the supervision of the government's Office of Contract Compliance. As black activists began organizing labor rights demonstrations at federal job sites, eighteen building trades unions agreed to end discrimination in apprenticeship training and membership.[4]

The labor leaders whose organizations were potentially impacted by affirmative action comprised an important element of President Johnson's Great Society cadre. Over two thousand local AFL-CIO union heads served on antipoverty community action boards and ran programs like Headstart, VISTA, and the Youth Corps. Yet OEO's focus on job training threatened union control of work standards, seniority procedures, and apprenticeship awards. Seeking to protect the right of sons to succeed their fathers and other prerogatives, building trades locals invoked grandfather clauses or resorted to other forms of nepotism that discriminated against African-Americans in apprenticeship and training programs. When Johnson created a mechanism for enforcing the equal employment provisions of the Civil Rights Act by issuing Executive Order 11246 in the fall of 1965, the Labor Department was assigned jurisdiction over federal construction contracts. Successful bidders now were required to submit evidence of compliance with government affirmative action standards before undertaking federal projects. The department soon created its own Office of Federal Contract Compliance (OFCC) to administer the hiring program.[5]

Between 1966 and 1967, the Johnson administration required construction contractors in St. Louis, San Francisco, and Cleveland to commit equal employment opportunity plans to writing, a practice that resulted in conferences in which employers agreed to minority hiring numbers. In September 1967, the Federal Executive Board of the Department of Housing and Urban Development (HUD) devised a plan for Philadelphia federal construction contractors that required low-bidders to be in compliance with OFCC minority hiring guidelines. The following year, the Labor Department ruled that contractors could be disqualified from federal projects unless they took "affirmative action" to include racial minorities in all phases of work. Justice Department lawyers now insisted that unions accept any African-American apprentice who possessed qualifications equal to the least qualified whites.[6]

Surprisingly, the election of a Republican president did little to change the federal government's embrace of affirmative action. Following Nixon's victory in 1968, Lyndon Johnson's outgoing Comptroller General ruled that the Philadelphia Plan was illegal because it compelled contractors to negotiate on minority hiring in postbid sessions. Yet as civil rights demonstrators threatened to shut down government construction sites if job demands were not met by the new administration, the Nixon White House supported the efforts of its Secretary of Labor, George P. Shultz, to revive the Philadelphia employment formula. A Princeton graduate who held a Ph.D. in labor economics from the Massachusetts Institute of Technology and a former fellow at the prestigious Center for Advanced Study in the Behavioral Sciences, the consensus-minded Shultz had served as the dean of the University of Chicago Business School. In June 1969, the Labor Department cited a "deplorably low rate" of minority employment in the building trades and announced that Under Secretary

Arthur A. Fletcher would reinstate the Philadelphia Plan across a five-county area. Under its terms an OFCC staff member would determine how many non-white construction workers were to be hired in each job category before federal contracts were signed.[7]

The new Philadelphia Plan, described by Shultz as "a fair and realistic approach, not an arbitrary imposition," complemented Nixonian economic thinking. The philosophy of the scheme was best described by Fletcher, an African-American who had shined shoes as a youth before becoming a professional football player and serving as special urban affairs aide to Washington governor Daniel J. Evans. Social legislation and litigation had opened up opportunities for racial minorities, the assistant labor secretary told the *New York Times*, but the Nixon administration intended to concentrate on equality of economic opportunity. In order to end high unemployment rates among non-whites, the government had to adopt "visible, measurable goals to correct obvious imbalances." Such an approach received endorsement from civil rights leader Whitney M. Young, Jr., executive director of the National Urban League, who viewed the construction hiring program as a possible model for the rest of the nation.[8]

Labor Department Solicitor Lawrence H. Silberman announced that the Philadelphia Plan fell within the Civil Rights Act of 1964 and derived from the presidential authority embodied in Franklin Roosevelt's Executive Order 8802 of 1941, which required federal defense contractors to practice equal employment. Nevertheless, the Nixon administration's adoption of affirmative action rivaled school busing as the most contentious legacy of the civil rights revolution. The controversy centered on a key section in Title VII of the Civil Rights Act, authored by Illinois Republican senator Everett M. Dirksen, that explicitly prohibited preferential employment on the basis of race, sex, or ethnicity, and outlawed quotas as a means of addressing work force imbalances. Although officials like Silberman insisted that affirmative action was a painless form of social intervention that required mere goals, not quotas, opponents argued that federal bureaucrats were compelling employers to hire without regard to individual merit.[9]

The brief against preferential treatment in affirmative action programs was taken up early in 1969 by Arizona Republican senator Paul J. Fannin. A Stanford graduate with experience in the oil business, Fannin supported feminist demands for an Equal Rights Amendment to erase gender bias. Yet he objected to rulings by President Johnson's Department of Labor that assumed that employment tests discriminated against racial minorities when nonwhites failed. Fannin asserted that government recruiting plans sought to accomplish "a so-called social purpose" without benefit of legislation. Accordingly, he introduced a Senate amendment to abolish Executive Order 11246 and to limit hiring programs to current law and the jurisdiction of the Equal Employment Opportunity Commission (EEOC), which Congress had created, instead of the executive branch OFCC. Noting that twenty-two federal agencies and thirty-five contract compliance officers already were involved in the affirmative action jobs bureaucracy, Fannin castigated arrogant and misguided "zealots" for fishing expeditions in which they acted as "judge and jury." Special treatment to redress past wrongs, he insisted, was "plainly unfair and un-American."[10]

As the administration prepared to authorize a new Philadelphia Plan in July 1969, Senate Minority Leader Dirksen and key Republicans asked for a delay. A month later Nixon controller general Elmer B. Staats responded to inquiries from Fannin and Arkansas Democrat John L. McClelland by informing Secretary Shultz that the affirmative action scheme violated civil rights legislation by requiring employers to make race a factor in hiring. Following Labor Department hearings, input from civil rights groups, and September protests by black activists at building sites in Pittsburgh and Chicago, however, Shultz ordered the plan into effect in six skilled construction crafts in federally assisted projects in Philadelphia. As Attorney General John Mitchell ruled that the jobs formula did not violate the quota provisions of the Civil Rights Act, Nixon officials committed themselves to "good faith efforts" to increase the ratio of the building industry's nonwhite workers from 4 percent to 26 percent and pledged to apply the affirmative action hiring plan to nine other cities.[11]

***

The most vociferous opposition to the Philadelphia Plan emerged in the AFL-CIO, a longtime civil rights ally in favor of broad limitations on workplace discrimination and a stronger EEOC. Using a $1.5 milllion Labor Department grant in 1968, the Federation had established the Human Resources Development Institute to promote the recruitment, training, hiring, and upgrading of jobless or underemployed workers in cities with large African-American populations. The AFL-CIO's Building and Construction Trades Department featured a federally funded Apprenticeship Outreach training program designed to target minority groups. In Chicago, construction unions responded to job site protests by black activists in September 1969 by announcing a plan to work with the Nixon administration and the Urban League in bringing twenty-five thousand nonwhites into the apprenticeship program within five years.[12]

Although labor leaders acknowledged the need to open up job opportunities for nonwhites, they objected to control of apprenticeships by either civil rights advocates or federal bureaucrats. Participants in the September 1969 convention of the AFL-CIO Building and Construction Trades asked local unions to recruit "qualified minority journeymen," but voted unanimously to oppose contractor "quota" systems or "unsound or unlawful" measures like the Philadelphia Plan. "We support the right of the Negro to justice," stated the delegates. "But we cannot accept the simplistic idea that the arithmetic of a population ratio should become the standard for selection and entry into employment." Union representatives insisted that construction trainees needed four years of apprenticeship before promotion to skilled positions. Noting that the mere assertion of a proposal by a minority group did not necessarily equate with the interests of all workers, the resolution condemned the legal verbiage of the Philadelphia Plan for disguising quotas.[13]

The building trades also took issue with government figures concerning minority participation. The "hard research" behind a Labor Department Manpower Administration Survey, complained union representatives, amounted to a pencilled notation in the corner of an official memorandum quoting another bureaucrat's "conservative estimate." AFL-CIO leaders disputed Nixon administration contentions that African-Americans comprised less than 2 percent of Philadelphia building trade workers. Federation president George Meany countered that 12 percent of the city's construction employees and 30 percent of its unionized workers in skilled trades were black. Meany told the building trades convention that the Nixon White House was using the construction unions as a "whipping boy" for reckless charges of racial discrimination while ignoring school segregation in the South. Delegates at the AFL-CIO's October national conference declared that the Philadelphia Plan masked efforts to divide racial minorities, liberals, and organized labor, thereby enhancing Republican political interests.[14]

The controversy over affirmative action in the construction industry took on added drama when the Senate Judiciary Committee's Subcommittee on the Separation of Powers opened hearings on the Philadelphia Plan in late October 1969. The panel was chaired by constitutional expert and North Carolina Democrat Sam J. Ervin, Jr., and included John McClellan and Republicans Quentin N. Burdick of North Dakota and Roman L. Hruska of Nebraska. Citing the controller general's opinion that the hiring scheme set up illegal quotas, Ervin asked whether the Shultz plan discriminated against white workers and if it violated congressional authority. The senator used a Brookings Institution report of 1967 to suggest that the Labor Department's compliance specialist often applied subjective quotas in deciding how hard to push contractors. "One thing that I have never been quite able to understand," declared Ervin, was "why public officials have such an insatiable thirst for power." Construction union leaders played upon such concerns by arguing that the Philadelphia Plan's broad statutory language contradicted the intent of Congress.[15]

With congressional prerogatives still an issue in December 1969, the Senate Appropriations Commttee reported out an amendment by Paul Fannin that prohibited funds for any program or contract ruled illegal by the controller general. Although President Nixon urged aides to press for a reversal and Secretary Shultz and Attorney General Mitchell both condemned the proviso, the Senate used only four hours of debate to approve the measure in a 73 to 13 vote. The next day Nixon issued a written statement defending the Philadelphia Plan. "Nothing is more unfair than that the same Americans who pay taxes should by any pattern of discriminary practices be deprived of an equal opportunity to work on Federal construction contracts," he declared. As the proposal moved to the House, presidential aides persuaded NAACP head Roy Wilkins to endorse the hiring scheme. The House faced "the most important civil rights vote in a long, long time," declared Shultz as he emerged from an Oval Office meeting. The Philadelphia Plan was "our last opportunity" to narrow the income distribution between whites and African-Americans, concurred Assistant Labor Secretary Fletcher.[16]

Nixon's embrace of affirmative action played havoc with conventional alignments over race. On the day of the House debate on the Fannin amendment, another White House statement threatened an appropriations veto if the "historic and critical civil rights vote" went the wrong way. Republicans such as Michigan floor leader Gerald R. Ford supported the president's stance on "civil rights and jobs," while Democrats like House Appropriations Committee chair George H. Mahon of Texas viewed the Philadelphia Plan in terms of congressional control of spending. In the end, administration mobilization of liberal opinion enabled the House to defeat the rider, 208 to 156. The Senate immediately reversed its earlier support of the Fannin measure in a 39 to 29 vote. Key to the dramatic White House victory was the conversion of five previously hostile northern Republican senators and one Democrat.[17]

By invoking the rhetoric of civil rights, the Nixon administration managed to orchestrate a stunning defeat for organized labor. The AFL-CIO fought back, denouncing the Philadelphia Plan as "a political gambit" of little practical value designed to confuse the public and hide the president's domestic failures. George Meany told the National Press Club in January 1970 that the scheme was a "concoction and contrivance of a bureaucrat's imagination." Employers would achieve compliance by shifting minority workers to government contracts, claimed Meany. The one-time plumber's apprentice insisted that the Labor Department's outreach training program, with which the Federation cooperated, offered the only viable means of bringing nonwhites into the work force. "There seems to be a belief among a large number of people," lamented Meany, "that anybody can be a plumber, anybody can be a sheet metal worker, anybody can be an electrician, with very little preparation or training."[18]

Just as Congress appeared to reconcile itself to affirmative action in employment, Senator Ervin revealed that in November 1969 OFCC Director John Wilks had issued a nonpublicized order establishing minority hiring quotas. Ervin noted that the Nixon administration had assured Congress that the Philadelphia Plan merely required good faith efforts by employers. Yet the Labor Department document stated that "the rate of minority applicants recruited should approximate or equal the ratio of minorities to the applicant population in each location." The North Carolina senator now charged that legislators had acted on false assumptions when rescinding the Fannin amendment a month earlier. Wilks acknowledged that the draft statement had been "circulated prematurely" but insisted that all Labor Department mandates had their legal precedence in President Johnson's executive orders.[19]

Following Ervin's outburst, OFCC Director Wilks and Secretary Shultz signed a modified version of the affirmative action directive in late January 1970. The long-awaited Order No. 4 gave all federal contractors 120 days to set up goals and timetables to ensure that the percentage of minority workers in their employ approximated the ratio of nonwhites in the surrounding work force. Employers who failed to show "good cause" for deficiencies could have their service contracts cancelled. In contrast to previous mandates that limited coverage to government construction bids exceeding $500,000, the new order applied to any federal contract involving at least $50,000 and fifty workers.[20]

***

While the controversial affirmative action program revealed the extent to which the Nixon administration had turned to government involvement in race relations, federal officials quietly cooperated with union leaders in efforts to integrate the nation's work force. In Chicago, Mayor Richard Daley brokered a deal between civil rights activists, building trades locals, and construction contractors that promised to bring four thousand black employees into a union-supervised training program for skilled jobs. The Labor Department helped to arrange a similar agreement in Pittsburgh to employ 1,250 African-Americans as construction journeymen. In the Washington, D.C. area, the AFL-CIO Building and Construction Trades Council responded to Secretary Shultz's threat of hiring quotas by pledging to train and place at least five hundred minority workers in one year. By the summer of 1970, over one hundred cities were considering voluntary plans to integrate the construction trades. Significantly, the minority share of overall union apprenticeships jumped from 6 percent to 14 percent between 1967 and 1973.[21]

Informal efforts to promote racial integration in the workplace were supplemented by an activist government. Nixon's Supreme Court endorsed affirmative action in *Griggs v. Duke Power Company* (1971), when it unanimously ruled against preemployment tests unrelated to job skills with a discriminatory impact. The president signed the Equal Employment Act of 1972, which extended EEOC jurisdiction. As the commission's annual budget approached $30 million, the number of attorneys on its staff tripled to three hundred in three years. Minority procurement set-asides by federal agencies also leaped from $8.2 million in fiscal 1972 to $242 million two years later. Meanwhile, Nixon approved OFCC directives that brought women workers under equal protection guidelines. By 1979, Labor Department hiring regulations would cover nearly seventeen thousand companies employing over twenty-six million people.[22]

Disagreements over affirmative action quotas, poor enforcement by contracting agencies, and inadequate staffing by federal compliance units contributed to the virtual erosion of the expanded Philadelphia Plan in Nixon's first term. Nevertheless, the administration's management of employment race relations placed it in the position of embracing the social regulation promoted by the cosmopolitan political class its rhetoric denounced. By focusing on broad rule-making and compensation for past damages instead of resolution of individual civil rights cases, federal agencies now de-emphasized the importance of personal intent and conscious wrongdoing in workplace conflicts. Under affirmative action procedures, government administrators potentially had the power to award economic benefits to members of groups that had suffered historic racial discrimination at the hands of employers. In effect, the new regulations appeared to require white workers to absorb penalties for the past wrongs of the market. In a period in which federal construction contracts substantially declined and in which inflation led to a loss of real wages, labor leaders predictably denounced racial preferences in hiring and promotion as a violation of traditional standards of equal opportunity and fair play.[23]

Nixon's support for workplace affirmative action, no matter how limited, complicated his courtship of organized labor and his obsession with Wallace voters. Seeking to recruit socially conservative, "uneducated," white-ethnic, and blue-collar Democrats to the Republican fold, the chief executive frequently sought the White House counsel of union leader Meany, a religiously devout and patriotic Irish-Catholic. Nixon cleverly used such meetings to tap working-class animosity to the adversarial subculture of the 1960s to which many post-World War II "baby boomers" were attracted. Anticipating professional careers in government, social services, communications, and the knowledge sector, an articulate minority of secular and socially liberal university students and academics had turned at middecade to an emancipatory counterculture defined by rock music, consciousness-altering drugs, and sexual experimentation. In politics, idealistic sympathy for the civil rights crusade led progressive-minded activists into the New Left, a movement spanning the collective struggles of African Americans, Hispanics, American Indians, feminists, students, and the poor. The broadly defined struggle also embraced radical environmentalism, opposition to U.S. policy in Vietnam and the Third World, and participation in a communitarian social revolution that sought to decentralize power and restructure capitalism.[24]

Nixon's attempt to win the hearts and minds of labor leaders reflected his understanding of the ideological war spawned by the predominantly upper-middle-class activists of the New Left and counterculture. Radical organizers in Students for a Democratic Society (SDS) and the University of California at Berkeley's Free Speech Movement (FSM) had pictured college students as future knowledge producers and technicians who ultimately would comprise a key sector of a newly defined and revolutionary working class. New Left theorists assumed that industrial workers would serve as willing allies and loyal cadres in the inevitable confrontation against the corporate elite. Yet movement leaders tended to view blue-collar workers and members of the lower-middle class as unenlightened defenders of the racial and political status quo whose social consciousness had to be elevated if they were to play a progressive role in history. Such condescension prompted many Americans to dismiss the affluent militants as an arrogantly self-important and contemptuously disrespectful branch of the American Establishment whose disdain for working people reflected ignorance of the importance of traditional social values to democratic society.[25]

Organized labor's anger at the movement surfaced most dramatically on the racial front. Following the conversion of the Student Nonviolent Coordinating Committee to African-American nationalism and black power in 1966, many white New Left activists aligned themselves with the Black Panthers, a military-style organization that sought to transform race pride into community control of ghetto policing and local institutions by self-selected leaders. Accepting guilt for "white skin privilege" and seeking to vindicate their own political fervor and historic role, white radicals uncritically accepted Panther hyperbole about working-class racism and the need for armed revolution. Such posturing infuriated labor leaders. Middle-class students were spreading the view that union loyalists were "largely reactionaries and even 'honkies,' " complained the editors of the *AFL-CIO News*. The new radicals were "elite liberals" who represented "paper" organizations nurtured on foundation grants and ample publicity, charged the Federation's Lane Kirkland. Civil rights veteran and labor crusader Bayard Rustin dismissed New Left dreams of revolution as the product of "a small and sick and sorry lot" whose inflated notion of strength came "from seeing themselves too often on television."[26]

Cultural critiques of the working class by student radicals and lifestyle dissidents further alienated the labor movement. Anarchic denunciations of patriotism, the police, conventional sexuality, the work ethic, and social authority appeared condescending, self-indulgent, and irresponsible to those who cherished traditional ties and obligations to families, neighborhoods, ethnic identities, religious faiths, and national unity. Ronald Reagan's attack on the "beatniks and malcontents" of the University of California at Berkeley in 1966 demonstrated how successfully such sentiments could be exploited. As noted by Tom Kahn, executive director of the socialist League for Industrial Democracy and a frequent contributor to AFL-CIO publications, disrespect for core values often reflected a privileged position. Kahn remarked that while an invisible half of the population went directly to work following high school, affluent youth were segregated in prestigious colleges and universities, where their views mirrored those of the academics who studied and theorized about them. New inventions and cultural styles, he observed, usually were "acquired first by society's chief beneficiaries, the well-to-do and their children."[27]

For many labor leaders, the New Left was a sectarian and narrowly based movement that appealed to aspiring intellectuals and elites in the humanistic professions by invoking the moral superiority of its followers over the nation's working class. Describing student activists as the first generation of American radicals out of sympathy with organized labor, Kahn chastized SDS and other groups for a lack of interest in the material aspirations and needs of ordinary people. The movement's rhetoric about powerlessness and participatory decision making, he contended, was merely a projection onto the poor of frustrations over its own unappreciated place in society. Targeting the planning proclivities of would-be social service providers and policy interventionists, Kahn declared that poor people were more interested in escaping poverty than in "joining committees and experiencing the dubious pleasure of endless meetings and discussions."[28]

***

By courting organized labor, the Nixon White House hoped to gain additional political capital by exploiting sharp divisions between student radicals and the working class over the Vietnam War. Although the liberal Kennedy and Johnson administrations had been responsible for escalating the conflict, U.S. involvement in East Asia long had been the favored cause of the nationalists and anticommunists who most strongly opposed the professionals and knowledge elites of the political class. Significantly, the antiwar movement thrived on college campuses, where students began to mount peaceful teach-ins, demonstrations, marches, and antidraft protests in 1965. As the New Left began to depict Vietnam as the ultimate symbol of U.S. brutality and oppression, however, antiwar theatrics became more disruptive. By 1967, radical activists were taking control of university offices, harassing government speakers and military recruiters, occupying armed forces induction centers, burning selective service registration cards, burglarizing and destroying draft board files, rallying behind the banners of the Communist Viet Cong, incinerating American flags, and engaging in violent street actions against police. By the end of the decade, militant elements of SDS had joined secret affinity groups in the Weather Underground, where they staged bombings of symbolic government targets and prepared for urban guerrilla warfare.[29]

From its inception in the early 1960s, the New Left pictured itself as a besieged minority that saw through the exploitation of the capitalist order and the false consciousness it attributed to American workers and consumers. As the death toll in Vietnam mounted and antiwar demonstrations reached fervor pitch in the Nixon years, protestors faced increasing skepticism from a frustrated public caught midway between an untrustworthy government and a radical intelligentsia with whom it was difficult to identify. Activists further alienated themselves from mainstream opinion by depicting U.S. foreign policy as an extension of society's pervasive greed, arrogance, and moral decay. Aligning with the armed struggles of Third World anti-imperialists, SDS dedicated itself to "bringing the war home" to confront the evil power of the empire from within. Revolutionary communiques from the Weather Underground and Black Panthers added a threatening tone to the movement by associating it with extremist ideologies and virulently anti-American and antidemocratic rhetoric.[30]

President Nixon's strategy for containing anti-Vietnam War sentiment had to contend with the reality of widespread disaffection with the military effort. Contrary to conventional assumptions, working people often were more opposed to the war than those of higher economic sectors. As early as September 1966, Gallup polls found that only 44 percent of manual employees supported Lyndon Johnson's handling of the conflict as opposed to 48 percent of business and professional respondents. By 1970, 48 percent of northern workers endorsed an immediate withdrawal of troops in contrast to 40 percent of the white middle class. Two years later, only 47 percent of blue-collar workers approved of Nixon's Vietnam policies in contrast to 50 percent of the general sample.[31]

Despite considerable disenchantment over the crusade in Vietnam, however, large proportions of the American working class remained bitterly estranged from the antiwar movement. As historian Christian G. Appy has noted, over 80 percent of the 2.5 million soldiers who served in Vietnam came from poor or working-class families. In contrast, educational deferments provided college and university students with exemptions during the heaviest years of the draft before 1969. Sensitive about the class privilege of aspiring professionals and intellectual elites, ordinary Americans frequently saw campus protests as disloyal attacks on troops by those whose affluence enabled them to avoid military service. Many were angered further by strikes against tax-supported institutions of higher learning which they were unable to attend. Veterans often resented media compliance in singling out antiwar leaders as representatives of their generation and believed that a corrupt and decadent Establishment had betrayed them by surrendering to the anti-Americanism and class prejudices of the educated sector. Gallup pollsters found a 3 to 1 unfavorable response to antiwar demonstrations at the height of Vietnam protest in November 1969. "Working-class anger at the antiwar movement," concluded Apply, "often represented class conflict, not conflict over the legitimacy of the war."[32]

The class tensions of the Vietnam era exploded in April 1968 when an "action faction" of SDS led a student protest against Columbia University's sponsorship of war-related research. Advocating the use of disruptive tactics to change social consciousness, radical leaders engineered an eight-day occupation of university adminstration offices. When campus officials called in one thousand members of the New York City tactical police force in a late-night raid, 692 activists were arrested and over one hundred students and several faculty intermediaries injured by antiriot clubs, brass knuckles, and extremely rough police tactics. The confrontation, recalled sociologist and former SDS leader Todd Gitlin, involved a "class war" between privileged youth of the upper-middle class and working-class police.[33]

Campus disruptions like Columbia provided an additional backdrop for George Wallace's independent campaign for the presidency in 1968. Rather than portraying the Vietnam War as a political controversy, Wallace cleverly focused on the antiwar movement as a symptom of the nation's alleged departure from traditional cultural values and respect for law. Targeting protesters as "silver-spooned brats" who rejected patriotism and social authority, the third-party candidate offered the chance to strike back rhetorically and symbolically against the professional elite and its offspring. Wallace's message seemed particularly geared toward blue-collar sensibilities. Appearing on television's *Meet the Press* in June 1968, the Alabama governor denounced college professors who supported the Communist cause in Vietnam as unworthy of academic freedom protections. "When I become your president," Wallace assured a crowd in Missouri, "I'm going to ask my attorney general to seek an indictment against any college professor who calls for a communist victory. . . . That's treason."[34]

Similar antagonism toward aspiring guardians erupted during antiwar demonstrations in Chicago during the 1968 Democratic National Convention. Participating in a "festival of life" that sought to unite countercultural and radical adherents and embarrass the Democrats as the war party, thousands of protesters engaged in nightly rounds of street warfare after Chicago city police used tear gas and clubs to clear them out of public parks. The widely televised disturbances climaxed on the night of the presidential nomination with a police attack on demonstrators and media outside the main delegates' hotel. When the week was over, 668 arrests had been made, over four hundred protesters had been given first aid, and 192 police had been injured. New Leftists rejoiced that Mayor Richard Daley's police had been exposed as a repressive instrument of the state. Yet most Americans sympathized with the use of official force and resented radical derision of the working-class police as "pigs." Only 10 percent of the public supported the demonstrators and a mere 25 percent of Vietnam doves condemned Daley's officers. "The confrontation at Chicago probably etched the lines of social class as sharply as they have ever been drawn in America," concluded two of the era's top political observers.[35]

Chicago helped to place Richard Nixon in the White House and contributed to his administration's politicized approach to the Vietnam War controversy. Like George Wallace, whose cultivation of social issues he continued to emulate, Nixon blamed an affluent liberal-intellectual Establishment for encouraging social unrest and contributing to moral decay and the collapse of the American spirit. Once in office, the veteran Republican planned to disengage the United States from Indochina without appearing to cave in to the antiwar critics his constituents despised. Nixon's strategy emerged as Vietnam activists planned a war moratorium day for October 1969 and the presidents of seventy-nine colleges signed an appeal for accelerated U.S. withdrawal from Southeast Asia. By then, polls showed 57 percent public support for gradual disengagement and 55 percent in favor of reduced military efforts. Seeking to shift attention from an unpopular war, White House speechwriters Pat Buchanan and William Safire composed a series of addresses for Vice President Spiro Agnew. Recent demonstrations had been organized by "an effete corps of impudent snobs who characterized themselves as intellectuals," Agnew assured a gathering of

New Orleans Republicans. Warning of "a spirit of national masochism," the vice president attacked the toleration of "hard-core dissidents and professional anarchists."[36]

Shortly before a second moratorium in November 1969, Nixon took his campaign against the political intellectuals of the antiwar movement to television. The president solemnly promised to reject "precipitate withdrawal" and proposed a measured disengagement from Vietnam according to a secret timetable. Requesting support from "the great Silent Majority," he vowed that his actions would not be dictated by "mounting demonstrations in the street." "If a vocal minority prevails over reason and the will of the majority," warned Nixon, "this nation has no future as a free society." A special Gallup survey revealed that 77 percent of those who listened to the speech approved of the president's approach. Yet support may have been based on the assumption that the White House soon would end the military involvement in Vietnam. When the chief executive returned to television the following April 30th to announce that U.S. troops had moved into Cambodia, the nation faced a new round of protests. At Kent State University near Cleveland, Ohio, the Republican governor summoned the National Guard after antiwar rioters trashed the local business district and burned a Reserve Officers' Training Corps (ROTC) building. When guardsmen ordered the dispersal of a noon rally on campus and a few demonstrators tossed rocks and bottles, the troops fired across the university commons, killing four young people and wounding nine.[37]

***

Kent State symbolized the polarization of a nation unable to extricate itself from the divisive military stalemate in Indochina. By focusing on disruptive elements of the antiwar movement, the Nixon administration hoped to gain political points and be able to negotiate a favorable settlement of the war. Accordingly, Vice President Agnew responded to the Ohio shootings by condemning "elitists" who encouraged campus activists and shielded "psychotic and criminal elements." As student strikes shut down 536 campuses and protests erupted at 1,300 institutions in May 1970, surveys revealed that more than half the public blamed the Kent State demonstrators for the killings. Half of working-class respondents in favor of immediate withdrawal also expressed hostility to antiwar demonstrators. The class dynamics of Vietnam protest resurfaced four days after Kent State when more than five hundred New York City construction workers disrupted an antiwar rally on Wall Street and beat up over seventy demonstrators and bystanders, including four police. One worker claimed that the brawl began when a middle-aged protestor spit on the American flag. When the crowd moved to City Hall, it forced officials to raise a flag that had been lowered to half-mast in memory of the Kent State victims. Provoked by a display of peace banners, the workers then smashed windows and attacked terrorized students at nearby Pace College.[38]

Although construction workers had led the resistance to the Nixon administration's affirmative action programs, New York building trade unions rallied
to the defense of the president's Vietnam War policy. Seeking to demonstrate
"love of country and respect for our country's flag," labor leaders organized
a massive parade of one-hundred thousand working people down Broadway–
the nation's largest pro-government rally in memory. Framing the event as
a "Worker's Woodstock," *Time* described plumbers, bricklayers, steamfitters,
and ironworkers striding under "God Bless America" banners to the cheers of
Lower Manhattan office employees, Teamsters, and longshore workers. In an
expression of defiance toward campus protestors, longhaired youth, and upper-
middle-class liberals and intellectuals, marchers burned an effigy of New York
reform mayor John Lindsay. Less than a week later President Nixon invited a
construction union delegation to the White House and was presented with a
hard hat in a private ceremony.[39]

Having aroused the opposition of AFL-CIO leaders through sponsorship
of affirmative action in construction and other fields, the White House now
welcomed organized labor as a foreign policy ally and political partner in the
struggle against political intellectuals and antiwar elements. On Labor Day, 1970,
Nixon hosted a dinner for seventy-five union leaders and toasted George Meany,
the pro-war AFL-CIO chief who had supported the Cambodian incursion. Vice
President Agnew continued to court working-class votes when he opened the
fall congressional campaign. "The time has come for someone . . . to represent
the workingmen of this country, the forgotten men of American politics," declared Agnew. "Written off by the old elite, the workingman has become the
cornerstone of the New Majority." The next day the vice president advanced
the administration's rhetorical class war by denouncing "the pampered prodi-
gies" of the U.S. Senate. In October, Agnew told Delaware Republicans that a
"haughty clique" with a "shockingly warped sense of values" had legitimized social permissiveness. In contrast to the American majority, the new elite consisted
of "the raised-eyebrow cynics, the anti-intellectual intellectuals, the pampered
egotists who sneer at honesty, thrift, hard work, prudence, common decency,
and self-denial."[40]

Republican politicians like Agnew and Nixon had done much to reverse
the historic alliance between New Deal political intellectuals and the working
class. Yet George Wallace offered the most effective fusion of culture class war
and populist politics. Renewing his assaults on student demonstrators in the
1972 Democratic presidential primaries, Wallace restated the common fear of
working people that unchecked protest by middle-class dissenters and social
interventionists was a symptom of the nation's moral decline and encroaching
weakness. By tying the antiwar and civil rights movements to the alien bureaucracy in Washington, Wallace gave vent to the feelings of powerlessness
experienced by many of his followers. The average citizen who worked, paid
taxes, and held the country together, the candidate told a rally in Bradenton,

Florida, was "fed up with much of this liberalism and this kowtowing to the exotic few." Wallace charged that the Demoratic Party had betrayed ordinary people when it became the agent of the "so-called intelligentsia," "intellectual snobs," "hypocrites," and "briefcase-carrying bureaucrats." Democrats had succumbed to the liberal dogma that worshipped human intelligence at the expense of all other values.[41]

One day before winning the Maryland and Michigan primaries and weeks after a stunning victory in Florida, Wallace was shot and partially paralyzed in an attempted assassination with no apparent political motive. Once the Alabama governor withdrew from the Democratic race, Richard Nixon was free to claim his populist constituency. In a confidential 1972 campaign memo, the president targeted the social issues of crime, busing, drugs, welfare, and inflation as the "gut" concerns of the coming contest. Although Nixon requested $2.5 billion for remedial education in disadvantaged schools as his first term ended, he called for a congressional moratorium on busing. Denouncing "arbitrary" federal requirements, "whether administrative or judicial," the chief executive now attacked the racial quotas his administration earlier had promoted. "The way to end discrimination against some," he insisted, was "not to begin discrimination against others." Mandatory quotas were a "dangerous detour away from the traditional value of measuring a person on the basis of ability."[42]

Republican campaign strategy in 1972 was enhanced by the emergence of South Dakota senator George McGovern, a history Ph.D. and critic of the Vietnam War, as the Democratic candidate. Nixon's reluctance to withdraw from Vietnam had strengthened the position of affluent and culturally progressive Democrats opposed to the war. Procedural rule changes after 1968 further shifted the party's balance of power. Following the recommendations of a commission chaired by McGovern, primaries and open caucuses played a larger role in the selection of convention delegates. Affirmative action guidelines also mandated specific quotas to guarantee representation for African-Americans, Hispanics, Asians, females, and youth. Indeed, the 1972 convention expelled Mayor Daley's elected delegation of Chicago political veterans and white ethnics for insufficient numbers of blacks and women. The new rules empowered upper-middle-class reformers at the expense of the white working class: over 40 percent of McGovern delegates had post-baccalaureate degrees. Accordingly, floor debate included calls for more affirmative action, recognition of homosexual rights, school busing, and legalization of marijuana.[43]

Like George Wallace, Nixon pictured McGovern and the antiwar crowd as a privileged elite remote from the sentiments and concerns of ordinary citizens. The president was furious that nearly 90 percent of university student body leaders and college newspaper editors supported the Democratic candidate, while the margin was 698 to 131 for Harvard law students and 34 to 4 for their professors. Sensing that McGovern's weak spot was his "pretentious moralism," Nixon ordered campaign staffers to cultivate the "New American Majority" and capture the Wallace vote with appeals to patriotism, anti-permissiveness, religiosity, and moral values. People in the big cities and surrounding suburbs were "soft," he confided, unlike the southerners, residents of the mountain and farm states, and white ethnics, who had not been "poisoned by the elite universities and the media." Five days before the 1972 election, Nixon went on radio to condemn liberal elites and bureaucrats for believing that "people just do not know what's good for them." The president sought to marginalize McGovernites by assuring voters that they had no reason to feel guilty about enjoying what they earned or wanting their children to be in good schools close to home.[44]

***

Amassing the support of nearly 80 percent of Wallace voters from 1968, a majority of the white working class, and two-thirds of all professionals, Nixon and Agnew won a record victory with a near-61 percent landslide. The White House rejoiced that the electorate had rejected the politics of the New Left and counterculture and believed it finally had received the mandate to roll back the welfare state, trim the federal bureaucracy, and conduct its own foreign policy. Since the 1940s, populists from Joe McCarthy to George Wallace had complained of an eastern liberal Establishment that included influential think tanks and foundations, Ivy League universities, elite journals and periodicals, and powerful Washington public interest law firms. Perceived as a semi-official government, the informal network was tied to the civil rights movement, the social welfare state, and the European focus of U.S. international relations. Nixon was convinced that four remnants of the power bloc—the press, the bureaucracy, Congress, and the intelligence community—were particularly hostile to his administration. The Establishment hated him, the president told aides, because he never had been "captured by them."[45]

As the White House basked in the electoral victory of 1972, Nixon conveyed his passionate contempt for the guardian class, a fury partly rooted in the distant controversies of the Alger Hiss case. While top conservatives went into big law firms and corporations, the president explained to his staff, the best liberals found their way into public service or teaching. More than half the career people in the State Department came from the Ivy League, he complained, where they played "those frilly games" like squash and crew. "No Godamn *Harvard* men," Nixon insisted as aides considered plans to reorder the executive agencies (more than half the administration's first-term cabinet appointments had been Ivy League graduates, four from Harvard).[46]

Nixon's hatred of social service professionals had played an important role in his surprising support of the Family Assistance Plan (FAP) in 1969. Following endorsement of a guaranteed annual income for the poor by one thousand academic economists, the president sent a landmark welfare reform measure to Congress. Designed by holdover officials from President Johnson's Department of Health, Education, and Welfare and promoted by Daniel Patrick Moynihan, the executive secretary of Nixon's Council on Urban Affairs, the proposal offered $1,600 a year to families of four with additional food stamp allotments. The president's sympathy for the working poor in preference to welfare recipients underscored the plan since its "workfare" provisions encouraged beneficiaries to find jobs. FAP also reflected Nixon's impatience with the federal welfare bureaucracy since it accompanied a proposal to dismantle OEO. Such sentiments were graphically illustrated when the president asked Moynihan if the program would "get rid of social workers?" "It will wipe them out," the aide replied. When a Senate committee demanded higher benefits for recipients, however, the White House lost interest in FAP and let a coalition of liberals and conservatives kill the plan.[47]

Beyond domestic issues, Nixon blamed the cowardice of liberal professionals for the failures of Vietnam. The president's disdain for his adversaries surfaced in the widely quoted comments that Chief of Staff H. R. Haldeman attributed to his boss in a personal White House diary entry in July 1971. Meetings with college presidents, the new managerial business class, and scientific advisers, Nixon told staffers, left him "concerned whether the country really has the character to do what really has to be done." Haldeman remembered the president as musing that the nation's leaders and educated classes were decadent and overly permissive. "Whenever you ask for patriotic support, they all run away: the college types, the professors, the elite, etc." The more people were educated, continued Nixon, the more they became "brighter in the head and weaker in the spine. When you have to call on the nation to be strong–on such things as drugs, crime, defense . . . the educated people and the leader class no longer have any character and you can't count on them." In another conversation, Nixon complained that the offspring of "the elite" never served in Vietnam. Instead, they defended their lack of courage "on the basis of principled opposition to the war." Immersed in a moral crisis, American society could expect no help from a professional upper-middle class that did not "give a damn about this country."[48]

One day after his reelection, Nixon told a reporter that Washington's habit of throwing money at problems in the 1960s had produced a breakdown in national leadership. Empowered by the landslide, the president met with aides at Camp David to initiate a reorganization of government agencies. "The sprawling federal bureaucracy had to be streamlined and brought under control," remembered Haldeman. Nixon hoped to restructure government and tighten White House influence through four domestic "super-cabinet" offices. Although such plans did not materialize, the administration moved in 1973 to impound congressionally appropriated funds for social programs and virtually abandoned public housing. It also sought to dismantle OEO's Office of Legal Services. The White House already had transferred Head Start, the Job Corps, and Manpower training to other agencies and diverted war on poverty funding to revenue-sharing schemes. Angry that "middle level burocrats" in legal services were channeling money to American Indian activists and welfare rights groups, Nixon sought to convert the agency into a government corporation supported by local jurisdictions. Yet the effort failed in 1973 when a federal court ordered that OEO be left intact.[49]

Reorganization also provided a means of evening the score with the president's longstanding political adversaries. White House counsel John Dean had created an administration "enemies list" in 1971. "We'll have a chance to get back at them one day," Nixon promised Dean in an Oval Office meeting in September 1972. The chief executive hinted that aides could use the Federal Bureau of Investigation (FBI) and other departments to harass liberal antagonists. One of the first agencies discussed at the Camp David session was the Internal Revenue Service (IRS). Nixon was obsessed with the entrenched bureaucrats in IRS, whom he suspected of singling out key Republican financial donors for audits. By placing administration loyalists in the tax bureau, the president hoped to orchestrate similar treatment of Establishment icons like the Ford Foundation and the Brookings Institution, non-profit and tax-exempt organizations allegedly used for "partisan, left-wing purposes." Nixon also relished the thought of auditing key Democratic donors, particularly "the big Jewish contributors."[50]

Nixon's reorganization efforts were part of the embattled president's ideological and partisan war on political intellectuals, social interventionists, and cultural liberals. During the president's first term the White House had deployed the IRS and FBI in illegal surveillance and covert harassment of antiwar dissenters, hostile journalists, and suspect national security staffers. When former Defense Department planner and antiwar convert Daniel Ellsberg, a Jew, leaked the contents of a secret Pentagon history of the Vietnam War to the *New York Times*, which published it in June 1971, the Justice Department indicted the activist and a cohort for espionage and conspiracy. Not content with FBI performance in the case, Nixon officials sought to gain derogatory information on Ellsberg's character by using a White House Special Investigations Unit (the "plumbers") to burglarize the office of the defendant's psychiatrist. "We're up against an enemy, a conspiracy," the president told top aides. "They're using any means, *We are going to use any means*." Enraged at the *Washington Post* for publishing the Pentagon Papers, Nixon proposed a break-in at the liberal Brookings Institution to obtain confidential documents on John Kennedy's handling of Cuba relations to leak to the press to "embarrass members of the establishment."[51]

White House operations against liberal social interventionists and political intellectuals also extended to election competitors. After mounting a series of "dirty tricks" against the opposition's front-running primary candidates, all but assuring George McGovern's nomination, Republican campaign director John Mitchell approved a covert entry at the Watergate offices of Democratic National Committee chair Larry O'Brien to gather sensitive political intelligence. In June 1972, an attempt to repair a faulty electronic listening device on O'Brien's telephone resulted in the arrest of five burglars. Washington, D.C. police soon traced the illegal operation to the White House "plumbers" responsible for the break-in at Ellsberg's psychiatrist. With the full participation of the president, Nixon aides immediately began a criminal coverup that involved the destruction of campaign records and incriminating evidence, perjury before the FBI and a federal grand jury, the payment of hush money to the burglary team, and unlawful influence on law enforcement investigators.[52]

As the case against the Nixon administration emerged in the spring of 1973, the White House clung to the bitter hatred of political intellectuals, cultural liberals, and social guardians that lay at the root of its imminent demise. The president complained to special national security assistant Henry Kissinger that "your Harvard friends" still were upset about the Alger Hiss case but had nothing to say about the way a federal judge imposed long prison sentences on the Watergate burglars to force them to talk. Two days later Nixon explained to aide John Ehrlichman that "we've been trying to run this town by avoiding the Jews in the government" who leaked information. Once a select Senate Watergate committee, chaired by Philadelphia Plan opponent Sam Ervin, began public hearings in May 1973, the Nixon team saw itself under siege from the very adversaries it had sought to neutralize. The great power blocs in Washington, recalled former Chief of Staff Haldeman, had awakened to the fact that Richard Nixon was politically vulnerable. On 9 August 1974, four months after the Watergate grand jury charged seven of his former aides and named him as an unindicted co-conspirator, the thirty-seventh president of the United States resigned as an alternative to certain impeachment and conviction.[53]

In the mold of populist conservatives like Hiram Wesley Evans, William Lemke, Joe McCarthy, and George Wallace, Nixon celebrated the toughness of working-class survival. Viewing upper-middle-class cosmopolitanites as effete, self-indulgent, and removed from appreciation of hard challenges and demands, he privately characterized McGovern peace activists and radical professors as frustrated and alienated "haters" who blamed others for their failures. On a Black Sea boat ride with Soviet leader Leonid Brezhnev weeks before he left office, Nixon complained to a sympathetic host that the younger generation was "almost totally obsessed with self, selfishness, and every kind of abstract idea." As he delivered an impromptu farewell to staffers gathered on the White House lawn on the eve of his resignation, the doomed chief executive implicitly contrasted such defects with the traditional virtues he associated with his own upbringing. In an emotional tribute to the self-sacrifice of his struggling parents, Nixon recalled his mother as a "saint." His father, to whom he referred as "my old man," was someone supposed to be a "sort of a little man, a common man" because he had been a streetcar motorman, a poor lemon rancher, a small-time grocer. "But he was a great man," Nixon blurted out with unusual feeling, "because he did his job, and every job counts up to the hilt, regardless of what happens."[54]

Despite such philosophizing, Nixon seldom directed high-minded scrutiny at his own life. He failed, for example, to acknowledge the moral dimensions to his participation in the Watergate scandal or to speculate on the human costs of the Vietnam War he helped to prolong. Violating the lessons a seasoned politician should have taken to heart, the president could not control his personal rage toward policy intellectuals, social interventionists, and liberal elites he considered enemies. Only at the bitter end did Richard Nixon acknowledge that resentment of New Class adversaries had led him to embrace criminal practices that struck at the core of American traditions of constitutional democracy and fair play. "Always remember," he told supporters on August 9th, "others may hate you, but those who hate you don't win unless you hate them, and then you destroy yourself."[55]

***

Stunned by the traumas of Vietnam and Watergate, voters turned against the Republican Party in 1976 by sending former Georgia governor and nuclear engineer Jimmy Carter to the White House. Yet waning U.S. influence in global affairs and a stagnant economy renewed criticism of the sociopolitical sector and increased resentment toward the knowledge professionals and cultural liberals that George Wallace and Richard Nixon had denigrated. Beginning in 1973, declining corporate profits, increased global competition, and rising energy prices brought the end of the golden age of prosperity inaugurated at the close of World War II. As automation and plant closings decimated the industrial sector, American workers increasingly found themselves relegated to low-paying service jobs and downward social mobility. Meanwhile, federal spending reached an annual $400 billion (nearly one-third the gross national product) at middecade, threatening the middle class with crippling inflation and high taxation.[56]

Welfare spending, the most controversial legacy of New Deal social interventionists, attracted particular criticism during the economic downturn. Between 1965 and 1975, the number of households on public assistance tripled to nearly 3.5 million, while the population receiving food stamps quadrupled in the five years preceding 1975. Conservative critics argued that ordinary taxpayers simultaneously subsidized the poor and middle-class bureaucrats by funding programs that merely encouraged waste, dependency, poor self-discipline, and lack of accountability. While welfare programs remained highly unpopular among many voters, the federal government's reputation was further tarnished by the fact that White House and Congress had turned to the courts to administer controversial civil rights and affirmative action programs.[57]

The most bitterly contested extension of federal judicial power in the 1970s involved compulsory public school busing, a program designed to achieve racial balance in the primary grades of northern educational facilities. The dispute erupted when a federal judge designed a racial integration plan for a white ethnic neighborhood in Boston in 1974, and grassroots opponents responded with school boycotts, street demonstrations, and intensive political lobbying. Echoing the sentiments of Wallace and Nixon, local activist Louis Day Hicks characterized the contest as one between "rich people in the suburbs" and "the workingman and woman, the rent payer, the home owner, the law abiding, tax-paying, decent-living, hard-working forgotten American." Although racial antagonisms undoubtedly contributed to opposition to busing, public criticism of the practice also reflected genuine concerns over the safety of children and neighborhoods. As court-ordered busing served as a metaphor for the erosion of parental control in the face of outside experts and authorities, the dispute became the wedge issue separating the Democratic Party's upper-middle-class social innovators and its white, working-class constituents.[58]

Affirmative action also contributed to increasing criticism of the federal government's social interventionists. Between 1972 and 1980, Washington prosecuted fifty-one city, county, and state governments for inadequate hiring of racial minorities. Many of these suits involved disputes with local police and fire departments over seniority practices, ability testing, educational requirements, union membership policies, and alleged nepotism. Other race-based formulas were applied to government contract set-asides, admissions to federally funded universities, and congressional redistricting. Public opinion registered widespread disapproval of such programs, even among racial minorities. For example, one study in 1980 found less than 20 percent of respondents in support of government efforts to aid the social and economic position of minorities. Americans favored the principle of equality, yet opposed enforcement of collective entitlement by the courts and bureaucracies as "special preference" and a violation of merit-based democratic principles. Nevertheless, African-American and Hispanic organizations joined with sympathetic elected leaders and agency officials in backing affirmative action.[59]

The heated political and cultural debates of the 1970s often centered on the role of social regulationists, lobbyists, and knowledge professionals–the host of engaged media, administrators, think tank consultants, social scientists and educators, public advocacy lawyers, urban planners, mental health workers, and others whose personal interests and ideological convictions were tied to an expanding public sector. Imbued with an abiding faith in administrative expertise, these Washington insiders worked closely with interest groups and political action committees representing-African Americans, Hispanics, feminists, consumer organizations, and environmental lobbies. By forging ties to powerful congressional subcommittee chairs, social and political activists were able to erect a powerful and lucrative entitlement apparatus and legislative network that made them a major force on Capitol Hill.[60]

The presumed affinity between the political class and special interests contributed to an unprecedented level of voter apathy and alienation in the late-1970s. Popular targets of such animosity focused on bureaucratic regulation, government social engineering, public spending, and taxation. In California, an angry electorate limited property assessments and levies by passing a comprehensive ballot initiative in 1978. A Republican proposal in Congress soon seized upon antigovernment sentiment by calling for a 30 percent federal income tax cut. Many working-class and middle-class constituents expressed frustration at being caught between the power of the wealthy and those whose militant organizations gave them "special treatment" from a paternalistic state. To critics, the "unholy alliance" between liberal and minority establishments appeared to favor educated social service professionals instead of the needy. One public opinion survey concluded that government planners appeared to have "monumental contempt for the people," defined as the majority of Americans who never attended college. Public agencies often created the problems they sought to fix, an Oklahoma woman told an interviewer in 1975, "so they can perpetuate their bureaucracies, hire more 'experts,' confiscate more tax money and solve their own mental problem, which seems to be a lusting after personal power."[61]

Perceiving themselves as dominated by vested interests and powerless to affect social policy, many Americans of the late-1970s lost faith in the political system's ability to address their needs. Escalating gasoline prices, a bleak economy, and the capture of U.S. hostages by Iranian revolutionaries solidified the image of a Washington political class disinterested in or incapable of protecting its own people. Seeking to address the energy shortage plaguing the nation in 1979, President Carter delivered a special television address that acknowledged a "crisis of confidence" among the public. Noting rampant disrespect for government and other social institutions, the dismayed chief executive reported that the bridge between citizens and their leaders had "never been so wide." By 1980, populist distrust of political intellectuals, social interventionists, and cultural liberals, Carter included, appeared to dominate public discourse. As one political scientist has observed with wry understatement, Americans of the period were "more likely than not to express feelings of mistrust toward government and to doubt the integrity and capabilities of its leaders."[62]

9

Far from Paradise: Social Guardians in the Postmodern Era, 1980–2001

American economic and political reverses of the 1970s appeared to validate the assault on political intellectuals, social interventionists, and cultural liberals advanced by modern-day conservatives such as Barry Goldwater, George C. Wallace, and Richard M. Nixon. Frustration over Washington-centered politics and the liberationist tendencies of New Class professionals and social guardians played a major role in the restoration of Republican power to the White House in three national elections between 1980 and 1988. Ronald Reagan and George H. W. Bush now assumed leadership of the effort to discredit the knowledge professionals and public sector advocates associated with the dominant wing of the Democratic Party. Not until the presidential election of Arkansas governor Bill Clinton in 1992 did the Democrats find a way to reinvent themselves as a centrist and ideologically independent political force. Yet the Clinton administration floundered on a series of fiascos that tied New Democrats to the perceived sins of the political intelligentsia and the cultural liberalism of the "baby-boomer" generation.

***

Anti-intellectual fervor in the 1980s and 1990s was fueled by a popular conservative revolution in social mores that had its roots in the turmoil of the Vietnam War era. Cold War economic mobility had rested upon the expectation of increasing wages, not the abandonment of regional, ethnic, class, or cultural affinities. Yet the federal government's acceptance of rights-based interventionism in the 1960s appeared to threaten shared principles, traditions, and obligations revolving around the family, religion, education, and nationhood. Social conservatives tied perceived permissiveness and moral relativism in the schools, universities, media, and courts to the spread of countercultural and feminist values, the growth of the welfare state, and the rise of new professionals. Led by homemaker Phyllis Schlafly, antifeminist women successfully opposed ratification of the Equal Rights Amendment between 1972 and 1982. Shifting the debate from equality to preservation of traditional values, Schlafly portrayed upper-middle-class women in the professions as privileged and self-centered subverters of family solidarity. Anti-abortion activists used the same argument in grass-roots crusades to preserve the right to life of the unborn.[1]

Secularism, hedonism, and permissiveness were the main targets of the social crusade inaugurated in the late-1970s by evangelical and fundamentalist Protestant ministers Jerry Falwell and Pat Robertson. The main beneficiary of Christian Right political involvement was former California governor, Ronald Reagan. As unemployment rose to 7 percent, inflation ballooned to 13.5 percent, and interest rates soared above 20 percent in 1980, Reagan leaped onto the post-Watergate political stage. Long known for his anticommunist views, the affable Californian had built a public persona on opposition to government bureaucrats and planners. During his televised endorsement of Barry Goldwater in 1964, Reagan had warned that "government can't control the economy without controlling the people." The governor continued to oppose Great Society social spending. "It should be obvious by now," he told Republicans across the race-conscious South in 1967, "that a self-appointed group of experts operating out of either Washington or Sacramento cannot have all the answers to the problems that beset us."[2]

Speaking before the largest political fundraising gathering in South Carolina history in 1967, Reagan accused the Democratic Party of betraying its supporters by deciding "that a few men in Washington knew better than we do what is good for us and know better than we do how to spend all our money." Voters would have to remove "the little intellectual elite" leading the country, the governor told a Republican fundraising rally in Louisville, in order to honor the "forgotten men and women who work and support the communities and pay for all the social experimenting." Addressing 1,200 guests of the Economic Club of New York early in 1968, Reagan lamented that Americans were experiencing "a feeling of helplessness, a feeling that government is now a separate force beyond the people's control."[3]

In eight years as California governor, Reagan more than doubled the state budget deficit, tightened environmental regulations, and generously increased public education spending. Yet in 1980 the Republican presidential candidate campaigned as an outsider representing ordinary people in the fight against "special interests" and untrustworthy cultural elites. Reagan claimed that a career of film acting had taught him to be in touch with audiences so that his speeches rang with "certain basic truths" recognized by average citizens. He rejected the moral relativism of academics who saw "just shades of gray in a world where discipline of any kind is an intolerable interference with the right of the individual." It was foolish to deny there were any absolutes, a "black and white of right and wrong," the governor informed the California Federation of Republican Women in 1970. Ten years later, Reagan sought to lead Americans into "an era of national renewal" to "revitalize the values of family, work, and neighborhood" and free citizens from government bureaucracy.[4]

As historian Christopher Lasch suggested, the Republican candidate never acknowledged how consumer capitalism eroded the traditional values he invoked. Nor did Reagan reveal the extent to which his conservative views resonated with the free market ideology of the corporate-financed think tanks and foundations calling for less government in the 1970s. Nevertheless, by equating liberal programs with inegalitarian attempts to impose racial preferences and "reverse discrimination," the former governor succeeded in attacking rule by interventionist political intellectuals and knowledge professionals while avoiding the nasty connotations of race-baiting. The cheerful and optimistic Californian built a powerful electoral coalition by promising to protect both working-class voters and corporate interests from excessive government regulation, wasteful welfare spending, and burdensome taxation. As Reagan rode to easy victory in 1980 against the hapless Jimmy Carter, exit polling showed that one-fourth of Democrats and 41 percent of union households voted Republican. The new president's inaugural address sustained the populist distinction between ordinary people and "government by an elite group." Promising to curb the size and influence of the "federal establishment," Reagan insisted that working people were "a special interest group" that had been "too long neglected." Government itself had become the problem.[5]

Reagan bonded with supporters by attributing common sense to ordinary people in contrast to the impractical ideologies he assigned to political intellectuals and cultural guardians. "This administration is motivated by a political philosophy that sees the greatness of America in you, her people, and in your families, churches, neighborhoods, communities," he told a 1983 meeting of the National Association of Evangelicals in Orlando, Florida. The president portrayed liberal policy planners and social interventionists as creatures of a spiritually empty and materialist Marxist vision. The national renaissance would not be achieved "by those who set people against people, class against class, or institution against institution," he assured the Conservative Political Action Conference in 1981. Reagan teased the financial technicians of the International Monetary Conference by suggesting that an economist was "the only professional who sees something working in practice and then seriously wonders if it works in theory." But the president was serious in 1985 when he introduced a simplified federal tax structure (lowering rates on the affluent but eliminating many deductions) and attacked "Washington sophisticates" and "special interest lobbyists" for opposing the plan supposedly backed by ordinary citizens.[6]

The emotional resonance of Reagan's persona rested on a profound rejection of the moral claims of the interventionist political class, whom the president equated with the cosmopolitan intelligentsia. Average Americans "held true to certain beliefs and principles" dismissed by intellectuals as "hopelessly out of date, utterly trite, and reactionary," he told the Conservative Political Action Conference in 1985. Reagan asserted that cultural experimenters believed that "only the abnormal was worthy of emulation," while they viewed religious devotion and adherence to traditional verities as "primitive" and "antimodern." Such thinkers saw people "only as members of groups," not as individuals. The president insisted that Americans either must side with "pipe dreamers and margin scribblers" or place their faith "in the common sense of the people." Taking aim at social welfare and civil rights policies most strongly identified with Great Society political intellectuals, Reagan followed through on his commitment to lower taxes, initiated major cuts in social services, restrained the regulatory agencies, opposed busing and mandated efforts at school desegregation, reduced budgets for legal services to the poor, substantially curtailed the implementation of affirmative action, and stacked the U.S. Commission on Civil Rights and Equal Employment Opportunity Commission with conservative appointees.[7]

**

Republican presidents of the 1980s skillfully exploited hostility to the interventionist political intelligentsia. When Reagan sought a second term in 1984, he faced a strong contender in former senator and Carter vice-president Walter F. Mondale, a career liberal with strong ties to organized labor, the civil rights movement, and feminist groups. Yet Mondale appeared overly beholden to women's rights lobbies when he named Geraldine A. Ferraro, a relatively inexperienced member of the House, as his vice-presidential running mate. The Minnesotan suffered an additional blow when he indicated that he might approve tax increases to reduce spiraling budget deficits, a gesture that backfired because it appeared to question the nation's ability to generate strong economic growth without inflation or the intrusion of technocrats. Mondale also failed to assure working-class voters that they would not shoulder added revenue burdens in a tax system that favored both the rich and special interest groups. Amid increased prosperity and national optimism, Reagan and Vice President George H. W. Bush eased to victory with 59 percent of the popular vote.[8]

When Bush ran for president on his own account in 1988, he guaranteed voters that he would adhere to Reaganomics and supply-side financing by opposing any tax increases or unnecessary growth in the public sector. Once again, the Republicans were challenged by an impressive rival in Massachusetts governor Michael S. Dukakis. A Greek American who taught university seminars on public administration and the efficient use of government, Dukakis claimed to have restored his state economy through astute fiscal management and recruitment of new businesses. Facing a deficit hawk who also talked about the need to create economic opportunity for working people, the Bush camp shifted the debate away from bread-and-butter issues and tax-and-spend liberals. Instead, White House strategists mounted a brilliantly conceived attack on the cultural mores and reformist tendencies of New Class professionals and liberal political insiders.[9]

Playing upon a tangled set of sentiments concerning crime, race, patriotism, and cultural permissiveness, Bush focused on Dukakis's opposition to the death penalty, his veto of a state bill to require public school teachers to lead students in the Pledge of Allegiance, his administration of a convict furlough program, and his membership in the rights-oriented American Civil Liberties Union.

The governor's positions on capital punishment and compulsory flag saluting reflected a profound reverence for constitutional protections and procedures. Yet many Americans wondered if affluent liberals and technocrats excessively fixated on process and individual rights and ignored the need to enforce widely shared moral commitments. Social conservatives believed that patriotism was a traditional obligation that should be taught in the schools if the excesses of fashionable self-indulgence were to be avoided. Support of the death penalty, in turn, reflected widespread frustration with the perceived failures of the criminal justice system and anxiety over lawlessness as a symptom of social disorder.[10]

The Bush campaign climaxed when a Republican political action committee aired a television commercial dramatizing the case of Willie Horton, an African-American convict serving a murder sentence in Dukakis's Massachusetts. Released on a weekend furlough permissable under state law, Horton had raped a white woman in Maryland and brutally beaten her fiancé. The widely distributed video implied that rights-oriented liberals lacked common sense as well as reverence for traditional values. It underscored the suspicion that interventionist political intellectuals and government planners were more concerned with social experiment and the perogatives of criminals than with protecting the safety, interests, and values of ordinary citizens. "I don't understand the type of thinking," Bush told a North Carolina rally, "that lets first-degree murderers who haven't even served enough time to be eligible for parole out on parole so they can rape and plunder again, and then isn't willing to let the teachers lead the kids in the Pledge of Allegiance." The vice-president described Dukakis as a "know nothing, believe nothing, feel nothing candidate," an "ice man."[11]

Exploitation of these powerful social issues enabled George H. W. Bush to rebound from a seventeen-point polling deficit in 1988 to an easy Election Day victory over the pragmatic but cerebral Dukakis. The new administration soon clarified its distance from the social interventionists and planning professionals of the Democratic Party. "The New Paradigm," an address delivered in 1990 by Bush policy planning assistant James Pinkerton, laid to rest the reformist aura of the Lyndon Johnson years. The Great Society was "a continuing, if well-intentional failure," stated Pinkerton, because it falsely assumed "that experts, wise bureaucrats in league with university professors and politicians," could "administer supply and demand, prosperity and equality, from an office building far away."[12]

President Bush appeared to close the door permanently on the politically divisive and culturally polarized 1960s and 1970s when he led a twenty-eight nation coalition in repelling Iraqi leader Saddam Hussein's armed aggression against oil-rich Kuwait in 1991. Relocating American strength in the principled use of military force instead of the sociopolitical sector, the administration claimed that the Persian Gulf War had extinguished the so-called Vietnam Syndrome—the paralysis in the nation's foreign policy that accompanied the humiliating defeat in Southeast Asia. As commentators observed a domestic "tidal wave of good feeling" following the successful campaign against Iraq, Bush's personal approval ratings soared to over 90 percent. Yet a sagging economy and an image of White House inaction made it difficult for the administration to take political advantage of the postwar euphoria.[13]

Reagan and Bush had cultivated a winning electoral constituency by insisting on lower taxes and reduced reliance on the social programs associated with the interventionist political class. As unemployment pushed toward 8 percent in the election year of 1992, however, many Americans wondered why the president did not apply his abilities to reversing the economic decline. When Bush honored the Reagan legacy by enacting a ninety-day moratorium on all new government regulations, public opinion viewed the White House as disengaged from domestic problems. This perception was skillfully exploited by Governor Bill Clinton of Arkansas, a virtual political outsider who received the Democratic presidential nomination.[14]

***

Seeking to free the Democratic Party from its association with the professional political class, Clinton offered a "third way" of governing, which he described in campaign speeches as the "New Covenant." By rejecting tax-and-spend liberalism, the candidate framed himself as a centrist on fiscal policy who promised to reinvent the welfare system, reduce the size of government, and pare down the federal budget deficit. In order to distinguish himself from upper-middle-class cultural liberals, the nominee took moderate positions on social issues such as abortion, crime, and the death penalty. Portraying Bush as out of step with the demands of the global economy, he also called for government investment in hi-tech infrastructure, training, and education.[15]

Clinton and vice-presidential nominee Al Gore charged that Reagan and Bush had "served the rich and special interests" with tax breaks and "trickle-down" economics. *Putting People First*, the Democratic campaign document, even tied Republican Washington to "an entrenched bureaucracy." Such assertions removed the onus of elite rule from political interventionists. By focusing on the possibilities of economic growth through the computer economy, moreover, Clinton and Gore implicitly distanced themselves from the policy practitioners and planners normally associated with the liberal state. A complex mix of southern populist, intellectual cosmopolitan, and well-connected networker, Clinton successfully reintegrated middle-class and white working-class voters into the Democratic coalition, although he only managed to win 43 percent of the popular vote in a three-way race with Bush and Reform Party candidate H. Ross Perot.[16]

The new president's consensual politics produced substantial accomplishments, foremost among them a 1993 budget agreement that ultimately led to Treasury surpluses, reduced interest rates, and a sustained economic boom. Clinton also won ratification of the North America Free Trade Agreement

(NAFTA), a key factor in integrating the United States into the global economy. Further achievements included welfare reform, federal aid for hiring teachers and police, earned income and child tax credits, handgun control, family and medical leave, a children's health initiative, and a compensated public service program for college students. Under the supervision of Vice President Gore, the administration even made inroads into streamlining the federal bureaucracy.[17]

Despite a record of centrist accomplishments, the Clinton White House found it difficult to separate itself from the political intellectuals and social interventionists associated with the liberal wing of the Democratic Party. Journalists reported that the new president initially accepted the advice of congressional leaders, who told him that the best hope for enacting his programs was to rally the party's traditional constituencies and interest groups of women, racial minorities, and organized labor. Clinton's first executive appointments appeared to reflect this advice. As a candidate, he had dramatized the need for racial and gender diversity in government by promising to appoint a cabinet that "looks like America." Yet the president failed to anticipate the pitfalls of selecting affluent New Class professionals for top positions. When the new cabinet was chosen, all but four of its eighteen members turned out to be practicing attorneys, including a large dose of Yale Law graduates, Harvard professors, Rhodes scholars, and high-powered lobbyists and corporate figures.[18]

The privileged nature of the Clinton talent pool was dramatized when the president was forced to withdraw two attorney general selections because each of the two women nominees was discovered to have employed illegal aliens as "nannies" without paying their social security. Broadcast widely over talk radio, the furor over "Clinton's yuppies" centered on the assertion that two highly compensated and favored members of the legal establishment had solved child care difficulties by circumventing the rules and exploiting immigrant workers. The controversy graphically illustrated pundit Kevin Phillips's contention that the administration had tapped "a new portion of the existing political-governmental elite," one comprised of the resented insiders of professional culture.[19]

Accused of practicing affirmative action in the interest of the Democratic Party's social guardians, the White House faced a storm of protest when it nominated Lani Guinier, an African-American woman and law school colleague of Bill and Hillary Clinton, as assistant attorney general for civil rights. A special rights assistant in President Carter's Justice Department and a University of Pennyslvania professor, Guinier had published widely on the subject of black political empowerment. Her articles presented the view that majority rule in a racially divided society was not a reliable instrument of democracy and that the election of African-American legislators was not sufficient to guarantee minority rights. Seeing antidiscrimination as a matter of equal outcomes, not mere fair process, Guinier had proposed that federal voting rights acts require state legislative "super majorities" for passing laws and that vetoes by racial minorities be permittted in state and local governments.[20]

The Clinton administration was slow to realize that Guinier's abstract speculations conceivably violated democratic notions of due process and perpetuated an image of interventionist political intellectuals as threats to popular sovereignty. While James Coleman, the White House legal affairs adviser and a criminal law professor at Duke University, saw the nominee's writings as harmless ruminations, executive branch staffers never anticipated controversy about an appointment to a nonpolicymaking position. Yet the *Wall Street Journal* sounded the alarm in April 1993 with a blistering editorial about the Clinton "quota queen" who viewed health care, job training, and housing as "basic entitlements" and who sought to tamper with majority rule. Weeks after the *New York Times* editorialized that Guinier's ideas were inappropriate for a federal appointee, the president rescinded the appointment.[21]

***

Clinton's most problematic association with social guardians came with the administration's ill-fated attempt to legislate comprehensive health care reform. As middle-class Americans were exposed to the rising costs and vulnerabilities of the medical delivery system in the early 1990s, public opinion turned toward a tax-supported system of universal insurance. Within his first week of office, the president honored a campaign pledge to create such a program by announcing that Hillary Clinton would chair a special health care task force. Under Lyndon Johnson, key presidential assistants had used task forces as covers for the secret operation of small policy planning staffs. The Clinton commission was to be advised by a group of experts headed by Ira Magaziner, a business leader who had served as a Rhodes scholar with the president. Magaziner enlisted the aid of five hundred health specialists organized into thirty-four subgroups and clusters. Meeting behind closed doors, the experts were assigned deadlines or "tollgates" for reporting their progress.[22]

The Clintons and Magaziner were convinced that effective cost controls in health care were impossible without a comprehensive insurance system covering all Americans. Yet they did not want to create new entitlements or add to the federal budget deficit. The result was managed competition. Under this compromise between a market-oriented and government-centered solution, people were to be organized into health maintenance organizations (HMO's) and other large insurance purchasers, for whose business doctors and hospitals were to compete. The cost-conscious method of delivering health care had been developed by two political intellectuals—Stanford University economist and former Defense Department deputy Alan C. Enthoven; and Paul M. Ellwood, who had served as President Nixon's legislative adviser on health issues. Enthoven and Ellwood had been meeting periodically in Jackson Hole, Wyoming with about one hundred academics, policymakers, physicians, insurance executives, and medical industry administrators. Heralded by the White House as "the intellectual brain trust for the managed competition model," the consortium received press coverage as a "loose-knit group of experts" that had become "one of the most important influences in the shaping of the Clinton plan."[23]

As Hillary Clinton and Magaziner organized the task force, they established a complete news blackout on all proceedings. Magaziner believed that the protections of secrecy would enable panelists to challenge the conventional views of Washington bureaucrats and medical industry interests. Yet the crowded meetings were unwieldy and difficult to manage. In addition, participants were pressured to conform to the goal of comprehensive insurance coverage and found references to more limited reforms repeatedly dismissed as the work of "incrementalists." Once the First Lady and Magaziner brought their recommendations to cabinet members, Treasury officials, and White House staff, no one advocated reconsideration of the positions to which the duo already had committed.[24]

The political insularity of health care advocates produced disastrous results. Concerned that hidden costs in their proposal might incite resistance from members of Congress who already resented exclusion from the process, the Clinton administration set out to place the health care package into the 1993 budget reconciliation bill. Yet executive branch policymakers and planners once again found themselves confronting the jealously guarded prerogatives of the legislative branch when West Virginia's Robert Byrd, chair of the Senate Appropriations Committee, invoked a procedural rule that killed the measure. Only after Congress approved the budget did the president go on television to deliver an address supporting health care reform. Following a series of town meetings, conferences, and television appearances, Clinton formally introduced the outlines of the administration plan to Congress.[25]

Billed as the most comprehensive social legislation in U.S. history, the Clinton health measure called for the creation of state-run insurance pools or alliances to serve consumers who were not covered by existing plans or who were not members of health maintenance organizations. All Americans were to be assured of coverage that could be carried from one job to another, despite pre-existing conditions or illnesses. The federal government would regulate drug prices and provide medication to the elderly, offer insurance subsidies for early retirees, and extend assistance to seniors for long-term home care. Washington also would pay for coverage for the needy and unemployed, subsidize premiums for the working poor, and compensate small businesses for meeting the insurance payments of their low-wage workers. While the government would mandate employers to cover 80 percent of premium costs, a new federal agency would place caps on all insurance rates. New regulations, moreover, were to encourage a better racial and gender mix of medical school graduates, the training of general practitioners instead of specialists, and the placement of doctors and health centers in underserved localities. Any additional burdens on the federal Treasury were to be offset by increased tobacco taxes.[26]

As historian Theda Skocpol has suggested, the confidential sessions of Clinton health policy experts resembled the private hearings on social security held by President Franklin Roosevelt's Committee on Economic Security before 1935. Yet the contrasting political context of the two eras proved decisive. Social security planners relied on taxation and government spending instead of federal regulation. In contrast, Clinton policymakers sought to demonstrate that New Democrats could use the federal government's powers to promote cost-cutting in a vital industry and practice public fiscal responsibility. Consequently, the president's health care proposal substituted an interlocking system of government rules for funding. Task force managers overgeneralized about the program's contents, minimized its costs (an estimated $400 billion for the first six years), and underplayed the role to be assumed by administrative regulators.[27]

Health care planners utterly failed to appreciate the ambivalence toward federal regulation that underlay American society. As journalists Haynes Johnson and David Broder observed, the 1,342-page Clinton bill embraced systems management terms like alliances, mandates, cooperatives, and managed competition that lent themselves to "heavy, bureaucratic, authoritarian" associations. Administration policy intellectuals did not anticipate that consumers would see state-run insurance alliances as cumbersome government entities instead of stimulants to competition. Endorsing the idea of change but uneasy about expanding government management, many Americans wondered about the potential impact of health care reform on their families. Middle-class consumers worried that federal regulations might interfere with their right to choose a doctor or hospital, that medical services could be rationed, or that subsidies for the poor might result in increased taxes or insurance premiums. Not surprisingly, support for the scheme dropped from 73 percent to 59 percent between the fall and spring of 1993.[28]

***

Public nervousness about the Clinton health proposal was reinforced by the most heavily financed lobbying campaign in American history. Government mandates, open enrollment requirements, and federal price ceilings posed new threats to health service providers, insurance firms, drug companies, and private employers, particularly small businesses that would be forced to pay some employees' premiums. One leading critic of the plan was the Health Insurance Association of America (HIAA), a consortium of 270 small or medium-sized companies that supported universal coverage and employer mandates but objected to the rest of the health care package. Following Clinton's September 1993 address, HIAA spent $10.5 million on a television advertisement that portrayed "Harry and Louise," a middle-class couple discussing the president's proposal at the kitchen table. The ad featured an announcer's proclamation that "the government may force us to pick from a few health care plans designed by government bureaucrats." "They choose," commented "Harry;" "we lose," responded "Louise." Public distrust of the Washington bureaucracy became the main target of the $100 million lobbying effort against the Clinton bill.[29]

As public support for the medical insurance measure dropped another 20 percent by 1994, the issue became less important to voters than the deficit, government spending, or crime. By spring, a majority of Americans opposed the bill, with approval among the elderly plummeting to 37 percent. Nearly two-thirds of a national sample expressed the view that the Clinton scheme involved too much government interference. In June 1994, the Senate Finance Committee mirrored public opinion by voting, 12 to 8, for watered-down health insurance legislation with no employer mandate, no controls on premiums, and no goals of universal coverage. When Senate Democrats finally brought the mild package to the floor in August, Republicans talked of "a budgetary disaster." "Make no mistake," declared Wyoming's Malcolm Wallop, "this government does not seek to serve, but to control. Americans are frightened of it. We will let it control us at our peril." One month later, Democratic congressional leaders announced the abandonment of health care reform.[30]

The defeat of the health security bill, as Theda Skocpol has indicated, marked "a pivotal moment" in U.S. political history. It also served as a catastrophic reversal for the Clinton administration's policymakers, advisers, and reformist social planners. Offering an explanation for the public's disaffection from the plan, the centrist *New Republic* suggested that health insurance interventionists "were interested in conceiving of a total overhaul of the system according to the dictates of what a small group of experts deemed rational." Advocates "wrote memos, they wrote memos about memos. They held meetings, and held meetings about meetings. They generated clusters and toll-gates, dozens of working groups and countless position papers. They felt power and philosophical." The premise of the Clinton-Magaziner project, concluded the editors, was "that complex social problems are amenable to totalizing, intellectual solutions, and that democracy is an obstacle to implementing them."[31]

Republican politicians deployed the health care scheme as an ideal foil for anti-Washington sentiment. Former Dan Quayle aide William Kristol had authored a confidential memorandum in late 1993 that advised congressional Republicans to kill health reform of any kind. Kristol warned that enactment of a medical insurance measure would "re-legitimize middle-class dependence for 'security' on government spending and regulation" and hurt the party's reputation for "restraining government." Augmenting his views in a *Wall Street Journal* opinion piece, the conservative strategist argued that the Clinton bill "would signal a rebirth of centralized welfare-state policy." By the fall of 1994, Kristol's political instincts appeared to have been salient. The "incredibly bloated, complex, unresponsive, incomprehensible health plan came to symbolize everything people hated about government," chortled Utah Republican senator Robert Bennett.[32]

No critic exploited the health care debacle with as much skill as House Republican leader Newt Gingrich. A Georgia native and adopted son of a career Army officer, Gingrich received a Ph.D. in European history from Tulane University in

1971 and taught environmental studies and western civilization at a small college in his home state. After running two unsuccessful campaigns for Congress from an Atlanta suburban district, he won the seat in 1978. Five years later Gingrich joined House Republicans in the Conservative Opportunity Society, a political faction that aired attacks on the welfare state and Democratic congressional leaders on cable-television's C-SPAN. After forcing the resignation of Democratic House Speaker Jim Wright on ethics violations in 1989, the Georgia Republican was elected Minority Whip in a hotly contested vote. Five years later, at the age of fifty, he succeeded in retiring Republican Minority Leader Robert Michel.[33]

An advocate of new information technologies and sustained innovation in the global economy, Gingrich insisted that power had to be stripped from policymakers and planners in Washington. Contending that Republicans represented "middle-class working taxpayers," the conservative ideologue pictured the Democrats as the party of inflation, temporary make work, centralized and rigid government institutions, bureaucratic red tape, higher taxes, and permissive social policies. The symbol of liberal governance was the welfare state, an "obsolete system" that reduced citizens to dependent clients and subordinated them to a political class with a vested interest in the status quo. Denouncing those intellectual elites, social engineers, and special interests who profited from the idea that society was responsible for all behavior, Gingrich pleaded that America was "too big, too diverse, and too free to be run by bureaucrats sitting in office buildings in one city."[34]

As the 1994 congressional elections approached, Gingrich moved to exploit the antigovernment sentiments precipitated by the health care debate. On September 27th, one day after Democratic congressional leaders announced their abandonment of the Clinton plan, over three hundred Republican House candidates gathered on the steps of the Capitol to sign the Contract with America. Written mainly by Gingrich, the document pledged that adherents would work for a constitutional amendment to balance the federal budget and for legislation to cut taxes, to toughen criminal penalties, to reform welfare, to ban unfunded governnment mandates, to place caps on civil law suit damages, and to set congressional term limits. "We propose to cede back power from the hallowed halls of Congress to the more hallowed kitchen tables of America," announced Republican House conference chair Dick Armey. In November, the Republicans ended a forty-year Democratic reign in the House by gaining fifty-two seats and won control of the Senate as well. The most decisive shift in government direction since the 1930s was facilitated by substantial Republican majorities among men, whites, and Protestants.[35]

Republicans succeeded in 1994 because sufficient number of voters were angry at government and were willing to support attacks on liberal social interventionists and cultural guardians. Months earlier, a national poll had revealed that 57 percent of respondents believed that the capital was controlled by lobbyists and special interests. Voters were dissatisfied with the "misuse of government by elites to promote their own interests against the people's," suggested political writer Kevin Phillips By 1994, majorities of 69 percent saw government as wasteful and inefficient while 65 percent thought that the federal establishment controlled too much of daily life. Large numbers of citizens blamed the situation on a "corrupt elite" in Washington that used its entrenched position to serve its own ends, concluded political scientist Philip A. Klinkner. As White House pollster Stanley Greenberg admitted, many Americans desired "to hold the current political class accountable for the failure of politics."[36]

***

Although Congress received an unprecedented 79 percent disapproval rating among voters in 1994, commentators reported that concerns over big government were most explicitly tied to White House "social engineering" controversies like affirmative action and health care. Accordingly, Bill Clinton emerged as the key icon of the political and cultural liberalism attributed to the post-1960s Washington establishment. Newt Gingrich had built a political career by condemning "government and elite culture." Having engineered a major realignment of national politics, the prospective Speaker sought to lead a counterrevolution in culture by targeting President Clinton as the embodiment of the interventionist intelligentsia. Shortly before the 1994 election, Gingrich told a Republican gathering that Clinton was "the enemy of normal Americans." He later vowed to bury the remains of "the Great Society, counterculture, McGovernick" legacy and steer the country away from a "situation-ethics morality" he associated with the First Family. The Clintons were "left-wing elitists," part of a "very small counterculture elite," he charged, who generated bureaucratic schemes such as health care on the assumption that "it was their job to give the country the Government that they thought the country needed, even if they didn't want it."[37]

Although Gingrich contrived many of the ties between George McGovern's politics and counterculture lifestyles, Bill and Hillary Clinton inevitably carried the cultural baggage of those post–World War II baby-boomers who figured so strongly in the social divisions of the 1960s and 1970s. The first member of his generation to run for president, Clinton found it politically awkward to publicly admit that he had been philosophically opposed to U.S. involvement in the Vietnam War while an undergraduate at Georgetown University in the mid-1960s. During that time Clinton had served as a part-time staffer for Arkansan J. William Fulbright's Senate Foreign Relations Committee, an important vehicle for antiwar sentiment. As a Rhodes scholar at Oxford, England, moreoever, he had helped to draw up a peace petition by American fellows and attended a religious vigil protesting U.S. policy.[38]

Clinton's opposition to the war was complicated by his opportunism in avoiding military service. As he completed college in 1969, the young Arkansan sought to join the Reserve Officer's Training Corps as an alternative to conscription.

Despite "loathing the military," he acknowledged at the time, he desired to maintain his "political viability within the system." When Clinton received a low ranking in the draft lottery, however, he rescinded the ROTC commitment and signed up for Yale Law School. Evidence of such duplicity raised anxieties over the candidate's suitability for the presidency among an electorate that continued to be uneasy about the Vietnam era revolution in values. Draft-dodging charges were compounded by speculations over former marijuana use and by reports that the married governor had used Arkansas state troopers to arrange illicit sexual liaisons. When the candidate's responses were equivocating and quibbling, opponents mocked him as "Slick Willie" and charged that he could not be trusted to assume responsibility for his actions.[39]

Clinton's antiwar and counterculture credentials reverberated with disastrous results in the controversy over the role of homosexuals in the armed forces. In his first week in office, the president announced that he intended to honor a campaign pledge by issuing an executive order banning discrimination against gays and lesbians in the military. The idea undoubtedly stemmed from the conviction that an efficient society utilized the talents of all Americans. Yet Clinton appeared to be pandering to gay and lesbian rights campaign supporters. He also faced stringent opposition from Pentagon brass and congressional leaders who believed that his lack of military experience accounted for the inability to appreciate how homosexuals might threaten unit discipline and cohesion. Under fire from critics, the commander-in-chief backed down, eventually accepting Senate Armed Services Committee chair Sam Nunn's proposal for a "don't ask, don't tell" policy. Homosexuals now could remain in the service if they did not reveal their sexual orientation, remained celibate, and refrained from gay or lesbian activity. The compromise satisfied no one. While gays and lesbians continued to complain of abuse and pundits criticized Clinton for "waffling" on his convictions, conservatives rejected any acceptance of homosexuality.[40]

Critics of the intelligentsia were particularly enraged at widespread toleration for gays and lesbians. The issue was addressed in memorable fashion by Justice Antonin Scalia, a Ronald Reagan appointee to the Supreme Court. Four years after Colorado voters supported a 1992 amendment to the state constitution that precluded protected legal status for homosexuals, the Court sustained rulings by the state judiciary declaring the measure unconstitutional. Dissenting vigorously, Scalia protested that the Colorado law was designed to prevent "piecemeal deterioration" of the sexual morality favored by a majority of the state's residents. By equating animosity toward homosexuality with evil, he contended, the Court had invented "a novel and extravagant constitutional doctrine." Scalia underscored the cultural war over the issue by criticizing his colleagues for "imposing upon all Americans the resolution favored by the elite class from which the members of this institution are selected."[41]

Attacks on New Class cultural morality and political philosophy were a persistent theme of ideological conservatives and right-wing media, whose critique of socially interventionist strategies and cosmopolitan values had become increasingly strident since the 1960s. *Rambo* (1982), the popular Hollywood motion picture that achieved near-cult status, offered a violent portrait of an alienated Vietnam veteran who raged against amoral professionals accused of compromising military integrity and patriotism. More insidious attacks on the social liberalism of knowledge elites appeared in the novels of Andrew Macdonald, formerly an assistant professor of physics at Oregon State University. Publishing *The Turner Diaries* (1978) under the pseudonym William L. Pierce, Macdonald described a fictional "Day of the Rope" during which California vigilantes decked out a "batch" of robed academics from UCLA before they were "strung up." In *The Hunter* (1989), the fanciful storyteller depicted a charismatic militiaman who believed that "efforts were better spent going after the promoters of racial mixing than its practitioners." After killing a professor named Horowitz, the narrator confessed "a hankering ... to take out a Senator or a bishop or a university president."[42]

Endorsements of Macdonald's chilling scenarios largely were confined to extremist organizations such as The Order, a white supremacy group modeled on the warriors of *The Turner Diaries,* and a small number of right-wing militias and rural patriots. Yet hostility toward social interventionists and adherents of liberal values also found strong support in Christian popular culture. Religious crusader Beverly La Haye epitomized such criticism by denouncing an "intellectual class" that pretended to be "judge and final arbiter over the Word of God." Resentful academics tried "to impose their visions by law, usually favoring socialism and other forms of rule by intellectuals," agreed free-market advocate and moral traditionalist George Gilder. Evangelist John Hagee condemned the free-enterprise-hating "New World Order crowd," by which he meant "the eastern establishment and liberals in America and Europe." Christian author Connie Marshner mocked the social engineering of "professionally credentialed members of the helping professions." Castigating "social parenting," by which the state took the place of God, Marshner insisted that government support for child care mainly was designed to meet the needs of the social service establishment and assist those wishing to avoid child-rearing costs.[43]

Conservative Christians used pamphlets, videos, and televised sermons to warn that the secular intelligentsia's assaults on traditional values would produce an alien generation incapable of love, compassion, or emotional warmth. Marshner traced much of society's troubles to the postmodern principle that all relationships were political, and therefore arbitrary. Indeed, La Haye pictured feminists as metaphorical strangers–as self-centered individualists whose rejection of gender differences, cherished authority, and family responsibilities would destroy civility and courtesy in public life. Gilder's *Men and Marriage* (1993) spoke to these concerns when it depicted the cold-hearted nature of a liberated culture characterized by "young lady lawyers with brisk smiles and medicated wombs."[44]

The cultural assault on policymaking professionals reverberated in the forceful critiques of popular radio talk show host, Rush Limbaugh. Like Gingrich, Limbaugh traced the supposed dominance of the interventionist elite to the 1960s, which he denigrated as "an era that celebrated drug abuse, political alienation, antiwar protests, campus mayhem, flower power, and a self-centeredness and egomania that bordered on the absurd." In *See, I Told You So* (1993), a guide for faithful listeners, the conservative media hero accused Vietnam era activists of believing they "had a better understanding of the world and could accomplish more than any other generation." Like Gingrich, Limbaugh used Hillary Clinton as the perfect embodiment of the "messianic" radicalism attributed to social guardians. "She is so much smarter, so much more conscious of all that is good, decent, and virtuous in the world," he mocked. Manipulating and controlling liberals like the Clintons, charged Limbaugh, had a propensity to "overstate a problem and work society into a frenzied state in order to justify their invariable, big-government solution."[45]

***

Republican House leaders hoped to build a permanent majority in Congress and retake the White House by mobilizing populist sentiment behind an antigovernment coalition committed to lower taxes and reduced federal deficits. Yet as spending cuts threatened to vitiate Medicare and other programs, the impasse between the legislative and executive branches forced two government shutdowns in 1995. With public opinion blaming the fiasco on congressional Republicans, Clinton and Gore won reelection the following year with 49 percent of the popular vote and Democrats gained nine seats in the House.[46] Despite vindication at the polls, however, questions of moral authority and personal integrity continued to plague the Clinton administration, serving to reinforce public anxiety about the reliability of baby boomer guardians and the Washington governing class.

Following the 1996 election, Clinton and Gore found themselves involved in a series of embarrassing campaign finance scandals. Meanwhile, a Justice Department special prosecutor, appointed under pressure from Congress in 1994, continued to investigate "Whitewater"—a series of allegations over financial and political improprieties dating back to Clinton's tenure as Arkansas governor. Although the president and First Lady never were charged with legal wrongdoing in the case, their defensive and antagonistic approach to investigators convinced critics that they were covering up misdeeds. The appearance of deception meshed with the president's tendency to shade meanings, finesse issues, and concentrate on appearances instead of substance. Political opponents insisted that Clinton embodied an instrumentalist pattern that belied traditional virtues associated with integrity and character.[47] As troubling allegations began to emerge about the former governor's personal life, questions over the ethical compass of social interventionists and cultural liberals took on added meaning.

Were members of the guardian class capable of the self-control, the willingness to honor promises, and the consistency of ideals that Americans expected of their leaders?

The moral credentials of New Class professionals came under severe scrutiny as a result of revelations concerning Bill Clinton's sex life. A sexual harassment lawsuit filed in 1994 charged the former governor with improperly propositioning a female state worker. Forced to testify in the case in 1998, the president stated that he never had conducted sexual relations with any government employee. When leaks of taped telephone conversations revealed that a former intern and aide had confessed to having sex with Clinton in the vicinity of the Oval Office, the attorney general asked the Whitewater special prosecutor to investigate whether the president had committed perjury or obstructed justice in the civil lawsuit. Shortly thereafter, Clinton publicly denied participation in the White House affair. In August 1998 he made an unprecedented appearance before a federal grand jury in which he acknowledged an "inappropriate" relationship with the aide but insisted that his testimony in the Arkansas suit had been "legally correct" because of the definition of sexual relations used in the case. When the special prosecutor released a report to Congress the following month, the president was cited for eleven potential impeachable offenses, including perjury before the grand jury and obstruction of justice.[48]

The widely publicized Clinton scandal raised thorny issues concerning the private and public spheres of national leaders and the extent to which Republican conservatives had sought to frame the president on testimony tangential to a civil lawsuit ultimately dismissed by the courts. Despite the partisan features of the controversy, Democratic leaders such as Connecticut senator Joseph I. Lieberman expressed as much moral outrage about the case as their Republican counterparts. The chief executive was supposed to act as a role model who set the nation's standards of behavior, agonized the senator. Instead, Clinton had conducted an immoral and harmful extramarital affair close to the Oval Office with an employee half his age. Lieberman charged that Clinton's "deception" in not immediately acknowledging the transgression involved an "intentional and premeditated decision" that reflected poorly on his personal credibility and the integrity of the office.[49]

Much of the public frustration over Clinton's behavior focused on the duplicitous manner in which he appeared to use legalistic parsing to suit his interests. Having confined his White House assignations to oral sex, the chief executive could deny having sexual intercourse with his partner. His grand jury testimony also included caveats such as "it depends on how you define *alone*," and "it depends on what the meaning of the word *is* is." As newspaper columnist William Safire suggested, most Americans sensed that Clinton's language was "trickily misleading, deliberately deceptive or even perjurious." The administration had "turned weasal words and tortured legalisms into a way of life," concluded *Newsweek*'s Jonathan Alter.[50]

Although commentators attributed the president's studied phrasing to his legal background and sharp competitive instinct, critics found it easy to tie the White House baby boomers to the interventionist political intelligentsia and cultural liberalism associated with the 1960s. "Like so many of his generation," concluded Newsweek's Alter, Clinton seemed "to bring a sense of entitlement to his transgressions." Denunciations of this nature reached a fever pitch among social conservatives such as former jurist Robert H. Bork. Assessing the "costs of Clintonism," Bork renewed the argument that the youth rebellion had produced a culture "freed of normal restraints" such as obligation to truth and decent behavior. As a result of the decay in morals, the president's "sexual depravity and lies" and "reckless self-gratification" had "numbed our moral sense" and "inflicted enormous injury to the nation's character and culture," claimed Bork. Similar arguments were advanced by the Christian Coalition's Reverend Pat Robertson, who referred to the White House as a "playpen for the sexual freedom of the poster child of the 1960s."[51]

Following release of the special prosecutor's report, polling revealed that two-thirds of respondents did not believe that President Clinton shared their moral values. Yet 62 percent of the public gave the chief executive a favorable job rating and 60 percent wanted him to finish his term. Ignoring indications that voters did not see Clinton's transgressions as affecting his public duties, the Republican House approved two articles of impeachment that accused the president of perjury before the grand jury and obstruction of justice. Following Democratic House gains in the mid-term elections, however, the Senate failed to register majorities for conviction on either count in the impeachment trial held early in 1999. Nevertheless, 71 percent of a public sample said that the baby boomer chief executive would be remembered most for the White House sex scandal.[52]

As a New Democrat, Bill Clinton offered to distance his party from a long association with the nation's political interventionists and social service professionals. Confronted with an increasingly bureaucratized private health care system, however, Clinton relied on consultants and experts to create a universal reform package that would treat medical insurance like social security and assure an efficient delivery of services. Yet societal tensions over the role of the interventionist intelligentsia and big government subverted the president's efforts, leading to a political fiasco. Clinton's propensity for personal self-indulgence also contributed to the controversial status of New Class social guardians. Angry at the White House for betraying public trust and impatient with Republicans who politicized that betrayal, voters remained ambivalent over the role of public expertise at decade's end.

Conclusion: The Political Class and American Democracy

Politics and governmental affairs were "of limited salience" to many Americans, wrote political scientist Stephen C. Craig in 1993, because the public believed it no longer could control or direct the system. Craig's pessimism was echoed by Clinton pollster Stanley Greenberg, who described a "dispirited, alienated, and fragmented" citizenry in an environment in which "nobody seems to be in charge, nobody can be trusted to do what they say, and nobody is in position to see the country through." By the last decade of the twentieth century, social critics and political commentators like Christopher Lasch and Kevin Phillips were suggesting that the dysfunctional political system reflected the division of American society into two distinct and antagonistic factions. Beyond the reach of ordinary citizens and removed from the physical demands of the productive economy, a subculture of administrators, social service professionals, and academic consultants set public discourse and advised government leaders. Comprising a key element of a nationwide "guardian class," knowledge specialists and interest group advocates thrived upon an enhanced public sector. A progressive, rights-oriented philosophy and emancipatory cultural ideals further distanced the group from the majority of Americans. Lasch believed that conflict between the two groups amounted to "a form of class warfare" in national life.[1]

"The heart of every complaint I hear about our government today," amateur politician Jesse Ventura observed in 1999, was the conviction that the political system was controlled by "comfortably ensconced people who are many levels removed from the working people of this country." Convinced that the political class devoted too much energy to "keeping itself in business," Ventura won an independent race for Minnesota's governship in 1998 on the Reform Party ticket. Two years later, Republican senator John McCain of Arizona attracted the support of independents in an unsuccessful but widely publicized run for his party's presidential nomination that called for sweeping campaign finance reform and attacked special political interests. Meanwhile, fellow Republican George W. Bush, son of the former president, squeezed out a bitterly contested Electoral College victory over Democrat Al Gore by insisting on less government and more trustworthy leaders. Once Islamic terrorists mounted deadly suicide attacks on New York City and the Pentagon in 2001, Bush dedicated his presidency to the protection of citizens through increased homeland security and the deployment of U.S. military force in Afghanistan and Iraq.[2]

Ventura, McCain, and Bush each played upon suspicion of the guardians who comprised the nation's governing elites, social policy consultants, and opinion molders. The sentiments expressed by these political figures had an extended history, one which this book has sought to portray and explain. Hostility to the socially committed knowledge and professional sector first had erupted in Wisconsin, the laboratory of Progressive reform and the state where university specialists initially assisted in the formation of public policy. During the 1920s, contention over the societal role of intellectuals helped to engender bitter debates between modern secularists and moral traditionalists. Both the Leopold-Loeb case and the Scopes Monkey trial provided ample grounds for discussing the place of scientific and cultural experts in defining society's mores. Discomfort over rapid social change and the perceived influence of intellectual elites helped to shape the impassioned rhetoric of the 1920s Ku Klux Klan, whose leaders ostracized liberal opinion leaders as strangers to the American Way.

Impacted by the enormous demands of the Great Depression, President Franklin Roosevelt turned to a brains trust of academic and legal advisers after 1932. Yet by appearing to bypass the cumbersome legislative process and by concentrating policymaking in the White House, Roosevelt left his administration vulnerable to charges of undemocratic procedures. Criticism was particularly strong from representatives of small agriculture and independent business who sensed that the president's experts were ignorant of their problems, apathetic about their interests, and hostile to their needs. Anxiety over the role of executive branch consultants led to overstated charges of White House complicity in anti-capitalist conspiracies or other attempts to redesign and restructure the political system. Nevertheless, suspicions about the use of applied intelligence continued to complicate the Roosevelt administration's attempts to induce economic recovery and stabilize the country's institutions.

Once Roosevelt won reelection in a 1936 campaign in which the brains trust was a major issue, concerns over executive branch advisers and bureaucratic administrators contributed to a series of political crises that seriously marred the president's second term. Congress resisted White House reorganization, criticized the consumerist bias of Roosevelt economists, objected to the dominance of antibusiness attorneys affiliated with the National Labor Relations Board, demanded limits on the arbitrary power of executive agencies, worked to reduce the number of professional staffers in government bureaus, and sought to limit social experimentation in recovery programs like the Civilian Conservation Corps. Some critics of the New Deal went so far as to depict Washington's emerging political class as a haven for radical Jews.

The coming of World War II and the menace of foreign totalitarianism intensified concerns over the evolution of a permanent bureaucracy in Washington. Threatened by the executive branch's growing power, Congress mounted highly publicized investigations into the influence of academic and professional experts on domestic federal spending, social programs in the civil defense agencies, stateside propaganda activities, government price-fixing, and long-range economic and social welfare planning. Concern over the preservation of traditional economic virtues, democratic principles, and their own political power led congressional leaders like Martin Dies, Jr. to undertake inquiries into the alleged radicalism of a number of academics employed by the Roosevelt administration. By 1945, a majority in Congress had rejected the New Deal's flirtation with collectivist social experiment and high-minded reform.

With the onset of the Cold War, the philosophy and behavior of government managers, policy experts, and academic consultants came under increasing suspicion. Critics associated the intelligentsia with a communist movement that supposedly functioned as a strategic interest group for power-hungry knowledge elites impatient with democratic procedure. The postwar controversy over political intellectuals emerged full blown with questions concerning the character of New Deal manager David E. Lilienthal. A series of congressional inquiries into the alleged threat of Communist subversion intensified the growing chasm between New Class insiders and traditional power brokers in local politics and business. Distrust of cosmopolitan elites also shaped the House Un-American Activities Committee's investigations into the past conduct of the Hollywood Ten and Alger Hiss. Accusing Truman State Department officials, high-ranking military, and foreign policy advisers of insufficient awareness of the Cold War's moral implications, Joe McCarthy mounted a populist attack on the administration's alleged toleration of domestic Communists. McCarthy's portrait of arrogant, privileged, and unaccountable political academics received support when lengthy hearings by the McCarran committee led it to denounce the scholarly Owen D. Lattimore as a conscious instrument of the Communist conspiracy.

The debate over the security clearance of physicist and nuclear weapons consultant J. Robert Oppenheimer reintroduced doubts concerning the loyalty of intellectual elites to core national values during the Eisenhower era. Yet Republican occupation of the White House led to the demise of Joe McCarthy when the Wisconsin senator turned against the military establishment in the televised Army-McCarthy hearings. Meanwhile, congressional Republicans led an investigation into the alleged role of tax-exempt foundations and social science researchers in formulating collectivist government policies and influencing public education and social attitudes. In a period in which anticommunism appeared to incorporate deeply held anxieties over the intrusion of remote elites into daily existence, a series of grass-roots campaigns focused on the unseen dangers of fluoridated municipal water supplies.

The Cold War emphasized the extent to which the American public entertained profound suspicions concerning the cultural ideology of sociopolitical professionals and policymakers. The civil rights revolution of the 1960s shifted the grounds of such concern. By involving white professionals, intellectuals, and social activists as strategic allies, the crusade for racial justice intensified anxieties over the role of federal administrators and regulators in using state coercion to erase human distinctions. Threats of depersonalization and powerlessness became a major focus of George C. Wallace's presidential primary campaigns of 1964. In the general election, Republican Barry Goldwater charged that forgotten and silent Americans had been eclipsed by powerful social interest groups aligned with Lyndon B. Johnson's Great Society. Johnson's War on Poverty elicited fears among local politicians that administrators were building their own power bases in local communities by colonizing the poor and selecting favored clients for lucrative patronage awards. Accusing the Great Society of double standards of racial justice, governors Ronald Reagan and George Wallace tied a culturally permissive liberal elite to the social disruptions, crime, and street violence of the 1960s underclass. Such themes became the focal point for Richard M. Nixon's campaign for the presidency in 1968.

Despite Nixon's coolness to social programs, the new adminstration endorsed a controversial affirmative action plan in the construction industry bitterly opposed by organized labor. Yet the Republican president also courted working-class support for the Vietnam War and opposition to would-be members of the professional classes in the student New Left and peace movement. Expropriating themes from Goldwater, Reagan, and Wallace, the White House denounced campus dissidents as a radical elite whose cultural values defied basic decency and common sense. Nixon's hatred for perceived allies of the antiwar movement contributed to his fatal involvement in Watergate-related attacks on the Liberal Establishment. When Jimmy Carter rode a reform tide to the presidency in 1976, opponents effectively fused condemnations of special interests and opposition to progressive social values into a creed of populist conservativism that helped to bring the Carter administration to its political knees.

During the 1980s, Republican presidents Ronald Reagan and George H. W. Bush built powerful electoral coalitions on the demonization of big government and on public impatience with the nation's New Class guardians and political interventionists. Once Bill Clinton won the White House, he and his wife Hillary became the target of critics who saw post–World War II babyboomers as politically unreliable and tainted by cultural deviance. Although Clinton's affirmative action policies and interventionist health care proposals strengthened such sentiment, America's controversy with the guardian class appeared to peak at century's end with the culturally infused debate over the White House sex scandal and the subsequent impeachment of the president.

***

Originating in a variety of ideological perspectives across the twentieth century, the response to America's political class and social guardians has contained enormous contradictions. During the 1920s the Ku Klux Klan and other social conservatives charged that academic intellectuals were exerting an excessively liberal influence over the nation's cultural agenda and social morality. Yet Republican populists from rural states simultaneously denounced scholarly specialists who used their expertise to deliver pro-Wall Street testimony before congressional committees. When the Great Depression led to Franklin Roosevelt's New Deal, the Democratic White House relied on market-oriented economic advisers who sought to restore consumer prosperity through federal expenditures, reinvigoration of credit, social welfare programs, and legislation supportive of workers and organized labor. Yet the statist implications to Roosevelt's programs and the administration's alliance with the unions led modernizing intellectuals like H. L. Mencken and Walter Lippmann to join producer critics and others in condemning the New Deal as inordinately radical, even socialist. Another paradox emerged when Republican adversaries of the Roosevelt administration refashioned populist rhetoric to suit small business and farming interests during World War II, going so far as to argue that consumer-oriented programs like price controls were elitist.

The contradictory response to the guardian class took dramatic form during the Cold War when anticollectivist ideologues alleged that key governmental and cultural figures aspired to build an international Communist workers' state that would elevate intellectuals as a powerful elite. Although assertions over the foreign ties of the political intelligentsia were exaggerated, anxieties over the suspect orientation of policy intellectuals and knowledge professionals resonated deeply with the public. Such concerns resurfaced in the 1960s controversy over federal sponsorship of civil rights. When the quest for racial justice resulted in coercive government mandates such as affirmative action, civil liberties crusaders such as Sam Ervin and Paul Fannin viewed Washington bureaucrats as the problem. The paradoxical nature of race politics emerged when the Nixon administration compensated for an affirmative action alliance with social interventionists by courting organized labor, the former ally of 1930s political intellectuals, and called for moral unity in the Vietnam War against the cultural dissidents of the upper-middle class.

Ronald Reagan and George H. W. Bush further complicated the political landscape by expropriating the critiques of corporate-funded theorists to espouse a populist conservatism that marginalized rival policy administrators and social specialists as fiscally irresponsible and morally decadent. In an added irony, Bill Clinton sought to avoid the dangers of tax-and-spend liberalism by proposing a health care package that substituted government regulation of the private insurance market for huge Treasury expenditures. Yet distrust of political intellectuals and interventionist policies was so great that the Clinton plan suffered a humiliating defeat. Positioning himself as a centrist, the Democratic president nevertheless had to contend with pervasive discomfort with the dissident politics and culture of the 1960s, of which he remained an unlikely but cogent symbol.

Perhaps the greatest contradiction of the century-long campaign against America's political class has been the futility of much of its effort. Critics of social guardians found themselves opposing a host of decent and plausible causes, including scientific teaching in the public schools, improved working conditions for industrial labor, regulation of the stock market and public utilities, cooperative experiments by federal youth agencies, consumer price controls during wartime, assurance of intellectual freedom for academics and foundation-sponsored researchers, adoption of benign public health measures, enactment of civil rights gains and anti-bias laws, protection of programs to aid the poor, and inclusive efforts to spread equality of opportunity. Furthermore, dangerous portions of anti-intellectual discourse embraced unwarranted hyperbole, unreasoned argument, banal half-truths, crude exaggerations, narrow-minded prejudice, and inelegant conspiratorial thinking. Indeed, the frequent failure of those opposing the guardian class cannot be separated from the cruel excesses associated with such individuals as Father Charles Coughlin, Joseph McCarthy, and George Wallace; and such phenomena as the Scopes trial, the 1920s Ku Klux Klan, Depression-era anti-Semitism, antifluoridation paranoia, race supremacy ideology, the Vietnam War, Watergate, and the rejectionism of the late-century extreme right.

Even when opponents of the intelligentsia discredited their causes with bigotry, bullying, terror, or outright violence, however, challenges to America's twentieth-century guardians often touched on central social anxieties. The leading focus of such efforts appeared to be the perceived erosion of fundamental values related to individual autonomy, personal empowerment, family cohesion, religious devotion, community bonding, ethnic allegiance, and national loyalty. Often representing traditional producers and members of the old middle class, critics of the political intelligentsia denounced a social agenda that allegedly encouraged the erasure of human distinctions and the obliteration of cultural differences. They warned that the coercive and manipulative methods of the intellectual classes threatened ordinary citizens with mass depersonalization, powerlessness, and the eradication of vitality and meaning from democratic political life. Concerns of this nature help to explain why professional elites and knowledge experts repeatedly have been attacked as agents of modern social and cultural degradation.

For nearly one hundred years, public discourse in the United States has been marked by a continuing dispute over a broadly defined political class whose members have been castigated as strangers to the American Way. The stranger represented a cultural renegade, a shadowy suspect who assumed a powerful inside position and threatened to use the coercions of social authority and expertise to impose abstract creeds, whether they be statist, collectivist, internationalist, or multiculturalist. When socially involved intellectuals embraced admirable causes such as freedom of inquiry, support for organized labor, civil rights for racial minorities, or antimilitarism, their participation, alleged motives, and presumed interests often became the central target of ideological strife and intergroup conflict. Yet their adversaries have been frustrated by the perception that social interventionists and members of the political class often managed to overcome their detractors and perpetuate and expand the bureaucratic networks and careers associated with their ideology and rule.

It may be difficult to ascertain whether service professionals, policy planners, and socially oriented intellectuals constitute members of a New Class that monopolizes governance and opinion in modern society. Yet the troubled response to the interventionist intelligentsia in twentieth-century America illustrates the warning of one scholar that "knowledge and expertise are inherently suspect when they become a basis for claims of political influence." Bureaucrats, planners, experts, and social service professionals often have compounded the vulnerabilities of their position with condescending attitudes toward the people they were mandated to serve. As sociologist Alvin Gouldner noted, upper-middle-class practitioners tend to assume that the world should be governed by people such as themselves–"those possessing superior competence, wisdom, and science." Similar concerns marked the criticism of Christopher Lasch, who condemned the insularity of educated professionals and who questioned the tendency of experts and knowledge elites to equate dissent from their self-serving agenda with emotional and cultural backwardness.[3]

Given the legitimacy of such objections and the pointed quality of much of the protests treated in these pages, it nevertheless must be acknowledged that no civilization can thrive without affording an important role for educated experts, knowledge professionals, socially oriented intellectuals, public administrators, and human service practitioners. Certainly, if society is to accomplish more than assuring personal profit for the wealthy and defending vested economic interests, it must be open to sources of intelligent social change and reform with the hope of improving and elevating the human condition and alleviating the impact of severe social stratification. How, indeed, can important challenges surrounding medical health, psychological well-being, economic welfare, worker safety, the environment, and international relations be addressed unless trained and committed practitioners are mobilized to play a role in such endeavors?

If social guardians and members of the political class are to retain the confidence of society, however, their efforts must resonate with broader segments of the public. Although much of the criticism of their role has come from conservatives and antistatists, it is important to recognize the culturally significant sources of such discontent. Service intellectuals must succeed in lending their expertise to social problems without necessarily imposing their own needs and sensibilities upon the rest of the citizenry. Knowledge professionals must prove that they can play a genuine role in reforms that curb elites, special interests, and privileged classes of all kinds, including their own. The sociopolitical sector must demonstrate that it can refashion itself to serve all segments of society instead of the interest groups normally aligned with its agenda. In a nation comprised of individualists as well as participants in common endeavors, the frequently cited goal of cultural pluralism takes on added meaning. Indeed, the requirements of diversity may compel socially committed intellectuals to fuse their own modernizing cultural values with the more traditional ethics of small business, the military, the religious world, ethnic subcultures, and other cohesive communities.[4]

Too often, public debate has asked ordinary Americans to choose between reliance on the goodwill of narrowly focused business interests or dependence on the judgement of socially committed intellectuals and reformers immersed in their own worlds. Although knowledge professionals and elements of the political class offer liberation from the crueler consequences of the market, they often appear tainted by self-reflexive concerns and preferences or by commitment to favored protégés. Arguably, a healthy democracy needs practitioners who serve all elements of the social structure, not some. Indeed, society cries out for disinterested healers, reformers, and authors of consent, not ideological monitors or masters. If there are lessons to be learned from the debates and conflicts chronicled in these pages, they conceivably rest on the notion that even the brightest among us require a balanced perspective on the effect and legacy of our mutual endeavors. Failure to achieve such vision only can provide comfort to those elements of society whose intentions are far from benevolent.

Notes

Introduction

1. Hiram Wesley Evans, "The Klan's Fight for Americanism," *North American Review* 223 (March 1926): 38–39 (quote on 39); Richard Kirkendall, *Social Scientists and Farm Politics in the Age of Roosevelt* (Columbia: University of Missouri Press, 1966): 94; "'American Hitler' Pictured by Wirt," *New York Times*, 25 March 1934, 26; *Congressional Record*, 77th Cong., 1st sess. 87 (25 November 1941): 9124 (Dies quote), and 81st Cong., 2d sess. 96 (20 February 1950): 1954, 1957; U.S. House of Representatives, Special Committee to Investigate Tax-Exempt Foundations and Comparable Organizations, *Tax-Exempt Foundations: Final Report* (Washington, D.C.: Government Printing Office, 1954): 39, 17, 45, 31, 40 (quote); Dan T. Carter, *The Politics of Rage. George Wallace, the Origins of the New Conservatism, and the Transformation of American Politics* (New York: Simon and Schuster, 1995): 305 (Wallace quote); "Remarks in Columbus to Members of Ohio Veterans Organizations," 4 October 1982, in *Public Papers of the Presidents of the United States, Ronald Reagan, 1982*, (Washington, D.C.: Government Printing Office, 1983): 1262 (Reagan quote).
2. Elliot A. Rosen, *Hoover, Roosevelt, and the Brains Trust: From Depression to New Deal* (Columbia University Press, 1977): 160–61, 171, 316.
3. Ibid., 159, 168; Kirkendall, *Social Scientists and Farm Politics*, 64–67, 257, 94, 96–97; William J. Barber, *Designs within Disorder: Franklin D. Roosevelt, the Economists, and the Shaping of American Economic Policy, 1933–1945* (New York: Cambridge University Press, 1996): 63, 72, 74; "Tugwell Sets 1938 to Balance Budget," *New York Times*, 29 October 1935, 5.
4. James Burnham, *The Managerial Revolution* [1941] (Bloomington: Indiana University Press, 1960); Joseph A. Schumpeter, *Capitalism, Socialism, and Democracy* [1942] (New York, Harper, 3d ed., 1950). For discussion of Schumpeter, see Peter Brimelow, *Alien Nation: Common Sense About America's Immigration Disaster* (New York: Random House, 1995): 230, and Daniel Bell, "The New Class: A Muddled Concept," in B. Bruce-Briggs, ed., *The New Class?* (New Brunswick, N.J.: Transaction Books, 1979): 170.
5. Friedrich A. Hayek, *The Road to Serfdom* (Chicago: University of Chicago Press, 1944): 53–54, 70, 78, 101, 158; Milovan Djilas, *The New Class: An Analysis of the Communist System* (New York: Frederick A. Praeger, 1957): 38–39, 45, and *The Unperfect Society: Beyond the New Class* (New York: Harcourt, Brace and World, 1969): 7 (quote), 8.

For Hayek's influence, see Alan Brinkley, *The End of Reform: New Deal Liberalism in Recession and War* (New York, Vintage, 1995): 157–58.

6. John Kenneth Galbraith, *The Affluent Society* [1958] (Boston: Houghton Mifflin, 4th ed., 1984), and *The New Industrial State* [1967] (Boston: Houghton Mifflin, 4th ed., 1985); David T. Bazelon, *Power in America: The Politics of the New Class* (New York: New American Library, 1967); Daniel Bell, *The Coming of Post-Industrial Society: A Venture in Social Forecasting* [1967] (New York: Basic Books, 1973), "New Class," in Bruce-Briggs, ed., *New Class?* 175–77, and "The Dispossessed (1962)," in Daniel Bell, ed., *The Radical Right: The New American Right Extended and Updated* (Garden City, N.Y.: Doubleday, 1963): 16, 21–22; Barbara Ehrenreich and John Ehrenreich, "The Professional-Managerial Class," *Radical America* 11 (March-April 1977): 7–13 (quote on 11). See also Barbara Ehrenreich and John Ehrenreich, "The New Left: A Case Study in Professional-Managerial Radicalism," *Radical America* 11 (May-June 1977): 7–22. The two articles by Ehrenreich and Ehrenreich were reprinted as "The Professional-Managerial Class," in Pat Walker, ed., *Between Labor and Capital* (Boston: South End Press, 1979): 5–45.

7. Alvin W. Gouldner, *The Future of Intellectuals and the Rise of the New Class* (New York: Continuum, 1979): 11 (first quote), 17, 18 (second quote), 19–20, 61, 65, 84.

8. Milton Friedman, *Capitalism and Freedom* (Chicago: University of Chicago Press, 1962): 201; Irving Kristol, *Two Cheers for Capitalism* (New York: Basic Books, 1978): 27–29. For the views of 1970s neoconservatives see Norman Podhoretz, "The Adversary Culture and the New Class," in Bruce-Briggs, ed., *New Class?* 19–31, and B. Bruce-Briggs, "An Introduction to the Idea of the New Class," in Bruce-Briggs, ed., *New Class?* 1–2, 4.

9. David Lebedoff, *The New Elite: The Death of Democracy* (New York: Franklin Watts, 1978): 19–20, 43, 52, 55; Kevin P. Phillips, *Arrogant Capital: Washington, Wall Street, and the Frustration of American Politics* (Boston: Little, Brown, 1994): 5 (first and second quotes), 27 (third quote). For the assertion that federal bureaucrats, education officials, and media elites belonged to a unified and parasitic New Class, see Brimelow, *Alien Nation*, 230.

10. D. Bell, "New Class," in Bruce-Briggs, ed., *New Class?* 169 (quote), 181–87. Bell's essay was first published as "The New Class: A Muddled Concept," *Society* 16 (January-February 1979): 15–23.

11. Jean-Christophe Agnew, "A Touch of Class," *Democracy* 3 (Spring 1983): 59, 60 (quote), 70; Christopher Lasch, *The True and Only Heaven: Progress and Its Critics* (New York: W. W. Norton, 1991): 509, 512–13, 515, 518.

12. Lasch, *True and Only Heaven*, 468, 484 (quote), 527; Thomas L. Haskell, Introduction, in Haskell, ed., *The Authority of Experts: Studies in History and Theory* (Bloomington: Indiana University Press, 1984): ix (quote); Richard Hofstadter, *The Age of Reform: From Bryan to F.D.R.* (New York: Alfred A. Knopf, 1955). For Lasch's critique of the insularity of the educated and professional classes, see *The Revolt of the Elites and the Betrayal of Democracy* (New York: W. W. Norton, 1995).

13. Richard Hofstadter, *Anti-intellectualism in American Life* (New York: Random House, 1962): 7 (quote), 27, 47–51.

14. Ibid., 6, 34–36 (first quote on 35), 42 (second quote), 43 (third quote), 198, 407–408.

15. Ibid., 35–36, 42 (first and third quotes), 43–44, 133 (second quote).

16. Richard F. Hamilton, "Liberal Intelligentsia and White Backlash," *Dissent* 19 (Winter 1972): 225.

17. Catherine McNicol Stock, *Main Street in Crisis: The Great Depression and the Old Middle Class on the Northern Plains* (Chapel Hill: University of North Carolina Press, 1992): 209; Alan Brinkley, "The Problem of American Conservatism," *American Historical Review* 99 (April 1994): 409, and *Liberalism and Its Discontents* (Cambridge, Mass.: Harvard University Press, 1998): xii; David A. Horowitz, *Beyond Left and Right: Insurgency and the Establishment* (Urbana: University of Illinois Press, 1997).

Chapter 1

1. Hiram Wesley Evans, "The Klan's Fight for Americanism," *North American Review* 223 (March 1926): 38–39 (quote on 39).

2. Lynn Dumenil, *The Modern Temper: American Culture and Society in the 1920s* (New York: Hill and Wang, 1995): 7–12, 16–17, 88, 148 (quote), 149, 173–74; LeRoy Ashby, *William Jennings Bryan: Champion of Democracy* (Boston: Twayne, 1987): 187 (quote). For the loss of faith during the Jazz Age see Joseph Wood Krutch, *The Modern Temper: A Study and a Confession* [1929] (New York, Harcourt, Brace, 1956).

3. Daniel Bell, *The Cultural Contradictions of Capitalism* (New York: Basic Books, 1978): xxii–xxiv, 7, 21–22, 67–68, 74, 77–78; George M. Marsden, *The Soul of the American University: From Protestant Establishment to Established Nonbelief* (New York: Oxford University Press, 1994): 113, 115, 117–21, 130, 153, 182, 189, 289, 332, and "The Soul of the American University: An Historical Overview," in Marsden and Bradley J. Longfield, eds., *The Secularization of the Academy* (New York: Oxford University Press, 1992): 22.

4. Marsden, *Soul of American University*, 306 (Dewey quote), 307 (AAUP quote), 308.

5. Ibid., 25, 129, 132–33n (quote).

6. Ibid., 267 (quote), 318.

7. Ibid., 292–95 (quote on 294), 341. See James H. Leuba, *The Belief in God and Immortality: A Psychological, Anthropological and Statistical Study* (Boston: Sherman, French, 1916); James Bissett Pratt, "Religion and the Younger Generation," *Yale Review* 12 (April 1923): 594–613; and Robert Cooley Angell, *The Campus: A Study of Contemporary Undergraduate Life in the American University* (New York: D. Appleton, 1928).

8. Marsden, *Soul of American University*, 268 (Earp quote); Willard B. Gatewood, Jr., *Preachers, Pedagogues, and Politicians: The Evolution Controversy in North Carolina, 1920–1927* (Chapel Hill: University of North Carolina Press, 1966): 104–105, 114 (Bernard quote). See L. L. Bernard, "The Development of the Concept of Progress," *Journal of Social Forces* 3 (January 1925): 207–212.

9. Harry Elmer Barnes, "Sociology and Ethics: A Genetic View of the Theory of Conduct," *Journal of Social Forces* 3 (January 1925): 217 (first quote), 218 (second and third quotes); Gatewood, *Preachers, Pedagogues, and Politicians*, 115–17; Alvin W. Gouldner, *The Future of Intellectuals and the Rise of the New Class* (New York: Continuum, 1979): 32, 44–45; Dumenil, *Modern Temper*, 186.

10. Marsden, *Soul of American University*, 328; Dumenil, *Modern Temper*, 147 (Cohen quote); Christopher Lasch, *The Revolt of the Elites and the Betrayal of Democracy* (New York: W. W. Norton, 1995): 10. For academic immersion in "scientism," see Neil Postman, *Technopoly: The Surrender of Culture to Technology* (New York: Alfred A. Knopf, 1992): 147.

11. Gouldner, *Future of Intellectuals*, 32, 44–45. For the distrust of urban cosmopolitanism see Don S. Kirschner, *City and Country: Rural Responses to Urbanization in the 1920s* (Westport, Conn.: Greenwood Press, 1970).

12. Hiram W. Johnson, "Why 'Irreconcilables' Keep Out of Europe, Told by Hiram Johnson," *New York Times Magazine*, 14 January 1923, 1; Dumenil, *Modern Temper*, 187.

13. Irving Stone, *Clarence Darrow for the Defense: A Biography* (Garden City, N.Y.: Doubleday, Doran, 1941): 387, 388–89, 390, 391, 398; "The Facts," in *The Plea of Clarence Darrow, August 22nd, 23rd and 25th, 1924, In Defense of Richard Loeb and Nathan Leopold, Jr., On Trial for Murder* (Chicago: Ralph Fletcher Seymour, 1924): 1.

14. *Plea*, 2; Kevin Tierney, *Darrow, A Biography* (New York: Thomas Y. Crowell, 1979): 320, 326, 334; Stone, *Darrow*, 398, 405 (second quote); "Slayers of Franks Both Plead Guilty," *New York Times*, 22 July 1924, 1 (first quote).

15. Stone, *Darrow*, 400–401, 405, 407 (third quote), 413, 420; Clarence Darrow, *The Story of My Life* [1932] (New York: Charles Scribner's Sons, 1934): 241 (first quote); "Had Loeb's Brother on List of Victims," *New York Times*, 17 July 1924, 7 (second quote); "Diseased in Minds Will Be Defense of Franks Slayers," *New York Times*, 27 July 1924, 7.

16. Stone, *Darrow*, 382–83, 403–404; Clarence Darrow, *Crime, Its Cause and Treatment* (New York: Thomas Y. Crowell, 1922): 34 (first quote), 36 (second quote).

17. Darrow, *Crime*, 29, 30 (first and second quotes), 33, 34, 274, 275 (third quote).

18. Ibid., vii (fourth quote), 28 (second quote), 29 (first quote), 274 (third quote); Stone, *Darrow*, 401.

19. Stone, *Darrow*, 413–14 (quote). The undated Joliet speech was cited by Leopold-Loeb prosecutors.

20. "Diseased in Minds Will Be Defense of Franks Slayers," *New York Times,* 27 July 1924, 1; "All-Day Fight Opens Move To Gain Mercy For Franks Slayers," *New York Times,* 31 July 1924, 1 (first quote); *Plea,* 55 (second and fourth quotes), 61, 73–74 (third quote). Darrow's description of the defendants as emotionless may have been borne out by Leopold's acknowledgment of sitting in the courtroom and watching "the play as it progresses." See "Diseased in Minds," *New York Times,* 27 July 1924, 7.

21. Stone, *Darrow,* 387, 390 (first quote), 399 (second quote).

22. Garry Wills, *Under God: Religion and American Politics* (New York: Simon and Schuster, 1990): 106 (first Darrow quote) *Plea,* 77 (third Darrow quote), 79 (second Darrow quote), 81.

23. *Plea,* 78 (second quote), 81, 84 (first and fourth quotes), 85 (third and fifth quotes).

24. "Franks Slayers Get Life Imprisonment," *New York Times,* 11 September 1924, 1–2.

25. George W. Kirchwey, "Loeb Case Introduces New Psychology," *New York Times,* 7 September 1924, sec. 8: 3; Leonard Blumgart, "The New Psychology and the Franks Case," *The Nation* 119 (10 September 1924): 261, 262 (quote).

26. "Warning Left at Loeb's Home," *New York Times,* 19 August 1924, 6 (first quote); "Murder Most Foul," *The Outlook* 138 (24 September 1924): 115; "Rich and Poor Murderers," *Literary Digest* 82 (27 September 1924): 10 (second and third quotes).

27. Blumgart, "New Psychology," *Nation,* 261 (first quote); "The Loeb-Leopold Sentence," *World's Work* 45 (November 1924): 12 (second quote), 13; "Education and Murder," *Literary Digest* 83 (18 October 1924): 31 (third quote), 32 (fourth and fifth quotes).

28. "The Mercy of the Court," *New York Times,* 11 September 1924, 22.

29. George M. Marsden, *Fundamentalism and American Culture: The Shaping of Twentieth-Century Evangelism, 1870–1925* (New York: Oxford University Press, 1980): 141–95; Gatewood, *Preachers, Pedagogues, and Politicians,* 30, 34 (first quote), 230; Vernon Kellogg, "War and Human Evolution: Germanized," *North American Review* 207 (March 1918): 366 (second quote). Evolutionists such as paleonthologist Henry Fairfield Osborn, president of the New York Museum of Natural History and author of the preface to Madison Grant's *Passing of the Great Race* (1916), tied Darwinism to notions of racial superiority. See Lawrence W. Levine, *Defender of the Faith, William Jennings Bryan: The Last Decade, 1915–1925* (New York: Oxford University Press, 1965): 286–87, 287n. Scopes appeared in New York with Osborn and eugenicist Charles B. Davenport to support the cause of science. See Edward J. Larson, *Summer For the Gods: The Scopes Trial and America's Continuing Debate Over Science and Religion* (New York: Basic Books, 1997): 113.

30. Marsden, *Soul of American University,* 321–22, 325; Gatewood, *Preachers, Pedagogues, and Politicians,* 120 (first quote), 121 (second quote).

31. Marsden, *Soul of American University,* 325.

32. Paolo E. Coletta, *William Jennings Bryan: Political Puritan, 1915–1925* (Lincoln: University of Nebraska Press, 1969): 232–33; Dumenil, *Modern Temper,* 187 (quote); Jerry R. Tompkins, "John Thomas Scopes: A Profile," in Tompkins, ed., *D-Days at Dayton: Reflections on the Scopes Trial* (Baton Rouge: Louisiana State University Press, 1965): 11–12; Wills, *Under God,* 100; Ashby, *Bryan,* 199.

33. Tompkins, "Scopes," in Tompkins, ed., *D-Days at Dayton,* 10–11; Wills, *Under God,* 100; Marsden, *Soul of American University,* 326; Larson, *Summer for the Gods,* 36.

34. Wills, *Under God,* 97, 99, 106; John Thomas Scopes, "Reflections—Forty Years After," in Tompkins, ed., *D-Days at Dayton,* 21 (quote); Ashby, *Bryan,* 180; David A. Horowitz, *Beyond Left and Right: Insurgency and the Establishment* (Urbana: University of Illinois Press, 1997): 10.

35. John Reed, "Bryan on Tour," *Collier's* 57 (20 May 1916): 11–12; Ashby, *Bryan,* xvi, 187–90, 192.

36. Ashby, *Bryan,* 196; William Jennings Bryan, *In His Image* (New York: Fleming H. Revell, 1922): 186 (first quote); T. V. Smith, "Bases of Bryanism," *Scientific Monthly* 16 (May 1923): 506, 509; Levine, *Defender of the Faith,* 220, 224, 228; Wills, *Under God,* 102 (second quote), 111 (third quote); James Gilbert, *Redeeming Culture: American Religion in an Age of Science* (Chicago: University of Chicago Press, 1997): 24, 28, 30, 34.

37. Marsden, *Soul of American University,* 319–21; Wills, *Under God,* 100–101; Willard H. Smith, *The Social and Religious Thought of William Jennings Bryan* (Lawrence: University of Kansas Press, 1975): 182, 191; Coletta, *Bryan,* 201; Gatewood, *Preachers, Pedagogues,*

and Politicians, 56, 99; Larson, *Summer for the Gods,* 39–40. Bryan's 1922 address at Virginia's Union Theological Seminary was published as *In His Image.* See also "The Menace of Darwinisrn," *The Commoner* (April 1921): 5–8.

38. Levine, *Defender of the Faith,* 261–62, 264–65, 268–69; William Jennings Bryan, "God and Evolution," *New York Times,* 26 February 1922, sec. 7: 1 (first quote); William Jennings Bryan, "Mr. Bryan Speaks to Darwin," *The Forum* 74 (July 1925): 107 (second quote); Ashby, *Bryan,* 196 (third quote).

39. Coletta, *Bryan,* 205 (first quote), 207 (second quote), 209; Levine, *Defender of the Faith,* 279 (third quote).

40. Levine, *Defender of the Faith,* 279; Ashby, *Bryan,* 197 (first Bryan quote), 184 (second Bryan quote); "Bryan Attacks Colleges," *New York Times,* 1 June 1922, 19 (third Bryan quote).

41. Bryan, *In His Image,* 37–38 (first quote); William Jennings Bryan, "God and Evolution," *New York Times,* 22 February 1922, sec. 7: 1 (second quote); "Reply from Mr. Bryan," *New York Times,* 14 March 1922, 14 (third quote); Bryan, "Bryan Speaks to Darwin," *Forum,* 101 (fourth quote); Leslie H. Allen, ed., *Bryan and Darrow at Dayton: The Record and Documents of the "Bible Evolution Trial"* (New York: Arthur Lee, 1925): 8–9 (fifth quote).

42. Levine, *Defender of the Faith,* 289 (first and second quotes); Ashby, *Bryan,* 184 (fourth quote), 185 (third quote), 187; Marsden, *Soul of American University,* 320; Coletta, *Bryan,* 236 (fifth quote). Dayton city attorneys Sue and Herbert E. Hicks were brothers. See Larson, *Summer For the Gods,* 89.

43. Wills, *Under God,* 100, 107; William Jennings Bryan and Mary Baird Bryan, *The Memoirs of William Jennings Bryan* (Chicago: John C. Winston, 1925): 425; Ashby, *Bryan,* 198; T. Smith, "Bases of Bryanism," *Scientific Monthly,* 505 (first quote), 506, 513; Edward Mims, "Why the South is Anti-Evolution," *World's Work* 50 (September 1925): 548 (second quote), 551 (third quote).

44. Ashby, *Bryan,* 176, 202 (Mencken quotes); Wills, *Under God,* 109; H. L. Mencken, " 'The Monkey Trial': A Reporter's Account," and Watson Davis, "The Men of Science," in Tompkins, ed., *D-Days at Dayton,* 35, 61, 69.

45. Allen, ed., *Bryan and Darrow at Dayton,* 11, 15, 41–43, 45, 48 (quote), 50, 53.

46. Ibid., 54, 64 (first quote), 65 (second quote), 66 (third quote).

47. Ibid., 72, 73 (first quote), 74 (second and third quotes); Wills, *Under God,* 101–102 (fourth quote on 102).

48. Allen, ed., *Bryan and Darrow at Dayton,* 74 (first quote), 75, 76 (second and third quotes).

49. Ibid., 78 (first, second, and third quotes), 79 (fourth quote). See "Full Text of Mr. Bryan's Argument Against Evidence of Scientists," *New York Times,* 17 July 1925, 1–2.

50. Allen, ed., *Bryan and Darrow at Dayton,* 91–92, 93 (first quote), 96; Levine, *Defender of the Faith,* 347 (second quote). For transcripts of the statements of scientists and educators, see Allen, ed., *Bryan and Darrow at Dayton,* 112–32.

51. Allen, ed., *Bryan and Darrow at Dayton,* 133, 151 (quotes).

52. Ibid., 156–57, 159–61, 171 (quotes).

53. Frank R. Pattie, ed., "The Last Speech of William Jennings Bryan," *Tennessee Historical Quarterly* 6 (September 1947): 265; Coletta, *Bryan,* 271, 272 (first quote); Allen, ed., *Bryan and Darrow At Dayton,* 172, 173 (second quote), 182 (third quote), 185 (fourth quote), 186 (fifth quote). Pattie's article contains his own transcript of the Winchester speech. See also William Jennings Bryan, *The Last Message of William Jennings Bryan* (New York. Fleming H. Revell, 1925).

54. Allen, ed., *Bryan and Darrow at Dayton,* 187 (first quote), 188 (second quote), 189, 194.

55. Roger N. Baldwin, "Dayton's First Issue," in Tompkins, ed., *D-Days at Dayton,* 59–60; Coletta, *Bryan,* 279; Wills, *Under God,* 112–13; Tompkins, "Scopes," in Tompkins, ed., *D-Days at Dayton,* 15–16.

56. Wills, *Under God,* 98.

57. "Burns Crosses for Bryan," *New York Times,* 1 August 1925, 2; "40,000 Klansmen Parade in Washington As 200,000 Spectators Look On Quietly," *New York Times,* 9 August 1925, 1; "Klan's Big Rally Ends With Oratory," *New York Times,* 10 August 1925, 26.

58. Shawn Lay, "Introduction: The Second Invisible Empire," in Lay, ed., *The Invisible Empire in the West: Toward a New Historical Appraisal of the Ku Klux Klan of the 1920s*

(Urbana: University of Illinois Press, 1992): 1–9; D. A. Horowitz, *Beyond Left and Right*, 82–89; Kathleen M. Blee, *Women of the Klan: Racism and Gender in the 1920s* (Berkeley: University of California Press, 1991). For local Klan purity crusades, see Leonard J. Moore, *Citizen Klansmen: The Ku Klux Klan in Indiana, 1921–1928* (Chapel Hill: University of North Carolina Press, 1991): 11–12, 22–23, 188–89, and William D. Jenkins, *Steel Valley Klan: The Ku Klux Klan in Ohio's Mahoning Valley* (Kent, Ohio: Kent State University Press, 1990): 159, 161.

59.　Moore, *Citizen Klansmen*, 36–37; Mark N. Morris, "Saving Society Through Politics: The Ku Klux Klan in Dallas, Texas, in the 1920s" (Ph.D. diss., University of North Texas, 1997): 143; Robert A. Goldberg, "Denver: Queen City of the Colorado Realm," in Lay, ed., *Invisible Empire*, 42; David A. Horowitz, "Order, Solidarity, and Vigilance: The Ku Klux Klan in La Grande, Oregon," in Lay, ed., *Invisible Empire*, 204, 205; Blee, *Women of the Klan*, 39.

60.　Shawn Lay, *Hooded Knights: The Ku Klux Klan in Buffalo, New York* (New York: New York University Press, 1995):146–47; D. A. Horowitz, *Beyond Left and Right*, 87–88; Nancy McLean, *Behind the Mask of Chivalry: The Making of the Second Ku Klux Klan* (New York: Oxford University Press, 1994): 87; Morris, "Saving Society Through Politics," 40, 235 (first quote), 236 (second quote) 320–21, 333–34; Shawn Lay, "Imperial Outpost on the Border: El Paso's Frontier Klan No. 100," in Lay, ed., *Invisible Empire*, 72, 78, 90; Goldberg, "Denver: Queen City," in Lay, ed., *Invisible Empire*, 49; Christopher Cocoltchos, "The Invisible Empire and the Search for Orderly Community: The Ku Klux Klan in Anaheim, California," in Lay, ed., *Invisible Empire*, 99–100, 117; Robert A. Goldberg, "Invisible Empire: The Knights of the Ku Klux Klan," in *Grassroots Resistance: Social Movements in Twentieth Century America* (Belmont, Calif.: Wadsworth, 1991): 81; Grand Titan, Texas, in *Papers Read at the Meeting of Grand Dragons, Knights of the Ku Klux Klan, at their First Annual Meeting, Held at Asheville, North Carolina, July 1923* [1923] (New York: Arno Press, 1977): 55 (third quote).

61.　David A. Horowitz, "Social Morality and Personal Revitalization: Oregon's Ku Klux Klan in the 1920s," *Oregon Historical Quarterly* 90 (Winter 1989): 371 (first quote), 372 (second quote); Jenkins, *Steel Valley Klan*, 154 (third and fourth quotes); Goldberg, "Denver: Queen City," in Lay, ed., *Invisible Empire*, 49; MacLean, *Behind the Mask of Chivalry*, 77 (fifth quote), 78 (sixth quote). For Klan opposition to secular values, see Dumenil, *The Modern Temper*, 285.

62.　Morris, "Saving Society Through Politics," 184–88; Charles C. Alexander, *The Ku Klux Klan in the Southwest* (Lexington: University of Kentucky Press, 1965): 79–80.

63.　Stanley Frost, *The Challenge of the Klan* (Indianapolis: Bobbs-Merrill, 1924): 22, 23 (quote), and "When the Klan Rides," *Outlook* 135 (26 December 1923): 717; Morris, "Saving Society Through Politics," 187, 190, 229, 329–30. See also Stanley Frost, "The Masked Politics of the Klan," *World's Work* 55 (February 1928): 399–407. For Evans's role as a reliable conduit of national Klan ideology, see Brian Robert McGee, "Klannishness and the Ku Klux Klan: The Rhetoric and Ethics of Genre Theory" (Ph.D. diss., Ohio State University, 1996): 237, 335n.

64.　Alexander, *Klan in the Southwest*, 96; Moore, *Citizen Klansmen*, 36–37; Hiram Wesley Evans, *The Public School Problem in America: Outlining Fully the Policies and the Program of the Knights of the Ku Klux Klan toward the Public School System* (Atlanta: Ku Klux Klan, 1924): 3 (first quote), 4 (second quote).

65.　*Is the Ku Klux Klan Constructive or Destructive: A Debate Between Imperial Wizard Evans, Israel Zangwill, and Others* (Girard, Kans.: Haldeman-Julius, 1924): 21 (first quote); Hiram Wesley Evans, "The Klan of Tomorrow," *Imperial Night-Hawk* 2 (15 October 1924): 1 (third and fourth quotes), 2 (second quote), 3, and "The Klan, Defender of Americanism," *The Forum* 74 (December 1925): 808.

66.　Alexander, *Klan in the Southwest*, 233; Goldberg, "Invisible Empire," in *Grassroots Resistance*, 88; Morris, "Saving Society Through Politics," 267; "Klan Ranks Thinner in Capital Parade," *New York Times*, 14 September 1926: 1; Evans, "Klan's Fight for Americanism," *North American Review*, 33–63. For the Klan's ideological portrait of Evans in the periodical that succeeded the *Imperial Night-Hawk* as the official organ, see "The Man Every American Should Know," *The Kourier Magazine* 2 (September 1926): 2–4. *The North American Review* announced that its subsequent issue would feature assessments of the Klan by Father Martin J. Scott of the College of St. Francis Xavier,

Dr. W. E. B. DuBois of the National Association for the Advancement of Colored People, Rabbi Emeritus Joseph Silverman of the Temple Emanu-El of New York, and Professor William Starr Myers of Princeton University.

67. Hiram Wesley Evans, "Klan's Fight for Americanism," *North American Review*, 38 (first, second, and third quotes), 38–39 (fourth quote).
68. Ibid., 34 (first quote), 39 (third and fourth quotes), 58 (second quote).
69. Ibid., 35 (third quote), 38 (second quote), 42 (fourth, fifth, sixth, seventh, eight, and ninth quotes), 43 (first quote).
70. Ibid., 49 (first and second quotes), 51 (third quote). Evans's contempt for intellectuals extended to his prediction that amoral thinkers would "dig up . . . logic in support of the success" of any thriving movement of the "plain people," even the Klan. See ibid., 50. For the imperial wizard's celebration of the emotional and instinctive, and the belief that such qualities were inherited and essential, see MacLean, *Behind the Mask of Chivalry*, 131, and McGee, "Klannishness and the Ku Klux Klan," 295–98, 300–304.
71. Robert A. Garson, "Political Fundamentalism and Popular Democracy in the 1920s," *South Atlantic Quarterly* 76 (Spring 1977): 219, 220 (quote), 223.
72. Ibid., 219, 223, 230, 232 (first quote), 233 (second quote).
73. Malcolm Cowley, *Exile's Return: A Literary Odyssey of the 1920s* [1934] (New York: Penguin Books, 1976): 214; John Dos Passos, *The Big Money*, U. S.A. [1936] (New York: Random House, 1937): 462.
74. Leonard J. Moore, "Good Old Fashioned New Social History and the Twentieth-Century American Right," *Reviews in American History* 24 (December 1996): 560–61.

Chapter 2

1. Lynn Dumenil, *The Modern Temper: American Culture and Society in the 1920s* (New York: Hill and Wang, 1995): 186; James Allen Smith, *The Idea Brokers: Think Tanks and the Rise of the New Policy Elite* (New York: Free Press, 1991): 28, 30, 36, 49; Robert Wiebe, *The Search for Order, 1877–1920* (New York: Hill and Wang, 1967): 112, 123, 166.
2. Barry Karl, *Executive Reorganization and Reform in the New Deal* (Chicago: University of Chicago Press, 1963): 1; Richard Kirkendall, *Social Scientists and Farm Politics in the Age of Roosevelt* (Columbia: University of Missouri Press, 1966): 3–4; David Thelen, *Robert M. La Follette and the Rise of the Insurgent Spirit* (Boston: Little, Brown, 1976): 108–109; Robert S. Maxwell, *La Follette and the Rise of Progressivism in Wisconsin* (Madison: State Historical Society of Wisconsin, 1956): 59, 81, 138; J. A. Smith, *The Idea Brokers*, 35.
3. Joseph Ratner, ed., *Intelligence in the Modern World: John Dewey's Philosophy* (New York: Random House, 1939): 424, 426; J. Smith, *Idea Brokers*, 11, 63, 65, 67; Dumenil, *Modern Temper*, 40, 42, 47, 52–54.
4. Richard Hofstadter, *Anti-intellectualism in American Life* (New York: Random House, 1962): 209–210 (Wilson quote); Herbert F. Marguiles, *The Decline of the Progressive Movement in Wisconsin, 1890–1928* (Madison: State Historical Society of Wisconsin, 1968): 137, 138 (second quote), 143, 147 (fourth quote), 148 (fifth quote); Thelen, *La Follette and Insurgent Spirit*, 118 (third quote).
5. Dumenil, *Modern Temper*, 26, 27 (Borah quote), 29 (first quote).
6. Don S. Kirschner, *City and Country: Rural Responses to Urbanization in the 1920s* (Westport, Conn.: Greenwood Press, 1970): 5–8, 136, 137–49, 151–53, 170, 183, 215, 238.
7. Elliot A. Rosen, *Hoover, Roosevelt, and the Brains Trust: From Depression to New Deal* (Columbia University Press, 1977): 324; Steve Fraser, "The Labor Question," in Fraser and Gary Gerstle, eds., *The Rise and Fall of the New Deal Order, 1930~1980* (Princeton, N. J.: Princeton University Press, 1989): 59–62, 69.
8. Alan Brinkley, *The End of Reform: New Deal Liberalism in Recession and War* (New York, Vintage, 1995): 37, 38 (quote); Theodore Rosenof, *Patterns of Political Economy in America: The Failure to Develop a Democratic Left Synthesis, 1933–1950* (New York: Garland, 1983): 6–7; John Dewey, *Liberalism and Social Action* [1935] (New York: Capricorn, 1963): 54. See Adolf A. Berle and Gardiner C. Means, *The Modern*

Corporation and Private Property (New York: Macmillan, 1932); George H. Soule, *A Planned Society* (New York: Macmillan, 1932); and Stuart Chase, *A New Deal* (New York: Macmillan, 1932).

9. William J. Barber, *Designs within Disorder: Franklin D. Roosevelt, the Economists, and the Shaping of American Economic Policy, 1933–1945* (New York: Cambridge University Press, 1996):171; Paul Conkin, *The New Deal* (New York: Thomas Crowell, 1967): 163–64; Brinkley, *End of Reform*, 55–56, 64; Peter H. Irons, The New Deal Lawyers (Princeton, N.J.: Princeton University Press, 1982): 6–7, 10; Thurman Arnold, *The Folklore of Capitalism* (New Haven, Conn.: Yale University Press, 1937): 389 (first quote), and *The Symbols of Government* (New Haven, Conn.: Yale University Press, 1935): 271 (second quote).

10. Rosen, *Brains Trust*, 4, 113, 114, 120 (third quote), 126–28, 130 (first quote), 131, 138 (second quote), 174, 204–205.

11. "How Roosevelt Aides Became 'Brain Trust,' " *New York Times*, 29 June 1933, 3 (first quote); Rexford G. Tugwell, *The Battle for Democracy* (New York: Columbia University Press, 1935): 222 (second quote), 223; Rosen, *Brains Trust*, 4–5, 172, 305–306, 329; Brinkley, *End of Reform*, 38, 55; Barber, *Designs within Disorder*, 5, 21. For portraits of Moley, Berle, and Tugwell, see Barber, *Designs within Disorder*, 1–9; Rosen, *Brains Trust*, 115–50, 195–211, 151–94; and Rexford G. Tugwell, *The Brains Trust* (New York: Viking Press, 1968): xi–xii. For a view of Roosevelt advisers that included business leader Charles W. Taussig, see "The Brain Trust," *Business Week*, 22 March 1933, 16–18. The term "brains trust" quickly was shortened to "brain trust."

12. Arthur Krock, " 'Professor' Charts Goal of 'Brain Trust,' " *New York Times*, 4 May 1933, 16; "Hutchins Defends The 'Brains Trust,' " *New York Times*, 18 May 1933, 21; "Seabury Attacks O'Brien Tax Plan," *New York Times*, 7 June 1933, 25; "Professors at Washington," *Christian Century* 50 (31 May 1933): 711 (first quote); "Trust Brains," *Collier's* 93 (19 May 1934): 66; "Brain Trust Here To Stay, Roosevelt Says at Yale," *New York Times*, 21 June 1934, 1 (second quote). See also Russell Owen, "The 'Brain Trust' Mirrors Many Minds," *New York Times*, 11 June 1933, sec. 6: 1, 3, and "The President's 'Brain Trust' Again a Target for Critics," *New York Times*, 1 April 1934, sec. 9: 3; and R. L. Duffus, "Roosevelt's Advisers—Right or Left?" *New York Times*, 21 January 1934, 5, 18.

13. Ernest K. Lindley, "War on the Brains Trust," *Scribner's Magazine* 94 (November 1933): 257 (first quote); "The Brain Trust," *Business Week*, 22 March 1933, 16 (second quote); "Calls Socialism 'Brain Trust' Aim," *New York Times*, 31 May 1933, 18; "The Brain Trust," *New Republic* 75 (7 June 1933): 85; "The Hullabaloo over the 'Brain Trust,' " *Literary Digest* 115 (3 June 1933): 8 (third quote); Delbert Clark, "Dramatic Fade-Out of the Brain Trust," *New York Times Magazine*, 24 March 1935, 4 (fourth quote); "Robinson Renamed By Indiana Party," *New York Times*, 6 June 1934, 3 (fifth quote).

14. Brinkley, *End of Reform*, 39–40; Richard Kirkendall, *Social Scientists and Farm Politics in the Age of Roosevelt* (Columbia: University of Missouri Press, 1966): 12, 28–29, 45, 50–51, 60, 89–90; Rosen, *Brains Trust*, 176–78, 181–84. Rosen noted that Wilson had been converted to domestic allotment through economist John D. Black, whose work on agricultural reform had been financed by Beardsley Ruml, the consumer-oriented economist who headed the Laura Spelman Rockefeller Fund.

15. Kirkendall, *Social Scientists and Farm Politics*, 59, 259; Gilbert C. Fite, "Farmer Opinion and the Agricultural Adjustment Act," *Mississippi Valley Historical Review* 48 (March 1962): 660, 666–67, and "John A. Simpson: The Southwest's Militant Farm Leader," *Mississippi Valley Historical Review* 35 (March 1949): 577–79.

16. William Hirth to James M. Thompson, 9 November 1932 and S. D. Gleason to Franklin D. Roosevelt, 27 December 1932, in Kirkendall, *Social Scientists and Farm Politics*, 59, 93; (first and second quotes); "Democrats Offer $1,500,000 Bill to Aid Farmers," *New York Times*, 26 January 1933, 61; "Add Strike Threat to Farm Demands," *New York Times*, 13 March 1933, 11 (third quote); "Corn Belt Has Fill of Varied Holidays," *New York Times*, 19 March 1933, sec. 4: 7.

17. "Witnesses Clash on Farm Bill Help," *New York Times*, 25 March 1933, 5; Fite, "Simpson," *Mississippi Valley Historical Review*, 563–64, 574; Statement of John A. Simpson, U.S. Senate, Committee on Agriculture and Forestry, *Hearings on Agricultural Emergency Act to Increase Farm Purchasing Power* (Washington, D.C.: Government Printing Office, 1933): 104–107 (first quote on 106, second quote on 104), 121. See also "Runt Relief,"

Time 21 (3 April 1933): 12, and Fite, "Farmer Opinion," *Mississippi Valley Historical Review*, 662, 665.

18. Fite, "Simpson," *Mississippi Valley Historical Review*, 580, and "Farmer Opinion," *Mississippi Valley Historical Review*, 659, 668, 669 (Martin quote); Homer E. Socolofsky, *Arthur Capper: Publisher, Politician, and Philanthropist* (Lawrence: University of Kansas Press, 1962): 170 (Capper quote).

19. "Runt Relief," *Time* 21 (3 April 1933): 12 (quote); Fite, "Farmer Opinion," *Mississippi Valley Historical Review*, 668; Rosen, *Brains Trust*, 162–63, 316; Lindley, "War on the Brains Trust," *Scribner's*, 263; Rexford G. Tugwell, "The Principle of Planning and the Institution of Laissez-Faire," *American Economic Review* 22 (March 1932), Supplement: 83, 89; Kirkendall, *Social Scientists and Farm Politics*, 96.

20. Rosen, *Brains Trust*, 159; Kirkendall, *Social Scientists and Farm Politics*, 64–67, 257; Barber, *Designs within Disorder*, 63, 72. See also Mordecai Ezekiel, "If Every Household Had $2,500 a Year," *New York Times*, 9 December 1934, sec. 9: 4.

21. William E. Leuchtenburg, *Franklin D. Roosevelt and the New Deal, 1932–1940* (New York: Harper and Row, 1963): 75; Irons, *New Deal Lawyers*, 10 (Peek quotes); Kirkendall, *Social Scientists and Farm Politics*, 94 (Hirth quotes).

22. Kirkendall, *Social Scientists and Farm Politics*, 94 (first quote); John A. Simpson, Open Letter to Franklin D. Roosevelt, 14 September 1933, 2 (second quote), 3 (third quote), Box 3, Folder 32, Papers of John A. Simpson, Western History Collections, University of Oklahoma; Simpson to Roosevelt, 24 October 1933, 1, 2–3 (fourth quote), Box 3, Folder 33, Simpson Papers.

23. John A. Simpson, "Modern Shylock," radio address of 27 January 1934, in *Congressional Record* (hereafter *CR*), 73rd Cong., 2d sess. 78 (30 January 1934): 1548; Fite, "Simpson," *Mississippi Valley Historical Review*, 583.

24. Catherine McNicol Stock, *Main Street in Crisis: The Great Depression and the Old Middle Class on the Northern Plains* (Chapel Hill: University of North Carolina Press, 1992): 88, 129, 134, 135, 141, 142, 145, and *Rural Radicals: Righteous Rage in the American Grain* (Ithaca, N.Y.: Cornell University Press, 1996): 85 (quote).

25. Alan Brinkley, *Voices of Protest. Huey Long, Father Coughlin, and the Great Depression* (New York: Alfred A. Knopf, 1982): 156–57; Stock, *Main Street in Crisis*, 87 (quote), 97, 98–99, 100–101. For the initial resistance of Iowa dairy farmers to an official campaign to use veterinarians from the state agricultural college to test all cows for tuberculosis, see Stock, *Rural Radicals*, 81–82.

26. Stock, *Main Street in Crisis*, 96, 97 (quote), 98, 101–102, 107, 126.

27. Ibid., 102, 108–109, 110–12; David A. Horowitz, *Beyond Left and Right. Insurgency and the Establishment* (Urbana: University of Illinois Press, 1997): 94–95.

28. David H. Bennett, *Demagogues in the Depression: American Radicals and the Union Party, 1932–1936* (New Brunswick, N.J.: Rutgers University Press, 1969): 93–94 (first quote on 94); William Lemke to Arthur W. Watwood, 25 March 1933 (second quote), and Lemke to C. H. Hyde, 18 March 1933, Folder 8. Jan.-March 1933, Box 11, Papers of William Lemke, Department of Special Collections, Orin G. Libby Manuscripts Collection, Chester Fritz Library, University of North Dakota; Lemke to C. W. Fine, 2 May 1933 (third quote), Folder 10: May-June 1933, Box 11, Lemke Papers.

29. Edward C. Blackorby, *Prairie Rebel: The Public Life of William Lemke* (Lincoln: University of Nebraska Press, 1963): 195n, 217; Bennett, *Demagogues in the Depression*, 95 (first and second quotes), 96 (third quote); William Lemke to W. H. Harvey, 13 January 1934, attached to Lemke to Harvey, 26 May 1934, Folder 17: May 1934, Box 11, Lemke Papers.

30. D. A. Horowitz, *Beyond Left and Right*, 94–98.

31. William R. Brock, *Welfare, Democracy, and the New Deal* (New York: Cambridge University Press, 1988): 3, 4, 62, 64, 66, 67, 173–74, 335, 339; Stock, *Main Street in Crisis*, 125.

32. Joseph P. Lash, *Dealers and Dreamers: A New Look at the New Deal* (New York: Doubleday, 1988): 130; Brinkley, *End of Reform*, 50–51; Jordan A. Schwarz, *The New Dealers: Power and Politics in the Age of Roosevelt* (New York: Alfred A. Knopf, 1993): 123–25, 133, 135–36; Irons, *New Deal Lawyers*, 9.

33. Schwarz, *New Dealers*, 128 (quote); Lash, *Dealers and Dreamers*, 130–32; Brinkley, *End of Reform*, 51–53; Blair Bolles, "Cohen and Corcoran, Brain Twins," *American Mercury* 43 (January 1938): 42–44.

34. Beverly Smith, "Corcoran and Cohen," *American Magazine* 124 (August 1937): 125 (quote); Lash, *Dealers and Dreamers*, 9; Bolles, "Brain Twins," *American Mercury*, 41–43; Brinkley, *End of Reform*, 54.

35. Lash, *Dealers and Dreamers*, 131; Leuchtenburg, *Roosevelt and the New Deal*, 59; Felix Belair, Jr., "Two of the 'Selfiess Six,'" *Nation's Business* 25 (July 1937): 25; Brinkley, *End of Reform*, 54–55; Bolles, "Brain Twins," *American Mercury*, 40 (first quote), 39; B. Smith, "Corcoran and Cohen," *American Magazine*, 22 (second, third, and fourth quotes). See also "Who's Who at F. D. R.'s Ear," *Business Week*, 5 December 1936, 32–33.

36. Leuchtenburg, *Roosevelt and the New Deal*, 90–91; Fraser, "Labor Question," in Fraser and Gerstle, eds., *Rise and Fall of New Deal Order*, 69; Bolles, "Brain Twins," *American Mercury*, 40; Schwarz, *New Dealers*, 142 (quote).

37. "Whitney Sees Curb As Nationalization," *New York Times*, 1 March 1934, 16; "Federal Reserve For Exchange Curbs As In Pending Bill," *New York Times*, 24 March 1934, 1, 2 (Rand quotes).

38. Lash, *Dealers and Dreamers*, 177 (Mallon quote); "'Little Red House' Is Held To Rule Us," *New York Times*, 21 April 1934, 5 (Britten quotes). Britten lost his reelection bid later in the year. See "Britten, De Priest Routed In Illinois," *New York Times*, 7 November 1934, 17. See also entry on Frederick A. Britten, *Biographical Directory of the United States Congress, 1774–1989* (Washington, D.C.: Government Printing Office, 1989): 672.

39. "Curb on Exchange Is Certain to Pass By Big House Vote," *New York Times*, 3 May 1934, 1; *CR*, 73rd Cong., 2d sess. 78 (2 May 1934): 7933 (second quote), 7934 (third and fourth quotes), 7944 (first quote). For descriptions of the residences in question, see B. Smith, "Corcoran and Cohen," *American Magazine*, 23, 125, and Bolles, "Brain Twins," *American Mercury*, 45.

40. "Curb on Exchange," *New York Times*, 3 May 1934, 1 (Mapes quote), 2 (Pettengill quote); "Curb on Exchanges is Passesd By House," *New York Times*, 5 May 1934, 1; Clyde P. Weed, *The Nemesis of Reform: The Republican Party During the New Deal* (New York: Columbia University Press, 1994): 145; *CR*, 73rd Cong., 2d sess. 78 (12 May 1934): 8714.

41. "For Industrial Loan Group," *New York Times*, 15 February 1933, 8; "Vanderlip Favors End of Gold Basis," *New York Times*, 6 March 1933, 6; "Map 5-Point Plan to Restore Prices," *New York Times*, 6 April 1933, 27; "Industries Draft A Plan To Employ 3,000,000 Now Idle," *New York Times*, 7 May 1933, 1, 31; "Cutting Work Time Viewed As Useless," *New York Times*, 12 April 1933, 11; Schwarz, *New Dealers*, 183–84. See also "Rand Issues Statement Here," *New York Times*, 20 February 1934, 5.

42. Lash, *Dealers and Dreamers*, 176 (quote); "Dr. Wirt Founded New School Plan," *New York Times*, 24 March 1934, 2; "Federal Reserve For Exchange Curbs As In Pending Bill," *New York Times*, 24 March 1934, 1.

43. "Dr. Wirt's Statement on 'Brain Trust' Plans," *New York Times*, 24 March 1934, 2.

44. Ibid. Aleksandr F. Kerensky was a moderate Russian socialist whose government was overthrown in 1917 by Vladimir I. Lenin's Bolshevik Party.

45. Ibid.

46. "'American Hitler' Pictured by Wirt," *New York Times*, 25 March 1934, 26.

47. "'Brain Trust' Faces Inquiry By House," *New York Times*, 25 March 1934, 26 (McGugin quotes); "12 in 'Brain Trust' Called Socialists," *New York Times*, 28 March 1934, 3 (Fish quote).

48. Russell Owen, "The President's 'Brain Trust' Again A Target for Critics," *New York Times*, 1 April 1934, sec. 9: 3 (Berle quote); "'Brain Trust' Faces Inquiry By House on Alleged Aims," *New York Times*, 25 March 1934, 26, 1 (Bulwinkle quote).

49. "Dr. Wirt Attacks New Deal Bills," *New York Times*, 26 March 1934, 5; "Wirt's Pamphlet Expands Attack," *New York Times*, 2 April 1934, 5; "House to Inquire into 'Brain Trust,'" *New York Times*, 30 March 1934, 3; "Dr. Wirt Ordered to Appear Today," *New York Times*, 16 April 1934, 3.

50. "Wirt Hearing Broadcast," *New York Times*, 11 April 1934, 12; "Crowd at Hearing Fills Caucus Room," *New York Times*, 11 April 1934, 12 (Wirt quotes); "Wirt Names 'Satelliltes' Of Brain Trust as Source Of His Revolution Story," *New York Times*, 11 April 1934, 1. Wirt's earlier statement before the House Commerce Committee was reprinted

in "Dr. Wirt Declares Reed Was Retained By Henry Pope, a Warm Springs Trustee," *New York Times*, 11 April 1934, 12.

51. "Wirt Names 'Satellites' Of Brain Trust as Source of His Revolution Story," *New York Times*, 11 April 1934, 1 (first quote); "Crowd at Hearing Fills Caucus Room," *New York Times*, 11 April 1934, 12 (second quote).

52. "Crowd at Hearing Fills Caucus Room," *New York Times*, 11 April 1934, 12 (Wirt quotes); "Dr. Wirt Declares Reed Was Retained By Henry Pope," *New York Times*, 11 April 1934, 12.

53. "Assails Tugwell As Red," *New York Times*, 11 April 1934, 12 (Hayes quote); "Storm in House Over Wirt's Plot,'" *New York Times*, 12 April 1934, 8; "Wirt Names 'Satellites' Of Brain Trust As Source of His Revolution Story," New York Times, 11 April 1934, 1; "Dr. Wirt's Targets Swift In Denials," *New York Times*, 11 April 1934, 12; "Richberg Writes Verse on Wirt Hearing," *New York Times*, 11 April 1934, 12. McGugin was defeated for reelection in 1934. See entry on Harold C. McGugin, *Biographical Directory of Congress*, 1467. Tugwell's notions had been summarized in Rexford G. Tugwell, *The Industrial Discipline and the Governmental Arts* (New York: Columbia University Press, 1933).

54. "Miss Kneeland Adds Denial," *New York Times*, 11 April 1934, 12 (Howe quote); "Dr. Wirt's Targets Swift in Denials," *New York Times*, 11 April 1934, 12 (Rainey quotes); "All Talking by Wirt, Says Coyle," *New York Times*, 11 April 1934, 12.

55. "Dr. Wirt's Charges Are Held Unproved," *New York Times*, 27 April 1934, 3; "Wirt Is Ruled Out in House Report," *New York Times*, 3 May 1934, 2 (quote).

56. Kirkendall, *Social Scientists and Farm Politics*, 70–75, 77–78, 256; Barber, *Designs within Disorder*, 73–74.

57. Kirkendall, *Social Scientists and Farm Politics*, 96 (second quote), 97 (first quote), 102; Barber, *Designs within Disorder*, 74 (third quote).

58. "Tugwell Sets 1938 to Balance Budget," *New York Times*, 29 October 1935, 5.

59. "Smith Says New Deal Meddles And Competes With Business," *New York Times*, 25 October 1936, 1; "Calls Socialism 'Brain Trust' Aim," *New York Times*, 31 May 1933, 18; "Modified New Deal Urged by Banker," *New York Times*, 17 May 1934, 1 (quote); "Brain Trust Failure Predicted by Harvey," *New York Times*, 26 August 1934, 15. For an educator's skepticism about White House advisers from the academy, see "Calls for Retreat of the Brain Trust," *New York Times*, 12 May 1935, 21. For a municipal expert's point that brains trusters should be advisers, not administrators without responsibility to the electorate, see Arthur Krock, "Visitor Saw Weakness in Roosevelt's Brain Trust," *New York Times*, 13 March 1935, 22.

60. Barber, *Designs within Disorder*, 44; Brinkley, *End of Reform*, 51 (quote). See George N. Peek, *Why Quit Our Own* (New York: Van Nostrand, (1936): 20.

61. Bennett, *Demagogues in the Depression*, 95, 104 (first quote), 102 (second, third, and fourth quotes); poll of 5 January 1936, George H. Gallup, *The Gallup Poll. Public Opinion, 1935–1971* (New York: Random House, 1972): vol. 1: 9; *CR*, 74th Cong., 2nd sess. 80 (12 May 1936): 7097–7138, 7229; D. A. Horowitz, *Beyond Left and Right*, 97–98.

62. Entry on Allen T. Treadway, *Biographical Directory of Congress*, 1952; *CR*, 74th Cong., 1st sess. 79 (14 May 1935): 7513, 7514 (quote). See also "Answers Snell Attack," *New York Times*, 15 May 1935, 9.

63. Delbert Clark, "Dramatic Fade-Out of the Brain Trust," *New York Times Magazine* (24 March 1935): 4 (first quote), and "Washington Now Pauses to Take Stock," *New York Times*, sec. 7: 20; Ronald A. Mulder, *The Insurgent Progressives in the United States Senate and the New Deal, 1933–1939* (New York: Garland, 1979): 107–111 (second quote on 108); James T. Patterson, *Congressional Conservatism and the New Deal: The Growth of the Conservative Coalition in Congress, 1933–1939* (Lexington: University of Kentucky Press, 1967): 38–39, 55.

64. *CR*, 74th Cong., 1st sess. 79 (28 June 1935): 10354 (Huddleston quotes); "Brewster Makes Charge," *New York Times*, 3 July 1935, 1 (Brewster quotes); "House Orders Inquiry into Lobbying By Friends and Foes of Utilities Bill After Beating President Again, 258–147," *New York Times*, 7 July 1935, 1.

65. "Brewster Makes Charge," *New York Times*, 3 July 1935, 2 (Corcoran quote), 1; "House Passes Own Bill," *New York Times*, 3 July 1935, 1; "House Orders Inquiry into Lobbying By Friends and Foes of Utility Bill," *New York Times*, 3 July 1935, 2. See also Arthur

Krock, " 'Quoddy Project Charges Kindle Republican Hopes," *New York Times*, 3 July 1935, 16.

66. "Brewster Shouts 'Liar' at Corcoran in Lobby Hearing," *New York Times*, 10 July 1935, 1 (third and fourth quotes), 6 (first and second quotes).

67. Ibid., 6.

68. "Utility Lobby War Spreads in Senate to All Other Bills," *New York Times*, 11 July 1935, 4 (quote); "House Seeks Lobby Costs of Death Sentence Foes," *New York Times*, 12 July 1935, 1, 6; "Bogus Messages in Utility Bill Sent, Then Burned," *New York Times*, 17 July 1935, 15.

69. "B. V. Cohen May Get Post," *New York Times*, 21 June 1935, 12; Patterson, *Congressional Conservatism*, 57n (Byrnes quote); "Conferees Rebuff New Deal Experts on Utilities Bill," *New York Times*, 25 July 1935, 4.

70. "Patton Cigar Gift Not in Cigar Box," *New York Times*, 27 July 1935, 4; "Utility Deadlock," *New York Times*, 28 July 1935, sec. 4: 1 (Huddleston quote); "Senators Broaden Lobby Data Hunt," *New York Times*, 28 July 1935, 23; " 'Death Sentence' Defeated Again, House Voting 210-155," *New York Times*, 2 August 1935, 1; "Hurley, Tumulty Received Big Fees From the Utilities," *New York Times*, 8 August 1935, 1; "Compromise Voted on 'Death Clause' By House, 219 to 142," *New York Times*, 23 August 1935, 1; "Accord is Reached on Utilities Bill," *New York Times*, 24 August 1935, 3; "Utilities Measure Sent to President," *New York Times*, 25 August 1935, 1.

71. Leuchtenburg, *Roosevelt and the New Deal*, 124–25, 131–32, 150–51. For efficiency as a threat to democratic government, see Barry Karl, *Executive Reorganization and Reform in the New Deal* (Chicago: University of Chicago Press, 1963): 24.

72. Thurman Arnold, *The Symbols of Government* (New Haven, Conn.: Yale University Press, 1935): 259–60; Ronald Radosh, "The Myth of the New Deal," in Radosh and Murray Rothbard, eds., *A New History of Leviathan: Essays on the Rise of the Corporate State* (New York: Dutton, 1972): 186; Hofstadter, *Anti-intellectualism in American Life*, 218. For anti-New Dealism by independent producers and business interests see David A. Horowitz, "Senator Borah's Crusade to Save Small Business from the New Deal," *The Historian* 55 (Summer 1993): 693–708, and *Beyond Left and Right*, 91–161.

73. Weed, *Nemesis of Reform*, 207; Theodore Rosenof, *Dogma, Depression, and the New Deal: The Debate of Political Leaders over Economic Recovery* (Port Washington, N.Y.: National University Publications, 1975): 10, 11; Herbert Hoover, *The Challenge to Liberty* (New York: Charles Scribner's, 1934): 79.

74. "Platform Drafted By 'Grass Rooters' Opposes New Deal," *New York Times*, 9 June 1935, 1–2; Richard M. Fried, *Nightmare in Red; The McCarthy Era in Perspective* (New York: Oxford University Press, 1990): 45; "Fish Denies Aiding Hearst," *New York Times*, 24 August 1935, 9 (first and second quotes); "Fish Sees Tugwell 'Worse' Than Reds," *New York Times*, 7 March 1936, 5 (third quote); *CR*, 74th Cong., 2d sess. 80 (6 January 1936): 82 (fourth quote). Fish addressed the National Republican Club in New York City on January 4, 1936.

75. "Muir Urges Fight on Business Curbs," *New York Times*, 31 October 1935, 19 (McNair quote); "Chester Attacks Curb on Industry," *New York Times*, 31 March 1936, 39 (Chester quote); "Sees 'Jig Up' for New Deal," *New York Times*, 21 February 1936, 2 (first Mencken quote); H. L. Mencken, "The New Deal Mentality," *American Mercury* 38 (May 1936): 4 (second Mencken quote), 5 (third Mencken quote).

Chapter 3

1. Alvin W. Gouldner, *The Future of Intellectuals and the Rise of the New Class* (New York: Continuum, 1979): 17, 76. For the sociopolitical sector's ambivalent relationship to capitalism see Barbara Ehrenreich and John Ehrenreich, "The Professional-Managerial Class," *Radical America* 11 (March-April 1977): 7–31, and "The New Left: A Case Study in Professional-Managerial Radicalism," *Radical America* 11 (May-June 1977): 7–22, both reprinted as "The Professional-Managerial Class," in Pat Walker, ed., *Between Labor and Capital* (Boston: South End Press, 1979): 5–45.

2. "Landon Demands Monopolies' End and Escape from Bureaucracy," *New York Times*, 9 June 1936, 1 (quotes); Alan Brinkley, *Voices of Protest: Huey Long, Father Coughlin*,

and the Great Depression (New York: Alfred A. Knopf, 1982): ix, 144–45, 164, 196–203, 282–83; David A. Horowitz, *Beyond Left and Right. Insurgency and the Establishment* (Urbana: University of Illinois Press, 1997): 113–14.

3. D. A. Horowitz, *Beyond Left and Right*, 105; William E. Leuchtenburg, *Franklin D. Roosevelt and the New Deal, 1932–1940* (New York: Harper and Row, 1963): 102 (first and second quotes); David H. Bennett, *Demagogues in the Depression: American Radicals and the Union Party, 1932–1936* (New Brunswick, N.J.: Rutgers University Press, 1969): 78 (third quote), 227–28 (fourth and sixth quotes), 229 (fifth quote); "Coughlin Asserts Paganism is Issue," *New York Times*, 12 September 1936, 2. See also "Coughlin Declares Rome Report a Lie," *New York Times*, 7 September 1936, 1, 7.

4. Bennett, *Demagogues in the Depression*, 19 (first Smith quote), 114–15, 178 (Townsend quote), 228; F. Raymond Daniell, "Lemke Endorsed By Coughlinites," *New York Times*, 16 August 1936, 27 (second Smith quote); "Coughlin Bases Fight on Papal Encyclicals," *New York Times*, 23 September 1936, 17 (first and second Lemke quotes).

5. D. A. Horowitz, *Beyond Left and Right*, 115, 140; poll of 10 January 1937, George H. Gallup, *The Gallup Poll: Public Opinion, 1935–1971* (New York: Random House, 1972) vol. 1: 45.

6. Turner Catledge, "Drive On Spending Falters At Start As House Revolts," *New York Times*, 22 April 1937, 16 (Dies quotes), and "Half Billion Cut In Relief Spurned," *New York Times*, 4 May 1937, 13 (Byrnes quote); "Snell Asks Action To Block Inflation," *New York Times*, 9 May 1937, 4 (Snell quote); D. A. Horowitz, *Beyond Left and Right*, 148–50. For the antistatist suspicions of Senate western insurgents and progressive Republicans, see Ronald A. Mulder, *The Insurgent Progressives in the United States Senate and the New Deal, 1933–1939* (New York: Garland, 1979): 130, 182, 207–208, 212, and Otis L. Graham, Jr., *An Encore for Reform: The Old Progressives and the New Deal* (New York: Oxford University Press, 1967): 39–40, 48, 67–69, 182–83.

7. A. S. R. to Editor, "The Administration to Date," *New York Times*, 8 February 1937, 16; Arthur Krock, "Departing Pair Afford Brain Trust Contrast," *New York Times*, 17 January 1937, sec. 4: 3 (quotes); Delbert Clark, "Brain Trusters: President's Aides Work Quietly Behind Scenes," *New York Times Magazine*, 7 March 1937, 4 (quote).

8. Clark, "Brain Trusters," *New York Times Magazine*, 5 (quote); Jordan A. Schwarz, *The New Dealers: Power Politics in the Age of Roosevelt* (New York. Alfred A. Knopf, 1993): 139, 141.

9. Barry Karl, *Executive Reorganization and Reform in the New Deal* (Chicago: University of Chicago Press, 1963): 26; Alan Brinkley, *The End of Reform: New Deal Liberalism in Recession and War* (New York: Vintage, 1995): 21; Richard Polenberg, *Reorganizing Roosevelt's Government: The Controversy Over Executive Reorganization, 1936–1939* (Cambridge, Mass.: Harvard University Press, 1966): 3, 7, 15, 17.

10. Polenberg, *Reorganizing Roosevelt's Government*, 11–15; Karl, *Executive Reorganization and Reform*, 39.

11. Brinkley, *End of Reform*, 21–22; Polenberg, *Reorganizing Roosevelt's Government*, 16 (Merriam quote), 18–19; Karl, *Executive Reorganization and Reform*, 230 (quote).

12. James T. Patterson, *Congressional Conservatism and the New Deal: The Growth of the Conservative Coalition in Congress, 1933–1939* (Lexington: University of Kentucky Press, 1967): 215–16; Polenberg, *Reorganizing Roosevelt's Government*, 28, 31–34, 46 (McNary quote), 139–40; Clyde P. Weed, *The Nemesis of Reform: The Republican Party During the New Deal* (New York: Columbia University Press, 1994): 180.

13. Karl, *Executive Reorganization and Reform*, 256; D. A. Horowitz, *Beyond Left and Right*, 140–43; Brinkley, *End of Reform*, 22 (first quote); "Court Commission Urged By Dr. Dodds To Solve Conflict," *New York Times*, 25 March 1937, 20 (Wheeler quote).

14. Arthur Krock, "Are the Two 'Wunder Kinder' About to Re-emerge?" *New York Times*, 2 April 1937, 22.

15. Entry on Charles L. Gifford, *Biographical Directory of the United States Congress, 1774–1989* (Washington, D.C.: Government Printing Office, 1989): 1058; *Congressional Record* (hereafter *CR*), 75th Cong., 1st sess. 81 (27 July 1937): 7683 (quotes).

16. *CR*, 75th Cong., 1st sess. 81 (27 July 1937): 7683 (first and second quotes), 7684 (third quote). For rumors of Corcoran's expected appointment as a White House secretary for legal affairs, see Arthur Krock, "Further Obscurity for the Cabinet is Seen," *New York Times*, 10 August 1937, 18. For suggestions of Corcoran's phrasing in Roosevelt's

Supreme Court reorganization message, see S. T. Williamson, "The President's English: Aimed at Eye and Ear," *New York Times*, 1 May 1938, sec. 8: 11.

17. *CR*, 75th Cong., 1st sess. 18 (27 July 1937): 7683 (first, third, fourth, and fifth quotes), 7684 (second quote).

18. Entry on Dewey J. Short, *Biographical Directory of Congress*, 1807; *CR*, 75th Cong., 1st sess. 81 (27 July 1937): 7691 (first and second quotes), 7691–92 (third quote), 7692 (fourth quote), and 13 August 1937, 8860–61 (fifth quote).

19. " 'Pure, Plain Cussedness,' " *Time* 30 (9 August 1937): 9 (quote); Polenberg, *Reorganizing Roosevelt's Government*, 49–50, 130; *CR*, 75th Cong., 1st sess. 81 (13 August 1937): 8859 (Mott quote). James Wheaton Mott was a Columbia University graduate, a journalist, and an attorney. See *Biographical Directory of Congress*, 1544.

20. D. A. Horowitz, *Beyond Left and Right*, 57–58, 140–41, 143; *CR*, 75th Cong., 1st sess. 83 (8 March 1938): 3018 (first quote), 3020, 3021–22 (second quote), 3029 (third quote).

21. "Wheeler For Curb On Reorganization," *New York Times*, 9 March 1938, 4 (first and second quotes); *CR*, 75th Cong., 3d sess. 83 (8 March 1938): 3017, 3026, and (15 March 1938), 3384.

22. *CR*, 75th Cong., 3d sess. 83 (11 March 1938): 3235 (16 March 1938): 3460; and (18 March 1938): 3645.

23. Polenberg, *Reorganizing Roosevelt's Government*, 148; Patterson, *Congressional Conservatism and the New Deal*, 220–22; "Senate Acts Today on Reorganization," *New York Times*, 28 March 1938, 1–2; Ronald L. Feinman, *Twilight of Progressivism: The Western Republican Senators and the New Deal* (Baltimore: Johns Hopkins University Press, 1981): 141; "Reorganization Bill Passed By the Senate, 49 To 42," *New York Times*, 29 March 1938, 1.

24. Patterson, *Congressional Conservatism and the New Deal*, 226–28, 300–301; *CR*, 75th Cong., 3d sess. 83 (8 April 1938): 5123, and 76th Cong., 1st sess. 84 (8 March 1939): 2476 (quote); Weed, *Nemesis of Reform*, 181; David L. Porter, *Congress and the Waning of the New Deal* (Port Washington, N.Y.: Kennikat Press, 1980): 91–94; Brinkley, *End of Reform*, 22–23.

25. Theodore Rosenof, *Dogma, Depression, and the New Deal. The Debate of Political Leaders over Economic Recovery* (Port Washington, N.Y.: National University Publications, 1975): 40, 42; Weed, *Nemesis of Reform*, 193; Schwarz, *New Dealers*, xxiii; Steve Fraser, "The 'Labor Question,' " and Alan Brinkley, "The New Deal and the Idea of the State," in Steve Fraser and Gary Gerstle, eds., *The Rise and Fall of the New Deal Order, 1930–1980* (Princeton, N.J.: Princeton University Press, 1989): 60–62, 68, 70–71, 98; Richard N. Chapman, *Contours of Public Policy, 1939–1945* (New York: Garland, 1981): 10.

26. Brinkley, *End of Reform*, 246–47, 95–98; Chapman, *Contours of Public Policy*, 9–10; Schwarz, *New Dealers*, 187, xv; Brinkley, "The New Deal and the Idea of the State," in Fraser and Gerstle, eds., *Rise and Fall of New Deal Order*, 98.

27. Brinkley, "The New Deal and the Idea of the State," in Fraser and Gerstle, eds., *Rise and Fall of New Deal Order*, 89–94, and End of Reform, 61–62, 64, 66, 71, 104; "Roosevelt Accepts Business Aid in Offer to Help End Recession," *New York Times*, 30 April 1938, 1 (first quote); William J. Barber, *Designs within Disorder: Franklin D. Roosevelt, the Economists, and the Shaping of American Economic Policy, 1933–1945* (New York: Cambridge University Press, 1996): 2–3, 114, 116 (second quote); S. T. Williamson, "The President's English: Aimed at Eye and Ear," *New York Times*, 1 May 1938, sec 8: 11.

28. Brinkley, *End of Reform*, 4, 7, 122; Rosenof, *Dogma, Depression, and the New Deal*, 55; poll of 17 April 1938, Gallup, *Gallup Poll*, vol. 1: 97.

29. Brinkley, *End of Reform*, 63; Christopher Lasch, *The True and Only Heaven: Progress and Its Critics* (New York: W. W. Norton, 1991): 68, 70.

30. Joseph Alsop and Robert Kintner, "New Deal's Bright Young Men Win Voice Again in Shaping Policies," *New York Times*, 3 May 1938, 3.

31. Joseph Alsop and Robert Kintner, "We Shall Make America Over: The New Dealers Move In," *Saturday Evening Post* 211 (12 November 1938): 8, 9 (quotes).

32. Feinman, *Twilight of Progressivism*, 80–81; D. A. Horowitz, *Beyond Left and Right*, 148; polls of 20 October 1935, 23 December 1938, 4 June 1939, Gallup, *Gallup Poll*, vol. 1:1, 130–31, 157.

33. *CR*, 75th Cong., 1st sess. 81 (21 May 1937): 4905 (Bacon quote), 4907, 4907–08 (Griswold quote), 4910, Patterson, *Congressional Conservatism and New Deal*, 172, 303.

34. D. A. Horowitz, *Beyond Left and Right*, 152–54; John E. Miller, *Governor Philip F. La Follette, the Wisconsin Progressives, and the New Deal, 1930–1939* (Columbia: University of Missouri Press, 1982): 129.

35. Dorothy Thompson, "The National Progressives," *New York Herald Tribune*, 2 May 1938, 17; Max Lerner, "Phil La Follette—An Interview," *Nation* 146 (14 May 1938): 552–55; Donald R. McCoy, "The National Progressives of America, 1938," *Mississippi Valley Historical Review* 44 (June 1957): 85–86, 89–90; D. A. Horowitz, *Beyond Left and Right*, 156–58 (La Follette quote on 158).

36. Alsop and Kintner, "New Deal's Bright Young Men," *New York Times*, 3 June 1938, 3; "Primary Test," *New York Times*, 5 June 1938, sec. 4: 1; "President Revises His Travel Plans," *New York Times*, 11 June 1938, 2; Bruce J. Dierenfield, *Keeper of the Rules: Congressman Howard W. Smith of Virginia* (Charlottesville: The University Press of Virginia, 1987): 69–71; Alan Brinkley, *Liberalism and Its Discontents* (Cambridge, Mass.: Harvard University Press, 1998): 72; "Four Marked for a 'Purge,'" *New York Times*, 21 August 1938, sec. 4: 6.

37. "Two New Dealers Beat for House in Virginia Vote," *New York Times*, 8 August 1938, 1; Mulder, *Insurgent Progressives in Senate*, 277–79; Patterson, *Congressional Conservatism and New Deal*, 297, 330–31, 333–34.

38. Fraser, "Labor Question," in Fraser and Gerstle, eds., *Rise and Fall of New Deal Order*, 71–76; poll of 19 January 1938, Gallup, *Gallup Poll*, vol. 1: 85.

39. Fraser, "Labor Question," in Fraser and Gerstle, eds., *Rise and Fall of New Deal Order*, 69.

40. Ibid., 71; Peter H. Irons, *The New Deal Lawyers* (Princeton, N.J.: Princeton University Press, 1982): 300; Patterson, *Congressional Conservatism and New Deal*, 181–82, 317–18; U.S. House of Representatives, Intermediate Report of the Special Committee to Investigate the National Labor Relations Board, *Report on the Investigation of the National Labor Relations Board* (Washington, D.C.: Government Printing Office, 1940): 2.

41. Intermediate Report, *Investigation of NLRB*, 3–4; "NLRB Defended," *New York Times*, 4 February 1940, sec. 4: 1; "Labor Board Files Shown at Hearing; Dissension Bared," *New York Times*, 12 December 1939, 1, 18; "NLRB Job of Kin of Cohen Studied," *New York Times*, 23 January 1940, 12 (quote).

42. "NLRB Job of Kin of Cohen Studied," *New York Times*, 23 January 1940, 12 (Smith quote); Howard W. Smith to Benjamin V. Cohen, 23 January 1940, Correspondence with Ben V. Cohen, Box 220, Papers of Howard W. Smith, Special Collections Department, University of Virginia Library; Intermediate Report, *Investigation of NLRB*, 5, 7, 9, 13.

43. Intermediate Report, *Investigation of NLRB*, 18, 33–34, 35 (quotes).

44. Dierenfield, *Keeper of the Rules*, 91, 93 (quotes); Intermediate Report, *Investigation of NLRB*, 85–86, 89, 93, 88.

45. Chapman, *Contours of Public Policy*, 91–92; Henry N. Dorris, "Agency-Curb Bill Adopted By Senate in Surprise Move," *New York Times*, 27 November 1940, 1; "House Vote on Agencies Signalizes A New Trend," *New York Times*, 21 April 1940, sec. 4: 7; Kevin P. Phillips, *Arrogant Capital: Washington, Wall Street, and the Frustration of American Politics* (Boston: Little, Brown, 1994): 24; Porter, *Congress and the New Deal*, 89; Charles Cortez Abbott, "Federal Corporations and Corporate Agencies," *Harvard Business Review* 16 (Summer 1938): 436, 437 (quote), 445–49.

46. Walter Lippmann, *An Inquiry into the Principles of the Good Society* (Boston: Little, Brown, 1937): 106, 111, 128; Gerald P. Nye, radio address of 24 August 1939, 1 (quote), Addresses, Box 56, Papers of Gerald P. Nye, Herbert Hoover Presidential Library; *CR*, 76th Cong., 1st sess. 84 (18 January 1939): A188 (Mundt quote).

47. *CR*, 76th Cong., 1st sess. 84 (3 March 1939): 2307–2308; Taft speech before Young Republican Club, Lawrence County, Ohio, 4 April 1936, in Russell Kirk and James McClellan, *The Political Principles of Robert A. Taft* (New York: Fleet, 1967): 17; Staff Memo, 18 March 1940, 1–2, Bureaucracy, 1938–40, Box 503, Papers of Robert A. Taft, Library of Congress.

48. Chapman, *Contours of Public Policy*, 92–93, 96–97; "Senate Passes Bill For Curb on Agencies," *New York Times*, 19 July 1939, 6; "Agency Curb Bill Back on Calendar," *New York Times*, 2 August 1939, 5; "Backs Bill To Curb Federal Agencies," *New York Times*, 8 February 1940, 15 (quote); Arthur Krock, "The Bill to Regulate the Federal Agencies," *New York Times*, 5 March 1940, 22.

49. "New Deal Agencies Accused in Debate," *New York Times*, 16 April 1940, 16 (Walter quotes); entry on Edward Eugene Cox, *Biographical Directory of Congress*, 835; *CR*, 76th Cong., 3d sess. 86 (15 April 1940): 4531–32.

50. Entry on Albert Elmer Austin, *Biographical Directory of Congress*, 555; *CR*, 76th Cong., 3d sess. 86 (18 April 1940): 4724 (quotes); Chapman, *Contours of Public Policy*, 95; Henry N. Dorris, "House Votes 279-97 To Curb Agencies By Court Review," *New York Times*, 19 April 1940, 1.

51. "Puts Review Limit In Agency Measure," *New York Times*, 18 April 1940, 19; Dorris, "House Votes 279-97 To Curb Agencies By Court Review," *New York Times*, 19 April 1940, 1; Chapman, *Contours of Public Policy*, 98; "Balk At Scuttling Logan Agency Bill," *New York Times*, 7 May 1940, 11; "Rush Senate Vote on Agencies Curb," *New York Times*, 9 May 1940, 14; "Senators Debate Walter-Logan Bill," *New York Times*, 31 May 1940, 21 (Ashurst quote); Louis Stark, "Congress Is Asked to Limit Effect of Jackson Ruling," *New York Times*, 6 October 1940, 1 (Smith quotes).

52. Henry N. Dorris, "Agency-Curb Bill Adopted By Senate In Surprise Move," *New York Times*, 27 November 1940, 1; Chapman, *Contours of Public Policy*, 102 (quote), 103; Harold B. Hinton, "House Sustains President's Veto Of Agencies Bill," *New York Times*, 19 December 1940, 1.

53. Barber, *Designs within Disorder*, 117, 119, 120, 130, 130n (quote), 185. See Richard V. Gilbert, et al, *An Economic Program for American Democracy* (New York: Vanguard, 1938), 90.

54. "Senate Eases Up;—Votes Ship Funds," *New York Times*, 8 February 1940, 14; *CR*, 76th Cong., 3d sess. 86 (7, 26 February, 29 July 1940): 1192–93, 1959–60, 1966 (Holt quote), A4645 (Case quote), A4646; Barber, *Designs within Disorder*, 130.

55. "CCC Now To Admit Some College Boys," *New York Times*, 5 August 1940, 15; John A. Salmond, *The Civilian Conservation Corps, 1933–1942: A New Deal Case Study* (Durham, N. C.: Duke University Press, 1967): 201–204; *CR*, 76th Cong., 3d sess. 86 (10 September 1940): 11950; Chapman, *Contours of Public Policy*, 148.

56. "College Students Plan Rally to Start New Voluntary Work Service for Youth," *New York Times*, 22 September 1940, sec. 2: 5 (quote); Meyer Berger, "Pioneer CCC Plan Pushed in Vermont," *New York Times*, 2 February 1941, 40; Frederick R. Barkley, "CCC Faces Attack On Three Points," *New York Times*, 9 February 1941, sec. 4: 6. See also "Vermont Camp Ready for Test As 'Moral Equivalent for War,'" *New York Herald Tribune*, 29 December 1940, sec. 2: 1, 7. A complete account of the project's formation, the highly sympathetic article appeared without a byline, suggesting the possibility that it was written by Camp William James supporter and *Tribune* columnist Dorothy Thompson.

57. "Merger Is Asked for NYA and CCC," *New York Times*, 9 December 1940, 19; *CR*, 76th Cong., 3d sess. 86 (23 September 1940): 12483; Berger, "Pioneer CCC Plan Pushed in Vermont," *New York Times*, 2 February 1941, 40; Barkley, "CCC Faces Attack On Three Points," *New York Times*, 9 February 1941, sec. 4: 6 (first quote); Salmond, *CCC*, 206 (second quote).

58. Berger, "Pioneer CCC Plan Pushed in Vermont," *New York Times*, 2 February 1941, 40; "Vermont Camp," *New York Herald Tribune*, 29 December 1940, sec. 2: 7 (first quote); *CR*, 77th Cong., 1st sess. 87 (11 February 1941): 907–908 (Engel quotes on 908); Salmond, *CCC*, 206; "24 Enrollees Secede from Vermont Camp," *New York Times*, 7 March 1941, 23. The quote on the "educated classes" was attributed to Rosenstock-Huessy.

59. Salmond, *CCC*, 207.

60. Charles Hurd, "Independents Join to Back Roosevelt," *New York Times*, 25 September 1940, 1, 22; Felix Belair, Jr., "Brain Trust Far From Dead," *New York Times*, 17 September 1939, sec. 4: 7.

61. Myron I. Scholnick, *The New Deal and Anti-Semitism in America* (New York: Garland Publishing, 1990): 251n; Leonard Dinnerstein, *Uneasy at Home: Antisemitism and the*

American Jewish Experience (New York: Columbia University Press, 1987): 62–63, and *Anti-Semitism in America* (New York: Oxford University Press, 1994): 90, 108; Irons, *New Deal Lawyers,* 6, 126.

62. Irons, *New Deal Lawyers,* 124–26; Dinnerstein, *Anti-Semitism,* 125, 127; David H. Bennett, *The Party of Fear: From Nativist Movements to the New Right in American History* (Chapel Hill: University of North Carolina Press, 1988): 265.

63. Dinnerstein, *Anti-Semitism,* xix, xxvi, 81 (Ford quote); Werner J. Cahnman, "Socio-Economic Causes of Antisemitism," Social Problems 5 (July 1957): 22–27; Leo P. Ribuffo, *The Old Christian Right. The Protestant Far Right from the Great Depression to the Cold War* (Philadelphia: Temple University Press, 1983): 9; William Langer, "The Jews," 43 (Langer quote), attached to "TO WHOM IT MAY CONCERN," 3 September 1941, Folder 3, Speeches 1949–50, Box 274, Papers of William Langer, Department of Special Collections, Orin G. Libby Manuscripts Collection, Chester Fritz Library, University of North Dakota.

64. Dinnerstein, *Uneasy at Home,* 64 (quote); Scholnick, *New Deal and Anti-Semitism,* 63, 65, 79–80; "Scores Roosevelt Aides," *New York Times,* 11 December 1935, 8 (Hooker quote); Glen Jeansomme, "Combating Anti-Semitism: The Case of Gerald L. K. Smith," in David A. Gerber, ed., *Anti-Semitism in American History* (Urbana: University of Illinois Press, 1986): 83, 92, 154; Will Lissner, "Black Legion Spread Surprising to Midwest," *New York Times,* 31 May 1936, sec. 4: 6; "Dr. Clinchy Denies Black Legion Charge," *New York Times,* 15 June 1936, 13 (Legion quote).

65. James Allen Smith, *The Idea Brokers: Think Tanks and the Rise of the New Policy Elite* (New York: Free Press, 1991): 77, 79, 80, 87.

Chapter 4

1. *Congressional Record* (hereafter *CR*), 78th Cong., 2d sess. 90 (29 February 1944): A1020.

2. David A. Horowitz, *Beyond Left and Right: Insurgency and the Establishment* (Urbana: University of Illinois Press, 1997): 186, 189, 195; *CR,* 78th Cong., 1st sess. 89 (29 March 1943): A1541 (Lemke quote).

3. "$65,000,000,000 Debt Limit Voted," *New York Times,* 15 February 1941, 1, 27; "Byrd Decries Debt 'Popularizing,' " *New York Times,* 24 May 1939, 11; Alan Brinkley, *The End of Reform: New Deal Liberalism in Recession and War* (New York: Vintage, 1995): 140; Jordan A. Schwarz, *The New Dealers: Power Politics in the Age of Roosevelt* (New York: Alfred A. Knopf, 1993): 194; Richard N. Chapman, *Contours of Public Policy, 1939–1945* (New York: Garland, 1981): 44–48, 50, 53.

4. "New Group To Seek Non-Defense Cuts," *New York Times,* 8 July 1941, 1, 10; Henry N. Dorris, "Senators Move for Tax Savings By Budget Rule," *New York Times,* 29 August 1941, 1; Ronald L. Heinemann, *Harry Byrd of Virginia* (Charlottesville: University Press of Virginia, 1996): 219; "Byrd For Deep Cuts in Civil Outlays," *New York Times,* 30 October 1941, 20; Henry N. Dorris, "Asks Billion Cut From Nondefense," *New York Times,* 15 November 1941, 15; U.S. Senate, Joint Committee on Reduction of Nonessential Federal Expenditures, *Hearings on Reduction of Nonessential Federal Expenditures* (Washington, D.C.: Government Printing Office, 1941): 19–20.

5. U.S. Senate, Preliminary Report on Reduction of Nonessential Federal Expenditures, *Reduction of Nonessential Federal Expenditures* (Washington, D.C.: Government Printing Office, 1941): 2, 4 (Report quote), 3–6; C. P. Trussell, "Byrd Group Asks $1,716,965,061 Cuts," *New York Times,* 26 December 1941, 1, 28; Frank L. Kluckhorn, "Byrd Asks Nation to Center on War, End 'Confusion, Jealousy, Red Tape,' " *New York Times,* 13 February 1942, 1 (first Byrd quote), 1, 14 (second Byrd quote). See also Chapman, *Contours of Public Policy,* 140–41.

6. Chapman, *Contours of Public Policy,* 168–70.

7. Ibid., 170–71 (Taber quote on 171), 174 (Cox quote); *CR,* 77th Cong., 2d sess. 88 (9 February 1942): 1153 (Shafer quote).

8. *CR,* 77th Cong., 2d sess. 88 (24, 9 February 1942): A721, 1153 (Bennett quotes), 1116 (Ford quote), 1158 (Ford amendment); Chapman, *Contours of Public Policy,* 172.

9. Chapman, *Contours of Public Policy,* 172–73; Heinemann, *Byrd of Virginia,* 224 (Byrd quote).

10. *CR*, 77th Cong., 2d sess. 88 (24, 28 February 1942): A680, 4685 (Tydings quote); Heinemann, *Byrd of Virginia*, 224, 225; "Accuses Mellett Again On OGR Work," *New York Times*, 3 May 1942, 39 (first and second Byrd quotes).

11. Frank R. Kent, "The Great Game of Politics," *Washington Evening Star*, in *CR*, 77th Cong., 2d sess. 88 (15 May 1942): A1786; John A. Salmond, *The Civilian Conservation Corps, 1933–1942: A New Deal Case Study* (Durham, N. C.: Duke University Press, 1967): 211–13, 215–17.

12. Heinemann, *Byrd of Virginia*, 227 (Report quote), 228; D. A. Horowitz, *Beyond Left and Right*, 211; Alan Brinkley, *Liberalism and Its Discontents* (Cambridge, Mass.: Harvard University Press, 1998): 65.

13. Luther Huston, "No. 1 Word," *New York Times Magazine*, 31 January 1943, sec. 5: 10 (first quote); Louis Stark, "Rail Unions Angry, Harrison Asserts," *New York Times*, 15 October 1943, 13 (second quote); *CR*, 78th Cong., 1st sess. 89 (29 March 1943): A1541 (Lemke quotes); "Senator Assails Big U. S. Payrolls," *New York Times*, 28 June 1943, 27 (Langer quotes); "Bricker Outlines World Unity Plan," *New York Times*, 12 December 1943, 4.

14. *CR*, 78th Cong., 1st sess. 89 (8 January, 8 February 1943): 53 (Woodruff quotes), 698 (Hoffman quote); C. P. Trussell, "Full Budget Study Looms in Congress," *New York Times*, 12 January 1943, 1; Henry N. Dorris, "Office Funds Cut in House Passage," *New York Times*, 18 February 1943, 20 (fourth quote); Chapman, *Contours of Public Policy*, 217–23.

15. U.S. Senate, Additional Report on Reduction of Nonessential Federal Expenditures, *Reduction of Nonessential Federal Expenditures: Federal Personnel* (Washington, D.C.: Government Printing Office, 1943): 7, 11, 12; "Byrd Economy Body Urges Federal Cut of 300,000 Workers," *New York Times*, 17 June 1943, 1; "Roosevelt Signs Six Big Fund Bills," *New York Times*, 13 July 1943, 1; Heinemann, *Byrd of Virginia*, 228.

16. Allan M. Winkler, *The Politics of Propaganda: The Office of War Information, 1942–1945* (New Haven: Yale University Press, 1978): 68–69; *CR*, 78th Cong., 1st sess. 89 (18 June 1943): 6116 (quotes).

17. Winkler, *Politics of Propaganda*, 66, 70–71; *CR*, 78th Cong., 1st sess. 89 (18 June 1943): 6134 (first Starnes quote), 6133 (second Starnes quote), 5863 (first and second Bridges quotes), 6137, 6143, 30 June 1943, 6814; C. P. Trussell, "Roosevelt Signs Six Big Fund Bills," *New York Times*, 13 July 1943, 1, 26.

18. Winkler, *Politics of Propaganda*, 149; "Says 'Youngsters' Do Federal Hiring," *New York Times*, 14 October 1943, 1, 13; U.S. House, Report of the Committee on the Civil Service, *Investigation of Civilian Personnel and Study of all Matters Relating to the Number, Proper Use, and Recruiting of Said Personnel* (Washington, D.C: Government Printing Office, 1943): 2.

19. Poll of 22 December 1943, George H. Gallup, *The Gallup Poll. Public Opinion, 1935–1971* (New York: Random House, 1972): vol. 1: 422; Bruce J. Dierenfield, *Keeper of the Rules: Congressman Howard W. Smith of Virginia* (Charlottesville: The University Press of Virginia, 1987): 102, Chapman, *Contours of Public Policy*, 214–15.

20. "Asks House To Sift 'Rule' By Agencies," *New York Times*, 4 February 1943, 12 (first Smith quote); Dierenfield, *Keeper of the Rules*, 103 (second and third Smith quotes).

21. Dierenfield, *Keeper of the Rules*, 103; Chapman, *Contours of Public Policy*, 145–46, 179–85, 224–25; Michael Darrock, "What Happened to Price Control?" *Harper's* 187 (July 1943): 115.

22. Brinkley, *End of Reform*, 83–84, 146; William J. Barber, *Designs within Disorder: Franklin D. Roosevelt, the Economists, and the Shaping of American Economic Policy, 1933–1945* (New York: Cambridge University Press, 1996): 54.

23. Brinkley, *End of Reform*, 146–47; Barber, *Designs within Disorder*, 65, 142 (Henderson quote); 142–43 (Clark quotes).

24. Barber, *Designs within Disorder*, 141–43.

25. Darrock, "What Happened to Price Control?" *Harper's*, 119, 121 (quote); poll of 12 August 1942, Gallup, *Gallup Poll*, Vol. 1: 344; W. H. Lawrence, "Tough Man With Two Tough Jobs," *New York Times Magazine*, 15 February 1942, 16; James T. Patterson, *Mr. Republican: A Biography of Robert A. Taft* (Boston: Houghton Mifflin, 1972): 258; Edward C. Blackorby, *Prairie Rebel: The Public Life of William Lemke* (Lincoln: University of Nebraska Press, 1963): 195n (Lemke quote).

26. W. H. Lawrence, "Henderson Quits," *New York Times,* 18 December 1942, 1; Charles E. Egan, "Sales Prices, Rents, Service Charges Frozen," *New York Times,* 29 April 1943, 1; Chapman, Contours of Public Policy, 226–27; D. A. Horowitz, *Beyond Left and Right,* 199; "OPA Policies Scored By Retailers," *New York Times,* 8 June 1943, 15 (quote); *CR,* 78th Cong., 1st sess. 89 (6 May 1943): A3410 (first and third Sikes quotes), A3411 (second Sikes quote).

27. Chapman, *Contours of Public Policy,* 215–16; *CR,* 78th Cong., 1st sess. 89 (18 June 1943): 6117 (Vursell quote).

28. Luther Huston, "GHQ for Our Daily Life," *New York Times Magazine,* 10 May 1942, 5; Chapman, *Contours of Public Policy,* 215–16, 227–28; C. P. Trussell, "Congress Recesses Until Sept. 14," *New York Times,* 9 July 1943, 1, 13.

29. U.S. House of Representatives, Second Intermediate Report of the Select Committee to Investigate Executive Agencies, *Report of the Select Committee to Investigate Executive Agencies* (Washington, D.C.: Government Printing Office, 1943): 2 (first quote), 4, 5, 12, (second quote), 19.

30. C. P. Trussell, "Smith Committee Denounces OPA and Is Attacked by House Group," *New York Times,* 16 November 1943, 1 (second quote), 17 (first quote); Dierenfield, *Keeper of the Rules,* 103–104.

31. *CR,* 77th Cong., 1st sess. 87 (25 November 1941): 9122 (first quote), 9123, 9124 (second quote).

32. *CR,* 78th Cong., 1st sess. 89 (7 April, 11 October 1943): 3093, 8195 (Bradley quote); Thomas N. Guinsburg, *The Pursuit of Isolationism in the United States Senate from Versailles to Pearl Harbor* (New York: Garland, 1982): 243 (Shipstead quote); William Pencak, *For God and Country: The American Legion, 1919–1941* (Boston: Northeastern University Press, 1989): 17, 266 (Legion quote), 268.

33. William Gellerman, *Martin Dies* [1944] (New York. Da Capo Press, 1972): 16–22, 33, 35, 36–38, 49, 53, 55; entry on Martin Dies, Jr., *Biographical Directory of the United States Congress* (Washington, D.C.: Government Printing Office, 1989): 909–910.

34. Gellerman, *Martin Dies,* 39 (quote), 61, 63, 65; Thomas C. Reeves, *The Life and Times of Joe McCarthy: A Biography* (New York: Stein and Day, 1982): 207–208.

35. Reeves, *Life and Times of McCarthy,* 208; U.S. House of Representatives, Report of the Special Committee on Un-American Activities, *Investigation of Un-American Activities and Propaganda* (Washington, D.C.: Government Printing Office, 1939): 31, 68, 119; Charles W. Hurd, "563 Federal Aides Put in 'Red Front,'" *New York Times,* 26 October 1939, 1, 14; U.S. House of Representatives, Hearings Before a Special Committee of the House of Representatives, *Investigation of Un-American Propaganda Activities in the United States* (Washington, D.C: Government Printing Office, 1938): 438–39.

36. Report of Special Committee, *Un-American Activities and Propaganda,* 10–12, 26–29, 118–19, and Special Committee on Un-American Activities, *Investigation of Un-American Propaganda in the United States* (Washington, D.C.: Government Printing Office, 1941): 1.

37. Ellen Schrecker, *Many Are the Crimes: McCarthyism in America* (Boston: Little, Brown, 1998): 110; *CR,* 77th Cong., 2d sess. 88 (15 January 1942): 409–410 (first quote), and 78th Cong., 1st sess. 89 (1 February 1943): 478 (second and third quotes), 475.

38. *CR,* 78th Cong., 1st sess. 89 (1 February 1943): 481 (second quote), 485 (first quote); "Dies Denounces New List of 'Reds,'" *New York Times,* 2 February 1943, 40; "House Won't Stop Pay of 40 Named By Dies," *New York Times,* 6 February 1943, 28; "Vote Pay Inquiry on Subversives," *New York Times,* 10 February 1943, 1; "House Votes, 302-4, For Dies Extension," *New York Times,* 11 February 1943, 1; "Dies To Check on 1,200," *New York Times,* 12 February 1943, 14.

39. U.S. House of Representatives, Special Committee on Un-American Activities, *Investigation of Un-American Propaganda Activities in the United States: Hearings before the Special Committee on Un-American Activities* (Washington, D.C.: Government Printing Office, 1943): 3236–3249, 3252, 3257–59, 3262, 3264, 3265 (quote). See also *CR,* 78th Cong., 1st sess. 89 (1 February 1943): 479–80.

40. Special Committee Hearings, *Un-American Propaganda Activities,* 3242, 3243 (quotes), 3265–66. Dies was furious at a press leak from an official at the Foreign Broadcast Intelligence Service falsely stating that his name was more frequently cited by Axis

radio broadcasts than that of any living American. See *CR*, 78th Cong., 1st sess. 89 (1 February 1943): 475.

41. Special Committee Hearings, *Un-American Propaganda*, 3366, 3371, 3375, 3377, 3501–3502, 3509, 3511, 3516, 3523 (quote), 3524. See also *CR*, 78th Cong., 1st sess. 89 (1 February 1943): 480, 483. Among the targets of the Dies Committee was Maurice Parmelee, a former employee of the Board of Economic Warfare and the author of *Nudism in Modern Life*, described by the chair as an obscene, antireligious, and "revolutionary" tract advocating "universal nudism in office and factory." See "Dies Denounces New List of 'Reds,' " *New York Times*, 2 February 1943, 40.

42. Special Committee Hearings, *Un-American Propaganda Activities*, 3525, 3526; U.S. House of Representatives, Special Subcommittee of Committee on Appropriations, *Report on the Fitness for Continuance in Federal Employment of Dr. Goodwin B. Watson, Dr. Frederick L. Schuman, and Dr. William E. Dodd, Jr., All of the Federal Communications Commission* (Washington, D.C.: Government Printing Office, 1943): 5 (quote), 4. See also "Watson, Dodd Held 'Unfit' For U.S. Jobs," *New York Times*, 22 April 1943, 25.

43. House Appropriations Subcommittee, *Report on Watson, Schuman, and Dodd*, 5–6; U.S. House of Representatives, Committee on Appropriations, Report on *the Fitness for Continuance in Federal Employment of Goodwin B. Watson and William E. Dodd, Jr., Employees of the Federal Communications Commission, and Robert Morss Lovett, Arthur E. Goldschmidt, and Jack Bradley Fahy, Employees of the Department of the Interior* (Washington, D. C.: Government Printing Office, 1943): 1–2, "Watson, Dodd Held 'Unfit' For U.S. Jobs," *New York Times*, 22 April 1943, 25; "Fight on Pay for Watson, Dodd, and Lovett Is Carried to Floor by House Committee," *New York Times*, 15 May 1943, 30; "Two Agencies Cut in Deficiency Bill," *New York Times*, 19 May 1943, 13; "Funds of 5 Billion Still Deadlocked in Congress Jam," *New York Times*, 3 July 1943, 1; "Roosevelt Signs Six Big Fund Bills," *New York Times*, 13 July 1943, 1.

44. "The New Red Network," *New Republic* 109 (2 August 1943): 136–37; "House Asked to Make Inquiry In Alleged Civil Service 'Gag,' " *New York Times*, 30 November 1943, 1; *CR*, 78th Cong., 1st sess. 89 (29 November 1943): 10099.

45. "Lovett Sues To Test Congress Ban on Pay," *New York Times*, 4 December 1943, 11; "Federal Officials To Get Back Pay," *New York Times*, 6 November 1945, 17; "Watson Denounces Report," *New York Times*, 22 April 1943, 25.

46. U.S. House of Representatives, Hearings Before a Special Committee on Un-American Activities, *Investigation of Un-American Propaganda Activities in the United States* (Washington, D. C.: Government Printing Office, 1939): 6355.

47. David Cushman Coyle, "The Twilight of National Planning," *Harper's* 171 (October 1935): 558–59; Samuel Barrett Pettengill, *Smokescreen* (New York: Southern Publishers, 1940: 11–12, 21–23.

48. Brinkley, *End of Reform*, 108, 248–49, 256; Philip W. Warken, *A History of the National Resources Planning Board, 1933–1943* (New York: Garland, 1979): 107, 111–12, 132–33, 135–81, 182; Barber, *Designs within Disorder*, 127.

49. Brinkley, *End of Reform*, 7–8, 139, 171, 250–54, 257, "The New Deal and the Idea of the State," in Steve Fraser and Gary Gerstle, eds., *The Rise and Fall of the New Deal Order, 1930-1980* (Princeton: Princeton University Press, 1989): 106–108, and *Liberalism and Its Discontents*, 89–90; "$7,695,000,000 Set in Post-War Plans for Public Works," *New York Times*, 28 April 1943, 1 (quote).

50. Brinkley, *End of Reform*, 176, 226, and "New Deal and Idea of State," in Fraser and Gerstle, eds., *Rise and Fall of New Deal Order*, 109; Barber, *Designs within Disorder*, 159 (quote); Chapman, *Contours of Public Policy*, 28–29; "New Deal Plans Industry Control," *Business Week* (20 March 1943): 15–16.

51. Theda Skopcol (with Edwin Amenta), "Redefining the New Deal: World War II and the Development of Social Provision in the United States," in Theda Skopcol, *Social Policy in the United States: Future Possibilities in Historical Perspective* (Princeton, N.J.: Princeton University Press, 1995): 193–94, 195, 198.

52. Chapman, *Contours of Public Policy*, 245–49; "Senate and House Pass Fund Bills Cut Below Budget," *New York Times*, 9 February 1940, 1; *CR*, 77th Cong., 2d sess. 88 (19 February 1942): 1491–94 (quote on 1494).

53. Chapman, *Contours of Public Policy*, 252, 256–57; "Byrd Disputes Post-War Planning Role," *New York Times*, 19 February 1943, 13; "M'Nutt Loses Plea on Manpower Fund,"

New York Times, 25 February 1943, 15; Louis Stark, "Congress At Odds on Security Plan," *New York Times*, 12 March 1943, 1, 7 (quote); Ralph Robey, "Postwar Bureaucratic Utopia: Part II," *Newsweek* 21 (10 May 1943): 62.

54. Robert A. Taft, "American Progress after the War," *Vital Speeches* 9 (15 June 1943): 539–41, and *CR*, 78th Cong., 1st sess. 89 (27 May 1943): 4924 (quote).

55. Taft, "American Progress," *Vital Speeches*, 538–40 (first and second quotes on 540).

56. Chapman, *Contours of Public Policy*, 258–59; "Abolition of NRPB Voted By Congress," *New York Times*, 19 June 1943, 1, 7; poll of 22 August 1943, Gallup, *Gallup Poll*, vol. 1: 402–403. Fifty-eight percent of respondents opposed postwar reforms, but half of the 32 percent who favored change wanted regulation of labor unions, less government meddling, lower taxes, and a free hand for business enterprise. For the relationship of the NRPB controversy to popular fears concerning bureaucracy, state power, and agency independence from Congress, see Brinkley, *End of Reform*, 255–56.

57. "Aubrey Williams Named Head of REA," *New York Times*, 23 January 1945, 11; Schwarz, *New Dealers*, xv; "Doubled Activity Predicted for REA," *New York Times*, 8 February 1945, 34; Chapman, *Contours of Public Policy*, 276.

58. John A. Salmond, "Postcript to the New Deal. The Defeat of the Nomination of Aubrey W. Williams as Rural Electrification Administrator in 1945," *Journal of American History* 61 (September 1974): 418–19; "Aubrey Williams Named Head of REA," *New York Times*, 23 January 1945, 11.

59. "Williams Opposed By 3 Farm Groups," *New York Times*, 2 February 1945, 13; Salmond, "Defeat of Williams," *Journal of American History*, 419; "Williams Denies He Is Communist," *New York Times*, 7 February 1945, 23 (quote).

60. "Williams Denies He Is Communist," *New York Times*, 7 February 1945, 23 (quote); "M'Kellar Presses Williams Attack," *New York Times*, 10 February 1945, 24; "Doubled Activity Predicted for REA," *New York Times*, 8 February 1945, 34; "Williams 'Waster,' M'Kellar Asserts," *New York Times*, 9 February 1945, 32. See also Salmond, "Defeat of Williams," *Journal of American History*, 423–25.

61. "M'Kellar Presses Williams Attack," *New York Times*, 10 February 1945, 24; "Williams Defends Foregoing Pulpit," *New York Times*, 20 February 1945, 17; Lansing Warren, "Senate Group, 12-8, Opposes Williams," *New York Times*, 3 March 1945, 1; "Vote on Williams Slowed By Debate," *New York Times*, 21 March 1945, 40; *CR*, 79th Cong., 1st sess. 91 (20 March 1945): 2463 (quote); entry on Raymond E. Willis, *Biographical Directory of Congress*, 2064.

62. *CR*, 79th Cong., 1st sess. (20 March 1945): 2464 (first quote), 2465 (second quote), 2469 (third quote).

63. Ibid., 2468, 2470 (first, second, and third quotes).

64. William S. White, "Senate, By 52 To 36, Rejects Williams As Director of REA," *New York Times*, 24 March 1935, 1, 15 (quote); Chapman, *Contours of Public Policy*, 276; Brinkley, *Liberalism and Its Discontents*, 71, 75, 77, 78; "Vote To Make REA Independent Unit," *New York Times*, 29 April 1945, 35; "$520,000,000 To REA Passed By Senate," *New York Times*, 15 May 1945, 20; Bertram D. Hulen, "Truman Changes Cabinet," *New York Times*, 24 May 1945, 1; "Senate Accepts Wickard," *New York Times*, 22 June 1945, 16.

65. Barber, *Designs within Disorder*, 160–61; Brinkley, *End of Reform*, 257, 259, 262–63; Stephen K. Bailey, *Congress Makes a Law: The Story behind the Employment Act of 1946* (New York: Columbia University Press, 1950): 117–18.

66. Bailey, *Congress Makes a Law*, 144–45; Barber, *Designs within Disorder*, 166, 167 (quotes).

67. Brinkley, *End of Reform*, 263 (quote); Bailey, *Congress Makes a Law*, 164–67, 233; Barber, *Designs within Disorder*, 167.

68. "Urges Court Curbs Upon U.S. Agencies," *New York Times*, 26 August 1944, 11; *CR*, 79th Cong., 1st sess. 91 (18 June 1945): 6236 (quote); Harl A. Dahlstrom, " 'Remote Bigness' as a Theme in Nebraska Politics: The Case of Kenneth S. Wherry," *North Dakota Quarterly* 38 (Summer 1970): 27–28; James Reston, "OPA Defiance is Widespread," *New York Times*, 29 June 1946, 1–2.

69. *CR*, 79th Cong., 1st sess. 91 (10 December 1945): 11706, 23 June, 27 September, 19 December 1945, A3021, A4065 (Schwabe quote), A5674–75; John D. Morris, "OPA Compromise Sent to President," *New York Times*, 29 June 1946, 1–2; "OPA Price Controls End at Midnight Tonight," *New York Times*, 30 June 1946, 1, 29; John D. Morris,

"House Votes To Control Prices, Rents," *New York Times,* 24 July 1946, 1–2, and "OPA Revival Bill Goes to Truman," *New York Times,* 25 July 1946, 1, 13.

70. Brinkley, *End of Reform,* 105.

Chapter 5

1. David A. Horowitz, *Beyond Left and Right: Insurgency and the Establishment* (Urbana: University of Illinois Press, 1997): 218.

2. Ibid., 216; entry on John W. Bricker, *Current Biography* (New York: H. W. Wilson, 1943): 73.

3. D. A. Horowitz, *Beyond Left and Right,* 218; Hugh Butler, "Government Grads Get Juicy Jobs," *American Magazine* 149 (April 1950): 25–26. For more on the revolving door syndrome for the period's government officials, see Peter H. Irons, *The New Deal Lawyers* (Princeton, N.J.: Princeton University Press, 1982): 298.

4. Entry on David E. Lilienthal, in John A. Garraty and Jerome L. Sternstein, eds., *Encyclopedia of American Biography* (New York: Harper Collins, 1996): 684; Jordan A. Schwarz, *The New Dealers: Power Politics in the Age of Roosevelt* (New York: Alfred A. Knopf, 1993): xv, 195–96.

5. Alan D. Harper, *The Politics of Loyalty: The White House and the Communist Issue, 1946–1952* (Westport, Conn.: Greenwood Press, 1969): 62–63; *Congressional Record* (hereafter *CR*), 80th Cong., 1st sess. 93 (24 March 1947): 2451; "Lilienthal Scored At Senate Meeting," *New York Times,* 11 February 1947, 10; Cabell Phillips, "Lilienthal Case Becomes a Political Issue," *New York Times,* 16 February 1947, 3 (quote); Anthony Leviero, "Lilienthal Rejects Red Aims," *New York Times,* 5 February 1947, 1, 3, and "Lilienthal's Fate Uncertain," *New York Times,* 12 February 1947, 1, 6; "M'Kellar Resumes Lilienthal Battle," *New York Times,* 18 February 1947, 17.

6. Anthony Leviero, "Lilienthal 'Veto' Asked by McKellar," *New York Times,* 6 February 1947, 1; David E. Shi, *The Simple Life: Plain Living and High Thinking in American Culture* (New York: Oxford University Press, 1985): 235–38; Schwarz, *New Dealers,* 219–20, 223, 226, 232; Thomas K. McCraw, *Morgan vs. Lilienthal: The Feud within the TVA* (Chicago: Loyola University Press, 1981): 72–73, 79, 82.

7. D. A. Horowitz, *Beyond Left and Right,* 221; Leviero, "Lilienthal's Fate Uncertain," *New York Times,* 12 February 1947, 6.

8. D. A. Horowitz, *Beyond Left and Right,* 221 (quote). See also *CR*, 80th Cong., 1st sess. 93 (2 April 1947): 3022–24.

9. "Text of Taft and Compton Messages," *New York Times,* 22 February 1947, 4 (Lilienthal quote); *CR*, 80th Cong., 1st sess. 93 (2 April 1947): A1463 (McKellar quote). Taft's statement and supporting documents also appear in *CR*, 80th Cong., 1st sess. 93 (3 April 1947): 3022–29.

10. D. A. Horowitz, *Beyond Left and Right,* 222; *CR*, 80th Cong., 1st sess. 93 (26 March 1947): 2594 (quotes).

11. Anthony Leviero, "Lilienthal Wins Senate Vote, 50-31," *New York Times,* 10 April 1947, 1; *CR*, 80th Cong., 1st sess. 93 (2 April 1947): 3028.

12. Richard M. Fried, *Nightmare in Red: The McCarthy Era in Perspective* (New York: Oxford University Press, 1990): 60–61, 67–68; David A. Oshinsky, *A Conspiracy So Immense: The World of Joe McCarthy* (New York: Free Press, 1983): 95–96.

13. Ellen Schrecker, *No Ivory Tower: McCarthyism and the Universities* (New York: Oxford University Press, 1986): 24, 31, 85, and *Many Are the Crimes: McCarthyism in America* (Boston: Little, Brown, 1998): 30; Fried, *Nightmare in Red,* 12–13; Malcolm Cowley, *The Dream of the Golden Mountains: Remembering the 1930s* (New York: Viking Press, 1964):158; Robbie Lieberman, *"My Song Is My Weapon": People's Songs, American Communism, and the Politics of Culture, 1930–50* (Urbana: University of Illinois Press, 1989): 87. For the leadership of working-class movements for revolution by middle-class intellectuals, see Alvin W. Gouldner, *The Future of Intellectuals and the Rise of the New Class* (New York: Continuum, 1979): 9–12, 17.

14. Schrecker, *Many Are the Crimes,* 5; M. J. Heale, *American Anticommunism: Combating the Enemy Within, 1830–1970* (Baltimore: Johns Hopkins University Press, 1990): 111; Schrecker, *No Ivory Tower,* 75, 76.

15. Schrecker, *Many Are the Crimes*, xiii, 5–6, and *No Ivory Tower*, 25, 74; William Gellerman, *Martin Dies* [1944] (New York: Da Capo Press, 1972): 81, 82; Fried, *Nightmare in Red*, 15.

16. J. Edgar Hoover, speech before International Association of Police Chiefs, 10 December 1945, in *CR*, 79th Cong., 1st sess. 91(17 December 1945): 12219 (quote); Schrecker, *Many Are the Crimes*, x–xi, xiii, 46–47, 85. For critiques of communism during World War II, see Heale, *American Anticommunism*, 5–121, and John E. Haynes, *Red Scare or Red Menace? American Communism and Anticommunism in the Cold War Era* (Chicago: Ivan R. Dee, 1996): 3–17. The continuities between wartime and postwar anticommunism are discussed in D. A. Horowitz, *Beyond Left and Right*, 189–93, 196, 211, 214, 217–20.

17. Schrecker, *No Ivory Tower*, 85–86, James F. O'Neill, "How You Can Fight Communism," *American Legion Magazine* 45 (August 1948): 16, 17 (quote), 44.

18. Schrecker, *Many Are the Crimes*, 142, 145; Robert E. Stripling, *The Red Plot Against America* [1949] (New York: Arno Press, 1977): 90; Eugene Lyons, *The Red Decade: The Stalinist Penetration of America* (Indianapolis: Bobbs-Merrill, 1941): 324 (first and second Lyons quotes), and "Our New Privileged Class," *American Legion Magazine* 51 (September 1951): 11–13, 37, 39 (third Lyons quote); Paul Harvey, *Remember These Things* (Chicago: Heritage Foundation, 1952): 76 (Harvey quotes).

19. *Is This Tomorrow: America Under Communism* (St. Paul: Catechetical Guild, 1947), 6 (first and second quotes), 48, in (1945–47) Folder, OF 263, Presidential Papers of Harry S. Truman, Harry S. Truman Presidential Library.

20. Ibid.

21. *CR*, 79th Cong., 1st sess. 91 (8 March 1945): A1093 (Dondero quote); D. A. Horowitz, *Beyond Left and Right*, 217, 218, 269 (second quote). For background on Dondero, see *Biographical Directory of the United States Congress*, 1774–1989 (Washington, D.C.: Government Printing Office, 1989): 920.

22. Fried, *Nightmare in Red*, 73; D. A. Horowitz, *Beyond Left and Right*, 223–24; Schrecker, *Many Are the Crimes*, 122–23; J. Edgar Hoover, HUAC testimony, 26 March 1947, in Ellen Schrecker, *The Age of McCarthyism: A Brief History with Documents* (Boston: Bedford Books, 1994): 116–17.

23. Victory S. Navasky, *Naming Names* (New York: Penguin Books, 1980): 78; Lyons, *Red Decade*, 38; D. A. Horowitz, *Beyond Left and Right*, 224; Robert K. Carr, *The House Committee on Un-American Activities, 1945–1950* (Ithaca, N.Y.: Cornell University Press, 1952): 55–56, 57.

24. Ronald Reagan, *An American Life* (New York: Simon and Schuster, 1990): 105, 107–109, 112–13, and Reagan with Richard G. Hubler, *Where's the Rest of Me: The Autobiography of Ronald Reagan* [1965] (New York: Karz Publishers, 1981): 168.

25. Reagan, *Where's the Rest of Me*, 168, and *An American Life*, 111, 113–14, 115 (quote); U.S. House of Representatives, *Hearings Before the Committee on Un-American Activities, Hearings Regarding the Communist Infiltration of the Motion Picture Industry* (Washington, D.C.: Government Printing Office, 1947): 214, 217–18.

26. Navasky, *Naming Names*, 80, 419, 82; Fried, *Nightmare in Red*, 76.

27. Navasky, *Naming Names*, 81–82; HUAC *Hearings*, 290–91, 293, 333–35.

28. Navasky, *Naming Names*, 80; Carr, *House Committee on Un-American Activities*, 76–77; HUAC *Hearings*, 364–66, 384 (quote); Fried, *Nightmare in Red*, 76.

29. Carr, *House Committee on Un-American Activities*, 70, 72–73, 76; Navasky, *Naming Names*, 83, 87; Reagan, *An American Life*, 115; Schrecker, *Age of McCarthyism*, 217–18.

30. Poll of 30 November 1947, in George H. Gallup, *The Gallup Poll: Public Opinion, 1935–1971* (New York: Random House, 1972): Vol. 1: 689–90; Lyons, "Our New Privileged Class," *American Legion Magazine*, 38 (first quote), 39 (second quote); Navasky, *Naming Names*, 138, 140, 143, 239–45, 202, 205, 258–59, 262, 264, 266. Support for the ten contempt citations was 62 percent among farmers, 49 percent among manual workers, 41 percent among business people and professionals, and 36 percent among white-collar employees. Of the ten witnesses, Lester Cole had never gone to college and Dalton Trumbo had worked as a baker for eight years before going to Hollywood. See Navasky, *Naming Names*, 80–82.

31. Earl Latham, *The Communist Controversy in Washington: From the New Deal to McCarthy* (Cambridge, Mass.: Harvard University Press, 1966): 39; Fried, *Nightmare in Red*, 18–19.

32. Whittaker Chambers, *Testimony before HUAC*, 3 August 1938, in Schrecker, *Age of McCarthyism*, 138–39; Stripling, *Red Plot*, 98 (quote); Whittaker Chambers, *Witness* (New York: Random House, 1952): 9; Fried, *Nightmare in Red*, 18–19. Chambers's philosophy is discussed in Marvin N. Olasky, "Liberal Boosterism and Conservative Distancing: Newspaper Coverage of the Chambers-Hiss Affair, 1948–1950," *Continuity* 15 (Fall-Winter 1991): 41n, 43–44.

33. Fried, *Nightmare in Red*, 20–21.

34. Ibid., 20; D. A. Horowitz, *Beyond Left and Right*, 226.

35. Navasky, *Naming Names*, 4, 7–8, 21; Fried, *Nightmare in Red*, 17–18.

36. Olasky, "Liberal Boosterism," *Continuity*, 33, 34, 42–43.

37. Karl Mundt, "What the Hiss Trial Actually Means," *CR*, 81st Cong., 2d sess. 96 (25 January 1950): 889, 891 (quote); "Bridges and Hiss and an Awakening People," *Detroit Free Press*, 6 April 1950, 6.

38. *CR*, 81st Congress, 1st sess. 95 (20 June 1949): A4409; D. A. Horowitz, *Beyond Left and Right*, 160.

39. Oshinsky, *A Conspiracy So Immense*, 104; D. A. Horowitz, *Beyond Left and Right*, 238, 253.

40. Stanley I. Kutler, *The American Inquisition: Justice and Injustice in the Cold War* (New York: Hill and Wang, 1982): 187–88; Athan Theoharis, *The Yalta Myths: An Issue in U. S. Politics, 1943–1955* (Columbia: University of Missouri Press, 1970): 45.

41. John T. Flynn, *While You Slept* (New York: Devin-Adair, 1951); D. A. Horowitz, *Beyond Left and Right*, 252.

42. "Senator Butler of Nebraska Dies," *New York Times*, 2 July 1954, 19; Eric F. Goldman, *The Crucial Decade and After: America, 1945–1960* (New York: Alfred A. Knopf, 1960): 125 (quote). Butler joined eleven other senators in a losing effort in 1945 to recommit Acheson's nomination for Under Secretary of State and was one of twenty-five senators who then refused to cast a vote on the matter. See *CR*, 79th Cong., 1st sess. 91 (24 September 1945): 8915–16. Nevertheless, Goldman provided no citation for the senator's alleged outburst and a survey of the *Congressional Record, New York Times Index*, and other sources failed to confirm that the quote was ever made. The cultural symbolism of the Cold War State Department is discussed in Edward A. Shils, *The Torment of Secrecy: The Background and Consequences of American Security Policies* (Glencoe, Ill.: Free Press, 1956): 88–89, and Talcott Parsons, "McCarthyism and American Social Tensions: A Sociologist's View," *Yale Review* 44 (Winter 1955): 239.

43. Thomas C. Reeves, "Joe: The Years Before Wheeling," in Reeves, ed., *McCarthyism* (Malabar, Fla.: Robert E. Krieger Publishing, 1982): 11–16; Oshinsky, *A Conspiracy So Immense*, 43; Jack Anderson and Ronald W. May, *McCarthy, the Man, the Senator, the "Ism"* (Boston: Beacon Press, 1952): 105.

44. Anderson and May, *McCarthy, the Man*, 107 (first quote), 108 (second quote), 110 (third and fourth quotes). When McMurray responded that Commerce Secretary Wallace would "discuss his view on Russia in words that the people of Wisconsin can understand," a heckler responded, "he don't have to talk down to us."

45. Oshinsky, *A Conspiracy So Immense*, 108–110, 112 (quote); Robert Griffith, *The Politics of Fear: Joseph R. McCarthy and the Senate* [1970] (Amherst: University of Massachusetts Press, 1987): 49–51, 71–72, 94; James Gilbert, *Redeeming Culture: American Religion in an Age of Science* (Chicago: University of Chicago Press, 1997): 182.

46. Thomas C. Reeves, *The Life and Times of Joe McCarthy: A Biography* (New York: Stein and Day, 1982): 249, 287, 323; *CR*, 81st Cong., 2d sess. 96 (20 February 1950): 1964 (quote); Griffith, *Politics of Fear*, 54–57.

47. John W. Dower, *War Without Mercy: Race and Power in the Pacific War* (New York: Pantheon, 1986): 15–17; Jordan Braverman, *To Hasten the Homecoming: How Americans Fought World War II through the Media* (Lanham, N.Y.: Madison Books, 1996): 143 (quotes).

48. *CR*, 81st Cong., 2d sess. 96 (20 February 1950): 1954.

49. Ibid., 1954 (first and second quotes), 1957 (third, fourth, and fifth quotes), 1968 (sixth quote).

50. Griffith, *Politics of Fear*, 59, 67–72.

51. Oshinsky, *A Conspiracy So Immense*, 137; Kutler, *American Inquisition*, 185–87.

52. Griffith, *Politics of Fear*, 77, 79 (first quote); "M'Carthy Labels Marshall 'Unfit,' " *New York Times*, 21 April 1950, 3 (second, third, fourth, and fifth quotes).

53. *CR*, 81st Cong., 2d sess. 96 (9, 19 May, 2 June 1950): A3427 (first, second, third, fourth, and fifth quotes), A3428 (sixth and seventh quotes), A3787 (eighth quote), A4161 (ninth quote). The Midwest Council of Young Republicans met in Chicago on 6 May 1950. The Sons of the American Revolution speech was delivered on 15 May 1950 at the organization's Atlantic City, New Jersey annual convention. The third McCarthy address was dated 25 May 1950.

54. Polls of 21 May, 7 July 1950, Gallup, *Gallup Poll*, vol. 2: 911–12, 924; Griffith, *Politics of Fear*, 100; *CR*, 81st Cong., 2d sess. 96 (21 July 1950): 10792 (quote).

55. Reeves, *Life and Times of McCarthy*, 319, 335 (first, second, and fifth quotes); *CR*, 81st Cong., 2d sess. 96 (23 September 1950): 6899 (fourth quote); 6901 (third quote). McCarthy addressed a Republican rally at Hyattsville, Maryland, on 22 September 1950.

56. D. A. Horowitz, *Beyond Left and Right*, 249, 250 (MacArthur quote), 251 (McCarthy quotes).

57. Douglas MacArthur, *Reminiscences* (New York: McGraw-Hill, 1964): 414 (quotes), 417–18.

58. Griffith, *Politics of Fear*, 143–44, Oshinsky, *A Conspiracy So Immense*, 197.

59. *CR*, 82nd Cong., 1st sess. 97 (24 May 1951): 5779 (quotes); Oshinsky, *A Conspiracy So Immense*, 200; Joseph Raymond McCarthy, *America's Retreat from Victory: The Story of George Catlett Marshall* (New York: Devin-Adair, 1951): 3, 4, 84, 165. See also "The History of George Catlett Marshall," *CR*, 82nd Cong., 1st sess. 97 (14 June 1951): 6556–6603.

60. McCarthy, *America's Retreat from Victory*, 100 (second quote), 167, 168 (first quote), 171.

61. Oshinsky, *A Conspiracy So Immense*, 210 (first quote); Anderson and May, *McCarthy, the Man*, 225–28, 230 (second quote), 233; Griffith, *Politics of Fear*, 146–51; "Text of Address by McCarthy Accusing Governor Stevenson of Aid to Communist Cause," *New York Times*, 28 October 1952, 26 (third and fourth quotes).

62. Heale, *American Anticommunism*, 184 (quote), 185–86; Schrecker, *Age of McCarthyism*, 84; Sidney Hook, "Heresy Yes—But Conspiracy, No," *New York Times Magazine*, 9 July 1950, 12, 38–39.

63. Joe McCarthy, *McCarthyism: The Fight for America* (New York: Devin-Adair, 1952): 101 (quotes).

64. John Whiteclay Chambers II, entry on Patrick Anthony McCarran, *Dictionary of American Biography, Supplement Five* (New York: Charles Scribner's Sons, 1977): 443–44.

65. Fried, *Nightmare in Red*, 116–17, 145; Schrecker, *No Ivory Tower*, 161, and *Age of McCarthyism*, 13.

66. Schrecker, *No Ivory Tower*, 161–62, 164, 167; Fried, *Nightmare in Red*, 145, 153; U.S. Senate, Report of the Committee on the Judiciary, *Institute of Pacific Relations* (Washington, D.C.: Government Printing Office, 1952): 2.

67. Fried, *Nightmare in Red*, 146, 148; Kutler, *American Inquisition*, 185, 200–201; 213 (quote).

68. Kutler, *American Inquisition*, 193, 199–200; U.S. Senate, Hearings before the Internal Security Subcommittee of the Committee on the Judiciary, *Institute of Pacific Relations* (Washington, D.C.: Government Printing Office, 1952): 2900, 2903 (first quote), 2905, 2906, 2907, 2914 (second quote), 2983. Former New Dealer Thurman Arnold was a member of the Fortas law firm, which represented corporate clients in dealings with the federal government.

69. SSIS Hearings, *IPR*, 2922, 2923, 2927 (quote), 2932, 2953, 2983, 2984–85.

70. Ibid. 2996, 3178, 3179 (second quote), 3180, 3238 (first quote).

71. Ibid. 2916, 2983, 2996 (first quote), 2998, 3430 (second quote); Fried, *Nightmare in Red*, 146, 150; Kutler, *American Inquisition*, 213.

72. SSIS Hearings, *IPR*, 3674 (first quote), 3675 (second and third quotes), 3676 (fourth quote), 3677, 3679. For a sympathetic treatment of the committee's conclusions, see John T. Flynn, *The Lattimore Story* (New York: Devin-Adair, 1953): 95–102.

73. Judiciary Committee Report, *IPR*, 74, 76, 84, 223, 225; Kutler, *American Inquisition*, 202–203.

74.   SSIS Hearings, *IPR*, 3676, 3677; Judiciary Committee Report, *IPR*, 224 (quote).
75.   Kutler, *American Inquisition*, 202–204, 206.
76.   Ibid., 203–211.

Chapter 6

1.   Daniel Bell, "The New Class: A Muddled Concept," in B. Bruce-Briggs, ed. *The New Class?* (New Brunswick, N.J.: Transaction Books, 1979): 174–76.
2.   Victor S. Navasky, *Naming Names* (New York: Penguin Books, 1980): 232, 235 (quote), 236–38.
3.   Ibid., 200–206, 239–46, 252–57, 258–62, 320–21.
4.   Entry on Adlai Ewing Stevenson, in John A. Garraty and Jerome L. Sternstein, eds., *Encyclopedia of American Biography* (New York. Harper Collins, 1996): 1067–68; Ellen W. Schrecker, *No Ivory Tower: McCarthyism and the Universities* (New York: Oxford University Press, 1986): 194–95, 340. Populist suspicion of the media and educational elite is described in M. J. Heale, *American Anticommunism: Combating the Enemy Within, 1830–1970* (Baltimore: Johns Hopkins University Press, 1990): 185–88.
5.   Ellen W. Schrecker, *The Age of McCarthyism: A Brief History with Documents* (Boston: Bedford Books, 1994): 32–34.
6.   Schrecker, *No Ivory Tower*, 131–33; Richard M. Fried, *Nightmare in Red: The McCarthy Era in Perspective* (New York: Oxford University Press, 1990): 179–80; Barton J. Bernstein, "The Oppenheimer Loyalty-Security Case Reconsidered," *Stanford Law Review 42* (July 1990): 1383 (Borden quote), 1389–90, 1400.
7.   B. Bernstein, "Oppenheimer Loyalty-Security Case," *Stanford Law Review*, 1383–84.
8.   Ibid., 1406–1407, 1416, 1419–20, 1444, 1448, 1451, 1461–65, 1463, 1469, 1480.
9.   Ibid., 1393–1395, 1397, 1398, 1403–1404, 1465, 1468 (quote), 1468. See also James Reston, "Dr. Oppenheimer Is Barred From Security Clearance, Though 'Loyal,' 'Discreet,' " *New York Times*, 2 June 1954, 1.
10.   B. Bernstein, "Oppenheimer Loyalty-Security Case," *Stanford Law Review*, 1468–70, 1478 (first quote), and "In the Matter of J. Robert Oppenheimer," *Historical Studies in the Physical Sciences* 12, Part 2 (1982): 226–27, 242 (second quote).
11.   B. Bernstein, "In Matter of Oppenheimer," *Historical Studies in the Physical Sciences*, 246, and "Oppenheimer-Loyalty Security Case," *Stanford Law Review*, 1386, 1467, 1484.
12.   James Gilbert, *Redeeming Culture: American Religion in an Age of Science* (Chicago: University of Chicago Press, 1997): 37–40, 48–50; Edward A. Shils, *The Torment of Secrecy: The Background and Consequences of American Security Policies* (Glencoe, Ill.: Free Press, 1956): 43, 122, 125, 131 (quote), 135, 181, 183–84.
13.   David Oshinsky, *A Conspiracy So Immense: The World of Joe McCarthy* (New York. Free Press, 1983): 250–51.
14.   John T. Flynn, *The Lattimore Story* (New York: Devin-Adair, 1953): 1 (first quote), 2, 111 (second quote); Oshinksy, *A Conspiracy So Immense*, 507; U. S. Senate, *Annual Report of the Committee on Governmment Operations Made by the Senate Permanent Subcommittee on Investigations* (Washington, D.C.: Government Printing Office, 1954): 1. For a description of the manner in which liberal elites have come under suspicion on the communist issue, see Jeane J. Kirkpatrick, "Politics and the New Class," in B. Bruce-Briggs, ed., *The New Class?* (New York: McGraw-Hill, 1981): 42-43; Jerome L. Himmelstein, *To the Right: The Transformation of American Conservatism* (Berkeley: University of California Press, 1990): 21, 77; Shils, *Torment of Secrecy*, 207n; and David Danzig, "The Radical Right and the Rise of the Fundamentalist Minority," *Commentary* 33 (April 1962): 296.
15.   *Annual Report of Government Operations Committee*, 2, 3, 5 (quote), 10; Oshinsky, *A Conspiracy So Immense*, 266, 271–76.
16.   Oshinsky, *A Conspiracy So Immense*, 277–85; *Annual Report of Government Operations Committee*, 26–27.
17.   Oshinsky, *A Conspiracy So Immense*, 322, 332–44; Schrecker, *No Ivory Tower*, 202, 203 (quote). Thirty-eight engineers and others were suspended at the Fort Monmouth Army laboratories following McCarthy's investigation. See Ellen W. Schrecker, *Many Are the Crimes: McCarthyism in America* (Boston: Little, Brown, 1998): 370.

18. Robert Griffith, *The Politics of Fear. Joseph R. McCarthy and the Senate* [1970] (Amherst: University of Massachusetts Press, 1987): 216–17; *Annual Report of Government Operations Committee*, 45–46; Oshinsky, *A Conspiracy So Immense*, 323–35; 366–68, 376, 377.
19. Richard H. Rovere, *Senator Joe McCarthy* (New York: Harcourt Brace Jovanovich, 1959): 26 (quote), 28; Oshinsky, *A Conspiracy So Immense*, 431, 433.
20. Shils, *Torment of Secrecy*, 99–101, 112–14, 119; Peter Viereck, "The New American Radicals," *Reporter* 11 (December 1954): 42; Barbara Ehrenreich and John Ehrenreich, "The New Left: A Case Study in Professional-Managerial Radicalism," *Radical America* 11 (May-June 1977): 20; Samuel Francis, "The Evil That Men Don't Do: Joe McCarthy and the American Right," *Chronicles* 10 (September 1986): 16–21; Richard Hofstadter, *Anti-intellectualism in American Life* (New York: Random House, 1962): 39–42. For a description of American anticommunism as an anticapitalist reaction to the corporate, bureaucratic, centralizing, and statist tendencies of modern society, see Steve Fraser, "The Labor Question," in Fraser and Gary Gerstle, eds., *The Rise and Fall of the New Deal Order, 1930–1980* (Princeton, N.J.: Princeton University Press, 1989): 73.
21. Poll of 15 January 1954, in George H. Gallup, *The Gallup Poll: Public Opinion 1935–1971* (New York: Random House, 1972): Vol. 2: 1201; Michael P. Rogin, *The Intellectuals and McCarthy: The Radical Specter* (Cambridge, Mass.: MIT Press, 1967): 5, 30–31, 65, 72, 171. Rogin tied McCarthy to politically conservative Republican constituencies in Wisconsin whose penchant for moral protest was contrasted to the legitimate populism and statist agenda of the anticapitalist working class. For further discussion of McCarthy and populism, see David A. Horowitz, *Beyond Left and Right. Insurgency and the Establishment* (Urbana: University of Illinois Press, 1997): 268–70.
22. Fried, *Nightmare in Red*, 158; Thomas C. Reeves, "Introduction," in Reeves, ed., *Foundations under Fire* (Ithaca, N.Y.: Cornell University Press, 1970): 26–27; *Congressional Record* (hereafter *CR*), 83rd Cong., 1st sess. 99 (27 July 1953): 10016.
23. *CR*, 83rd Cong., 1st sess. 99 (27 July 1953): 10015 (quote), 10016; John Lankford, *Congress and the Foundations in the Twentieth Century* (River Falls, Wisc.: Wisconsin State University, 1964): 58. For a report of Reece's views, see Leo Egan, "Number and Size of Foundations Up," *New York Times*, 3 March 1954, 20.
24. C. P. Trussell, "Democrat Assails Attack on Funds," *New York Times*, 13 May 1954, 26, and "Tax-Free Foundations Held Threat to Education in U.S." *New York Times*, 12 May 1954, 1, 23.
25. C. P. Trussell, "Tax-Free Foundations Held Threat," *New York Times*, 12 May 1954, 23; U.S. House of Representatives, Special Committee to Investigate Tax-Exempt Foundations and Comparable Organizations, *Relations between Foundations and Education and between Foundations and Government*, Staff Report No. 3 (Washington, D.C.: Government Printing Office, 1954): 469, 467, 475 (first quote), 476 (second quote), 477 (third quote), 480 (fourth quote).
26. Lankford, *Congress and the Foundations*, 83; "Foundations Face 'Propaganda' Test," *New York Times*, 21 May 1954, 14; C. P. Trussell, "Power of Grants Scored in Inquiry," *New York Times*, 20 May 1954, 26. See Albert H. Hobbs, *Social Problems and Scientism* (Harrisburg, Pa.: Stackpole, 1953).
27. Trussell, "Power of Grants Scored in Inquiry," *New York Times*, 20 May 1954, 26; U. S. House of Representatives, Special Committee to Investigate Tax-Exempt Foundations and Comparable Organizations, *Tax-Exempt Foundations: Hearings before the Special Committee to Investigate Tax-Exempt Foundations and Comparable Organizations* (Washington, D.C.: Government Printing Office, 1954): 117, 123, 124, 126, 129, 130, and *Tax-Exempt Foundations: Final Report* (Washington, D.C.: Government Printing Office, 1954): 68.
28. Special Committee to Investigate Tax-Exempt Foundations, *Hearings*, 131 (quotes), and *Final Report*, 72.
29. Special Committee to Investigate Tax-Exempt Foundations, *Final Report*, 85–87, and *Hearings*, 139.
30. C. P. Trussell, "Democrat Assails Attack on Foundations," *New York Times*, 13 May 1954, 26; "Foundations Defended," *New York Times*, 30 May 1954, 14; Irving Spiegel, " 'Unfair' Methods Of Inquiry Scored," *New York Times*, 6 June 1954, 29; "Inquiry On

Grants Closes Hearings," *New York Times,* 7 July 1954, 1, 6; Editorial, "Another Reply to Reece," *New York Times,* 6 August 1954, 16.

31. C. P. Trussell, "Foundations Help Subvert Country, House Study Says," *New York Times,* 20 December 1954, 1 (second quote); Special Committee to Investigate Tax-Exempt Foundations, *Final Report,* 54 (first quote), 154–56. See also "Excerpts From Report on Congressional Investigation of Tax-Exempt Foundations," *New York Times,* 20 December 1954, 21.

32. Special Committee to Investigate Tax-Exempt Foundations, *Final Report,* 17, 31, 39, 40 (quote), 45; Trussell, "Foundations Help Subvert Country," *New York Times,* 20 December 1954, 1.

33. Special Committee to Investigate Tax-Exempt Foundations, *Final Report,* 17, 18, 30, 31, 32, 61, 73, 77; Trussell, "Foundations Help Subvert Country," *New York Times,* 20 December 1954, 20.

34. Special Committee to Investigate Tax-Exempt Foundations, *Final Report,* 18, 60, 78.

35. Ibid., 72 (second quote), 88 (first quote).

36. Ibid., 40 (Report quote); René A. Wormser, "Foundations: Their Power and Influence," in Reeves, ed., *Foundations under Fire,* 100, 103, 104 (Worsmer quote). See also René A. Wormser, *Foundations: Their Power and Influence* (New York: Devin-Adair, 1958): 178–81.

37. Special Committee to Investigate Tax-Exempt Foundations, *Final Report,* 20–22; Reeves, "Introduction," in Reeves, ed., *Foundations under Fire,* 26; Charles Grutzner, "Foundations Call Charges Untrue," *New York Times,* 20 December 1954, 1, 20; Lankford, *Congress and Foundations,* 88.

38. Robert D. Johnston, "The Myth of the Harmonious City: Will Daly, Lora Little, and the Hidden Face of Progressive-Era Portland," *Oregon Historical Quarterly* 99 (Fall 1998): 270, 276–78 (quote on 276), 281–83, and "Middle-Class Political Ideology in a Corporate Society: The Persistence of Radicalism in Portland, Oregon, 1883–1926" (Ph.D. diss., Rutgers University, 1993): 249, 253.

39. Robert L. Crain, et al, *The Politics of Community Conflict: The Fluoridation Decision* (Indianapolis, Ind.: Bobbs-Merrill, 1969): 4, 17, 19, 20, 30, 81.

40. Ibid., 4, 18, 21, 22, 24; Donald R. McNeil, *The Fight for Fluoridation* (New York: Oxford University Press, 1957): 127, 142; Morris Davis, "Community Attitudes toward Fluoridation," *Public Opinion Quarterly* 23 (Winter 1959): 475; Leverett G. Richards, "Many Vast Organizations Back Plan for Protective Fluoridation of City Water Supplies," *Oregonian,* 22 October 1956, 12; "Schrunk, Bowes Lead; City Measures Trail," *Oregonian,* 7 November 1956, 1; James Rorty, "Introduction," in Frederick B. Exner and G. L. Waldbott, *The American Fluoridation Experiment* (New York: Devin-Adair, 1957): 10. Rorty was a nationally known magazine contributor.

41. McNeil, *Fight for Fluoridation,* 122, 128, 134–35, 157–59; Crain, *Politics of Community Conflict,* 4; Bernard Mausner and Judith Mausner, "A Study of the Anti-Scientific Attitude," *Scientific American* 192 (February 1955): 35; Rorty, "Introduction," in Exner and Waldbott, *American Fluoridation Experiment,* 1–2, 13–16. Waldbott was a Detroit physician who specialized in allergy treatments and who published a newsletter that served as a nationwide clearinghouse for anti-fluoridation information.

42. McNeill, *Fight for Fluoridation,* 145–50. See also U. S. House of Representatives, Select Committee to Investigate the Use of Chemicals in Foods and Cosmetics, *Hearings* (Washington, D.C.: Government Printing Office, 1952).

43. McNeil, *Fight for Fluoridation,* 146, 149, 188–90; *CR,* 82nd Cong., 2d sess. 98 (24 March 1952): A1833 (first and third quotes), A1834, 2762 (second quote).

44. "Fluoridation Safe," *New York Times,* 27 September 1952, sec. 4: 11; "City Club Voices Support for Fluoridation Proposal," *Oregonian,* 13 October 1956, 5; McNeil, *Fight for Fluoridation,* 187 (first quote); Mausner and Mausner, "Anti-Scientific Attitude," *Scientific American,* 35 (second quote). For perspective on the fluoridation controversy at the height of the debate, see Donald R. McNeil, "Fluoridation's Pro and Con," *New York Times Magazine,* 3 March 1957, 15.

45. Arnold Green, "The Ideology of Anti-Fluoridation Leaders," *Journal of Social Issues* 17 (No. 4, 1961): 13; Crain, *Politics of Community Conflict,* vi , 3–4, 97–98; "A Two-Part Report on Fluoridation, Part 1: The Cancer Scare," *Consumer Reports* 43 (July 1978): 393; "A Two-Part Report on Fluoridation. Part II: The Misleading Claims," *Consumer*

Reports 43 (August 1978): 482 (quote); Tom Alkire, "Fluoride Debate Won't Decay," *Willamette Week,* 30 October 1978, 1.

46. James O. Wilson, "Preface," in Crain, *Politics of Community Conflict,* xi, xii; Crain, *Politics of Community Conflict,* 67–69, 148.

47. Green, "Ideology of Anti-Fluoridation Leaders," *Journal of Social Issues,* 14, 16, 23.

48. Ibid., 15, 16, 21 (quote), 22, 24–25.

49. Crain, *Politics of Community Conflict,* 145–46; Davis, "Community Attitudes toward Fluoridation," *Public Opinion Quarterly,* 482; Mausner and Mausner, "Anti-Scientific Attitude," *Scientific American,* 35–39; John P. Kirscht and Andie L. Knutson, "Science and Fluoridation: An Attitude Study," *Journal of Social Issues* 17 (No. 2, 1961): 39.

50. William A. Gamson, "The Fluoridation Dialogue: Is It an Ideological Conflict?" *Public Opinion Quarterly* 25 (Winter 1961): 533; Green, "Ideology of Anti-Fluoridation Leaders," *Journal of Social Issues,* 21 (first quote); McNeil, *Fight for Fluoridation,* 108 (second quote), 109; Exner and Waldbott, *American Fluoridation Experiment,* 1, 2, 23, 129 (third quote), 131.

51. Crain, *Politics of Community Conflict,* 6; McNeil, *Fight for Fluoridation,* 198; Mausner and Mausner, "Anti-Scientific Attitude," *Scientific American,* 36–39; Gamson, "Fluoridation Dialogue," *Public Opinion Quarterly,* 535 (first quote), 537; Herman F. Strongin to the Editor, *New York Times,* 16 January 1957, 30 (second quote).

52. Crain, *Politics of Community Conflict,* 46–47; McNeil, *Fight for Fluoridation,* 123 (Franzen quote), 124 (Michigan quotes). For Hoffman's insertion, see *CR,* 83rd Cong., 2d sess. 100 (1 June 1954). A4069–70.

53. McNeil, *Fight for Fluoridation,* 186; Clarence Dean, "Hundreds Crowd All-Day Hearing on Fluoridation," *New York Times,* 7 March 1957, 1, 14; Walter Sullivan, "Fluoride Battle To Resume Today, Approval Likely," *New York Times,* 18 November 1963, 1, 25; Peter Kihss, "Experts Divided on Fluoridation At City Hearing," *New York Times,* 19 November 1963, 1, 27; "Fluoride Backed By Council, 19–4," *New York Times,* 11 December 1963, 1, 39; Charles G. Bennett, "Final Won By Fluoridation; Fight Will Go On," *New York Times,* 13 December 1963, 1, 38; "City Council Against Fluoridation Measure," *Oregonian,* 27 August 1964, 27; Alkire, "Fluoride Debate," *Willamette Week,* 30 October 1978, 1, 4; Ann Sullivan, "Opponents Plan Fluoridation Challenges," *Oregonian,* 9 November 1978, sec. C: 1; Steve Jenning, "City Approves Ballot Title for Fluoride Repeal Attempt," *Oregonian,* 15 February 1979, sec. B: 1; "Fluoridation Foes Petition for Vote, *Oregonian,* 4 July 1979, sec. D: 1, and "Fluoridation Forces Say Issue Fading," *Oregonian,* 22 May 1980, sec. B: 1; "Multnomah Co. Voting," *Oregonian,* 21 May 1980, sec. B: 4; Susan C. Orlean, "A Case of Moral Decay," *Willamette Week,* 1 December 1981, 4.

54. "Two-Part Report on Fluoridation," *Consumer Reports,* 394 (quote); Davis, "Community Attitudes toward Fluoridation," *Public Opinion Quarterly,* 474; Alan Keith-Lucas, "The Political Theory Implicit in Social Casework Theory," *American Political Science Review* 47 (December 1953): 1091 (quotes). For the social and political alienation of antifluoridation activists, see Arnold Simmel, "A Signpost for Research on Fluoridation Conflicts: The Concept of Relative Deprivation," *Journal of Social Issues* 17 (No. 2, 1961): 36. For the tension between experts and traditionalists, see William R. Brock, *Welfare, Democracy, and the New Deal* (New York: Cambridge University Press, 1988): 366.

55. Green, "The Ideology of Anti-Fluoridation Leaders," *Journal of Social Issues,* 16 (quote), 25.

Chapter 7

1. E. L. Taylor to Lyndon B. Johnson, 15 July 1957, Civil Rights, Correspondence Relating to LBJ's Senate Bill, Box 3, Senate Papers of LBJ Relating to Civil Rights, Lyndon Baines Johnson Presidential Library (LBJPL).

2. Harvard Sitkoff, *A New Deal for Blacks: The Emergence of Civil Rights as a National Issue* (New York: Oxford University Press, 1978): 142–43, 145–49, 171–73, 260.

3. Ibid., 35; Alan Brinkley, *Liberalism and Its Discontents* (Cambridge, Mass.: Harvard University Press, 1998): 63–65, 71, 75–77.
4. John Morton Blum, *V Was For Victory: Politics and American Culture During World War II* (New York: Harcourt Brace Jovanovich, 1976): 185–88, 215–18; Steven F. Lawson, *Running for Freedom: Civil Rights and Black Politics in America Since 1941* (New York: McGraw-Hill, 1991): 11–12, 15–19.
5. Alan Brinkley, *The End of Reform: New Deal Liberalism in Recession and War* (New York. Vintage, 1995): 170; Lawson, *Running for Freedom*, 20, 32–40.
6. Brinkley, *Liberalism and Its Discontents*, 295; Jerome L. Himmelstein, *To the Right: The Transformation of American Conservatism* (Berkeley: University of California Press, 1990): 100; David Lebedoff, *The New Elite: The Death of Democracy* (New York: Franklin Watts, 1978): 21. See also Alan Brinkley, "The Problem of American Conservatism," *American Historical Review* 99 (April 1994): 295.
7. Brinkley, *Liberalism and Its Discontents*, 78 (Glass quote); Lawson, *Running for Freedom*, 27, 39; Sitkoff, *New Deal for Blacks*, 71–72; Allan M. Winkler, *The Politics of Propaganda: The Office of War Information, 1942–1945* (New Haven, Conn.: Yale University Press, 1978): 67–68; *Congressional Record* (hereafter *CR*), 78th Cong., 1st sess. 89 (1 February 1943): 478 (Dies quote); "Senate Group, 12-8, Opposes Williams," *New York Times*, 3 March 1945, 18.
8. John T. Flynn to Archbishop Francis J. Spellman, 29 January 1946, "S" Correspondence, Flynn to Styles Bridges, 1 March 1949, 1 (first quote), 2 (second quote), and Flynn to Walter F. George, 24 March 1949, 1 (third quote), Senate, Papers of John T. Flynn, University of Oregon Special Collections.
9. Brinkley, *Liberalism and Its Discontents*, 100–101; *CR*, 83rd Cong., 1st sess. 99 (27 July 1953): 10016; U.S. House of Representatives, Special Committee to Investigate Tax-Exempt Foundations and Comparable Organizations, *Tax-Exempt Foundations: Final Report* (Washington, D.C.: Government Printintg Office, 1954): 72 (quote).
10. Lawson, *Running for Freedom*, 28, 47–48; David A. Horowitz, *Beyond Left and Right: Insurgency and the Establishment* (Urbana: University of Illinois Press, 1997): 277 (first quote), 278; "Southern Congressmen Present Segregation Manifesto," *Congressional Quarterly Almanac* 12 (1956): 416 (second quote). The manifesto was published on 12 March 1956.
11. T. G. Tilford, "Common Sense and Integration," *Daily Sentinel* (Nacogdoches, Tex.), 14 August 1957, 1 (first quote), 2; Dr. Paul H. Power to Lyndon B. Johnson, 21 September 1957 (second quote), Civil Rights, Correspondence Relating to LBJ's Senate Bill, Box 3, Senate Papers of LBJ, LBJPL. Portions of this and the following sections are from D. A. Horowitz, *Beyond Left and Right*, 277–81, 284, 286–93, and "White Southerners' Alienation and Civil Rights: The Response to Corporate Liberalism, 1956–1965," *Journal of Southern History* 54 (May 1988): 174–87, 194–200.
12. D. A. Horowitz, *Beyond Left and Right*, 278, 279 (quotes).
13. Dr. John R. Brown to President Eisenhower, 29 September 1957 (first quote), Faubus File Opposing Eisenhower, A-D, Box 394, Senate Papers of LBJ, LBJPL; Tilford, "Common Sense and Integration," *Daily Sentinel*, 1 (second and third quotes), 2 (fourth quote), 3.
14. Lawson, *Running for Freedom*, 56–58; Velva Otts to LBJ, 26 September 1957 (quote), Civil Rights, Correspondence Relating to LBJ's Senate Bill, Box 3, Senate Papers of LBJ, LBJPL.
15. Roland Roggenbrod to LBJ, 27 June 1957 (quote), Civil Rights Correspondence Relating to LBJ's Senate Bill, 2 of 2, Box 3, LBJ Senate Papers, LBJPL; Lawson, *Running for Freedom*, 45–47, 64–65, 72, 80–81.
16. Lawson, *Running for Freedom*, 92–96; David J. Garrow, *Bearing the Cross: Martin Luther King, Jr. and the Southern Christian Leadership Conference* (New York: W. Morrow, 1986): 231–64, 266–67, 269, 271–86.
17. Frank E. Land and Donald Lee Blagg to Vice President Johnson, 28 August 1963 (quote), Civil Rights, August 1963, Box 5, Vice Presidential Papers Open for Civil Rights, LBJPL; Hugh Davis Graham, *The Civil Rights Era: Origins and Development of National Policy, 1960–1972* (New York: Oxford University Press, 1990): 456–57; Rhoda Lois Blumberg, *Civil Rights: The 1960s Freedom Struggle* (Boston: Twayne, 1984): 106–107.

18. Irwin Unger, *The Best of Intentions: The Triumph of the Great Society Under Kennedy, Johnson, and Nixon* (New York: Doubleday, 1996): 79, 80–81, 83–85.

19. Ibid., 86, 92–94, 97, 99–100.

20. Lawson, *Running for Freedom*, 48, 94–95.

21. Ibid., 98–99; David Chalmers, *And the Crooked Places Made Straight: The Struggle for Social Change in the 1960s* [1991] (Baltimore: Johns Hopkins University Press, 1996): 26–27; Frederick M. Wirt, *The Politics of Southern Equality: Law and Social Change in a Mississippi County* (Chicago: Aldine, 1970): 133, 136; George E. Reedy to President, 2 October 1965 (quote), attached to Memo, Joe Califano to President, 25 October 1965, CF HU2, Equality of Races, 1964–1966, Box 56, White House Central Files (WHCF), LBJPL.

22. Confidential Memorandum, George E. Reedy to LBJ [1963], Confidential Memoranda—Reedy, Box 6, Vice Presidential Papers Open for Civil Rights, LBJPL; George C. Wallace, *Stand Up for America* (Garden City, N.Y.: Doubleday, 1976): 10, 22, 24, 26, 43, 51, 57, 65–69, 75 (quote).

23. Stephen Lesher, *George Wallace: American Populist* (Reading, Mass.: Addison-Wesley, 1994): 174 (first quote), 273–74; Wallace, *Stand Up for America*, 78–79, 81 (second quote), 83, 86, 88.

24. Christopher Lasch, *The Revolt of the Elites and the Betrayal of Democracy* (New York: W. W. Norton, 1995): 91; Ben A. Franklin, "Maryland's Vote Held Anti-Negro," *New York Times*, 21 May 1964, 1; Lesher, *Wallace*, 273 (first quote), 280 (third quote), 283 (second quote), 298.

25. Dan T. Carter, *George Wallace, Richard Nixon, and the Transformation of American Politics* (Waco, Tex.: Markham Press Fund, 1992): 9 (first quote), 10, 12–13; Wallace, *Stand Up for America*, 178 (second and third quotes).

26. George Wallace, speech at Whitewater State College, Wisconsin, 23 March 1964, quoted in Jody Carlson, *George C. Wallace and the Politics of Powerlessness: The Wallace Campaigns for the Presidency, 1964–76* (New Brunswick, N. J.: Transaction Books, 1981): 64 (first quote), 65 (third quote); Lesher, *Wallace*, 271 (second quote), 278.

27. Lesher, *Wallace*, 284, 295, 303; Himmelstein, *To the Right*, 63–64, 68, 77; Robert Alan Goldberg, *Barry Goldwater* (New Haven, Conn.: Yale University Press, 1995): x, 49, 120.

28. Goldberg, *Goldwater*, 92, 95–96 (first quote), 120 (second quote), 127, 138–40.

29. Ibid., 150–51. The manifesto was delivered on 11 January 1961.

30. Ibid., 151, 219; Thomas Byrne Edsall with Mary D. Edsall, *Chain Reaction: The Impact of Race, Rights, and Taxes on American Politics* (New York: W. W. Norton, 1991): 38–44; Kent Schuparra, *Triumph of the Right. The Rise of the California Conservative Movement, 1945–1966* (Amonk, N.Y.: M. E. Sharpe, 1998): 92, 96 (quote); Himmelstein, *To the Right*, 69.

31. Adrienne R. Spivack to Jack Valenti, 20 July 1964, attached to Valenti to Spivack, 22 July 1964 (quote), PL2, 7/21/64—7/23/64, WHCF, Box 93, LBJPL; Goldberg, *Goldwater*, 217 (fourth quote) 222, 229 (third quote); speech at Minneapolis, 10 September 1964, Supplement E–Additional September Quotes, "What Barry Goldwater Has Said," 6 (first quote), Box 26, Office Files of George Reedy, LBJPL; speech at Illinois State Fair, 19 August 1964, quoted in *Chicago Tribune*, 20 August 1964, Supplement C, Goldwater Quotes, Sept. 1–15, 1964, 5 (second quote), Box 28, Reedy Office Files, LBJPL.

32. Goldwater Position Papers, Goldwater for President Committee, 1964, in "What Goldwater Said," 206, Box 28, Reedy Office Files, LBJPL; Edsall, *Chain Reaction*, 7–8; Goldberg, *Goldwater*, 205 (quotes).

33. Goldberg, *Goldwater*, 232–36.

34. Lawson, *Running for Freedom*, 101–102, 107, 110–11.

35. Ibid., 112–13; David J. Garrow, *Protest at Selma: Martin Luther King, Jr., and the Voting Rights Act of 1965* (New Haven, Conn.: Yale Univesity Press, 1978): 91, and *Bearing the Cross*, 396, 405–407, 413.

36. Mrs. H. B. McConnell to LBJ, 29 March 1965 (first and second quotes), Civil Rights, Public Opinion Mail, Box 179, LBJPL; Mrs. B. Westedorf to President, 28 March 1965 (third quote), Civil Rights, Public Opinion Mail, Box 145, LBJPL; Don F. Wasson, "Selma Inscribes Note of Reason in History Text," *Montgomery Advertiser*, 31 January 1965 (fourth quote), attached to Lawrence F. O'Brien to Sen. John Sparkman, 23 February 1965, HU 2/ST1, 2/15/65-3/8/65, WHCF, Box 27, LBJPL.

37. Reprint of radio address by Reverend and Bob Marsh, 28 March 1965, 1 (first and third quotes), 2 (second quote), attached to Lawrence F. O'Brien to Sen. John Sparkman, HU 2/ST1, 4/19/65-4/24/65, WHCF, Box 28, LBJPL.

38. Ibid., 3.

39. Ibid., 1, 2 (quote).

40. Lawson, *Running for Freedom,* 113–15; Garrow, *Bearing the Cross,* 380–81, 406, 395, and *Protest at Selma,* 98.

41. David Horowitz and David Kolodney, "The Foundations," *Ramparts* 7 (April 1969): 44; Hugh Davis Graham, *Civil Rights and the Presidency: Race and Gender in American Politics, 1960–1972* (New York: Oxford University Press, 1992): 6 (quotes).

42. Lawrence H. Fuchs, *The American Kaleidoscope: Race, Ethnicity, and the Civic Culture* (Hanover, N.H.: University Press of New England, 1990): 406; Unger, *Best of Intentions,* 328; H. Graham, *Civil Rights and Presidency,* 6, 151, 155, and *Civil Rights Era,* 3.

43. Unger, *Best of Intentions,* 58–59, 63, 153–54.

44. Ibid., 150–51 (first quote on 150), 164, 173 (second quote).

45. Ibid., 152, 159–60, 172–73. For OEO's problems with local officeholders, see James T. Patterson, *America's Struggle Against Poverty, 1900–1994* (Cambridge, Mass.: Harvard University Press, 1994): 142–48, and David Zarefsky, *President Johnson's War on Poverty, Rhetoric and History* (University City: University of Alabama Press, 1986): 120–59.

46. Unger, *Best of Intentions,* 155–56.

47. Ibid., 158, 161–64, 230–31.

48. Ibid., 157–58; Jill Quadagno, *The Color of Welfare: How Racism Undermined the War on Poverty* (New York: Oxford University Press, 1994): 47–52.

49. E. J. Dionne, Jr., *Why Americans Hate Politics* (New York: Simon and Schuster, 1991): 74; Unger, *Best of Intentions,* 166; F. J. Williams to LBJ, 25 March 1965 (quote), Civil Rights, Public Opinion Mail, Box 145, LBJPL; Marjorie Hunter, "Cleveland Antipoverty Group Accused of Ignoring Poor for Fear of Political Power," *New York Times,* 15 April 1965, 23. Even in Syracuse, where the community action board was controlled by the mayor, $7 million of the antipoverty program's $8 million funding had gone to salaries by mid-1967. See Unger, *Best of Intentions,* 160.

50. Hunter, "Cleveland Antipoverty Group," *New York Times,* 15 April 1965, 23 (quote); Unger, *Best of Intentions,* 159.

51. Bob Finch, "Yorty Wants Poverty Funds To Aid Needy," *Los Angeles Herald-Dispatch,* 8 May 1965, in U.S. House of Representatives, Hearings Before the Subcommittee of the War on Poverty Program of the Committee on Education and Labor, *Examination of the War on Poverty Program* (Washington, D.C.: Government Printing Office, 1965): 853, 854 (quote); "Syracuse Hits Poverty Program," *New York Times,* 24 June 1965, 13.

52. Ben A. Franklin, "Mayors Challenge Antipoverty Plan," *New York Times,* 1 June 1965, 30 (first quote), and "Mayors Shelve Dispute on Poor," *New York Times,* 2 June 1965, 20 (second quote); Unger, *Best of Intentions,* 167, 171–72.

53. Joseph A. Loftus, "Antipoverty Bill Withstands Foes," *New York Times,* 22 July 1965, 28, "House Approves Expanded Drive Against Poverty," *New York Times,* 23 July 1965, 1; Joseph A. Loftus, "Senate Approves Funds to Extend Poverty Program," *New York Times,* 20 August 1965, 1; Quadagno, *Color of Welfare,* 57; Unger, *Best of Intentions,* 173–74.

54. Unger, *Best of Intentions,* 196, 213–15; Joseph A. Loftus, "U.S. May Curb Aid to Syracuse Poor," *New York Times,* 2 December 1965, 83; "Shriver Rejects Syracuse Plea," *New York Times,* 9 December 1965, 58; "Wide Policy Role For Poor Opposed By Budget Bureau," *New York Times,* 5 November 1965, 1; Nan Robertson, "15 Sites Can Veto Poverty Project," *New York Times,* 25 March 1966, 27.

55. "Poverty Hearings Called 'Whitewash,'" *New York Times,* 26 March 1966, 14 (quote); "Republicans Assail Poverty Program," *New York Times,* 29 March 1966, 36; Unger, *Best of Intentions,* 214–16. By 1967, two-thirds the OEO budget went to Headstart and other non-political programs. See Quadagno, *Color of Welfare,* 57.

56. Fred Powledge, "Antipoverty Program Criticized at Teach-in Here," *New York Times,* 6 December 1965, 22 (quote); Unger, *Best of Intentions,* 236–37.

57. Schuparra, *Triumph of the Right,* 81 (Rafferty quote), 82; Max Rafferty, "What Happened to Patriotism," *Reader's Digest* 79 (October 1961): 108–109.

58. Ronald Reagan, *An American Life* (New York: Simon and Schuster, 1990): 147 (first quote), 152; Schuparra, *Triumph of the Right*, xxix, 128 (second and third quotes).

59. Schuparra, *Triumph of the Right*, xviii, xxxix, 113, 124, 138, 149.

60. Ronald Reagan, address before the National Sand and Gravel Association, Los Angeles, 8 Febuary 1967, and address before Republican State Convention, Anaheim, n.d., in Reagan, *The Creative Society: Some Comments on Problems Facing America* (New York: Devin-Adair, 1968): 17, 75 (first quote), 77 (second quote).

61. Edsall, *Chain Reaction*, 9–10, 77–78, 85; Carlson, *Wallace and Politics of Powerlessness*, 15, 17.

62. George Wallace, address before Fraternal Order of Police, 29 August 1966, Miami, Fla., in Dan T. Carter, *The Politics of Rage. George Wallace, the Origins of the New Conservatism, and the Transformation of American Politics* (New York: Simon and Schuster, 1995): 305 (first quote); George Wallace, Report to the Alabama Legislature, 10 January 1967, in Lesher, *Wallace*, 369 (second and third quotes).

63. George Wallace, *Meet the Press*, 23 April 1967, in Lesher, *Wallace*, 390 (first and second quotes); Richard M. Scammon and Ben J. Wattenberg, *The Real Majority* (New York: Coward-McCann, 1970): 43 (third quote), Wallace, *Stand Up for America*, 87 (fourth quote).

64. Wallace, *Stand Up for America*, 122, 124; D. Carter, *Politics of Rage*, 313–14, 345; Lesher, *Wallace*, 417; Jonathan Rieder, "The Rise of the Silent Majority," in Steve Fraser and Gary Gerstle, eds., *The Rise and Fall of the New Deal Order, 1930–1980* (Princeton, N.J.: Princeton University Press, 1989): 250–52, 254, 261; Harris poll of 12 September 1968, in Fred Panzer, Memo to the President, 16 September 1968, EX PL (Wallace, George), WHCF, Box 27 LBJPL; Edsall, *Chain Reaction*, 77.

65. William C. Berman, *America's Right Turn: From Nixon to Bush* (Baltimore: Johns Hopkins University Press, 1994): 8–9; Rieder, "Silent Majority," in Fraser and Gerstle, eds., *Rise and Fall of New Deal Order*, 260 (quote).

66. Berman, *America's Right Turn*, 9–10; Rieder, "Silent Majority," in Fraser and Gerstle, eds., *Rise and Fall of New Deal Order*, 244 (quote), 248; Dionne, *Why Americans Hate Politics*, 193.

Chapter 8

1. Kurt Schuparra, *Triumph of the Right: The Rise of the California Conservative Movement, 1945–1966* (Amonk, N.Y.: M.E. Sharpe, 1998): 146; Hugh Davis Graham, *The Civil Rights Era: Origins and Development of National Policy, 1960–1972* (New York: Oxford University Press, 1990): 463–64; Irwin Unger, *The Best of Intentions: The Triumph of the Great Society Under Kennedy, Johnson, and Nixon* (New York: Doubleday, 1996): 302; Thomas Byrne Edsall with Mary D. Edsall, *Chain Reaction: The Impact of Race, Rights, and Taxes on American Politics* (New York: W. W. Norton, 1991): 106; James Allen Smith, *The Idea Brokers: Think Tanks and the Rise of the New Policy Elite* (New York: Free Press, 1991): 13, 149.

2. Edsall, *Chain Reaction*, 75; H. Graham, *Civil Rights Era*, 4, and *Civil Rights and the Presidency: Race and Gender in American Politics, 1960–1972* (New York: Oxford University Press, 1992): 138–39, 147–49.

3. Jill Quadagno, *The Color of Welfare: How Racism Undermined the War on Poverty* (New York: Oxford University Press, 1994): 79; J. Larry Hood, "The Nixon Administration and the Revised Philadelphia Plan for Affirmative Action: A Study in Expanding Presidential Power and Divided Government," *Presidential Studies Quarterly* 23 (Winter 1993): 149; Joan Hoff, *Nixon Reconsidered* (New York: Basic Books, 1994): 91–92; Allen J. Matusow, *Nixon's Economy: Booms, Busts, Dollars, and Votes* (Lawrence, Kans.: University Press of Kansas, 1998): 28–29. See also Dean J. Kotlowski, *Nixon's Civil Rights: Politics, Principle, and Policy* (Cambridge, Mass.: Harvard University Press, 2001): esp. 97–124.

4. Hood, "Nixon Administration and Affirmative Action," *Presidential Studies Quarterly*, 145; Quadagno, *Color of Welfare*, 62–64, 71.

5. Quadagno, *Color of Welfare*, 64–65, 66, 67, 69, 73; H. Graham, *Civil Rights and Presidency*, 154–55.

6. Hood, "Nixon Administration and Affirmative Action," *Presidential Studies Quarterly*, 146–47; H. Graham, *Civil Rights and Presidency*, 157–58; Quadagno, *Color of Welfare*, 75.

7. Hood, "Nixon Administration and Affirmative Action," *Presidential Studies Quarterly*, 145–47; Matusow, *Nixon's Economy*, 27; David R. Jones, "Mild Labor Secretary," *New York Times*, 1 March 1969, 17; "U.S. Plans Formula To Get Contractors to Hire Minorities," *New York Times*, 28 June 1969, 61 (quote); Roy Reed, "New U.S. Job Plan for Negroes Set," *New York Times*, 18 July 1969, 10.

8. "Shultz Defends New Plan To Get Jobs for Negroes," *New York Times*, 6 July 1969, 37 (Shultz quote); "Negro Gets Key Post In Labor Department," *New York Times*, 15 March 1969, 33; James M. Naughton, "U.S. To Start Plan Giving Minorities Jobs In Building," *New York Times*, 24 September 1969, 1, 18; H. Graham, *Civil Rights and Presidency*, 161 (Fletcher quote); Reed, "New Job Plan for Negroes," *New York Times*, 18 July 1969, 10.

9. Hood, "Nixon Administration and Affirmative Action," *Presidential Studies Quarterly*, 150–51; H. Graham, *Civil Rights and Presidency*, 159, 226.

10. Entry on Paul Jones Fannin, *Biographical Directory of the U.S. Congress, 1774–1989* (Washington, D.C.: Government Printing Office, 1989): 981; *Congressional Record* (hereafter *CR*), 91st Cong., 1st sess. 115 (9 June, 31 January, 4, 7 February, 24 March, 1 April 1969): 15174, 2395–96, 2639 (first quote), 3110, 3112–13, 7334 (second quote), 8269 (third quote), 8270 (fourth quote).

11. "Dirksen Asks Delay on Negro Jobs Plan," *New York Times*, 9 July 1969, 24; *CR*, 91st Cong., 1st sess. 115 (5, 11, 13 August 1969): 22332–33, 22346–50, 23268–69, 23740–41; "Controller Scores Negro Hiring Plan," *New York Times*, 6 August 1969, 43; Donald Janson, "Construction Jobs Rights Plan Backed at Philadelphia Hearing," *New York Times*, 27 August 1969, 24; Naughton, "U.S. To Start Plan Giving Minorities Jobs," *New York Times*, 24 September 1969, 1, 18 (quote).

12. Saul Miller, "Labor, Civil Rights Coalition Reaffirms Randolph's Goals," *AFL-CIO News* 14 (10 May 1969): 1, 3; "House, Senate Panel Back Bill To Strengthen Ban on Job Bias," *AFL-CIO News* 15 (6 June 1970): 12; "Labor Asks Stronger Curbs on Job Bias," *AFL-CIO News* 14 (20 September 1969): 8; " 'Human Resources' Job Plan Gets Under Way in Nine Cities," *AFL-CIO News* 14 (4 January 1969): 3; Eugene A. Kelly, "Building Crafts Vote Plan to Spur Jobs for Negroes," *AFL-CIO News* 14 (27 September 1969): 1; "Chicago Building Trades Promote Job Opportunities for 4,000 Blacks," *AFL-CIO News* 14 (13 September 1969): 3. For organized labor's embrace of civil rights, see Lane Kirkland, "Labor and the Liberal Tradition," *AFL-CIO American Federationist* 76 (December 1969): 12–15. A 1968 survey of blue-collar workers outside the South revealed that nearly 90 percent supported legislation to eliminate racial discrimination in employment. See Richard F. Hamilton, "Liberal Intelligentsia and White Backlash," *Dissent* 19 (Winter 1972): 226.

13. "Chicago Building Trades Promote Opportunities," *AFL-CIO News* 14 (13 September 1969): 3; Kelly, "Spur Jobs for Negroes," *AFL-CIO News* 14 (27 September 1969): 1 (first, second, and third quote), 5 (fourth quote). See also "Affirmative Action: Building Trades Cite Record in Recruiting Negroes for Jobs," *AFL-CIO News* 14 (27 September 1969), 7, and Statement of Policy on Equal Employment Opportunity Adopted by the 55th Convention of the Building and Construction Trades Department (AFL-CIO), 22 September 1969, Atlantic City, N.J., in Statement of Louis Sherman, U.S. Senate, Hearings before the Subcommittee on Separation of Powers of the Senate Committee on the Judiciary on the Philadelphia Plan and S. 931, *The Philadelphia Plan: Congressional Oversight of Administrative Agencies* (Washington, D.C.: Government Printing Office, 1970): 178.

14. Resolution No. 270, AFL-CIO Building and Construction Trades Department, 22 September 1969, in Sherman Statement, Hearings, *Philadelphia Plan*, 179 (first and second quotes); Damon Stetson, "Meany Criticizes Nixon on Racism," *New York Times*, 25 September 1969, 25; Kelly, "Spur Jobs for Negroes," *AFL-CIO News* 14 (27 September 1969): 5 (third quote); "Labor Affirms Commitment to Civil Rights Progress," *AFL-CIO News* 14 (11 October 1969): 11. See also "Excerpts from Building Trades' Statement on Hiring Minorities," *New York Times*, 23 September 1969, 56.

15. Opening Statement of Sam J. Ervin, Jr., Statement of Harry P. Taylor, and Statement of Building and Construction Trades Department, AFL-CIO, Hearings, *Philadelphia Plan*,

1–4, 85 (quote), 172. See also "Trades Score Racial Quotas in Hiring Plan," *AFL-CIO News* 14 (1 November 1969): 7.

16. *CR*, 91st Cong., 1st sess. 115 (18 December 1969): 39975; Robert M. Semple, Jr., "Philadelphia Plan: How White House Engineered Major Victory," *New York Times*, 26 December 1969, 20; John W. Finney, "Nixon Is Upheld in House As Integration Curb Loses," *New York Times*, 19 December 1969, 1, 27; David E. Rosenbaum, "Shultz Appeals to House on Jobs," *New York Times*, 21 December 1969, 39 (quotes); "Negro Rights: Mr. Nixon vs. Labor," *Newsweek* 75 (5 January 1970): 49–50.

17. Warren Weaver, Jr., "Congress Avoids Tie-Up on Rights," *New York Times*, 23 December 1969, 1, 14 (quotes); *CR*, 91st Cong., 1st sess. 115 (22 December 1969): 40749, 40921–22; Robert M. Semple, Jr., "Philadelphia Plan: How White House Engineered Major Victory," *New York Times*, 26 December 1969, 20.

18. "Nixon's Score on Civil Rights Shows 'Pretty Bad' First Year," *AFL-CIO News* 15 (10 January 1970): 5 (first quote); "Meany Says Nixon is Using Jobs Plan As a Political Tool," *New York Times*, 13 January 1970, 28 (second quote); George Meany, speech before National Press Club, 12 January 1970, in Meany, "The Outreach Program," *Vital Speeches* 36 (1 February 1970): 230–34 (third quote on 230). See also "Philadelphia Plan Assailed As Masking Rights Retreat," *AFL-CIO News* 15 (17 January 1970): 1, 11.

19. "Ervin Criticizes Orders on Hiring," *New York Times*, 16 January 1970, 15,

20. "Labor Department Issues New Rules on Minority Hiring by Firms," *AFL-CIO News* 15 (7 February 1970): 2 (quote); Hoff, *Nixon Reconsidered*, 92. See also H. Graham, *Civil Rights and Presidency*, 167–68.

21. Seth S. King, "Chicago Negroes Win Accord on Construction Jobs," *New York Times*, 13 January 1970, 28; George Meany, "To End Job Bias," *New York Times*, 7 February 1970, 28; "Negroes in Pittsburgh Achieve Accord on Jobs in Construction," *New York Times*, 31 January 1970, 20; "D.C. Construction Unions Protest New Racial Quota Hiring Directive," *AFL-CIO News* 15 (6 June 1970): 11; Paul Delaney, "Nixon Plan for Negro Jobs In Construction Is Lagging," *New York Times*, 20 July 1970, 1; Quadagno, *Color of Welfare*, 80–81.

22. H. Graham, *Civil Rights and Presidency*, 180–87, 200, 205, 214, 217, 218; Nathan Glazer, *Affirmative Discrimination: Ethnic Inequality and Public Policy* (New York: Basic Books, 1975): 38; Hood, "Nixon Administration and Affirmative Action," *Presidential Studies Quarterly*, 162.

23. Delaney, "Nixon Plan," *New York Times*, 20 July 1970, 18; H. Graham, *Civil Rights and Presidency*, 225–26; Edsall, *Chain Reaction*, 122–24; "Union Leader Says Building Cut Could Keep Jobs From Negroes," *New York Times*, 5 September 1969, 23; Stephen Steinberg, *Turning Back: The Retreat from Racial Justice in American Thought and Policy* (Boston: Beacon Press, 1995): 213.

24. Matusow, *Nixon's Economy*, 3 (quote), 28; Jerome L. Himmelstein, *To the Right: The Transformation of American Conservatism* (Berkeley: University of California Press, 1990): 77, 100; Maurice Isserman and Michael Kazin, "The Failure and Success of the New Radicalism," in Steve Fraser and Gary Gerstle, eds., *The Rise and Fall of the New Deal Order, 1930–1980* (Princeton, N.J.: Princeton University Press, 1989): 236; William C. Berman, *America's Right Turn: From Nixon to Bush* (Baltimore: Johns Hopkins University Press, 1994): 9–10; Alvin W. Gouldner, *The Future of Intellectuals and the Rise of the New Class* (New York: Continuum, 1979): 71; Barbara Ehrenreich and John Ehrenreich, "The New Left: A Case Study in Professional-Managerial Radicalism," *Radical America* 11 (May-June 1977): 8–9; Peter L. Berger, "The Worldview of the New Class: Secularity and Its Discontents," in B. Bruce-Briggs, ed., *The New Class?* (New York: McGraw-Hill, 1981): 53; Jean-Christophe Agnew, "A Touch of Class," *Democracy* 3 (Spring 1983): 71; Alan Brinkley, *Liberalism and Its Discontents* (Cambridge, Mass.: Harvard University Press, 1998): 223; Edsall, *Chain Reaction*, 258–59, 273; Peter B. Levy, *The New Left and Labor in the 1960s* (Urbana: University of Illinois Press, 1994): 5–6, 117–19. For the New Left and counterculture see David Chalmers, *And the Crooked Places Made Straight: The Struggle for Social Change in the 1960s* [1991] (Baltimore: Johns Hopkins University Press, 1996).

25. Christopher Lasch, *The True and Only Heaven: Progress and Its Critics* (New York: W. W. Norton, 1991): 510; Leo P. Ribuffo, "Why Is There So Much Conservatism in the United States and Why Do So Few Historians Know Anything About It?" *American*

Historical Review 99 (April 1994): 445; Gouldner, *Future of Intelletuals,* 70–71; Donald I. Warren, *The Radical Center: Middle Americans and the Politics of Alienation* (Notre Dame, Ind.: University of Notre Dame Press, 1976): ix; Levy, *New Left and Labor,* 95, 110, 115, 120, 126; Andrew N. Greeley, "The War and White Ethnic Groups: Turning Off 'The People,' " *New Republic* 162 (27 June 1970): 15.

26. Levy, *New Left and Labor,* 81; "The New Left," *AFL-CIO News* 14 (15 March 1969): 6 (first quote); Kirkland, "Labor and Liberal Tradition," *AFL-CIO American Federationist* 76 (December 1969): 13 (third quote), 14 (second quote); "Bayard Rustin Warns Against Racial Division," *AFL-CIO News* 14 (11 October 1969): 11 (fourth quote).

27. Levy, *New Left and Labor,* 94, 102; Robert E. Lane and Michael Lerner, "Why Hard Hats Hate Hairs," *Psychology Today* 4 (November 1970): 45–46; Schuparra, *Triumph of the Right,* 117 (quote); Tom Kahn, "Youth: Protest and the Democratic Process," *AFL-CIO American Federationist* 76 (April 1969): 3, also in "Focus on Rebels Overlooks Non-Protesting Young Workers," *AFL-CIO News* 14 (26 April 1969): 5.

28. Kahn, "Youth," *AFL-CIO American Federationist,* 3–5 (quote on 4); "New Left," *AFL-CIO News* 14 (15 March 1969): 6; Greeley, "The War and White Ethnic Groups," *New Republic,* 14–15.

29. E. J. Dionne, Jr., *Why Americans Hate Politics* (New York: Simon and Schuster, 1991): 164; Todd Gitlin, *The Sixties: Years of Hope, Days of Rage* (New York: Bantam Books, 1987): 249–74. See also Tom Wells, *The War Within: America's Battle Over Vietnam* (Berkeley: University of California Press, 1994).

30. Dionne, *Why Americans Hate Politics,* 49–52; Gitlin, *The Sixties,* 381–32; Isserman and Kazin, "Failure and Success of New Radicalism," in Fraser and Gerstle, eds., *Rise and Fall of New Deal Order,* 213 (quote).

31. Poll of 21 September 1966, George H. Gallup, *The Gallup Poll: Public Opinion, 1935–1971* (New York: Random House, 1972): Vol. 3: 2027–28; Christian G. Appy, *Working-Class War: American Combat Soldiers and Vietnam* (Chapel Hill: University of North Carolina Press, 1993): 41; Richard Krickus, *Pursuing the American Dream: White Ethnics and the New Populism* (Garden City, N.Y.: Anchor Books, 1976): 239. While 50 percent of Gallup's 1966 college-educated respondents supported Johnson's handling of the war, approval ratings reached only 45 percent for those with high-school education and 36 percent for those with grade school background.

32. Appy, *Working-Class War,* 6, 41 (quote), 220; Richard Rogin, "Joe Kelly Has Reached His Boiling Point," *New York Times Magazine,* 28 June 1970, 16; Linda Kintz, *Between Jesus and the Market: The Emotions That Matter in Right-Wing America* (Durham, N.C.: Duke University Press, 1997): 239–40, 243, 246–47; Jerry Lee Lembke, "Myth, Spit, and Vietnam Veterans: More on the Politics of Memory," *Tikkun* 12 (March/April 1997): 11–13; Dionne, *Why Americans Hate Politics,* 44; poll of 27 November 1969, Gallup, *Gallup Poll,* Vol. 3: 2224–25. For a study of working-class responses to student activism, see H. Edward Ransford, "Blue Collar Anger: Reacting to Student and Black Protest," *American Sociological Review* 37 (June 1972): 333–46.

33. Gitlin, *The Sixties,* 306–308 (first quote on 307, second quote on 308); Irwin Unger and Debi Unger, *America in the 1960s* (St. James, N.Y.: Brandywine Press, 1988): 177–93.

34. Dan T. Carter, *George Wallace, Richard Nixon, and the Transformation of American Politics* (Waco, Tex.: Markham Press Fund, 1992): 26, 30 (first quote), 34, 339; Stephen Lesher, *George Wallace: American Populist* (Reading Mass.: Addison-Wesley, 1994): 420–21 (second quote).

35. Chalmers, *Crooked Places Made Straight,* 121–22; Gitlin, *The Sixties,* 326–27; Milton Viorst, *Fire in the Streets: America in the 1960s* (New York: Simon and Schuster, 1979): 460–61; Levy, *New Left and Labor,* 99–100, 102 (first quote); Greeley, "War and White Ethnic Groups," *New Republic,* 14; Richard M. Scammon and Ben J. Wattenberg, *The Real Majority* (New York: Coward-McCann, 1970): 62 (second quote).

36. Stepehn E. Ambrose, *Nixon: The Triumph of a Politician, 1962–1972* (New York: Simon and Schuster, 1989): 137, 301; polls of 12 October, 13 November 1969, Gallup, *Gallup Poll,* Vol. 3: 2218, 2222; H. R. Haldeman, *The Ends of Power* (New York: Times Books, 1978): 183; Marjorie Hunter, "Agnew Says 'Effete Snobs' Incite War Moratorium," *New York Times,* 20 October 1969, 1 (first and third quotes), 12 (second quote).

37. "Text of President Nixon's Address to Nation on U.S. Policy in the War in Vietnam," *New York Times,* 4 November 1969, 16 (quotes); special survey of 3 November 1969, Gallup,

Gallup Poll, Vol. 3: 2222; Kenneth J. Heineman, *Campus Wars: The Peace Movement at American State Universities in the Vietnam Era* (New York: New York University Press, 1993): 245–49. For a description of Nixon's speech, see Max Frankel, "Nixon Calls for Public Support As He Pursues His Vietnam Plan On a Secret Pullout Timetable," *New York Times,* 4 November 1969, 1, 17.

38. Wells, *War Within,* 424 (first quote), 425 (second quote); Greeley, "War and White Ethnic Groups," *New Republic* 14; Fred J. Cook, "Hard-Hats: The Rampaging Patriots," *The Nation* 210 (15 June 1970): 712–19; Rogin, "Joe Kelly," *New York Times Magazine,* 12–13; Appy, *Working-Class War,* 39–40.

39. "Workers' Woodstock," *Time* 95 (1 June 1970): 12 (quotes); Andy Logan, "Around City Hall," *New Yorker* 46 (6 June 1970): 104; Matusow, *Nixon's Economy,* 7.

40. Matusow, *Nixon's Economy,* 71, 80–81 (first, second, and third quotes on 81); Jonathan Rieder, "The Rise of the Silent Majority," in Fraser and Gerstle, eds., *Rise and Fall of the New Deal Order,* 262 (fourth and fifth quotes). For Nixon's appeal to the "majority of Americans," see Ambrose, *Nixon: Triumph of a Politician,* 392–93.

41. D. Carter, *Wallace, Nixon, and American Politics,* 13, 15, 425 (second, third, fourth, and fifth quotes); Lesher, *Wallace,* 430, 470, 471 (first quote), 475; "Wallace: Why I Run," *New York Times,* 1 March 1972, 39; George C. Wallace, *Stand Up for America* (Garden City, N.Y.: Doubleday, 1976): 92.

42. Berman, *America's Right Turn,* 16; H. Graham, *Civil Rights and Presidency,* 215, 216 (quotes).

43. Dionne, *Why Americans Hate Politics,* 48–59, 51, 198; Kevin P. Phillips, "Political Responses to the New Class," in Bruce-Briggs, ed., *The New Class?* 141; Berman, *America's Right Turn,* 15.

44. Ambrose, *Nixon: Triumph of a Politician,* 636 (second quote), 637 (fifth quote); H. R. Haldeman, *The Haldeman Diaries: Inside the Nixon White House* (New York: G. P. Putnam's, 1994): 519 (first, third, and fourth quotes).

45. Rieder, 'Silent Majority,' in Fraser and Gerstle, eds., *Rise and Fall of the New Deal Order,* 263, 262; Barbara Ehrenreich, *Fear of Falling: The Inner Life of the Middle Class* (New York: Pantheon Books, 1989): 124n; Berman, *America's Right Turn,* 18, 20; Haldeman, *Ends of Power,* 181; Stephen E. Ambrose, *Nixon: Ruin and Recovery, 1973–1990* (New York: Simon and Schuster, 1991): 20 (quote).

46. Ambrose, *Nixon: Ruin and Recovery,* 19, 20 (first quote); Haldeman, *Ends of Power,* 175 (second quote); Ambrose, *Nixon: Triumph of a Politician,* 543.

47. Melvin Small, *The Presidency of Richard Nixon* (Lawrence: University Press of Kansas, 1999), 187–89; Ambrose, *Triumph of a Politician,* 269 (quotes).

48. Entry of 21 July 1971, Haldeman, *Diaries,* 326; Nixon conversation with H. R. Haldeman and Charles Colson, 2 July 1971, in Stanley I. Kutler, ed., *Abuse of Power: The New Nixon Tapes* (New York: The Free Press, 1997): 17. Nixon sometimes distrusted Republican corporate leaders as well. See Ambrose, *Nixon: Ruin and Recovery,* 24–25.

49. Berman, *America's Right Turn,* 18; Haldeman, *Ends of Power,* 168 (second quote), 172 (first quote); George Lipsitz, *The Possessive Investment in Whiteness: How White People Profit From Identity Politics* (Philadelphia: Temple University Press, 1998): 144; Hoff, *Nixon Reconsidered,* 62–65 (third quote on 64), 73–76.

50. Stanley I. Kutler, *The Wars of Watergate: The Last Crisis of Richard Nixon* (New York: W. W. Norton, 1990): 4 (second quote), 105 (first quote); Ambrose, *Nixon: Ruin and Recovery,* 19 (third quote); Haldeman, *Ends of Power,* 169; Nixon conversations with John Ehrlichman and H. R. Haldeman, 8, 13 September 1971, in Kutler, ed., *Abuse of Power,* 29, 31 (fourth quote).

51. Kutler, *Wars of Watergate,* 4, 97, 101, 105–106, 108–116, 119–120, 123, 180; Nixon conversation with H. R. Haldeman and Charles Colson, 2 July 1971; Nixon conversation with Henry Kissinger and H. R. Haldeman, 1 July 1971; and Nixon conversation with H. R. Haldeman, John Ehrlichman, and Charles Colson, 1 July 1971, in Kutler, ed., *Abuse of Power,* 8 (first quote), 11 (second quote), 15–17.

52. Kutler, *Wars of Watergate,* 107, 198–99, 235, 200–241.

53. Nixon conversation with Henry Kissinger, 27 March 1973 and Nixon conversation with John Ehrlichman, 29 March 1973, in Kutler, *Abuse of Power,* 261 (first quote), 289 (second quote); Kutler, *Wars of Watergate,* 340–82, 464–65, 545–50; Haldeman, *Ends of Power,* 169, 182.

54. Ambrose, *Nixon: Triumph of a Politician*, 623 (first quote), and *Nixon: Ruin and Recovery*, 372, 378 (second quote), 441 (fourth quote), 442 (third quote).
55. Ambrose, *Nixon: Ruin and Recovery*, 444.
56. Thomas Ferguson and Joel Rogers, *Right Turn: The Decline of the Democrats and the Future of American Politics* (New York: Hill and Wang, 1986): 77–79; Himmelstein, *To the Right*, 6, 132–38; Peter Clecak, *Crooked Paths: Reflections on Socialism, Conservatism, and the Welfare State* (New York: Harper and Row, 1977): 73, 80–81, 90.
57. Edsall, *Chain Reaction*, 3–5, 7, 9, 11–12, 17, 106, 121, 122, 214, 236, 281–283; Clecak, *Crooked Paths*, 80–81, 90–91; Lasch, *True and Only Heaven*, 37.
58. Lasch, *True and Only Heaven*, 478 (quote), 504–505; Ronald P. Formisano, *Boston against Busing: Race, Class, and Ethnicity in the 1960s and 1970s* (Chapel Hill: University of North Carolina Press, 1991): 3, 119, 138–46, 187, 189–93.
59. Steinberg, *Turning Back*, 167; Edsall, *Chain Reaction*, 13, 123–24, 187 (quote); Sunita Parikh, *The Politics of Preference: Democratic Institutions and Affirmative Action in the United States and India* (Ann Arbor: University of Michigan Press, 1997): 141–42; H. Graham, *Civil Rights and Presidency*, 219.
60. Clecak, *Crooked Paths*, 82; Lasch, *True and Only Heaven*, 38; Rieder, "Silent Majority," in Fraser and Gerstle, eds., *Rise and Fall of New Deal Order*, 265; H. Graham, *Civil Rights and Presidency*, 223; Burdett A. Loomis, *The New American Politician: Ambition, Entrepreneurship, and the Changing Face of Political Life* (New York: Basic Books, 1988): 4, 13, 15, 17, 28–29, 161. See also Eugene Lewis, *Public Entrepreneurship: Toward a Theory of Bureaucratic Political Power; The Organizational Lives of Hyman Rickover, J. Edgar Hoover, and Robert Moses* (Bloomington: Indiana University Press, 1980): 1–20, 241.
61. Mona Harrington, *The Dream of Deliverance in American Politics* (New York: Random House, 1986): 191, 195; Phillips, "Political Responses to New Class," in Bruce-Briggs, ed., *The New Class?* 143–44; Edsall, *Chain Reaction*, 18; Warren, *Radical Center*, xi (third and fourth quotes), 1, 2, 3 (second quote), 12–13, 14 (first quote), 21, 29. The Oklahoma respondent's name was Anne V. Bowker.
62. Stephen C. Craig, *The Malevolent Leaders: Popular Discontent in America* (Boulder, Colo.: Westview Press, 1993): 1 (first and second quotes), 2 (third quote).

Chapter 9

1. Linda Kintz, *Between Jesus and the Market: The Emotions That Matter in Right-Wing America* (Durham, N.C.: Duke University Press, 1997): 56–57, 153; Thomas Byrne Edsall with Mary D. Edsall, *Chain Reaction: The Impact of Race, Rights, and Taxes on American Politics* (New York: W. W. Norton, 1991): 20, 108–109, 258–59; Jerome L. Himmelstein, *To the Right: The Transformation of American Conservatism* (Berkeley: University of California Press, 1990): 6, 71; E. J. Dionne, Jr., *Why Americans Hate Politics* (New York: Simon and Schuster, 1991): 107–108, 110, 112–13.
2. Himmelstein, *To the Right*, 97–100; Edsall, *Chain Reaction*, 17; Ronald Reagan, *Speaking My Mind: Selected Speeches* (New York: Simon and Schuster, 1989): 27 (first quote); Ronald Reagan, *Ronald Reagan Talks to America* (Old Greenwich, Conn.: Devin-Adair, 1983): 56 (second quote).
3. Gladwin Hill, "Reagan Aids G.O.P. In South Carolina," *New York Times*, 30 September 1967, 17 (first quote); Ben A. Franklin, "Reagan Assails Welfare Costs," *New York Times*, 15 October 1967, 41 (second and third quotes); Reagan, *Reagan Talks to America*, 61 (fourth quote); "Reagan Lays 'Insolvency' in U.S. to the President," *New York Times*, 18 January 1968, 24.
4. William C. Berman, *America's Right Turn: From Nixon to Bush* (Baltimore: Johns Hopkins University Press, 1994): 32, 88; Sidney Blumenthal, *The Rise of the Counter-Establishment* (New York: Times Books, 1986): 6, 321–22 (first quote on 321); Reagan, *Speaking My Mind*, 14 (second quote), and *Reagan Talks to America*, 186 (third and fourth quotes); John Kenneth White, *The New Politics of Old Values* (Hanover, N.H.: University Press of New England, 1988): 50 (fifth quote); Mona Harrington, *The Dream of Deliverance in American Politics* (New York: Random House, 1986): 259, 261. The heart of Reagan's 1980 campaign message was conveyed in his July 17th nomination

acceptance speech at the Republican National Convention and a November 3rd television address entitled "A Vision for America."

5. Christopher Lasch, *The True and Only Heaven: Progress and Its Critics* (New York: W. W. Norton, 1991): 516; Barbara Ehrenreich, *Fear of Falling: The Inner Life of the Middle Class* (New York: Pantheon Books, 1989): 145, 158, 194; Edsall, *Chain Reaction*, 10, 12–13, 14 (first quote), 144–46; William E. Pemberton, *Exit With Honor: The Life and Presidency of Ronald Reagan* (Armonk, N.J.: M.E. Sharpe, 1997): 91–92; Reagan Inaugural Address, 20 Janauary 1981, in *Public Papers of the Presidents of the United States, Ronald Reagan, 1981* (Washington, D.C.: Government Printing Office, 1982): 1 (second, fourth, and fifth quotes), 2 (third quote).

6. Remarks at the Annual Convention of the National Association of Evangelicals, Orlando, Florida, 8 March 1983, in *Public Papers of the Presidents of the United States, Ronald Reagan, 1983*, Book 1 (Washington, D.C.: Government Printing Office, 1984): 360; Remarks at the Conservative Political Action Conference Dinner, Washington, D.C., 20 March 1981, in *Public Papers, Reagan, 1981*, 278 (first and second quotes), 99–100; Remarks at the Annual Meeting of the Board of Governors of the International Monetary Fund and World Bank Group, Washington, D.C., 29 September 1987, in *Public Papers of the Presidents, Ronald Reagan, 1987*, Book 2 (Washington, D.C.: Government Printing Office, 1989): 1090 (third quote); George Skelton, "Tide of Mail Backs Tax Plan, Reagan Says," *Los Angeles Times*, 1 June 1985, 4 (fourth and fifth quotes). See also Robert S. McIntyre, "President Plays Populist With Rhetoric of Fairness," *Los Angeles Times*, sec. 4: 1, 3. For a critique of conservative attacks on the poor, immigrants, and racial minorities as a rhetorical mask for 1980s wage, investment, education, and tax policies that marginalized the non-affluent, see George Lipsitz, *The Possessive Investment in Whiteness: How White People Profit From Identity Politics* (Philadelphia: Temple University Press, 1998): xix, 15, 16–18, 66, 112, 144, 146.

7. Remarks at the Annual Dinner of the Conservative Political Action Conference, Washington, D.C., 1 March 1985, *Public Papers of the Presidents of the United States, Ronald Reagan, 1985* (Washington, D.C.: Government Printing Office, 1988): 227 (first, second, third, and fourth quotes); Remarks Accepting the Presidental Nomination at the Republican National Convention in Dallas, Texas, 23 August 1984, in *Public Papers of the Presidents of the United States, Ronald Reagan, 1984* (Washington, D.C.: Government Printing Office, 1987): 1174 (fifth quote); "Remarks in Columbus to Members of Ohio Veterans Organizations," 4 October 1982, *in Public Papers of the Presidents of the United States, Ronald Reagan, 1982,* (Washington, D.C.: Government Printing Office, 1983): 1262 (sixth quote); Kevin P. Phillips, *The Politics of Rich and Poor: Wealth and the Electorate in the Reagan Aftermath* (New York: Random House, 1990): 75; Pemberton, *Exit With Honor*, 138–39. In 1989 the Supreme Court declared that minority set-asides in construction were illegal. See Joan Hoff, *Nixon Reconsidered* (New York: Basic Books, 1994): 91.

8. "Landslide Victory By Reagan Underscores Democratic Ills," *Congressional Quarterly Almanac* (hereafter *CQA*) 40 (1984): 3:6B; Jeffrey Bell, *Populism and Elitism: Politics in the Age of Equality* (Washington, D.C.: Regnery Gateway, 1992): 100–101.

9. Dionne, *Why Americans Hate Politics*, 48, 123, 309, 313.

10. Ibid., 12, 78–79, 313–15; Edsall, *Chain Reaction*, 224; Berman, *America's Right Turn*, 140.

11. Berman, *America's Right Turn*, 140; Edsall, *Chain Reaction*, 224–26; Dionne, *Why Americans Hate Politics*, 301 (first quote), 314–16; Sidney Blumenthal, *Pledging Allegiance: The Last Campaign of the Cold War* (New York: Harper Collins, 1990): 264–66 (second quote on 264), 284–86, 295–96, 307–309.

12. Dionne, *Why Americans Hate Politics*, 310; Blumenthal, *Pledging Allegiance*, 318; Edsall, *Chain Reaction*, 274 (quote).

13. Michael Duffy and Dan Goodgame, *Marching in Place: The Status Quo Presidency of George Bush* (New York: Simon and Schuster, 1992): 247.

14. Elizabeth Drew, *On the Edge: The Clinton Presidency* (New York: Simon and Schuster, 1994): 62; Duffy and Goodgame, *Marching in Place*, 169, 255.

15. Drew, *On the Edge*, 19 (quotes); Governor Bill Clinton and Senator Al Gore, *Putting People First: How We Can All Change America* (New York: Times Books, 1992): 6, 9–10, 15.

16. Clinton and Gore, *Putting People First*, vii (first quote), 5 (second quote), 3 (third quote); Drew, *On the Edge*, 19, 70–71.

17. Drew, *On the Edge*, 70–71; Charles O. Jones, *Clinton and Congress, 1993–1996: Risk, Restoration, and Reelection* (Norman: University of Oklahoma Press, 1999): 62, 78–79, 84, 177.

18. Haynes Johnson and David S. Broder, *The System: The American Way of Politics at the Breaking Point* (Boston: Little, Brown, 1996): 493; Drew, *On the Edge*, 24 (quote); Martin Walker, *The President We Deserve: Bill Clinton, His Rise, Falls, and Comebacks* (New York Crown 1996): 180.

19. M. Walker, *The President We Deserve*, 179–80 (first quote on 180); Drew, *On the Edge*, 38–39, 53; Kevin P. Phillips, *Arrogant Capital: Washington, Wall Street, and the Frustration of American Politics* (Boston: Little, Brown, 1994): 39 (second quote).

20. Gary C. Jacobson, "The 1994 House Elections in Perspective," in Philip A. Klinkner, ed., *Midterm: The Elections of 1994 in Context* (Boulder, Colo: Westview Press, 1996): 5; Drew, *On the Edge*, 56, 198, 201, 210; H. Johnson and Broder, *The System*, 342; Bob Cohn, "Crowning a 'Quota Queen'?" *Newsweek* 121 (24 May 1993): 87.

21. Drew, *On the Edge*, 199–200, 204, 210–11; H. Johnson and Broder, *The System*, 342 (first quote); Cohn, "Crowning a 'Quota Queen'?" *Newsweek*, 87 (second quote).

22. Jacob S. Hacker, *The Road to Nowhere: The Genesis of President's Clinton's Plan For Health Security* (Princeton, N.J.: Princeton University Press, 1997): 16–17, 122, 123 (quote); Vincente Navarro, *The Politics of Health Policy: The U.S. Reforms, 1980–1994* (Cambridge, Mass.: Blackwell Publishers, 1994): 195–196, 198, 205; Lawrence R. Jacobs, "The Politics of American Ambivalence toward Government," in James A. Morone and Gary S. Belkin, eds., *The Politics of Health Care Reform: Lessons from the Past, Prospects for the Future* (Durham, N.C.: Duke University Press, 1994): 377–78; Drew, *On the Edge*, 189–90, 192.

23. Theda Skocpol, *Boomerang: Clinton's Health Security Effort and the Turn against Government`in U.S. Politics* (New York: W. W. Norton, 1996): 15, 17; Hacker, *Road to Nowhere*, 73–75, 134, 152; Drew, *On the Edge*, 191; Navarro, *Politics of Health Policy*, 206; Robin Toner, "Hillary Clinton's Potent Brain Trust on Health Reform," *New York Times* (28 February 1993): sec. C: 1 (second quote), C: 8 (first quote). See also Howard Fineman, "Clinton's Brain Trusters," *Newsweek* 121 (19 April 1993): 26–27.

24. H. Johnson and Broder, *The System*, 113, 129, 130–31, 140, 142; Hacker, *Road to Nowhere*, 123; Drew, *On the Edge*, 305 (quote), 193–95.

25. Hacker, *Road to Nowhere*, 131; H. Johnson and Broder, *The System*, 125–126, 133, 171–72, 174, 181–82, 190; Drew, *On the Edge*, 300, 302, 309–310.

26. Drew, *On the Edge*, 303–304; Skocpol, *Boomerang*, 64–66, 71.

27. Skocpol, *Boomerang*, xiii, 14–15, 108, 110, 177–78; Hacker, *Road to Nowhere*, 136, 139; Drew, *On the Edge*, 306; H. Johnson and Broder, *The System*, 230.

28. Drew, *On the Edge*, 307, 310; H. Johnson and Broder, *The System*, 152, 154 (quote); Stanley A. Renshon, *High Hopes: The Clinton Presidency and the Politics of Ambition* (New York: New York University Press, 1996): 271–72; Jacobs, "Politics of Ambivalence," in Morone and Belkins, eds., *Politics of Health Care Reform*, 375–76, 380–82; James A. Morone, "Nativism, Hollow Corporations, and Managed Competition: Why the Clinton Health Care Reform Failed," *Journal of Health Politics, Policy, and Law* 20 (Summer 1995): 392–93; Mollyann Brodie and Robert J. Blendon, "The Public's Contribution to Congressional Gridlock on Health Care Reform," *Journal of Health Politics, Policy and Law* 20 (Summer 1995): 404, 406; Skocpol, *Boomerang*, 8, 11–12, 167–68, 172; Robert J. Blendon, et al, "What Happened to Americans' Support of the Clinton Plan," *Health Affairs* 14 (Summer 1995): 12, 8.

29. H. Johnson and Broder, *The System*, 159, 199–201, 205 (quote), 206, 212, 318–21; Eugene Carlson, "Small Insurers Seek to Block Plan to Widen Coverage," *Wall Street Journal*, 8 April 1992, sec. B: 2.

30. Hacker, *Road to Nowhere*, 146; H. Johnson and Broder, *The System*, 264, 391–92, 485–86, 508–509, 527–28; Blendon, et al, "What Happened to Support of Clinton Plan," *Health Affairs*, 8–10.

31. Skocpol, *Boomerang*, xiii, 81; "Total Quality Madness," *New Republic* 211 (3 October 1994): 7.

32. H. Johnson and Broder, *The System*, 233–34 (first and second quotes on 234), 271; William Kristol, "How to Oppose the Health Plan–and Why," *Wall Street Journal*, 11 January 1994, sec. A: 14.

33. Entry on Newton Leroy Gingrich, in John A. Garraty and Jerome L. Sternstein, eds., *Encyclopedia of American Biography*, 2nd ed. (New York: HarperCollins, 1996): 443.

34. "The Washington Establishment vs the American People: A Report from the Budget Summit," lecture at the Heritage Foundation, Washington, D.C., 22 August 1990, and "The Survival of the Two-Party System," lecture at West Georgia College, Carrollton, Georgia, 1976, in Amy D. Bernstein and Peter W. Bernstein, eds., *Quotations from Speaker Newt: The Little Red, White and Blue Book of the Republican Revolution* (New York: Workman Publishing, 1995): 31, 77 (first quote); Mel Steely, *The Gentleman from Georgia: The Biography of Newt Gingrich* (Macon, Ga.: Mercer University Press, 2000): 141, 224–25; Dick Williams, *Newt: Leader of the Second American Revolution* (Marietta, Ga.: Longstreet Press, 1995): 38, 341, 351 (second quote); Newt Gingrich, *To Renew America* (New York: HarperCollins, 1995): 9 (third quote). See also Newt Gingrich, *Window of Opportunity: A Blueprint for the Future* (New York: Tor Publishing, 1984).

35. David Rosenbaum, "Republicans Offer Voters a Deal for Takeover of House," *New York Times*, 28 September 1994, sec. A: 16; John J. Pitney, Jr. and William F. Connelly, Jr., " 'Permanent Minority' No More: House Republicans in 1994," in Klinkner, ed., *Midterm*, 50 (Armey quote); "Rare Combination of Forces Makes '94 Vote Historic," *CQA* 50 (1994): 561–64; "After 40 Years, GOP Wins House," *CQA* 50 (1994): 570–71, 574–78.

36. Phillips, *Arrogant Capital*, 6, 168 (first quote); Blendon, et al, "What Happened to Americans' Support of the Clinton Plan," *Health Affairs*, 12–13; Philip A. Klinkner, "Court and Country in American Politics: The Democratic Party and the 1994 Election," in Klinkner, ed., *Midterm*, 63 (second quote); Stanley B. Greenberg, *Middle Class Dreams: The Politics and Power of the New American Majority*, rev. ed. (New Haven, Conn.; Yale University Press, 1996); 14–15, 272 (third quote), 304.

37. Jacobson, "The 1994 House Elections," in Klinkner, ed., *Midterm*, 3–7; Michael Kelly, "You Ain't Seen Nothing Yet," *New Yorker* 71 (24 April 1995): 46 (quote); Williams, *Newt*, 23 (first Gingrich quote); Michael Wines, "Clinton Delivers Sharp Jab at G.O.P. and 2 of Its Icons," *New York Times*, 22 October 1994, sec. A: 9 (second Gingrich quote); Maureen Dowd, "G.O.P.'s Rising Star Pledged To Right Wrongs of the Left," *New York Times*, 10 November 1994, sec. A: 1 (third Gingrich quote), sec. B: 3 (fourth, fifth, sixth, and seventh Gingrich quotes).

38. M. Walker, *The President We Deserve*, 5, 33.

39. Ibid., 32, 68, 124 (Clinton quotes); Drew, *On the Edge*, 376, 418 (quote). For the duplicity of Clinton's approach to the draft, see Renshon, *High Hopes*, 213–15.

40. Denise M. Bostdorff, "Clinton's Characteristic Issue Management Style: Caution, Conciliation, and Conflict Avoidance in the Case of Gays in the Military," in Robert E. Denton, Jr., and Rachel L. Holloway, eds., *The Clinton Presidency: Images, Issues, and Communication Strategies* (Westport, Conn.: Praeger, 1996): 190 (quote), 191, 196, 197, 199–200, 211; Drew, *On the Edge*, 42–46, 48, 249–51.

41. *Romer v. Evans*, 116 S. Ct. 1620 (1996), 1637 (first and second quotes), 1629 (third quote).

42. Kintz, *Between Jesus and the Market*, 245; Andrew Macdonald [William L. Pierce], *The Turner Diaries* (Washington, D.C.: National Alliance, 1980): 160–61, and *The Hunter* (Hillsboro, Wyo.: National Vanguard, 1989): 45.

43. Kintz, *Between Jesus and the Market*, 32 (La Haye quote), 41 (Marshner quotes), 137 (Hagee quote), 178 (Gilder quote).

44. Ibid., 19, 43, 72, 164 (Gilder quote).

45. Rush H. Limbaugh, III, *See, I Told You So* (New York: Pocket Star Books, 1993): 129 (first and second quotes), 143 (third quote), 144 (fourth quote), 144–45 (fifth quote), 149–50, 151 (sixth quote).

46. "We Are Really Catching a Wave," *Time* 145 (22 May 1995): 32; David Maraniss and Michael Weisskopf, *"Tell Newt to Shut Up!"* (New York: Simon and Schuster, 1996): 39, 147, 161; H. Johnson and Broder, *The System*, 575–77; "Voters Hand Clinton a Second

Term," *CQA* 52 (1996): 11:13–17; "GOP Retains House Majority," *CQA* 52 (1996): 11:23–27.

47. Paul Glastris and Bruce B. Auster, "Clinton's Next Trial," *U.S. News and World Report* 122 (10 February 1997): 26–27; Michael Duffy and Michael Weisskopf, "Let's Go to the Videtape," *Time* 150 (13 October 1997): 30–33; Marci McDonald, "The Cloud over Gore," *U.S. News and World Report* 125 (7 September 1998): 32; H. Johnson and Broder, *The System*, 259–61, 273–74, 277, 600; Renshon, *High Hopes*, 271, 274, 276, 297; David McCabe, "Character Counts," *Commonweal* 124 (11 April 1997): 10.

48. "Investigation of the President," *CQA* (1998): 12:4–5; "Clinton Address Fails to Defuse Ticking Time Bomb of Starr Report," *CQA* (1998): 12:7–9 (second quote on 8); "House of Representatives Casts Historic Vote To Impeach Clinton," *CQA* (1998): 12:3; Nancy Gibbs and Michael Duff, " 'I Misled People,' " *Time* 152 (31 August 1998): 30–32 (first quote on 32). See also Nancy Gibbs and Michael Duffy, "The Cost Of It All," *Time* 151 (24 August 1998): 36–44; Special Report, *Time* 151 (31 August 1998); and "The Starr Report," Special Issue, *Time* 151 (September 1998).

49. "Lieberman, Colleagues Respond," *CQA* (1998): D:13.

50. William Safire, "Alone with 'Alone' or What 'Is' Is," *New York Times Magazine*, 11 October 1998, 22; Jonathan Alter, "Spinning Out of Sinning," *Newsweek* 132 (21 September 1998): 45. See also Richard Lacayo, "When Is Sex Not 'Sexual Relations,' " *Time* 151 (24 August 1998): 38, and "A Lawyer's Loopholes," *Newsweek* 132 (14 September 1998):29.

51. Jonathan Alter, "The Two Mr. Clintons," *Newsweek* 132 (24 August 1998): 22; Robert H. Bork, "Counting the Costs of Clintonism," *American Spectator* 31 (November 1998): 57 (first quote), 56 (second, third, and fourth quotes); Richard I. Berke, "To Christians, G.O.P. Urges Punishment and Prayer," *New York Times*, 19 September 1998, sec. A: 9 (Robertson quote). See also "Citing 'Moral Crisis,' A Call to Oust Clinton," *New York Times*, 23 October 1998, 20.

52. Laurie Goodstein, "Christian Coalition Moans Lack of Anger at Clinton," *New York Times*, 20 September 1998, 34; "House of Representatives Casts Historic Vote," *CQA* (1998): 12:3; "Investigation of the President," *CQA* (1998): 12:5; Howard Fineman, "The Survivor," *Newsweek* 133 (22 February 1999): 20–22.

Conclusion

1. Stephen C. Craig, *The Malevolent Leaders: Popular Discontent in America* (Boulder, Colo.: Westview Press, 1993): 3, 4 (first quote), 17, 83; Stanley B. Greenberg, *Middle Class Dreams: The Politics and Power of the New American Majority*, rev. ed. (New Haven, Conn.: Yale University Press, 1996): x (second quote), 8 (third quote); Kevin P. Phillips, *Arrogant Capital: Washington, Wall Street, and the Frustration of American Politics* (Boston: Little, Brown, 1994): 5, 26, 27 (fourth quote), 33–34, 66, 82; Christopher Lasch, *The Revolt of the Elites and the Betrayal of Democracy* (New York: W. W. Norton, 1995): 5–6, 20 (fifth quote), 25, 29, 34, 43, 77. See also James Allen Smith, *The Idea Brokers: Think Tanks and the Rise of the New Policy Elite* (New York: Free Press, 1991): xii–xiv, 224–26, and James Davison Hunter, *Culture Wars: The Struggle to Define America* (New York: Basic Books, 1991): 42–46.

2. Jesse Ventura, *I Ain't Got Time To Bleed: Reworking the Body Politic From the Bottom Up* (New York: Villard, 1999): 7 (first quote, 13 (second quote), 16; Nancy Gibbs, et al, "McCain's Moment," *Time* 155 (14 February 2000): 26–36; "Bush Evokes Jefferson, Calls for Tackling Society's Problems 'One Person at a Time,' " *Congressional Quarterly Almanac* 56 (2000): D:105–106; "Bush Pledges Attack on Afghanistan Unless It Surrenders Bin Laden Now," *New York Times*, 21 September 2001, sec. A: 1, sec, B: 4. For a classic critique of the political class, see Matt Brai and David Brauer, "Jesse Ventura's 'Body' Politics," *Newsweek* 132 (16 November 1998): 32–42.

3. James Allen Smith, *The Idea Brokers: Think Tanks and the Rise of the New Policy Elite* (New York: Free Press, 1991): xvii (first quote); Alvin W. Gouldner, *The Future of Intellectuals and the Rise of the New Class* (New York: Continuum, 1979): 65 (second quote); Christopher Lasch, *The True and Only Heaven: Progress and Its Critics* (New York: W. W. Norton,

1991): 466–68, 526, and *The Revolt of the Elites and the Betrayal of Democracy* (New York: W. W. Norton, 1995): 80. See also Carl Boggs, *Intellectuals and the Crisis of Modernity* (Albany: State University of New York Press, 1993): 102, and Barbara Ehrenreich and John Ehrenreich, "The New Left: A Case Study in Professional-Managerial Radicalism," *Radical America* 11 (May-June 1977): 21–22.

4.   For contradictions between service to the entire population and representation of special interest groups and constituencies, see Vincente Navarro, *The Politics of Health Policy: The U.S. Reforms, 1980–1994* (Cambridge, Mass.: Blackwell Publishers, 1994): 27.

Bibliography of Archival Sources and Public Documents

Manuscripts

Flynn, John T. Papers. University of Oregon Special Collections, Eugene.
Johnson, Lyndon B. Senate Papers Relating to Civil Rights, Senate Papers, Vice Presidential Papers Open for Civil Rights, and Presidential Papers. Lyndon Baines Johnson Presidential Library, Austin, Tex.
Langer, William Papers. Department of Special Collections, Orin G. Libby Manuscripts Collection, Chester Fritz Library, University of North Dakota, Grand Forks.
Lemke, William Papers. Department of Special Collections, Orin G. Libby Manuscripts Collection, Chester Fritz Library, University of North Dakota, Grand Forks.
Nye, Gerald P. Papers. Herbert Hoover Presidential Library, West Branch, Iowa.
Reedy, George E. Papers. Office Files. Lyndon Baines Johnson Presidential Libary, Austin, Tex.
Simpson, John A. Papers. Western History Collections, University of Oklahoma, Norman.
Smith, Howard W. Papers. Special Collections Department, University of Virginia Library, Charlottesville.
Taft, Robert A. Papers. Library of Congress, Washington, D.C.
Truman, Harry S. Presidential Papers. Harry S. Truman Presidential Library, Independence, Mo.

Public Documents

Biographical Directory of the United States Congress, 1774–1989. Washington, D.C.: Government Printing Office, 1989.
Congressional Record. Washington, D.C.: Government Printing Office, 1934–1969.
U.S. House of Representatives. Committee on Appropriations. *Report on the Fitness for Continuance in Federal Employment of Goodwin B. Watson and William E. Dodd, Jr., Employees of the Federal Communications Commission, and Robert Morss Lovett, Arthur E. Goldschmidt, and Jack Bradley Fahy, Employees of the Department of the Interior.* Washington, D.C.: Government Printing Office, 1943.
U.S. House of Representatives. Hearings Before the Committee on Un-American Activities. *Hearings Regarding the Communist Infiltration of the Motion Picture Industry.* Washington, D.C.: Government Printing Office, 1947.

U.S. House of Representatives. Hearings Before a Special Committee of the House of Representatives. *Investigation of Un-American Propaganda Activities in the United States.* Washington, D.C.: Government Printing Office, 1938.

U.S. House of Representatives. Hearings Before a Special Committee on Un-American Activities. *Investigation of Un-American Propaganda Activities in the United States.* Washington, D.C.: Government Printing Office, 1939.

U.S. House of Representatives. Hearings Before the Subcommittee of the War on Poverty Program of the Committee on Education and Labor. *Examination of the War on Poverty Program.* Washington, D.C.: Government Printing Office, 1965.

U.S. House of Representatives. Intermediate Report of the Special Committee to Investigate the NLRB, *Report on the Investigation of the NLRB.* Washington, D.C.: Government Printing Office, 1940.

U.S. House of Representatives. Report of the Committee on the Civil Service. *Investigation of Civilian Personnel and Study of all Matters Relating to the Number, Proper Use, and Recruiting of Said Personnel.* Washington, D.C.: Government Printing Office, 1943.

U.S. House of Representatives. Report of the Special Committee on Un-American Activities. *Investigation of Un-American Activities and Propaganda.* Washington, D.C.: Government Printing Office, 1939.

U.S. House of Representatives. Second Intermediate Report of the Select Committee to Investigate Executive Agencies. *Report of the Select Committee to Investigate Executive Agencies.* Washington, D.C.: Government Printing Office, 1943.

U.S. House of Representatives. Select Committee to Investigate the Use of Chemicals in Foods and Cosmetics. *Hearings.* Washington, D.C.: Government Printing Office, 1952.

U.S. House of Representatives. Special Committee to Investigate Tax-Exempt Foundations and Comparable Organizations. *Relations between Foundations and Education and between Foundations and Government.* Staff Report No. 3. Washington, D.C.: Government Printing Office, 1954.

U.S. House of Representatives. Special Committee to Investigate Tax-Exempt Foundations and Comparable Organizations. *Tax-Exempt Foundations: Hearings before the Special Committee to Investigate Tax-Exempt Foundations and Comparable Organizations.* Washington, D.C.: Government Printing Office, 1954.

U.S. House of Representatives. Special Committee to Investigate Tax-Exempt Foundations and Comparable Organizations. *Tax-Exempt Foundations: Final Report.* Washington, D.C.: Government Printing Office, 1954.

U.S. House of Representatives. Special Committee on Un-American Activities. *Investigation of Un-American Propaganda in the United States.* Washington, D.C.: Government Printing Office, 1941.

U.S. House of Representatives. Special Committee on Un-American Activities. *Investigation of Un-American Propaganda Activities in the United States: Hearings before the Special Committee on Un-American Activities.* Washington, D.C.: Government Printing Office, 1943.

U.S. House of Representatives. Special Subcommittee of Committee on Appropriations. *Report on the Fitness for Continuance in Federal Employment of Dr. Goodwin B. Watson, Dr. Frederick L. Schuman, and Dr. William E. Dodds, Jr., All of the Federal Communications Commission.* Washington, D.C.: Government Printing Office, 1943.

U.S. Senate. Additional Report on Reduction of Nonessential Federal Expenditures. *Reduction of Nonessential Federal Expenditures: Federal Personnel.* Washington, D.C.: Government Printing Office, 1943.

U.S. Senate. *Annual Report of the Committee on Government Operations Made by the Senate Permanent Subcommittee on Investigations.* Washington, D.C.: Goverment Printing Office, 1954.

U.S. Senate. Committee on Agriculture and Forestry. *Hearings on Agricultural Emergency Act to Increase Farm Purchasing Power.* Washington, D.C.: Government Printing Office, 1933.

U.S. Senate. Hearings Before the Subcommittee to Investigate the Administration of the Internal Security Act and Other Internal Security Laws of the Committee on the Judiciary. *Institute of Pacific Relations.* Washington, D.C. Government Printing Office, 1952.

U.S. Senate. Hearings before the Subcommittee on Separation of Powers of the Senate Committee on the Judiciary on the Philadelphia Plan and S. 931. The *Philadelphia Plan:*

Congressional Oversight of Administrative Agencies. Washington, D.C.: Government Printing Office, 1970.

U.S. Senate. Joint Committee on Reduction of Nonessential Federal Expenditures. *Hearings on Reduction of Nonessential Federal Expenditures.* Washington, D.C.: Government Printing Office, 1941.

U.S. Senate. Preliminary Report on Reduction of Nonessential Federal Expenditures. *Reduction of Nonessential Federal Expenditures.* Washington, D.C.: Government Printing Office, 1941.

U.S. Senate. Report of the Committee on the Judiciary. *Institute of Pacific Relations.* Washington, D.C.: Government Printing Office, 1952.

Index

Domestic security. See Internal security
Dondero, George A., 116
Dos Passos, John, 35
Douglas, Melvyn, 87
Draft. See Conscription
Drug use, 187, 194, 196, 216, 218
Dukakis, Michael S., 206–207
Dumenil, Lynn, 13
Duran, Gustavo, 124

Earp, Edwin L., 15
Eastland, James O., 130
Economic Club of New York, 204
Economic Opportunity Act (1964), 162, 171
Economic Stabilization Board, 107
Ehrenreich, Barbara, 4
Ehrenreich, John, 4
Ehrlichman, John, 198
Einstein, Albert, 13
Eisenhower, Dwight David, 9, 136, 137–38, 142, 158–60; passim, 165, 223
Eisler, Gerhard, 116
Election (s): of 1896, 23; of 1912, 38; of 1924, 69, of 1932, 130; of 1936, 64, 222; of 1938, 74–76, 98, 102; of 1940, 79–80; of 1942, 89; of 1944, 114, 123; of 1946, 109–110, 123, 124; of 1948, 125; of 1950, 127; of 1952, 129, 136, 139, 165; of 1958, 165; of 1962, 175; of 1964, 164–67, 204, 224; of 1966, 175–76, 188; of 1968, 178–79, 181, 190–91; of 1972, 193–95; of 1976, 224; of 1980, 203–205; of 1984, 203, 206; of 1988, 203, 206–207; of 1992, 208; of 1994, 214–15; of 1996, 218; of 1998, 220, 222; of 2000, 222
Eliot, Charles W., 14
Ellsberg, Daniel, 197–98
Ellwood, Paul M., 210
Ely, Richard T., 37
Emergency Anti-Inflation Act (1942), 91
Emergency Price Control Act (1942), 91
Empiricism, 143, 145–46
Employment Act (1946), 106
Engel, Albert J., 81–82, 88
Enthoven, Alan C., 210
Equal Employment Act (1972), 186
Equal Employment Opportunity Commission (EEOC), 161, 182–83, 186, 206
Equal Rights Amendment (ERA), 182, 203
Ervin, Sam J., Jr., 184–86, 198, 225
Espionage, 113–14, 116, 119–22, 124–27, 129, 136–39, 142

Ethical relativism. See Moral relativism
Evans, Daniel J., 182
Evans, Hiram Wesley, 1, 8, 13, 32–36, 128, 198
Evers, Medgar, 162
Evolution. See Darwinism; Scopes trial; Social Darwinism
Executive Order 8802 (1941), 182
Executive Order 11246 (1965), 170, 181, 182
Executive Reorganization Bill (1937–39), 66–70
Exner, Frederick B., 148, 151
Extramarital sex, 143–44
Ezekiel, Mordecai, 42, 44, 71, 100

Faddis, Charles I., 102
Fair Employment Practices Committee (FEPC), 156, 157
Fair Labor Standards Bill (1937–38), 75
Falwell, Jerry, 204
Family Assistance Plan (FAP), 195–96
Fannin, Paul J., 182–85, 225
Farm Bureau Federation, 42
Farm reform. See Agricultural reform
Farmer-labor movement, 65, 73, 95, 96
Farmer-Labor Progressive Federation, 73–74
Farmers Holiday Association, 42–43, 46–47
Federal Bureau of Investigation (FBI), 113–14, 117, 120, 138, 197–98
Federal Employee Loyalty Program, 113
Federal Employment Relief Administration (FERA), 39, 48, 56, 103
Federal Theater Project (WPA), 96, 157
Federal Writers Project (WPA), 96
"Fellow-travelers," 96, 112–13, 121, 140
Fellowship for Reconciliation, 156
Feminism: opponents, 95, 203, 217; supporters, 182, 187, 194, 200, 206, 209
Ferguson, Homer, 112, 130
Ferguson, Miriam ("Ma"), 30
Ferraro, Geraldine A., 206
Fish, Hamilton, Jr., 53, 62, 85, 95, 104
Fletcher, Arthur A., 181–82, 185
Fluoridation controversy, 10, 135, 147–53, 155, 224, 226
Fly, James Lawrence, 98
Flynn, John T., 122, 139, 157–58
Foner, Philip, 140
Ford, Gerald R., 185
Ford, Henry, 83
Ford, Leland M., 87

New Democrats, 203, 208, 212, 220
New Frontier, 161
New Left: and antiwar protest, 10, 189–92,
215–16, 218, 227; and student activism,
172–73, 187–89; opponents, 187–89, 195,
197–98, 215, 218, 224
"New Paradigm," 207
New York Bureau of Municipal Research, 37
New World Order, 217
Nietzche, Friedrich, 19–20, 24, 27–28, 29
Nixon, Richard M.: as populist, 10, 120,
178–79, 189, 191–96, 199–200, 224; and
race, 10, 178–87; and Vietnam War,
189–99; and Watergate, 197–99;
mentioned, 203, 210
Nonpartisan League, 46
Norris, George, 58
North America Free Trade Agreement
(NAFTA), 208–209
Novak, Michael, 4
Nuclear weapons, 110, 127, 136–38
Nudism, 248n41
Nunn, Sam, 216
Nye, Gerald P., 53, 65, 78

O'Brien, Larry, 197–98
O'Connor, John, 60
O'Daniel, W. Lee, 105, 107
O'Donnell, John, 127
Odum, Howard W., 15
Office of Civilian Defense (OCD), 86–88, 95
Office of Contract Compliance, 180
Office of Economic Opportunity (OEO),
162, 170–76 passim, 181, 196–97. See also
War on Poverty
Office of Facts and Figures, 97
Office of Federal Contract Compliance
(OFCC), 181–82, 185–86
Office of Government Reports (OGR), 88
Office of Price Administration (OPA), 9, 85,
90–94, 106–107, 116
Office of War Information (OWI), 90–91,
126, 157
Ohio Public Utilities Commission, 119
Oliphant, Herman, 72
O'Neill, James F., 114
Oppenheimer, J. Robert, 9, 135, 137–39,
223
Order, The, 217
Order No. 4, 186
Organized labor. See Labor unions
Osborn, Henry Fairfield, 232n29
Overseas Library Program, 140

Parmalee, Maurice, 248n41
Peace Corps, 161, 171
Peace movement. See New Left, and antiwar
protest
Peek, George N., 44, 54, 57, 85
Pentagon Papers, 197
Peress, Irving, 141
Permanent Subcommittee on Investigations
(McCarthy committee), 139–40
Perot, H. Ross, 10, 208
Persian Gulf War (1991), 207–208
Pettengill, Samuel B., 50, 59, 100
Philadelphia Plan, 10, 181–86, 198
Phillips, Kevin, 5, 209, 215, 221
Pierce, William L. (Andrew Macdonald),
217
Pinkerton, James, 207
Pittman, Key, 70
Pledge of Allegiance, 206–207
Podhoretz, Norman, 4
Poll tax, 156
Popular Front, 113, 116
Populism: and KKK, 1, 33–36; and New
Deal opponents, 1–3, 44–48, 63–64, 105,
225; and anticommunism, 1, 9, 115–16,
119, 124–25, 138–39, 141–42, 223; and
knowledge elites, 2–3, 17, 225; and civil
rights opponents, 10, 155, 164–65, 166,
176, 179, 200; and Bryan, 23–25, 28–30;
in Progressive Era, 38–39, 43, 46, 255n21;
and antisemitism, 83; during World War
II, 89, 107, 124; during Cold War era,
115–16, 124–25; 141–42, 149–54; and G.
Wallace and Nixon, 155, 164–65, 177–78,
190–91, 193–94; since 1980, 201, 205–208
passim, 214–15, 218
Populist Party (1890s), 43
Pornography, 168–69
Porter, Noah, 14
Poverty. See Antipoverty; War on Poverty
Powell, Adam Clayton, 175
Premarital sex, 143–44
Price control, 91–95 passim, 106–107
Progressive Party (1912), 66
Progressive Party (1924), 69
Progressive Party (Wisconsin), 73–74
Progressive reform, 6, 8, 23, 37–39, 66,
222
Prohibitionism, 23, 31
Project Uplift, 172
Public Administration Clearing House
(Chicago), 66
Public health, 31, 101–102, 147–53